RYMES
OF ROBYN HOOD

RYMES
OF ROBYN HOOD,

*An Introduction
to the English Outlaw*

R. B. Dobson
and
J. Taylor

UNIVERSITY OF PITTSBURGH PRESS

Published in Great Britain in 1976 by William Heinemann Ltd

Published in the U.S.A. in 1976 by the University of Pittsburgh Press

Library of Congress Cataloging in Publication Data

Main entry under title:

Rymes of Robyn Hood.

Bibliography
Includes index.
1. Robin Hood—Legends. 2. English poetry.
I. Dobson, Richard Barrie. II. Taylor, John, 1925—
PR2125.D6 1976   820'.8'0351   75-31564
ISBN 0-8229-1126-4

Printed in Great Britain by
W & J Mackay Limited, Chatham

TO
Mark and Michelle,
Donald and Richard

CONTENTS

		Page
Preface		ix
List of Abbreviations		xi

INTRODUCTION
I.	The Genesis of Robin Hood	1
II.	The Medieval Background	17
III.	The Legend since the Middle Ages	36

| *Note on the Texts of the Ballads* | | 65 |
| *Map: Sherwood and Barnsdale* | | 69 |

A. 'RYMES OF ROBYN HOOD'
1.	A Gest of Robyn Hode	71
2.	Robin Hood and the Monk	113
3.	Robin Hood and the Potter	123
4.	Robin Hood's Death	133
	(a) Percy Folio Version	134
	(b) Robin Hood Garland Version	137
5.	Robin Hood and Guy of Gisborne	140
6.	The Jolly Pinder of Wakefield	146
	(a) Broadside Version	147
	(b) Percy Folio Version	148
7.	Robin Hood and the Butcher	150
	(a) Percy Folio Version	152
	(b) Broadside Version	155
8.	Robin Hood and the Curtal Friar	158
	(a) Percy Folio Version	159
	(b) Broadside Version	161
9.	Robin Hood and Little John	165
	(a) Chapbook Version	166
	(b) Virginian Version	170
10.	Robin Hood and Allen A Dale	172
11.	Robin Hood and Maid Marian	176
12.	The Noble Fisherman (Robin Hood's Preferment)	179
13.	Robin Hood and the Valiant Knight	183
14.	The opening and closing stanzas of Martin Parker's 'A True Tale of Robin Hood'	187
15.	Robin Hood and the Duke of Lancaster, 1727	191

16. The Birth of Robin Hood (*Willie and Earl Richard's Daughter*)   195
17. John Keats, 'Robin Hood: To A Friend'   198
18. Alfred Noyes, 'Sherwood'   200

B. *'PLAYS OF ROBIN HOOD'*
19. The Play of 'Robin Hood and the Sheriff', *c*. 1475   203
20. The Play of 'Robin Hood and the Friar', *c*. 1560   208
21. The Play of 'Robin Hood and the Potter', *c*. 1560   215
22. Extracts from Anthony Munday's 'The Downfall' and 'The
     Death of Robert, Earl of Huntington' (1597–8)   220
23. Extracts from 'The Sad Shepherd' (Ben Jonson)   231
24. 'Robin Hood and his Crew of Souldiers': Nottingham, 1661   237
25. Extracts from 'The Foresters' (Alfred Tennyson)   243

C. *OTHER OUTLAW SONGS*
26. An Outlaw's Song of Trailbaston, *c*. 1305.   250
27. Robyn and Gandeleyn   255
28. Adam Bell, Clim of the Clough, and William of Cloudesly   258
29. Marsk Stig Made An Outlaw   274
30. The Death of Jesse James   278

APPENDICES
I.   Titles and First Lines of Robin Hood Ballads   281
II.   Note on the Sloane Manuscript Life of Robin Hood   286
III. A Selection of Proverbs of Robin Hood   288
IV.   A Select List of Robin Hood Place-Names   293

SELECT BIBLIOGRAPHY   312

INDEX   324

PREFACE

'For many men speketh wyth wondring of Robyn Hood, and of his Bowe, Whych never shot therin I trowe'. It is with some diffidence that two teachers of history present a selection of texts to illustrate the growth of one of England's most complex as well as most famous legends. The difficulties and dangers inherent in taking too serious an interest in tales of Robin Hood, proverbially only 'good enough for fools', have been apparent since they first emerged in the later middle ages. Only in very recent years have historians and literary critics begun to study the legend of Robin Hood with the attention it deserves and to rescue its hero from the not always helpful clutches of the local enthusiast, the ballad scholar and the writer of children's stories. Of course stories of Robin Hood will continue to be told again and again and in every possible way; and the myth will always be more potent than the highly controversial facts which provide its historical framework. Yet the sources on which all tales of Robin Hood ultimately depend have often been allowed to remain in a quite unnecessary obscurity, and are accessible only in the large and at times outdated collections of Joseph Ritson and Francis Child. Although the task of compiling this anthology has served only to increase our respect for the remarkable talents of those two scholars, there remains a need for a simpler guide than theirs to the literature of Robin Hood. The lack of such a guide has prompted us to produce this selection of 'rymes of Robyn Hood', designed not for specialists but for those who would like to trace for themselves the main steps in the evolution of England's most complex and perennially appealing legend.

Whether or not, in Professor Child's famous phrase, 'Robin Hood is absolutely a creation of the ballad-muse', any anthology of greenwood literature is bound to devote most of its space to the ballads on which—until at least the early nineteenth century—Robin Hood's fame was always based. Of the thirty-eight surviving 'traditional' Robin Hood ballads, we have printed fourteen, selected either for their antiquity, their literary merit, or their illumination of the later development of the legend. Four other poems, ranging from a political satire of 1727 to Alfred Noyes's 'Sherwood', illustrate some of the later changes in popular attitudes to the medieval greenwood hero. Similar vicissitudes in taste are even more apparent in the seven items (including extracts from plays by Anthony Munday, Ben Jonson and Alfred Tennyson) chosen to represent Robin Hood's long history as a dramatic character on the English stage. Our collection concludes with a very small selection of five other outlaw songs or ballads which may help to place Robin Hood more firmly in the context of his own late medieval English forest as well as to provide a comparison with some 'noble bandits' of other periods.

The four appendices include a list of the titles of known Robin Hood ballads together with collections, by no means comprehensive, of Robin Hood proverbs and place-names in England. The aim throughout (never difficult where Robin Hood is concerned) has been rather to ask questions than to answer them; but in our introduction we summarize the still very imperfect state of present knowledge about the origins and later development of the greenwood legend. An earlier and at times somewhat different version of our views on the genesis of Robin Hood may be found in our article, 'The Medieval Origins of the Robin Hood Legend: A Reassessment', *Northern History*, VII, 1972, pp. 1–30.

The obligations incurred by us during the compilation of this book are too numerous to be acknowledged as fully as they deserve. But we should especially like to thank Professor D. C. Fowler, Professor J. C. Holt and Professor E. Miller for their most helpful comments on our interpretations of the Robin Hood legend. Dr C. E. Challis, Mr John Harvey, Dr David Palliser, Dr John Maddicott, Mr John Scattergood and Professor R. M. Wilson provided us with a number of important references to Robin Hood in documentary and literary sources. We are also very indebted to the staff of the British Library manuscript room, York Minster Library, York City Library, and the University Libraries of Leeds and York. In addition R. B. Dobson would wish to express his appreciation to the British Academy for the award of a Visiting Overseas Fellowship at the Folger Shakespeare Library, Washington D.C., in the autumn of 1974: this Fellowship enabled him to consult the Folger Library's extensive holdings of Robin Hood material, ranging from an early printed fragment of the *Gest* of Robin Hood to William Stukeley's own heavily annotated copy of the Robin Hood Garland. Although our editions of the Robin Hood ballads in this anthology are designed for the general reader rather than the linguistic scholar, our aim throughout has been to present reliably accurate versions of what are often highly complex primary texts. Thanks to the expert advice of Professor Arthur Cawley, Miss Betty Hill, Mrs Karen Stern, Dr P. J. Jones and Mr Derek Pearsall on literary and textual problems, we hope we may have come closer to achieving this objective than would otherwise have been possible. On matters of historical interpretation we are of course especially indebted to the important contributions to the study of the Robin Hood legend made by Professor J. C. Holt, Dr M. H. Keen and Professor R. H. Hilton a dozen years ago. We would also like to thank Mrs Vicky Liversidge for her labours at the typewriter, Professor George Potter for his invaluable help with the proofs, Mr Nicholas Skelton for his cartographical work on our behalf, and Mr Roger Smith of William Heinemann Ltd for his interest and support during the preparation of this book.

LIST OF ABBREVIATIONS

Arber	E. Arber, *A Transcript of the Registers of the Company of Stationers of London, 1554–1640*. 5 vols, 1875–94.
B.L.	British Library.
Child	F. J. Child, ed., *The English and Scottish Popular Ballads*. 5 vols, 1882–98.
C.P.R.	*Calendar of Patent Rolls*.
D.N.B.	*Dictionary of National Biography*.
E.H.R.	*English Historical Review*.
Evans	T. Evans, *Old Ballads, Historical and Narrative*. Editions of 1777, 1784, 1810.
Gable	J. H. Gable, *A Bibliography of Robin Hood* (University of Nebraska, Studies in Language, Literature and Criticism, No. 17, 1938).
Gutch	J. M. Gutch, ed., *A Lytell Geste of Robin Hode, with other ancient and modern ballads and songs relating to this celebrated yeoman*. 2 vols, 1847.
Keen, *Outlaws*	M. Keen, *The Outlaws of Medieval Legend*. 1961.
Leach	MacEdward Leach, ed., *The Ballad Book*. 1955.
O.E.D.	*Oxford English Dictionary*.
P.N.S.	English Place-Name Society.
Pepys	Samuel Pepys's collection of ballads in Magdalene College Library, Cambridge.
Quiller-Couch	A. Quiller-Couch, ed., *The Oxford Book of Ballads*. 1910.
Ritson	J. Ritson, *Robin Hood: A collection of all the ancient poems, songs, and ballads*. Editions of 1795, 1820, 1832, 1846.
Roxburghe	The Roxburghe collection of ballads in the British Museum Library.
Roxburghe Ballads	*The Roxburghe Ballads*. 9 vols, published by Ballad Society, 1871–99.
T.R.H.S.	*Transactions of the Royal Historical Society*.
V.C.H.	*Victoria History of the Counties of England*.
Y.A.S.	Yorkshire Archaeological Society.
Y.A.J.	*Yorkshire Archaeological Journal*.

❡ Here begynneth a gest of Robyn Hode

'Here begynneth a gest': the first page of the *Gest of Robin Hood* among the Chepman and Myllar tracts (National Library of Scotland). This woodcut of a mounted archer had already been used to illustrate Chaucer's 'Yeoman' in Richard Pynson's 1491 printed edition of *The Canterbury Tales*.

INTRODUCTION

I. *The Genesis of Robin Hood*

'If I shulde deye bi this day · me liste noughte to loke;
I can noughte perfitly my pater-noster · as the prest it syngeth,
But I can rymes of Robyn hood · and Randolf erle of Chestre,
Ac neither of owre lorde ne of owre lady · the leste that evere was made.'[1]

With these famous words, spoken by William Langland's character of Sloth
in his capacity as the personification of negligent Christian priesthood, any
investigation of the origins of the Robin Hood legend must inevitably begin.
Over two centuries have elapsed since Bishop Percy first drew public attention
to this passage from *The Vision of William concerning Piers Plowman*;[2] and
hope must now be abandoned that there survives an indisputably earlier
reference to England's greatest outlaw hero. The B-text of *Piers Plowman*
can be dated with a high degree of probability to or very near the year 1377.[3]
Before 1377 there lived many Robin Hoods in England but none who can be
certainly identified with the later legendary hero; before 1377 England
suffered from many outlaws but none whose exploits can be confidently
interpreted as the genesis of the greenwood legend. In the case of a myth
whose origins are so shrouded in mysterious ambiguity it is best to begin with
extreme caution. All we know for certain about the Robin Hood legend at
the beginning of Richard II's reign is that it existed, that it had found
expression in the form of 'rymes' or verses, and that it was regarded in at
least some quarters as a disreputably plebeian taste.

Nor is there any reason to believe that the attitude to the Robin Hood cult
first expressed by the author of *Piers Plowman* in the 1370s was at all untypical.
Indeed the critical tone adopted by William Langland in the first of all
recorded references to the outlaw hero continued to be characteristic of most
of the many allusions made to Robin Hood's popular appeal by fifteenth-
century writers. In the absence of any surviving text of a Robin Hood tale
or ballad before *Robin Hood and the Monk* (of *c.* 1450 or later; No. 2 below),
such references are the only secure guide we possess to the popularity of the
greenwood saga during the Lancastrian period. Thus the author of the
homiletic *Dives and Pauper*, probably a Franciscan friar writing between

---

[1] *The Vision of William concerning Piers the Plowman in three parallel texts*, ed. W. W. Skeat
(Oxford, 1886), I, 166 (B-text, Passus V, lines 400–3).

[2] *Percy's Reliques of Ancient Poetry* (Everyman edition, 1906), I, 117.

[3] Langland's reference to 'rymes of Robyn hood' naturally recurs in the later C-text of
Piers Plowman (Passus VIII, line 11) but is absent from the much slighter A-text of
c. 1362.

1405 and 1410, admonished those who 'gon levir to heryn a tale or a song of robyn hode or of sum rubaudry than to heryn messe or matynes'.[1] At about the same date, probably during the first decade of the fifteenth century, Hugh Legat, a Benedictine monk of St Albans Abbey, composed a vernacular sermon in which he quoted what was probably the oldest and certainly the most famous of all proverbial expressions associated with Robin Hood: 'for mani, manime seith, spekith of Robyn Hood that schotte never in his bowe'.[2] A popular variant of this proverb was almost certainly known to Geoffrey Chaucer when he was writing *Troilus and Criseyde* in the 1380s: in criticizing those who 'Defamen love, as nothing of it knowe; / Thei speken but thei benten nevere his bowe', Chaucer seems to have been consciously transferring the bow usually ascribed to Robin Hood into the hands of Cupid, a transference deliberately reversed by two early fifteenth-century copyists of the poem.[3] Not many years later, apparently in 1419–20, this particular proverb found its most perfect expression in the verse *Reply of Friar Daw Topias to Jack Upland*:

> 'On old Englis it is said
> Unkissid is unknowun;
> And many men speken of Robyn Hood,
> And shotte nevere in his bowe.'[4]

During the late fifteenth and early sixteenth centuries contemporary references to the popularity of the Robin Hood legend continued to proliferate without, however, becoming much more specific about that legend's subject matter. By the end of the middle ages there can be no doubt that knowledge of the outlaw was widely diffused throughout all levels of society. At one extreme, Robin Hood proverbs found their way into works as sophisticated as George Ripley's erudite *Compound of Alchemy* (1471) or John Skelton's satire *Why Come ye Nat to Court?* (1522–3).[5] At another, the singing or 'harping' of 'Robyn-Howde' figures as a popular pastime in late

---

[1] Chapter LI (on the First Commandment) of *Dives and Pauper*, first published by Pynson in 1493 but not reprinted since 1536. The view that it was written by Harry Parker, a Carmelite from Doncaster, has been discredited: see H. G. Pfander, '*Dives and Pauper*', *The Library*, 4th series, XIV (1934), pp. 299–312; H. G. Richardson, *Notes and Queries*, 11th series, IV, pp. 321–3; cf. *English Historical Documents* IV (1327–1485), ed. A. R. Myers (London, 1969), p. 707.

[2] *Three Middle English Sermons from the Worcester Chapter MS. F. 10*, ed. D. M. Grisdale (Leeds, 1939), p. 8.

[3] *The Book of Troilus and Criseyde* (Book II, lines 860–1), ed. R. K. Root (Princeton, 1926), p. 449.

[4] *Jack Upland, Friar Daw's Reply and Upland's Rejoinder*, ed. P. L. Heyworth (Oxford, 1968), p. 80. For later examples of this proverb, see Appendix III, pp. 289–90.

[5] George Ripley, *The Compound of Alchemy*, ed. by E. Ashmole, in *Theatrum Chemicum Britannicum* (London, 1652), p. 175; *The Complete Poems of John Skelton*, ed. P. Henderson (3rd edn., London, 1959), pp. 176, 314.

fifteenth-century poetic burlesques.[1] In almost every instance moreover the references to the popular enthusiasm for Robin Hood tales remain intensely disparaging. Thus Alexander Barclay, a monk of Ely who made more allusions to the outlaw legend than any other author before the Reformation, recognized the appeal of hearing 'some mery fit of Maide Marian, or els of Robin Hood' but had no doubt that these were 'fables', 'jests' and 'trifles', all 'ground of ribaudry'.[2] Similarly, in John Rastell's *Interlude of the Four Elements* (*c.* 1520), it is the character of Yngnoraunce who expresses enthusiasm for the outlaw hero: 'But yf thou wylt have a song that is good, / I have one of Robyn Hode, / The best that ever was made'.[3] In 1528 William Tyndale characteristically pushed these moral reservations to extremes with a blanket condemnation of those who forbade the laity to study the Bible in the vernacular but allowed them 'to read Robin Hood, and Bevis of Hampton, Hercules, Hector and Troilus, with a thousand histories and fables of love and wantonness, and of ribaldry, as filthy as heart can think, to corrupt the minds of youth withal'.[4] On the eve of the English Reformation Robin Hood had already clearly forced his way into the distinguished company of the greatest heroes of all time.

Whether these 'fables and jestes of Robin Hood' were in fact a corrupting or seditious influence on late medieval audiences is a much more debatable matter. Clerical censure of Robin Hood tales is best interpreted as a late manifestation of a long tradition, dating back to at least Saints Jerome and Gregory the Great, of Christian reprobation of secular and unholy stories. There is no evidence of any serious attempt on the part of the late medieval English ecclesiastical hierarchy to protect the common laity from the supposedly depraved and foolish tales of Robin Hood: indeed the stream of critical references already mentioned testify to their growing popularity. During the course of the fifteenth century moreover allusions to Robin Hood begin to appear in record as well as literary sources. The phrase, 'Robin Hode en Barnesdale stode', made the first of its many curious appearances as a legal formula in the English courts during a lawsuit of 1429.[5] Ten years later, a petition to the parliament of 1439 related some of the misdeeds of

---

[1] *How the Plowman learned his Pater Noster*, and an untitled burlesque, both printed in T. Wright and J. O. Halliwell, *Reliquiae Antiquae* (London, 1841–3), I, 43–7, 81, 85; cf. Child, III, 41.

[2] See Barclay's *The Shyp of Folys of the Worlde* (a translation of Sebastian Brant's *Narrenschiff*), ed. T. H. Jamieson (London, 1874), II, 155; cf. Ritson, 1846, p. 22.

[3] J. Rastell, *The Interlude of the Four Elements*, ed. J. O. Halliwell (Percy Society, vol. 22, 1848), pp. 50–1.

[4] *The Works of William Tyndale*, ed. G. E. Duffield (Courtenay Library of Reformation Classics, I, Appleford, Berks., 1964), p. 331. For a later version of the same complaint (by Nicholas Bownd in 1606), see K. Thomas, *Religion and the Decline of Magic* (London, 1971), p. 164.

[5] W. C. Bolland, *A Manual of Year Book Studies* (Cambridge, 1925), p. 107; cf. Ritson, 1846, p. 23.

Piers Venables of Derbyshire, a criminal who had helped to rescue a prisoner being taken to Tutbury castle: it was alleged that he had gathered around him a large number of misdoers, 'beyng of his clothinge, and in manere of insurrection wente into the wodes in that county like it hadde be Robyn Hode and his meynee'.[1] This appears to be the first of many recorded occasions when real criminals, rebels and outlaws were given the names of the legendary outlaws of the greenwood, perhaps the most famous example being Sir Robert Cecil's later condemnation of Guy Fawkes and his associates as 'Robin Hoods'. Before the end of the fifteenth century there is indeed some evidence that the leaders of criminal bands voluntarily chose aliases derived from the Robin Hood legend. As early as 1417 Robert Stafford, chaplain, the chief of a gang of thieves and marauders in Surrey and Sussex, assumed the name of 'Frere Tuck'; and in 1497 Robert Marchall of Wednesbury in Staffordshire had to defend himself before Star Chamber against the allegation that under the name of 'Robyn Hood' he had led a group of more than a hundred men to a riotous assembly at Willenhall.[2] More notorious still were the exploits, five years later, of 'a felowe, whych had renued many of Robin Hodes pagentes, which named himself Grenelef' and so had presumably read or heard the *Gest of Robyn Hode*.[3]

Yet another, and in many ways more informative, insight into the development of the Robin Hood legend in the fifteenth century is provided by writers north of the border, and in particular by the three Scottish chroniclers, Andrew of Wyntoun, Walter Bower and John Major.[4] Andrew of Wyntoun, whose verse *Original Chronicle* of Scotland to 1408 was probably completed before 1420, ascribed the exploits of Robin Hood and Little John to the years between 1283 and 1285:

'Litil Johun and Robert Hude
Waythmen war commendit gud,
In Ingilwode and Bernysdaile
Thai oyssit all this tyme thar trawale'.[5]

Wyntoun is the only writer to name Inglewood in Cumberland, the home of Adam Bell (No. 28), in this connection; and it may be that he had confused the setting of two separate cycles of outlaw stories. The better informed

---

[1] *Rotuli Parliamentorum* (Record Commission, 1767–77), V, 16.

[2] *C.P.R., 1416–22*, pp. 84, 141; *1429–36*, p. 10; *Staffordshire Suits in the court of Star Chamber* (Staffordshire Historical Collections, X, Pt. I, 1907), p. 81. We owe this last reference to the generosity of Dr David Palliser.

[3] See below, p. 90; Robert Fabyan, *Cronycle* (London, 1559), p. 533.

[4] The contribution of these three Scottish chroniclers to the Robin Hood legend is assessed by Keen, *Outlaws*, pp. 176–8, and J. B. Bessinger, Jr., 'Robin Hood: Folklore and Historiography, 1377–1500', *Tennessee Studies in Literature*, XI (1966), pp. 61–9.

[5] *The Original Chronicle of Andrew of Wyntoun*, ed. F. J. Amours (Scottish Text Society, 1903–14), V, 136–7.

Walter Bower, in his continuation of John Fordun's *Scotichronicon* written in the 1440s, remarked that it was the foolish people, the '*stolidum vulgus*', who preferred tales, mimes and songs about the deeds of 'Robertus Hode and Littill Johanne' to those about the heroes of other romances. In an entry inserted under the year 1266 Bower wrote, 'Then arose the most famous murderer, Robert Hood, as well as Little John together with their accomplices from among the dispossessed and the banished, whom the foolish people are so inordinately fond of celebrating in tragedy and comedy'.[1] Scottish enthusiasm for tales of Robin Hood continued to be intense during the next century. Nor was it confined to the '*stolidum vulgus*': a reference within Gavin Douglas's *Palice of Honour*, composed in or near 1501, to 'Robene Hude, and Gilbert with the quhite hand' makes it virtually certain that the Scottish poet was familiar with a version of the *Gest of Robyn Hode*.[2] And it was a Scottish author, John Major, who in 1521 first fully articulated the view that Robin Hood was a noble outlaw. In a well-known passage of his Latin *History of Greater Britain*, Major was at pains to stress that '*Robertus Hudus Anglus et Parvus Joannes*' (whom he assigned to the period of Richard I's imprisonment in Germany during the early 1190s) assaulted only the wealthy. 'He would allow no woman to suffer injustice, nor would he spoil the poor, but rather enriched them from the plunder taken from abbots. The robberies of this man I condemn, but of all robbers he was the most humane and the chief'.[3]

With the exceptionally influential eulogy of Robin Hood by John Major, the first man of letters known to have expressed a positive admiration for Robin Hood, this survey of pre-Reformation references to the outlaw hero may be appropriately drawn to a close. Although the Robin Hood legend was still at a comparatively early stage of its development in the 1520s, it is clear enough that its central theme—the exploits of an outlaw who could do violence yet retain sympathy—had come into permanent existence. Nor can there be any doubt that Major had derived his belief in Robin Hood as the 'prince of thieves' directly from those 'songs' which, as he himself wrote, were 'told all over Britain' in his own day. All the early comments on the Robin Hood legend leave one with the inescapable conclusion that the reciting or singing of tales and 'rymes' had been the primary means of that legend's dissemination in the later middle ages. The product of a largely oral and therefore to us impenetrable culture, the medieval legend of Robin Hood can be sometimes glimpsed but never fully comprehended. It is indeed to the

[1] *Johannis de Fordun Scotichronicon*, ed. T. Hearne (Oxford, 1722), III, 774.

[2] *Shorter Poems of Gavin Douglas*, ed. P. J. Bawcutt (Scottish Text Society, 1967), p. 109. For further discussion of Scottish interest in Robin Hood at this period see below, p. 40.

[3] John Major, *Historia Majoris Britanniae*, ed. R. Freebairn (Edinburgh, 1740), p. 128; translated in A. Constable's edition of *A History of Greater Britain* (Scottish History Society, X, 1892), pp. 156–7.

exceptional cases of the very few early Robin Hood 'ballads' which were committed to writing that one is forced to turn in any attempt to trace the legend of the greenwood back to its original date and form. Hardly a single aspect of the early history of the English ballad remains uncontroversial, not even that of nomenclature. As is now well known, the word 'ballad', ultimately derived from the Latin *ballare* (to dance) and the Provençal *ballada* (dance-song), was not applied to popular English narrative songs of the Robin Hood type until the late sixteenth century. Although the practice of describing the earliest surviving Robin Hood stories as ballads is now too firmly established to be eradicated, readers of this selection of texts would do best to forget it altogether. The common belief that the early Robin Hood narratives form a distinctive category within the literary genre of 'traditional English ballads' has done more than almost anything else to becloud rather than clarify the important issues.[1]

Quite apart from the general problems of ballad origins in England, too complex a subject to be discussed here, the study of the early Robin Hood 'ballads' themselves is fraught with textual problems of exceptional difficulty and ambiguity. So formidable has been Francis Child's reputation as an editor that not one of the thirty-eight Robin Hood ballads printed in his *English and Scottish Popular Ballads* in 1888—with the single exception of the *Gest*—has been subjected to detailed literary analysis since that date. As Professor Holt has already suggested, the next move in the investigation of the Robin Hood legend would seem to lie with linguistic scholars rather than historians.[2] Admittedly no important early Robin Hood ballad has been discovered since Child's day, and his collated texts, although they fall a little short of perfection, have stood the test of time remarkably well. On the other hand it would now be fruitful to undertake a much more sophisticated study of the Middle English word-forms found in some of the ballads than was possible in the late nineteenth century—a study which could hardly fail to throw some light on the geographical provenance and date of composition of the earliest Robin Hood items in the Child canon. More generally, it is already clear that Child's personal approach to the task of ballad collecting and editing, based on a mixture of scholarship, connoisseurship and intuition, is often seriously at odds with the interests and needs of the historian. One obvious effect, for instance, of Child's preoccupations 'has been to encourage the study of ballads without respect to time and place'.[3] As the reader of the early Robin Hood songs in this collection will soon appreciate, their stanzas are normally written in so-called *Common Measure*, whereby the first and third lines of the

---

[1] The best introduction to these issues remains M. J. C. Hodgart, *The Ballads* (London, 1950); cf. the same author's introduction to *The Faber Book of Ballads* (London, 1965).

[2] J. C. Holt, 'Robin Hood: Some Comments', *Past and Present*, 19 (1961), p. 18.

[3] D. C. Fowler, *A Literary History of the Popular Ballad* (Durham, North Carolina, 1968), p. 3.

quatrain have four stresses and eight syllables, the second and fourth lines three stresses and six syllables; but Professor E. K. Chambers and, more recently, Professor David Fowler, have already launched formidable attacks on the view that the earliest surviving Robin Hood ballads were ever 'sung ballads' in Child's sense at all.[1] The possibility, indeed probability, that these pre-sixteenth-century works of 'yeoman minstrelsy' were recited and perhaps composed by itinerant professional entertainers makes Child's quasi-mystical concept of a 'ballad-muse' seem largely irrelevant. No longer can we be quite so confident as we would wish that the earliest Robin Hood ballads to survive bring us into immediate and undistorted contact with the thoughts and attitudes of the mass of the English population.

Such problems of origin and interpretation are rendered almost impossible to resolve because of the extreme rarity of authentically medieval Robin Hood ballads. For more than two centuries after the first known allusion to the outlaw by Langland, Robin Hood ballads are considerably less plentiful than the many literary references to the growth of the legend. Several of the later Robin Hood ballads admittedly do incorporate parts of an older and medieval tradition, most notably *Robin Hood and Guy of Gisborne* (No. 5) and *Robin Hood's Death* (No. 4). In many ways these two ballads are the most intriguing, as they are the most violent and tragic, items in the entire corpus of outlaw ballads. Untypical in that they are completely devoid of the characteristic earthy humour of the other Robin Hood ballads, they make their first known appearance—both in difficult, incomplete and partly corrupt texts—in the famous seventeenth-century Percy folio. Much more than any of the other ballads they urgently deserve the attention of modern linguistic scholarship. That these two ballads existed in some form during the fifteenth century is not of course in dispute. A medieval version of *Robin Hood and Guy of Gisborne* underlies a dramatic fragment of the 1470s (No. 19) and the Percy Folio version of *Robin Hood's Death* uses a legend clearly familiar to the compiler of the *Gest*. Until the apparently early word-forms of these two ballads are subjected to closer scrutiny than hitherto, any attempt to use *Robin Hood and Guy of Gisborne* or *Robin Hood's Death* as evidence for the origins of the medieval Robin Hood legend must however be made with considerable caution. In a very different category is that beautiful and haunting poem, *Robyn and Gandeleyn* (No. 27), which survives in a mid fifteenth-century Sloane manuscript in the British Museum and therefore has strong claims to be considered the first extant popular English ballad. However, although the stark tale of a double death related in *Robyn and Gandeleyn* throws an unusual and at times disturbing light upon the folk-lore of the medieval greenwood, there seems to be no reason at all to re-open the hypothesis that this Robin is at all closely related to the Robin Hood of the

[1] E. K. Chambers, *English Literature at the Close of the Middle Ages* (Oxford, 1945), pp. 129–37; Fowler, pp. 65–84.

other ballads.[1] Consequently only three (the *Gest*, *Robin Hood and the Potter*, *Robin Hood and the Monk*) of Child's Robin Hood ballads can be positively dated in their earliest recorded form to the period before the early sixteenth century.

Of these, much the longest, most complex and influential is the famous *Gest of Robyn Hode*, not strictly speaking a ballad in any conventional sense, but an ambitious attempt to construct a lengthy narrative of almost epic proportions by weaving together material from various now vanished smaller ballads or tales. Few of the problems surrounding the creation and dissemination of the *Gest* are simple, not even the date and identity of the earliest text of the work. No manuscript copy of the *Gest* survives and the most famous printed text (itself apparently a cheap reprint of a previous and now lost edition by Richard Pynson) is a solitary black-letter copy bound with ten other early printed tracts into a volume in the National Library of Scotland. This edition of the *Gest* was not itself however the product of the first Scottish press: it was probably printed on the continent, almost certainly by Dutch printers for the English as well as Scottish market, during the second decade of the sixteenth century. There is consequently no absolute certainty that this copy of the *Gest* precedes another black-letter version of the same work, printed at London by Wynkyn de Worde at some time between 1492 and 1534 and now surviving in a single copy in the Cambridge University Library.[2] Collation of these two first printed editions of the *Gest* reveals numerous slight verbal but relatively few substantive textual variations, a fact which suggests that a fairly standardized version of the work was presumably circulating in manuscript form at the end of the fifteenth century.[3] More significantly still, both texts preserve so large a number of Middle English literary forms that they gave Child strong grounds for believing that 'the whole poem may have been put together as early as 1400, or before'.[4] If so, and Child's opinion has been tacitly accepted by all succeeding ballad scholars, the crucial place of the *Gest* in the development of the Robin Hood

---

[1] Child long ago pointed out that the differences between Robyn and Gandeleyn on the one hand and Robin Hood and Little John on the other are much more striking than their similarities. Although the former certainly enter the 'grene wode' to kill deer, it is by no means clear that they were intended to represent outlaws at all. According to the ballad itself 'Stronge theuys wern tho chylderin non, / But bowmen gode and hende' (p. 256 below).

[2] For a more detailed discussion of the texts of the *Gest* see below, pp. 71–4.

[3] It seems highly likely that the copy of 'Roben Hod', priced at 2d., which occurs in the catalogue of an Oxford bookseller in 1520, was a printed edition of the *Gest* rather than of some smaller Robin Hood ballad: 'The daily ledger of John Dorne, 1520', ed. F. Madan, Oxford Historical Society, *Collectanea*, 1st series, III (1885), p. 79.

[4] Child, III, 40, where many of these antique forms are conveniently listed. W. H. Clawson, *The Gest of Robin Hood* (Toronto, 1909), p. 128, goes even further and argues, largely on the grounds of the frequent instances of a final—*e* word-ending, that the work was compiled in the fourteenth century.

legend needs no urging. An attractive and enjoyable work composed at so early a date may well have played an important role in stimulating and influencing the production of later Robin Hood ballads in a similar vein.[1]

The two other, much shorter and more 'conventional', fifteenth-century Robin Hood ballads raise other problems. Indisputably the earlier text is the poem or 'talkyng' of ninety verses, beginning with the line 'In somer, when the shawes be sheyne', now known as *Robin Hood and the Monk* (No. 2 below). In many ways the most artistically accomplished of all the Robin Hood ballads ('perfection of its kind' according to Child), this poem survives only in a manuscript of the mid-fifteenth century, whose miscellaneous contents were apparently prepared to serve the didactic purposes of an anonymous clerical compiler.[2] The manuscript contains several short devotional treatises as well as a series of metrical narratives such as *King Edward and the Shepherd*, a variation on the familiar theme of King and Subject, and the *Turnament of Tottenham*, a chivalric burlesque. Although in regular ballad stanza form, *Robin Hood and the Monk* was almost certainly designed to be recited by a minstrel rather than sung. To the student of ballad literature the chief interest of this first extant Robin Hood ballad may indeed be that 'it shows the lingering technique of later balladry beginning to emerge in late medieval minstrelsy'.[3] Its appearance in manuscript form proves that a Robin Hood ballad could occasionally be committed to writing as early as the mid-fifteenth century, but it remains extremely unlikely that there was ever a large audience of contemporary *readers* for the late medieval tales of Robin Hood. In the case of the only other extant medieval Robin Hood ballad, we are once again confronted with an isolated work of 'yeoman minstrelsy' inserted into a miscellaneous compilation of devotional and other pieces. *Robin Hood and the Potter* (No. 3) is preserved in another Cambridge University Library manuscript, to be dated—on palaeographical grounds—either to the very end of the fifteenth century or (more probably) to the early sixteenth century.[4] Like *Robin Hood and the Monk*, this ballad shows strong traces of minstrel technique, notably an *ABAB* rhyming pattern within many of its stanzas, and was apparently intended to be recited aloud rather than sung. Such recitation might of course have been delivered in a chanting tone and with the benefit of musical accompaniment; but it must have been far removed from the common measures and refrains of the later popular sung ballads.[5]

The fact that all the early surviving Robin Hood ballads bear the hallmarks

[1] For this and other reasons the highly theoretical discussion of the *Gest* by W. M. Hart, *Ballad and Epic* (Boston, 1907), pp. 88–109, seems extremely misguided.

[2] See below, pp. 113–15.

[3] Fowler, *Literary History of Popular Ballad*, p. 82.

[4] See below, p. 123.

[5] Chambers, *English Literature at the Close of the Middle Ages*, p. 148; and see below, p. 124.

of 'minstrel padding' throws at least some flickering light on the nature of
their audiences. Little enough is known about the practices of medieval
minstrelsy; but one would probably be safe to assume that works like *Robin
Hood and the Monk* and *Robin Hood and the Potter* were recited by itinerant
minstrels whose livelihood depended on their ability to serve a comparatively
wide audience, composed no doubt of peasants and townsmen as well as
members of the gentry. Within the first few stanzas of the *Gest* Robin Hood
is immediately identified as a friend of the 'husbonde' and 'yeman' as well as
of those knights and squires 'that wol be a gode felawe'. All allowances made
for the ambiguities of these terms, 'yeoman minstrelsy' remains the most
appropriate description for the *Gest*, *Robin Hood and the Monk* and *Robin
Hood and the Potter*, all works which reflect a deliberate appeal to the patronage of the yeoman rather than of the landed nobleman. The Robin Hood of
the early ballads is emphatically not a knight himself and his followers
certainly do not belong to the aristocratic section of society. Yet the 'curteyse
outlawe' of the *Gest* has many of the attributes of the well-born chivalric hero
of medieval tradition.[1] In other words the contents as well as the form of the
early Robin Hood ballads reveal the strong influence upon them of the conventions of late medieval English romance. For all we know, the 'rymes of
Robyn hood' so familiar to the Sloth of *Piers Plowman* and significantly
associated by him with those of 'Randolf erle of Chestre', may have been even
more akin to the highly conventionalized metrical tale than the surviving
Robin Hood narratives of the following century.[2] As it is, the *Gest*, *Robin
Hood and the Monk* and *Robin Hood and the Potter* provide classic examples
of the difficulties of disentangling 'popular' from 'aristocratic' elements in
medieval literature.[3] The literary 'ballad form' in which the Robin Hood
legend is first expressed may well derive, as modern scholars are at pains to
stress, from the courtly French romance and *carole* rather than the communal story-telling of the English peasantry: but this leaves entirely open the
important issue as to whether the protagonist himself originated as a popular
or aristocratic hero.[4]

In no sense therefore do the surviving Robin Hood ballads present us with

[1] J. C. Holt, 'The Origins and Audience of the Ballads of Robin Hood', *Past and Present*,
18 (1960), pp. 93–101; and see below, p. 32.

[2] Although none of the 'rymes' of Rannulf de Blundeville, Earl of Chester (d. 1232)
survive, the broad outlines of two lost romances about him can be reconstructed from
later sources: see R. M. Wilson, *The Lost Literature of Medieval England* (London,
1970), pp. 117–18.

[3] For some of these difficulties see the short discussion in G. Duby, 'The Diffusion of
Cultural Patterns in Feudal Society', *Past and Present*, 39 (1968), pp. 3–10.

[4] The fact that the heroes of the late medieval Danish *riddarvisor* or 'knight ballads' are
very aristocratic indeed is certainly worth noting; but there are good reasons for
believing that the 'ballad community' served by these Danish *folkeviser* was much more
like that which promoted the Scottish Border ballads than the audience for 'rymes' of
Robin Hood (see below, pp. 274–6).

the 'original' Robin Hood legend, a legend whose origins are indeed lost beyond recall. Nevertheless it is as well to remember that the outlaw hero in pre-industrial societies has rarely, if ever, been a purely fictional creation. In cases as dissimilar as those of Marsk Stig of thirteenth-century Denmark (No. 29) and Jesse James of nineteenth-century America (No. 30), the activities of a historical individual underlay the later legend. Indeed the remarkable uniformity of the process whereby a noted rebel or criminal has been posthumously transformed into the stereotyped role of a 'social bandit' can hardly fail to tempt one into the belief that a 'real' Robin Hood must have existed. Moreover medieval English narrative tales can themselves often be interpreted as an early form of popular history, designed to perpetuate as well as to embroider the genuine exploits of the famous dead. At a period when few laymen could have read or indeed understood the Latin chronicles produced by monastic and secular clerks for ecclesiastical audiences, the act of reciting a romance or singing a ballad was itself a 'remembrance of things past' as well as an act of entertainment. As will be seen in the next section of this introduction, the geographical allusions in the early Robin Hood ballads, and especially in the *Gest*, are sufficiently specific to suggest that the exploits of a real Barnsdale outlaw lay behind the later Robin Hood saga. Despite Professor Holt's salutary warning that 'any effort to penetrate behind the *Gest* leads us, not to rustic figures, but to the knightly heroes of the thirteenth-century romances and *gestes*', the probability remains that the early Robin Hood ballads present us with a glamorized and 'gentle' version of a historic outlaw who had indeed begun his legendary career as 'some primitive social rebel'.[1]

Needless to say, the search for this 'real' Robin Hood has long been the most obsessive aspect of the modern enthusiasm for the greenwood legend. On the whole it has proved to be a peculiarly fruitless quest. As is now well known, the copious records of thirteenth- and fourteenth-century England present us with not one Robin Hood but a bewildering variety of persons of that name. Francis Child discovered no less than 'six Robin Hoods between 30 Edward I and 10 Edward III, a period of less than forty years'.[2] Nor is this surprising. Robert was one of the five or six commonest male Christian names in post-Conquest England; and in the thirteenth century its diminutive form of Robin was even more usual than Robert itself.[3] The surname Hood or Hude is also familiar enough to all readers of medieval archives.[4] Far from being related to Germanic or Scandinavian deities like Woden, Hodr, or

---

[1] Holt, 'Origins and Audience of the Ballads of Robin Hood', p. 102.

[2] Child, III, 56.

[3] *Oxford Dictionary of Christian Names*, ed. E. G. Withycombe (2nd edn., 1950), p. 243; cf. R. B. Dobson, *Durham Priory, 1400–1450* (Cambridge, 1973), p. 56.

[4] Six individuals with that surname (one a 'Robertus Hude, barbour') were received into the freedom of the city of York between 1272 and 1558: see *Register of the Freemen of the City of York* I (Surtees Society, XCVI, 1897), pp. 126, 148, 181, 189, 241, 248.

Hodeken, the name of Hood in English must mean a head-covering. Its application to individuals can only have arisen in one of two ways—either as a metonymy for the occupational 'Hooder' (a maker of hoods) or as a nickname. In both cases it was a surname which readily lent itself to the making of compounds like Greenhood, a name easily confused with and absorbed by the still common Greenwood.[1] On several occasions in the sixteenth and seventeenth centuries, the legendary Robin Hood was himself transformed into Robin Wood or Whood, a complication which does not however appear to apply to the medieval period where all the sources agree on a spelling like Hood, Hude or (most common in the *Gest* and the early ballads) Hode.

The conclusion must be that the discovery of the name Robert or Robin Hood in a medieval English document is not in itself of particular significance. Somewhat more intriguing is the use of the compound 'Robynhod' as a surname. Only three examples of this usage have yet been discovered for the period before Langland's first reference to the legend in or about 1377. In 1296 a 'Gilbert Robynhod' was recorded at Fletching, Sussex, and thirty-six years later (in 1332) a 'Robert Robynhoud' occurs at Harting in the same county.[2] Any hopes raised by the possibility that these two men bore surnames derived from the legendary Robin Hood (whose origins would then need to be firmly placed earlier than the late thirteenth century) are somewhat dashed by the remaining example. For a 'Katherine Robynhod' recorded in the London coroner's roll for 1325 can almost certainly be identified as his daughter of that Christian name mentioned in the will of 'Robert Hod', a Common Councillor for the Vintry Ward who died shortly before May 1318.[3] It seems clear enough that the surname 'Robynhod', like 'Hod' or 'Hood' itself, could be used in late medieval England as a heritable family surname quite without benefit of any deliberate allusion to the outlaw of legend.

For obvious reasons most attempts to identify the historical Robin Hood in surviving record sources have tended to concentrate upon the northern parts of England. Of the many possible candidates perhaps the least likely is the Robin Hood imprisoned in 1354 on a charge of trespass of vert and venison in the forest of Rockingham.[4] Apart from the fact that this Northamptonshire forest fails to appear in early Robin Hood literature, it is difficult to believe

---

[1] G. Redmonds, *English Surname Series, I: Yorkshire, West Riding* (Chichester, 1973), pp. 16–17; cf. Chambers, *English Literature at the Close of the Middle Ages*, pp. 129–30.

[2] *The Three Earliest Subsidies for the County of Sussex, 1296, 1327, 1332* (Sussex Record Society, X, 1910), pp. 33, 236. We are most grateful to Professor R. M. Wilson for this and the following reference. Cf. Child, IV, 496, for a Thomas Robinhood of 1381.

[3] *Calendar of Coroners' Rolls of the City of London, A.D. 1300–1378*, ed. R. R. Sharpe (London, 1913), pp. 125–6; cf. *Calendar of London Letter-Book B*, ed. R. R. Sharpe (London, 1900), p. 238. We have had the benefit of consulting an unpublished paper by John Harvey on this London Robert or Robin Hood of *c.* 1300.

[4] As suggested by Chambers, *English Literature at the Close of the Middle Ages*, p. 130.

that the historical genesis of a legend so well established (on Langland's evidence) by the 1370s can date from a period later than the early fourteenth century. The most famous and most circumstantially detailed of all attempts to identify Robin Hood does in fact assume that he was the 'Robyn Hode' who received daily payment as one of Edward II's *'valets de chambre'* during 1324. This familiar hypothesis, first put forward by Joseph Hunter in 1852, rests on a quite remarkable belief in the historical accuracy of the *Gest*. Hunter asks us to believe, on no direct evidence at all, that this Robin Hood had supported the anti-royalist cause of Earl Thomas of Lancaster and on the latter's defeat at the battle of Boroughbridge (1322) took to an outlaw's life in Barnsdale: it could then follow that on Edward II's visit to the north of England in 1323 he was pardoned and received into royal service.[1] This thesis was developed in great detail during the 1940s and 1950s by Mr J. W. Walker, whose major new contribution was the highly dubious identification of the 'Robyn Hode' who served Edward II with a Robert Hood who bought a plot of land on Bickhill, the market place of Wakefield, in 1316.[2] In the wake of this supposed discovery, the identification of other characters in the *Gest* with various personages (Roger of Doncaster, Richard of the Lee, Gilbert Withondes) mentioned in the Wakefield court rolls and other records has become something of a local sport in the area.[3] The weight of ingeniously applied learning on this topic has tended to conceal the theory's central flaw: there is no direct evidence whatsoever that the Wakefield Robin Hood(s) of the early fourteenth century was ever an outlaw, or indeed a criminal, at all.

A persuasive case can moreover be advanced to suggest that the historical genesis of the Robin Hood legend lay in the thirteenth rather than the fourteenth century. As this argument rests on deductions drawn from references within the *Gest*, *Robin Hood and the Monk* and *Robin Hood and the Potter*, it may be as well to stress that the adventures related in these texts can emphatically not be ascribed to a precise period. All we know of the frequency of thematic variation and name transference in popular ballad literature would lead us to expect that the surviving 'rymes' of the fifteenth century contain within them an inextricably confused series of different chronological layers. The continual re-shaping of the outlaw saga in more modern times should

---

[1] J. Hunter, 'The Great Hero of the Ancient Minstrelsy of England: Robin Hood, his period, real character, etc.' (*Critical and Historical Tracts*, No. 4, 1852), pp. 28–38. For the most devastating demonstration of Hunter's 'uncommon insensibility to the ludicrous' see Child, III, 55–6.

[2] J. W. Walker, 'Robin Hood Identified', *Y.A.J.*, XXXVI (1944–7), pp. 4–46, and *The True History of Robin Hood* (Wakefield, 1952). See the detailed criticisms offered by Keen, *Outlaws*, pp. 183–7; R. H. Hilton, 'The Origins of Robin Hood', *Past and Present*, 14 (1958), pp. 33–4; Holt, 'Origins and Audience of the Ballads of Robin Hood', pp. 104–5.

[3] P. V. Harris, *The Truth about Robin Hood* (Mansfield, 1973), and 'Who was Robin Hood?', *Folk-Lore Quarterly*, LXVI (1955), pp. 288–94.

warn us that it can never have been a static legend in the middle ages. It would therefore be perfectly legitimate to suppose that the earliest surviving ballad texts capture that legend as it had been re-worked to suit the tastes of a late fourteenth- or fifteenth-century audience but may still contain allusions to an earlier and more 'original' stage of its development. One possible allusion of this sort occurs in the forty-fifth stanza of the *Gest* where Robin Hood expresses a doubt as to whether the impoverished knight brought before him may not have been 'made a knyght of force': it has been argued that such a reference to the practice of distraint of knighthood 'leads us most obviously to the time of Henry III or Edward I'.[1] Similarly the *Gest's* account of the deliberate foreclosing on the impoverished knight's debt to the abbot of St Mary's, York, points to a period before 1300 for the simple reason that after that date few English monasteries were ever in a position to advance large amounts of money to members of the English gentry. Even more intriguing is the complete absence in the *Gest* and the early ballads of any reference to justices of peace, known to be among the chief agents of royal authority in the English localities from the early fourteenth century onwards.[2] Does the appearance of the sheriff of Nottingham as the villain of the Robin Hood saga imply that the legend came to birth in a period, before rather than after the reign of Edward I, when that officer's authority and unpopularity were apparently at their height? However that question (one upon which historical opinion is still very much divided) comes to be answered, the part played by the sheriff in the outlaw legend deserves attention in its own right.

The central position of the sheriff of Nottingham as the anti-hero of the Robin Hood legend throughout its history needs no particular urging. The common feature of all those ballads which place Robin Hood in Sherwood Forest is the outlaw's obsessional enmity with the sheriff of Nottingham; indeed the latter plays so fundamental a role in the legend that he may have been even more crucial to its origins than Robin Hood himself. In the *Gest*, for example, one is left with an overall impression that it was the sheriff's presence in Nottinghamshire that drew Robin to that county rather than that it was Robin's activities in Sherwood which compelled the local royal agent to move into the centre of the legend. Although Nottingham is the only English town to be afforded a prominent role in the Robin Hood ballads, there can be little doubt that it owes this prominence less to its importance as the outlaws' hypothetical local market town than to its verbal association with the sheriff of that name. For these and other reasons the possibility that a series of adventurous and probably scurrilous tales about an anti-hero, the sheriff of Nottingham, arose independently from and perhaps even preceded those concerning Robin Hood deserves consideration. The theory, speculative as it is, that the late medieval Robin Hood legend was an amalgam of two

---

[1] Holt, 'Origins and Audience of the Ballads of Robin Hood', p. 103; cf. Child, III, 51.
[2] Holt, 'Robin Hood: Some Comments', p. 18; Keen, *Outlaws*, p. 135.

originally distinct story cycles (one centred on a Barnsdale outlaw, the other on the sheriff of Nottingham) has the advantage of making several other features of the antagonism between the two adversaries a little more intelligible than it can otherwise hope to be. Apart from the well-known difficulty of understanding why a sheriff of Nottinghamshire should come to be the persecutor and butt of an outlaw leader living outside his county in southern Yorkshire, this sheriff never seems quite the official enemy appropriate to any forest bandit. Control over the forest was the subject of intense governmental interest throughout the middle ages, but from the mid-thirteenth century at least it was rarely a duty entrusted to a county sheriff. In these circumstances therefore it might well be that a quest for a historical sheriff of Nottingham could prove less illusory than the perennial search for a 'real' Robin Hood.

As with the historical originals of Robin Hood there have been no lack of candidates for the original sheriff of the ballads. Professor Owen, the most lucid exponent of the view that the Robin Hood legend was a fusion of two separate adventure cycles, believed that some unknown constable of Nottingham castle during the twelfth or thirteenth century may well have served as the model.[1] Mr Valentine Harris put forward the claims of John de Segrave who in the reign of Edward II was Justice of the Forests beyond Trent and Constable of Nottingham castle.[2] Another fourteenth-century possibility is Sir Robert Ingram, mayor of Nottingham and sheriff of the county on several occasions: he appears to have been an ally of the famous Coterel gang whose activities centred upon Nottinghamshire and Derbyshire.[3] Yet as Professor Holt has pointed out, the number of historical sheriffs of Nottinghamshire with a recorded interest in forest administration seems very restricted. His own two candidates, Philip Mark, who combined the Nottinghamshire shrievality with the custody of Sherwood from 1212 to 1217, and Brian de Lisle, Chief Justice of the Forest from 1221 to 1224 and sheriff of Yorkshire a decade later, still appear to be the best in the field.[4] Although (for reasons already discussed) there is no *a priori* reason why a 'real' sheriff of Nottingham should be a contemporary of a 'real' Robin Hood, this particular line of investigation also points to the thirteenth rather than the fourteenth century for the origins of the greenwood legend.

Unfortunately not one of the many attempts to identify a historic Robin Hood in the period before 1300 carries conviction. According to Walter Bower, the outlaw rose to prominence in 1266 as the leader of a group of dis-

---

[1] L. V. D. Owen, 'Robin Hood', *Chambers's Encyclopaedia* (1950 edn.), XI, 733–4; and cf. Child, III, 51.
[2] Harris, *The Truth about Robin Hood*, p. 97.
[3] J. Bellamy, *Crime and Public Order in England in the Later Middle Ages* (London, 1973), p. 75.
[4] Holt, 'Origins and Audience of the Ballads of Robin Hood', p. 104.

inherited followers of Simon de Montfort, killed at the battle of Evesham in the previous year. Despite the fact that Bower was writing almost two centuries later, this dating of the origins of the greenwood legend to the 1260s has exerted considerable influence, especially among Victorian writers.[1] It still deserves consideration. One of Simon de Montfort's adherents, Roger Godberd, did indeed become an outlaw in Sherwood forest; and his robberies and murders of travellers within that forest became so notorious that Henry III's government offered a remarkably large sum of 100 marks to Reynold de Grey, constable of Nottingham castle, for his capture.[2] Although it seems not unreasonable to suppose that Roger Godberd's activities over a period of four years or so in Sherwood may have had some effect on the development of the greenwood legend, there is no evidence that he ever adopted the alias of Robin Hood. Nor does the *Gest* or any other Robin Hood ballad refer to the political issues at stake in the England of the 1260s.

The same argument applies much more forcefully to the famous belief, first recorded by John Major and later popularized by Anthony Munday and Sir Walter Scott, that the historical Robin Hood flourished during the reigns of Richard I and John.[3] For this view there is no evidence whatsoever; all allowances made for the possible longevity of oral traditions in medieval England, it is hard to associate any of the incidents or references in the surviving ballad literature with a period as early as the 1190s. We are left, if only for the present, with one final possibility—a candidate for the role of the historical Robin Hood first put forward in 1936 by Professor Owen and championed more recently by Professor Holt. In the governmental Pipe Roll of 1230 the sheriff of Yorkshire accounted for 32s. 6d. '*de catallis Roberti Hood fugitivi*'. Similar references to this Robert Hood or Hod appear in the Pipe Rolls of 1228 (where he is given the alternative nickname of *Hobbehod*) and 1231.[4] Interesting as it is to discover 'the one historical Robin Hood we know of as an outlaw', it has to be remembered that we have at present no evidence that this 'fugitive' was at all a violent outlaw. As was perhaps inevitable from the start, the quest for an original Robin Hood peters out at a stage of profound uncertainty. On balance it has always been a search more capable of generating heat than light. We may derive some consolation from the fact that the popular audience for the Robin Hood legend in the later middle

---

[1] See especially the references collected by Gutch, I, pp. ix, 77–8, 128.

[2] *C.P.R.*, *1266–72*, pp. 633–4; Bellamy, *Crime and Public Order*, pp. 83–4.

[3] Few modern writers have ever favoured a twelfth-century date for the birth of the Robin Hood legend. On this issue critical and imaginative treatments of the Robin Hood legend have nearly always parted company. The only serious scholar to accept a twelfth-century date for Robin Hood in recent years was Professor W. Entwistle in his book on *European Balladry* (Oxford, 1939), p. 232.

[4] *Pipe Roll 14 Henry III* (Pipe Roll Society, XLII, 1927), p. 274; Owen, 'Robin Hood', pp. 733–4; Holt, 'Origins and Audience of the Ballads of Robin Hood', pp. 104–7.

ages, wise in their time perhaps, undoubtedly soon 'forgot . . . in the darling of their fancy . . . the original forester of the West Riding.'[1]

II. *The Medieval Background*

'Such severe measures against criminals ought to keep the English in check, but, for all this, there is no country in the world where there are more thieves and robbers than in England; insomuch that few venture to go alone in the country, excepting in the middle of the day . . .'[2]

The impossibility of tracing the Robin Hood legend backwards to its original forms not only renders the certain identification of a 'real' Robin Hood impossible but also bedevils all attempts to place him within a firm historical context. The early Robin Hood ballads present the historian with a *locus classicus* of the perils which lie in wait for him who would wish to relate literature to life. Nevertheless there is no need for absolute defeatism. Recent studies of local government and society in late medieval England have begun to make the appeal of the greenwood legend a little more intelligible than used to be the case. Similarly a close attention to the texts of the *Gest of Robyn Hode* and the other ballads provides some clues to the origins and nature of that appeal. To take the most obvious approach first, it now seems clear that Robin Hood originally emerged as an intensely local hero figure. 'Full thirteene yeares and something more / These northerne parts he vexed sore.'[3] In view of the incessant variations in place nomenclature to which popular legends and ballad literature are both notoriously prone, it is worth emphasis that Robin Hood has always been a northern English hero. Apart from such late and minor eccentricities as his visits to the royal court or to Scarborough in *Robin Hood and Queen Katherine* (Child 145) and *The Noble Fisherman* (No. 12 below), the legendary outlaw has never been the victim of any serious attempt to wrench him out of the context of a Yorkshire or Nottinghamshire forest. Indeed the association of Robin and his band of outlaws with a comparatively confined area of northern England is one of the most distinctive features of the greenwood ballads, a feature shared by few of the other items in the repertory of so-called traditional ballads. It is hard not to draw the obvious conclusion that by at least the late fourteenth century, the concept of a 'northern' Robin Hood had become so deeply impressed on popular imagination that he could never thereafter be transferred to a different part of England.

[1] *Bishop Percy's Folio Manuscript*, ed. J. W. Hales and F. J. Furnivall (London, 1867–8), I, 6.

[2] *A Relation of the Island of England, c. 1500*, ed. C. A. Sneyd (Camden Society, Old Series 37, 1847), p. 34, reprinted in *English Historical Documents, 1485–1558*, ed. C. H. Williams (London, 1967), p. 199.

[3] See below, pp. 186, 190.

However Robin Hood is and was more than just an indisputably northern hero: he has been inseparably associated from a very early date with not only one but two different regions—Sherwood Forest in Nottinghamshire, and Barnsdale north of Doncaster in the West Riding of Yorkshire. The once popular debate about which of these two areas deserves historical precedence as the original home of the legendary outlaw is of more than antiquarian interest.[1] A close scrutiny of all early references to Robin Hood's geographical milieu leaves little doubt that in the later middle ages he was more often associated with Barnsdale than Sherwood.[2] Admittedly it may be urged in favour of the latter that the very first poem on the subject of Robin Hood, preserved in three and a half lines of doggerel English scribbled into a Lincoln Cathedral manuscript soon after 1400, begins with an unequivocal 'Robyn hod in scherewod stod'.[3] But at about the same date the Scottish chronicler Andrew of Wyntoun reported that Little John and Robin Hood were outlaws who had once operated 'In Ingilwode and Bernysdaile'.[4] Barnsdale was once again firmly attached to Robin Hood's persona during the course of a lawsuit in 1429 when the curious legal maxim, 'Robin Hode en Barnesdale stode' made an early appearance in an English court.[5] Writing in the 1440s, Walter Bower illustrated the adventurous reputation of Robin Hood by paraphrasing a now lost ballad whose theme was the outwitting of 'a certain sheriff' in 'Barnisdale'.[6] And when, in a famous letter to his brother John of 16 April 1473, Sir John Paston complained that he had been deserted by the servant whom he had employed 'to pleye Seynt Jorge and Robyn Hod and the Shryff off Nottyngham', he jocularly accused him of having 'goon into Bernysdale'.[7]

On balance therefore these fifteenth-century references to the Robin Hood legend seem to suggest that during the later middle ages the outlaw hero was more closely related to Barnsdale than Sherwood. The evidence of the earliest extant ballads points a little less certainly to the same conclusion. The 'feyre foreste' mentioned in the famous opening line of *Robin Hood and*

---

[1] The rivalry between Barnsdale and Sherwood appears to have reached its climax in the seventeenth century when travellers in both regions were encouraged to join, on payment of a fee, the 'Renowned Brotherhood' of Robin Hood after a ceremonial enthronement in the outlaw's supposed chair. Detailed descriptions of these two rituals are printed in *Old Yorkshire*, ed. W. Smith (London, 1884), V, 251; *A Relation of a Short Survey of 26 Counties, 1634*, ed. L. G. Wickham Legg (London, 1904), p. 13; James Brome, *Travels over England, Scotland and Wales* (2nd edn. London, 1707), pp. 75–6.

[2] For a slightly more detailed account than the one which follows here see Dobson and Taylor, 'Medieval Origins of the Robin Hood Legend', pp. 10–20.

[3] G. E. Morris, 'A Ryme of Robyn Hod', *Modern Language Review*, XLIII (1948), pp. 507–8; cf. R. M. Wilson, *The Lost Literature of Medieval England* (2nd edn, London, 1970), p. 130.

[4] See above, p. 4.   [5] See above, p. 3.

[6] *Scotichronicon*, ed. Hearne, III, 774.

[7] *The Paston Letters*, ed. J. Gairdner (London, 1904), V, 185.

the Monk (No. 2) is certainly explicitly identified as 'mery Scherwode' in the sixteenth stanza of that poem. But whereas the adventures described in *Robin Hood and the Potter* (No. 3) appear at first sight to take place within and immediately around the town of Nottingham, that ballad begins with Little John's account of his unfortunate encounter with the 'prod potter' at 'Wentbreg', a place which can only be Wentbridge ten miles north of Doncaster and at the northern limits of Barnsdale.[1] The later but exceptionally precise *Robin Hood and Guy of Gisborne* (No. 5) is more specific still. Here the 'fayre fforest' of the courtly introductory stanza rapidly takes concrete form not as Sherwood but as Barnsdale, the gates of which Little John 'knowes eche one'; when challenged by Sir Guy to reveal his identity, the hero declares simply that 'My name is Robin Hood of Barnesdale, / A ffelow thou has long sought'.[2] But the most interesting, because probably the earliest, of all geographical references in medieval Robin Hood literature are the ones provided by those sections of the *Gest of Robyn Hode* (the first and fourth fyttes) which deal with Robin's befriending of the impoverished knight.

Nowhere does the *Gest* mention Sherwood Forest as such, and from his very first appearance in the third stanza ('Robyn stode in Bernesdale, / And lenyd hym to a tre') the outlaw is firmly identified with the region north of Doncaster. The modern reader of the *Gest*, like its medieval audience, is made immediately aware that the outlaw has a permanent headquarters within Barnsdale, even if it can only take the form of a 'grene-wode tre' at which he can be contacted 'This day twelve moneth' (stanza 79). Only at a much later stage of the *Gest*, and one derived from a different tale or ballad, does the sheriff of Nottingham make his semi-obligatory appearance; and it is not until the fifth fytte of the work that Robin finally goes to Nottingham himself to take part in an archery contest (stanza 289). It is at Nottingham again that the king makes his six months' stay during his personal attempt to apprehend the outlaw. More significantly however, the author of the *Gest* makes Robin retire to Barnsdale for the last twenty-two years of his life after his chastening experience of life at the royal court. It was presumably from Barnsdale too that Robin Hood set out on his famous last journey, described in the cryptic last six verses of the *Gest*, to death by treachery at the neighbouring nunnery of 'Kyrkesly' four miles north of Huddersfield. The widespread later popular belief that the greatest English outlaw hero died at Kirklees priory—which finds its fullest but most mysterious expression in the haunting *Robin Hood's Death* (No. 4) is at least geographically in line with the prevailing tradition.[3]

---

[1] See below, p. 126.   [2] See below, pp. 142, 144.

[3] In the early sixteenth century John Leland was already convinced that that Kirkley or Kirklees was the '*monasterium Monialium ubi Ro. Hood nobilis ille exlex sepultus*': Leland's *Collectanea*, ed. T. Hearne, I (London, 1774), p. 54. The best introduction to the extraordinary series of legends which sprang up around the reputed site of Robin's death still remains the references collected by Ritson, *Robin Hood*, I, pp. xliv-xlix. The much mutilated and controversial gravestone of Robin Hood survives in a reconstructed

Robin appropriately meets his death at the end of the *Gest* as the result of nefarious collusion between a West Riding prioress and a knight, Sir Roger, of 'Donkesly', 'Donkestere' or Doncaster, immediately south of Barnsdale. The final impression left by both the *Gest* and the other early ballads is therefore of a legendary outlaw based reasonably firmly in the Barnsdale area but capable of expeditions southwards in pursuit of his arch-enemy, the sheriff of Nottingham.

There is of course no easy solution to the problem presented by these descriptions of a Robin Hood whose exploits alternated between Barnsdale and Sherwood Forest. Even if we are led by the weight of surviving evidence to a belief that the former was the more popular traditional home of the outlaw, it is clear that both areas were identified with the legendary 'greenwood' long before the end of the middle ages. Admittedly Sherwood and Barnsdale are less than forty miles apart and the two areas may have become confused in popular imagination at an early date. A more probable explanation for the two distinct geographical backgrounds to the Robin Hood legend is that the latter had already crystallized, at the time of its first recorded appearance, out of two even earlier and separate cycles, one of Barnsdale and one of Sherwood.[1] In the circumstances such a hypothesis is almost impossible to prove, even without benefit of the problems created by name-transference in ballad literature; but certainly the motives and achievement of the author of the *Gest* in particular become more intelligible if we suppose that his source-material included both a Nottinghamshire and a Barnsdale outlaw, possibly still relatively distinct. To suggest that the accomplished compiler of the *Gest* was the first person to fuse the two heroes into the one Robin Hood of the later legend, although not absolutely unreasonable, is however to go further than the insecure evidence allows.

While it is not at all surprising that Sherwood, one of the most famous of English forests at all periods (it was selected by Edward III as one of the venues for the extravagant hunting-parties at which he entertained his French hostages and English magnates in 1363),[2] should have been chosen as the backcloth to a medieval outlaw legend, Barnsdale presents us with a more baffling problem. An obscure and small area, Barnsdale never seems to have had fixed geographical boundaries but was usually understood to comprise the district, four or five miles from north to south and about the same from east to west, stretching southwards from the river Went to the villages of Skelbrooke and Hampole, six miles north of Doncaster. The name itself, although quite

---

form in the grounds of Kirklees Hall, but not the 'statue of this renowned freebooter, large as life, leaning on his unbent bow, with a quiver of arrows by his side, which formerly stood at one side of the entrance into the old hall': T. Allen, *New and Complete History of the County of York* (London, 1831), V, 476–7. Also see below, p. 309.

[1] See above, pp. 14–15.
[2] *Chronicon Henrici Knighton*, ed. J. R. Lumby (Rolls Series, 1889–95), II, 118–19.

ancient and probably derived from the Old English 'Beorn's Valley', scarcely occurs at all before the fifteenth century and owes nearly all of its prominence to the Robin Hood legend.[1] A magnesian limestone area, probably not much more heavily wooded in the later middle ages than it is today, Barnsdale does not appear to have ever been a forest in either the literal or the legal sense. When Leland visited southern Yorkshire in the early sixteenth century, he observed (or so he wrote) 'Along on the lift hond a iii miles of betwixt Milburne and Feribridge . . . the wooddi and famose forest of Barnesdale, wher they say Robyn Hudde lyvid like an owtlaw'.[2] However Leland's sense of direction is demonstrably at fault here, and when Henry VIII and Bishop Tunstall passed through southern Yorkshire at about the same period, it was described as 'one of the greatest and richest valleys in Europe'.[3] How had this obscure if relatively prosperous and well-settled area come to be made the home of England's greatest forest hero?

The possibility that Barnsdale was chosen more or less at random as the scene of Robin Hood's exploits would seem inherently unlikely; and a study of the various references to other places in the West Riding provided by the *Gest* leaves absolutely no doubt that the region was intended to be a good deal more than merely Robin's 'airy nothing, a local habitation and a name'. Not only Doncaster and Kirklees priory but also Wentbridge—the village on the Went through which travellers from the north entered 'Bernysdale'—figure in the *Gest*.[4] Much more intriguing, because more specific, are the places mentioned by Robin himself when he gave Little John the instructions from which the future action of the poem was to follow:

'And walke up to the Saylis,
And so to Watlinge Strete,
And wayte after some unketh gest,
Up chaunce ye may them mete.'[5]

---

[1] *The Place-Names of the West Riding of Yorkshire*, ed. A. H. Smith (P.N.S., XXXI, 1961), II, 37.

[2] *The Itinerary of John Leland, in England and Wales*, ed. L. Toulmin-Smith (London, 1906–10), IV, 13.

[3] Joseph Hunter, 'Account of King Henry the Eighth's Progress in Yorkshire', *Memoirs illustrative of the History and Antiquities of the County and City of York communicated to the Annual Meeting of the Archaeological Institute at York, July 1846* (London, 1848), p. 3.

[4] Admittedly the reference to Wentbridge in the *Gest* ('as he went at a brydge ther was a wrastelyng'—stanza 135) is so cryptic as to be debatable; but *Robin Hood and the Potter*, as has been seen, mentions 'Went-breg' *eo nomine*. A small hamlet throughout the later middle ages, Wentbridge had acquired its modern name form by 1302 and a leper-house by 1385, but was unlikely to be widely known except to travellers on the great north road. For evidence that by at least 1487 Wentbridge possessed 'an in' capable of providing beds for overnight accommodation, see *York Civic Records*, ed. A. Raine, II, (Y.A.S., Record Series, CIII, 1941), p. 5.

[5] *Gest*, stanza 18, repeated at stanza 209.

At first sight this order to apprehend an unsuspecting wayfarer on Watling Street might not seem topographically helpful: by the fifteenth century the name of the famous Roman road from Dover to Wroxeter via London had long been applied to many other stretches of road in various parts of the country. Among the oldest and best-documented examples of this practice, however, is the old Roman road (A639, still known as 'Roman Ridge') which runs north-west from Barnsdale towards Pontefract; the section of this road immediately to the north of the village of Wrangbrook was termed *Watling-stret* as early as the thirteenth century. Moreover in 1433 the whole of the road from Ferrybridge through Barnsdale to Worksop in Nottinghamshire was described as 'the highway called Watlyngstrete'.[1] At the very least, therefore, the 'Watlinge Strete' of the *Gest* was a particularly appropriate choice: at the most it reveals genuine familiarity with the detailed topography of Barnsdale on the part of the original author or composer of this section of the *Gest*. That the latter is the more likely alternative is proved by the immediately preceding allusion to 'the Saylis', without doubt the most important place reference in the entire corpus of Robin Hood ballads. To Joseph Hunter is due the credit for being able to identify this extremely elusive place-name with Sayles, a small and obscure tenancy of the late medieval manor of Ponte-fract which contributed towards the feudal aid granted to Edward III in 1346–7 for the knighting of his eldest son, the Black Prince.[2] Although Hunter and his successors have never established the exact whereabouts of the late medieval Sayles, this is not in fact a particularly arduous task. Never a village nor apparently even a hamlet, the name and location of Sayles, a land-holding within the parish of Kirk Smeaton, has yet survived almost un-changed to the present day. An 'acre in the Sailes' listed in a Kirk Smeaton glebe terrier of 1688 can be safely identified with the plot of land referred to as 'Sailes Close' almost two centuries later in a glebe terrier of 1857.[3] Thanks to this evidence of continuity, there can be no reasonable doubt that 'the Saylis' so well known to the Robin Hood of the *Gest* is still partly preserved as 'Sayle's Plantation', on the very northern edge of Barnsdale and five hundred yards east of Wentbridge.[4] It is hard not to believe that the medieval Sayles had gained some notoriety as a possible scene for highway robbery during the later middle ages, whatever the detailed origins of its association

---

[1] *Place-Names of West Riding* (P.N.S., XXXVI, 1962), VII, 145; I. D. Margary, *Roman Roads in Britain* (London, 1967), p. 415.

[2] It was assessed as one-tenth of a knight's fee: J. Hunter, 'The Great Hero of the Ancient Minstrelsy of England', pp. 15–16.

[3] Borthwick Institute of Historical Research, St Anthony's Hall, York: R. III. F 1 xlvi b; R. III. F. 16 xlvi (Kirk Smeaton Glebe Terriers of 7 June 1688 and 10 June 1857).

[4] Map Reference (Ordnance Survey, 6″ Yorkshire Sheet 41 NE) SE 495171. The high ground of Sayles, 120 feet above the surrounding plain, commands an extensive view, even to Market Weighton in the East Riding: see 'Dodsworth Yorkshire Notes', ed. R. Holmes (*Y.A.J.*, XII, 1893), p. 65.

with Robin Hood. Even today its potentialities as a place for concealed ob-
servation are obvious enough: the high ground of Sayle's Plantation ('up to'
which Little John may once have walked) is most readily visible to the south-
bound motorist on the modern A1 as he looks left or eastwards immediately
after crossing the new viaduct over the Went.

However 'the Saylis' and 'Watlinge Strete' of the *Gest* were not the only
places within Barnsdale to be associated with Robin Hood before the close of
the middle ages. By the eastern side of the great north road, four miles south
of Wentbridge and the Sayles, stands the most historically significant of all
the physical memorials to the outlaw legend—Robin Hood's Well. The latter
now takes the form not of a well but of a well-house, a 'rustic dome' designed
by Sir John Vanbrugh for the Earl of Carlisle in the early eighteenth century.[1]
Throughout the seventeenth and eighteenth centuries, that is both before and
after the construction of Vanbrugh's well-house, Robin Hood's Well was one
of the most celebrated halting-places on the great north road, familiar to
'drunken Barnabee', John Evelyn and countless other travellers.[2] First
recorded as 'Robbinhood-well' by Roger Dodsworth, the site has however a
history and an association with the outlaw legend which can be traced backwards into the fifteenth century under its earlier name of Robin Hood's Stone.
Within the context of a detailed description of estate boundaries, the cartulary
of Monkbretton Priory records the existence of a 'stone of Robin Hood' lying
near the 'Lynges' of Slepill and in close proximity to 'the king's highway', a
site which must be identical, or very nearly so, with that on which the later
Robin Hood's Well was to stand.[3] Much to the confusion of recent investiga-
tions of the Robin Hood legend, the copy of this deed in the Monkbretton
cartulary is assigned to Trinity Sunday 1322 ('*Millesimo III^{mo} Vicesimo
Secundo*'), a date which, if valid, would undoubtedly force us to recognize that
Robin Hood had become a name with which to conjure half a century before
he was first mentioned by Langland. It is however absolutely clear, from the
internal evidence of this deed and a comparison with adjoining items in the
cartulary, that—as its editor recognized—the correct date is not 1322 but 1422.

Even at this point in the early fifteenth century a 'stone of Robin Hood'

---

[1] See Appendix IV, p. 310 below.

[2] *Barnabae Itinerarium or Barnabee's Journal by Richard Brathwait*, ed. J. Haslewood and
W. C. Hazlitt (London, 1876), II, G6; *The Diary of John Evelyn*, ed. E. S. de Beer
(London, 1955), III, 128; *Stukeley's Diaries and Letters*, III (Surtees Society, LXXX,
1887), p. 373; cf. the map and itinerary of the great north road in *Ogilby's Traveller's
Guide* (London, 1699 and other edns). A small inn of the same name stood near the site
of Robin Hood's Well at the beginning of the nineteenth century: E. Miller, *History and
Antiquities of Doncaster* (Doncaster, *c.* 1804), p. 343.

[3] *Abstracts of the Chartularies of the Priory of Monkbretton*, ed. J. W. Walker (Y.A.S.,
Record Series, LXVI, 1924), p. 105. Cf. A. H. Smith's notes on 'Robin Hood' in
Modern Language Review, XXVIII (1933), pp. 484–5, and *Place-Names of the West
Riding*, Part II, p. 36.

within Barnsdale has given considerable cause for reflection—understandably enough when one appreciates that it stood only a mile south of Barnsdale Bar, where the great north road forked into two branches, one leading through Pontefract and Wetherby to Boroughbridge and the extreme north, the other via Wentbridge and Sherburn-in-Elmet to York.[1] Whichever route the traveller followed, he was compelled to pass through Barnsdale, inevitably the most frequented passage into the Vale of York and in a real sense the gateway to north-eastern England and to Scotland. Appropriately enough it was at Barnsdale Bar that several members of the English royal family were ceremonially welcomed on their progresses to the north in the later middle ages.[2] Not surprisingly it is a known fact that so popular a thoroughfare gave medieval highwaymen an opportunity they were very prepared to grasp: as Joseph Hunter was once again the first to demonstrate, Barnsdale was indeed a notoriously dangerous stretch of the main road from northern to southern England in the early fourteenth century.[3] It can be regarded as a medieval equivalent to such celebrated later centres of armed robbery and ambush— all on arterial English roads—as Gad's Hill, Hounslow Heath, Watford Gap and Stangate Hole, areas dreaded by travellers of the sixteenth and seventeenth centuries. Without wishing to carry Hunter's arguments to his own perilous extremes (the identification of an historical 'Robyn Hode' in the person of a Wakefield tenant of the 1320s) the history of Robin Hood's Stone and, above all, the *Gest*'s reference to 'the Saylis' makes it only natural to believe that the legendary outlaw owed his association with Barnsdale to the memory of the exploits of the leader of a highway gang—a robber, whether called Robin Hood or not, who levied a kind of blackmail on travellers along the great north road. On this point history and legend would seem to most nearly, if not completely, meet.

---

[1] The former route, apparently always considered the most important, appears quite clearly in the Gough Map and Matthew Paris's even earlier map of England. Also see B. Dickins, 'Premonstratensian Itineraries from a Titchfield Abbey MS. at Welbeck', *Proceedings of the Leeds Philosophical and Literary Society*, iv, part 6 (1938), pp. 349–60; *Durham Account Rolls*, III (Surtees Society, CIII, 1901), p. 724.

[2] J. Hunter, *South Yorkshire* (London, 1828–31), II, 487–8; Leland's *Collectanea*, ed. Hearne, IV, 185–203, 265–80; S. Anglo, *Spectacle, Pageantry, and Early Tudor Policy* (Oxford, 1969), p. 22. According to the city of York's 'Memorandum Book', Mayor John Fereby met Edward IV in September 1478, at a place *'paulo minus duobus miliaribus ultra Wentbrig'*, i.e. undoubtedly at Barnsdale Bar: see *York Memorandum Book*, II (Surtees Society, CXXV, 1915), p. 240; R. Davies, *Extracts from the Municipal Records of the City of York* (London, 1843), p. 78.

[3] Towards the end of Edward I's reign the escort accompanying the bishops of St Andrews and Glasgow and the abbot of Scone while they passed between Pontefract and Tickhill was afforced by twenty archers 'propter Barnisdale': Hunter, 'Great Hero', p. 14. Dr John Maddicott has most kindly just informed us of his important new discovery of a privy seal warrant of 23 June 1329 (P.R.O., C.81/163/2703) which records a robbery at *'le Saylles'* by two men of Doncaster and others; cf. *C.P.R., 1327–30*, p. 432.

In idealizing the exploits of a highway robber the early Robin Hood ballads do not of course stand alone. Until the early nineteenth century highway robbery continued to hold pride of place as the most colourful, as well as one of the most common, forms of violent crime. To adopt Macaulay's description of the mounted highwayman of seventeenth-century England, 'A romantic interest therefore attached, and perhaps still attaches, to the names of freebooters of this class. The vulgar eagerly drank in tales of their ferocity and audacity, of their occasional acts of generosity and good nature, of their amours, of their miraculous escapes, of their desperate struggles, and of their manly bearing at the bar and in the cart'.[1] Robin Hood may be unique; but it would be unwise to forget that many of his qualities (including magnanimity to the poor and oppressed) were also attributed to the John Clavels, James Hinds, John Nevisons, Richard Turpins and Thomas Boulters of a later age. Indeed one of the reasons for the continued appeal of the medieval greenwood hero in the early modern period was that he could so readily be assimilated into the once famous but now largely forgotten popular tradition of 'the gentlemen of the road'.[2] Of all types of thief, the professional highwayman was the most likely to enjoy a more than local reputation—a generalization no doubt as applicable to the fourteenth as to the eighteenth century. In both periods the man who ambushed travellers on the highways of England enjoyed the glamour that derived from an exceptionally dangerous occupation: his was an offence for which juries were prepared to convict and judges eager to sentence to death.

Any attempt to relate the Robin Hood legend to its medieval social context should accordingly begin by emphasizing the extremely high incidence of highway robbery in fourteenth- and fifteenth-century England. Although the detailed history of this particular felony remains to be written, the frequency with which it occurs in legal records and royal pardons of the later middle ages is now well known. Governmental concern at the way in which 'various persons, in defiance of the law, have risen in large bands to prey on the King's liegemen, as also on the goods of the Holy Church, the royal justices and others' was reflected in a large number of parliamentary petitions and statutes of the fourteenth century; and on various occasions the judges of both Edward III and Henry IV made serious efforts to have highway robbery construed as treason so that its practitioners might be subjected to the ultimate penalties of the law.[3] All travellers along the roads of medieval England

---

[1] T. B. Macaulay, *The History of England from the Accession of James II* (Everyman edition, 1906), I, 295.

[2] Thus in 1714 Robin Hood found his way into Captain Alexander Smith's classic *A Complete History of the Lives and Robberies of the most notorious Highwaymen, Footpads, Shoplifts, and Cheats of both sexes* (ed. A. L. Hayward, London, 1933, pp. 408–12); cf. *The Highwaymen of Wiltshire* (N. B. Randle, Devizes, *c.* 1845), p. 3; *Bishop Percy's Folio Manuscript*, ed. J. W. Hales and F. J. Furnivall (London, 1867–8), I, 4.

[3] *Rotuli Parliamentorum* (Record Commission, 1783), II, 64; Keen, *Outlaws*, p. 193; Bellamy, *Crime and Public Order*, pp. 11, 42.

had reason to fear the depredations of armed gangs of highwaymen, perhaps their most famous victim being the poet Geoffrey Chaucer who was relieved of £20 near a certain 'Fowle Ok' in the autumn of 1390: it is not hard to understand why his 'felaweshipe' of pilgrims to Canterbury decided to ride 'nyne and twenty in a compaignye'.[1] The temporary removal of the major departments of national government from London to York in the 1330s provoked—as one of its inevitable consequences—an epidemic of armed robbers in the area, intent of 'beating, wounding and robbing . . . those coming and going to and from that city'.[2] Eighty years later (in 1411) the vicar of Kirkby Hill, near Boroughbridge on the great north road, actually petitioned the papacy for a dispensation from residence there on the explicit grounds of his sufferings at the hands of local highwaymen.[3] Similarly the confessions of men like Richard Bretoun and Thomas Morys, both of whom turned informers (or approvers) in early 1389, illustrate not only the ubiquity of highway robbers throughout midland and southern England but also the diversity of their victims (esquires, monks, chaplains, chapmen, dyers, fishermen and servants) and of their spoils (horses, books, swords, daggers, bows and arrows, bales of cloth and packs of shoes as well as money).[4] 'Tho roberdes knaves', to give the travelling highwaymen the colloquial name by which they were most often known for at least a hundred years after the appearance of the future 'roberdesmen and drawlatches' in the 1285 Statute of Winchester, were an only too familiar component of the late medieval social scene. Although Sir Edward Coke was almost certainly mistaken in his belief that these *Roberdsmen* 'took their denomination' from the greenwood hero, it is fair to say that Robin Hood's Christian name provides a symbolically appropriate allusion to the criminal milieu his legend has since immortalized.[5]

Ambush on the king's highway was however a crime which could be committed for a variety of widely differing reasons, many of which appear to have no direct relevance to the themes of the early Robin Hood ballads at all. Extremely common, for example, was the use of armed ambush as an instrument in local vendettas and disputes between landlords and their tenants.

[1] *Life Records of Chaucer*, IV, ed. E. A. Bond and W. D. Selby (Early English Text Society, 1910), p. 292; *The Works of Geoffrey Chaucer*, ed. F. N. Robinson (2nd. edn., 1957), p. 17. Chaucer appears to have been ambushed while travelling near London on at least three separate occasions.

[2] *Calendar of Close Rolls, 1333–37*, pp. 294–5.

[3] *Calendar of Papal Letters*, VI (1404–15), p. 322; cf. A. H. Thompson, *The English Clergy and their Organization in the later Middle Ages* (Oxford, 1947), p. 121.

[4] E. Rickert, *Chaucer's World*, ed. C. C. Olson (New York, 1948), pp. 256–7. For a record of a group of common thieves and '*depredatores hominum*' who preyed on travellers across the north Yorkshire moors in the early 1360s, see *Yorkshire Sessions of the Peace, 1361–1364*, ed. B. H. Putnam (Y.A.S., Record Series, C, 1939), pp. 148–9.

[5] *The Vision of William concerning Piers the Plowman* (B-text), ed. W. W. Skeat (Oxford, 1869), pp. 2, 95. Other references to *Roberdsmen* are collected and discussed by Ritson, 1846, p. 34; Holt, 'Origins and Audience of Ballads of Robin Hood', p. 93.

Thus in the summer of 1419 two discontented tenants of Durham Cathedral Priory, Thomas Claxton and Thomas Billingham, deliberately terrorized that religious house by threatening to kill or wound any monk or monastic servant who left its precincts without adequate protection.[1] Forty years later a Durham monk was himself prepared to advocate the ambushing of one of the convent's adversaries by sending 'furth a trayst mane and gar hym be disgysed and waytte on hym . . . that he take gud seth on hyme that he passe noght'.[2] The employment of criminal bands by members of the English religious orders is indeed one of the undoubted, if most surprising, features of the period.[3] Even more common was the maintenance of companies of robbers by prominent lay lords, a phenomenon which reached its ultimate manifestation in the activities of the so-called 'gentry gangs' of the thirteenth and fourteenth centuries. The exploits of two such bands, the Folvilles of Ashby-Folville in Leicestershire and the Coterels of north Derbyshire, have now been analysed in considerable detail. The most remarkable feat of the Folvilles was the capture in 1332 of Sir Richard Willoughby, a Justice of the King's Bench, whom they held to ransom for no less than 1,300 marks; the Coterel gang, active between 1328 and 1333, maintained a spy in Nottingham itself.[4]

But of all the robber bands so far investigated perhaps the most relevant to the student of the Robin Hood legend is that which conducted a veritable private war against the officials of the duchy of Lancaster in and around Knaresborough forest between 1387 and 1392. Neither the members of this gang nor their leader, William Beckwith of Beckwith in Yorkshire, seem to have been men of financial substance let alone gentility.[5] Is this assorted band of lesser landholders, tradesmen, artisans and servants the best example yet unearthed of a 'yeomen gang'? And might William Beckwith, the would-be forester of Knaresborough, and his friends have found the adventures of Robin Hood, that greatest 'gode yeman' of them all, especially congenial? As Professor Bellamy has recently shown, there were certainly 'some adventures and situations which were common to both the outlaws of legend

[1] Dobson, *Durham Priory, 1400–1450*, pp. 50, 194.
[2] Dean and Chapter of Durham Muniments, Locellus XXV, no. 38.
[3] For cases involving the monasteries of Rufford in Nottinghamshire and Kirkstall in West Yorkshire see *C.P.R., 1317–21*, p. 93; *1354–58*, p. 498. Cf. Bellamy, *Crime and Public Order*, p. 73; J. M. Kaye, 'The Early History of Murder and Manslaughter', *Law Quarterly Review*, LXXXIII (1967), pp. 380–5.
[4] J. G. Bellamy, 'The Coterel Gang: An Anatomy of a band of fourteenth-century Criminals', *E.H.R.*, LXXIX (1964), pp. 698–717; E. L. G. Stones, 'The Folvilles of Ashby-Folville, Leicestershire, and their Associates in Crime', *T.R.H.S.*, 5th series, VII (1957), pp. 117–36. For the activities of 'gentry gangs' in the West Midlands at the beginning of the fourteenth century see R. H. Hilton, *A Medieval Society* (London, 1966), pp. 254–8.
[5] J. G. Bellamy, 'The Northern Rebellions in the Later Years of Richard II', *Bulletin of the John Rylands Library*, XLVII (1965), pp. 254–74; cf. *English Historical Documents, IV, 1327–1485*, ed. A. R. Myers (London, 1969), pp. 1221–2.

and the historical criminal bands'. Yet he is surely correct to remind us of the differences as well as the similarities between the reality and the myth. In particular, the early Robin Hood ballads lack the theme of feuding between neighbours which seems to have been such a dominant element in the exploits of the fourteenth-century gangs of well-connected misdoers. Confusion is only too likely to result from a failure to distinguish between the robberies of 'professional' highwaymen and the more sporadic lawlessness of the county gentry, between what Professor Hilton has called 'honest felons' and 'well-born bandits'. The evidence so far available suggests that few of the latter slept in the woods or lived the hard physical life of a real forest outlaw at all. 'The Coterels, Folvilles and Staffords (leaders of a notorious criminal band in Staffordshire during the 1320s) were unlikely to become folk heroes'; and it seems equally improbable that Robin Hood can be interpreted as an idealization of the leader of a 'gentry gang'.[1]

This is not to deny that the early Robin Hood ballads contained several themes likely to appeal to members of the English gentry as much as to their social inferiors. It is not hard to see why the knight of the *Gest* (stanza 324) is prepared 'to mayntene the outlawes stronge'. The medieval green-wood legend was rooted not only in the violent lawlessness of the age but in the corruption of its law and administration. It is important to remember that neither the violence nor the corruption was a new development in the four-teenth century. In K. B. McFarlane's words, 'It is odd that it is the very rich-ness of their sources which has given the later middle ages a bad name'.[2] At whatever point of time the Robin Hood legend first emerged, the popularity of a figure who embodied some notion of justice in an unjust society was assured. For a thoroughly detailed impression of the way in which legal mal-practice pervaded the conduct of public life at the local level the historian may have to await the evidence of the great letter-collections of the fifteenth century.[3] But it had probably always been true that the surest way to obtain a favourable verdict in the law courts of medieval England was through the assistance of a powerful patron. In particular, the office of sheriff had long been 'a focal point for corrupt interest to interfere with the working of

---

[1] Bellamy, *Crime and Public Order*, pp. 87-8. In his excellent survey of the activities of the criminal bands of late medieval England Professor Bellamy also concludes (p. 45) that 'normally those with gentle blood in their veins showed little inclination to be ['pro-fessional'] highway robbers'.

[2] K. B. McFarlane, *The Nobility of Later Medieval England* (Oxford, 1973), p. 114.

[3] The evidence of the Paston and Stonor letters on this subject is well known. An even more alarming commentary on the corruption of local jurors and sheriffs in northern England is provided by the somewhat neglected *Plumpton Correspondence* (of 1416-1552), ed. T. Stapleton (Camden Society, Old Series, IV, 1839), especially Letters 100-126. For the survival of similar acts of embracery and bribery in sixteenth-century Yorkshire see R. B. Smith, *Land and Politics in the England of Henry VIII : The West Riding of Yorkshire, 1530-46* (Oxford, 1970), pp. 146-51.

medieval justice'.[1] For a suitable consideration many a medieval sheriff showed himself prepared to empanel amenable jurors, to make false returns to writs, and to fail to release prisoners. Sheriffs such as Sir Robert Ingram of Nottinghamshire positively co-operated with gangs like the Coterels.[2] Small wonder that against this sort of background, a figure who in imagination remedied the deficiencies of the law, opposed the sheriff and achieved some kind of simple justice, should have gained the sympathy of gentry and commons alike.

In such circumstances it is hardly surprising that the outlaw figure, in fact as well as fiction, was one more likely to attract admiration than horror in the minds of contemporaries. In many ways the imposition of outlawry, a punishment rooted in Anglo-Saxon precedent, was bound to be an admission of governmental failure—the last resort of a legal system which lacked policing services adequate to bring notorious criminals to justice. As F. W. Maitland suggested, 'Outlawry is the last weapon of the ancient law, but one that it must often use'.[3] There can be no doubt that, as in the analogous employment of the supreme spiritual punishment of excommunication by the medieval church, the royal courts of medieval England degraded the severity of sentences of outlawry by over-use. By the early thirteenth century the legal view that the outlaw was a wild beast ('bearing the wolf's head') whose pursuit was the right and duty of every law-abiding man, was rarely observed in practice. During the course of the fourteenth century the application of the process of outlawry to cases of misdemeanour and even civil offences lessened its deterrent effect still further. At the end of Edward III's reign those who killed an outlaw were more likely to face trial themselves than to be congratulated. In an age when outlawed royal officials continued to hold their own positions with relative impunity, it is understandable that many criminals showed little concern at being outlawed at all.[4] Indeed the sentence of outlawry may have often brought a criminal as much sympathy as hostility. The author of the early fourteenth-century *Outlaw's Song of Trailbaston* (No. 26 below) had no difficulty in presenting himself as an unjustly oppressed victim of the inequities of the legal system in his area of England. It is now established that many real criminal bands enjoyed the active support—not always based on fear—of many members of society. In the early 1330s the Coterel gang is known to have been assisted by more than 150 'receivers', prepared

---

[1] M. Hastings, *The Court of Common Pleas in the Fifteenth Century* (Cornell, 1947), p. 224.

[2] Bellamy, *Crime and Public Order*, p. 75. For a general condemnation of the corruption of sheriffs in 1425, see *Rotuli Parliamentorum*, IV, 306.

[3] F. Pollock and F. W. Maitland, *The History of English Law before the time of Edward I* (Cambridge, 1898), I, 476.

[4] For a detailed discussion of 'what happened to the vast multitude of medieval outlaws', see especially R. F. Hunnisett, *The Medieval Coroner* (Cambridge, 1961), pp. 67–8; cf. Bellamy, *Crime and Public Order*, pp. 105–6, 201; R. L. Storey, *The End of the House of Lancaster* (London, 1966), p. 215.

to supply them with food, shelter and information.[1] Even so well-established an ecclesiastic as Henry Knighton, canon and chronicler of Leicester Abbey, wrote of the exploits of Richard de Folville in terms ('a fierce, daring and impudent man') which imply as much admiration as condemnation.[2]

That the early Robin Hood legend owed much of its appeal to contemporary dissatisfaction with the corruption of local law and administration can hardly be denied. What remains controversial is the extent to which the cult of the outlaw hero reflects a critique, whether conscious or not, of social as well as legal injustice. Is it really true, to put this fundamental problem in its simplest terms, that the medieval tales of Robin Hood provide 'a trustworthy index to the restiveness of the common people under political, economic and social abuses'?[3] Few historians would now accept H. C. Coote's crudely extreme interpretation of the medieval outlaw ballads as 'an epic of communism' which deliberately transmitted revolutionary ideas and memories of the French *Jacquerie* of 1358.[4] More intriguing is the possibility that the early versions of the Robin Hood legend may have been, at least in part, a by-product of the agrarian struggles over rents, services and social status which culminated in the Great Revolt of 1381. Yet, as Professor Holt demonstrated in a deservedly famous article, there are serious objections to the argument that the Robin Hood ballads consciously express social protest on the part of the English peasants.[5] Quite apart from Robin Hood's location in a part of England far removed from the known centres of revolt in 1381, the stories about him are scarcely an incitement to revolution as such. Neither the *Gest* nor the early ballads raise at all directly the question of the obligations of peasants to their lords, the theme which modern historians rightly see as the central element in social and economic relationships throughout the middle ages. They provide no references to the continuing exaction or re-imposition of labour services, to the payment of entry-fines and rents, or to merchet, heriot and the other incidents of servile tenure.[6] In particular the well-documented (both before and after 1381) contemporary agitation against villein status is conspicuous by its complete absence from the medieval outlaw legend. Life in the greenwood may offer a sort of Arcadian liberty to those who go there, but no one in the early narratives makes the point that such freedom might take the practical form of emancipation from manorial oppression. Nor are the individuals singled out for eternal enmity either in

---

[1] Bellamy, *Crime and Public Order*, p. 72.

[2] *Chronicon Henrici Knighton* (Rolls Series, 93, 1889–95), I, 460; Keen, *Outlaws*, p. 204.

[3] G. H. Gerould, *The Ballad of Tradition* (Oxford, 1932), p. 134.

[4] H. C. Coote, 'The Origin of the Robin Hood Epos', *Folk-Lore Journal*, III (1885), pp. 44–52.

[5] Holt, 'Origins and Audience of Ballads of Robin Hood', pp. 89–110, which develops at considerable length many of the arguments summarized here.

[6] The only criticism of oppression by manorial reeves in the ballads is voiced by Robin's monastic victim in the *Gest* (stanza 254).

Robin Hood's famous 'policy statement' (stanza 15 of the *Gest*) or elsewhere in the ballads—the sheriff of Nottingham, members of the religious orders, 'these bisshoppes and these archebisshoppes'—attacked for the abuse of their authority as landlords. It is a knight and not a peasant who suffers from the extortion of the abbot of St Mary's, York. The latter, like the sheriff of Nottingham himself, appears rather as a personification or 'ideograph' of such well-worn medieval themes as corruption in high places and clerical avarice than as a symbol of the exploitation of peasants by the landowning classes.

There are other reasons why it is difficult to see Robin Hood, however much his exploits may have appealed to all sections of the community, as a distinctively peasant hero and one who articulated grievances specific to the late medieval English peasantry. Although the figure of the peasant in medieval literature is often conspicuous by its absence, there is no lack of fourteenth- and fifteenth-century comment upon his place in society. Throughout western Europe it seems evident that the classical medieval tradition of portraying the peasant as a rude and gluttonous *rusticus*, the symbol of congenital ignorance, was giving way to a more complex and often sympathetic approach. By 1300 the composers of several French *fabliaux* as well as Willhelm der Gärtner, the author of the satirical German narrative poem, *Meier Helmbrecht*, already showed themselves capable of viewing the harsh realities of the peasant's lot with sardonic insight.[1] Even before William Langland elevated his own 'poor ploughman' to quasi-saintly status at the end of the fourteenth century there is evidence of similar realism in literary portraits of the English peasantry.[2] In every case the world we are invited to enter is infinitely far removed from that of Robin Hood. Thus the so-called *Song of the Husbandman*, probably written around 1300 by a south-western author, consistently puts forward the plight of poor tenant farmers, oppressed as much by manorial officials ('bailif', 'hayward' and 'wodeward') as by governmental taxation. Another poem in the same manuscript (British Library, Harley 2253) represents the 'Man in the moone' as a poverty-stricken peasant who has fled into permanent exile from his village after being victimized by the local hayward.[3] Towards the close of the fourteenth century the literary conven-

---

[1] See E. Power, 'Peasant Life and Peasant Conditions (*c.* 1100–*c.* 1500)', *Cambridge Medieval History* VII (1932), pp. 739–44; R. Taylor, 'German Literature in the Middle Ages', *Germany: A Companion to German Studies*, ed. M. Pasley (London, 1972), pp. 486–7.

[2] B. White, 'Poet and Peasant', *The Reign of Richard II*, ed. F. R. H. Du Boulay and C. M. Barron (London, 1971), pp. 58–74. English literature of the fourteenth and fifteenth centuries shows a marked tendency to distinguish sharply between the social stereotypes of the admirable ploughman and the disreputable labourer: see R. H. Hilton, *The English Peasantry in the Later Middle Ages* (Oxford, 1975), pp. 21–4.

[3] *The Oxford Book of Medieval English Verse*, ed. C. and K. Sisam (Oxford, 1970), pp. 111–14, 132–4; see the comments in V. J. Scattergood, *Politics and Poetry in the Fifteenth Century* (London, 1971), pp. 350–3.

tion of the poor but perfect ploughman had come to condition the attitudes of poets as different as Geoffrey Chaucer and the author of *Pierce the Plowman's Crede* and *The Plowman's Tale*. To the justifiable objection that such poems, like *Piers Plowman* itself, were not written by peasants and present an artificial stereotyped treatment of their social role, it may be answered that the few scraps of authentic peasant 'protest literature' to survive from later medieval England raise issues equally distant from those encountered in the early Robin Hood legend. The strong sense of Christian fraternity expressed in the mysterious letters (possibly written by John Ball) which circulated through England in 1381 has left little imprint on the outlaw ballads; nor do the latter articulate that more explicit revolutionary threat ('If thou art pore, than art thou fre, / If thou be riche, than woo is the') occasionally encountered in stray fifteenth-century verses.[1]

If not a specifically peasant hero, could Robin Hood be the hero of the late medieval English gentry? In fairness to Professor Holt, the first historian to raise this previously unexplored possibility, his own arguments have been directed to the more limited thesis 'that the chief topics of the *Gest*—ecclesiastical usury, the forest and the sheriffs—were such, or were presented in such a way, as to appeal more to the gentry than to any other group'.[2] Even this still controversial conclusion is bound to be subject to the general qualification that all literature of wish-fulfilment tends to take on unrealistic and socially ambitious forms: it was no accident that the author of the *Gest* invited his audience—in his very first lines—to think of themselves as 'gentilmen, That be of frebore blode'. There can however be no doubt that many members of the English gentry in the fifteenth century must have been familiar with tales of Robin Hood and that some (like Sir John Paston in 1473)[3] positively patronized the cult. We have already seen that Robin Hood possesses many of the knightly virtues and that much of his behaviour can be interpreted as that of a courtly hero transferred to a lower social plane. As the second stanza of the *Gest* makes absolutely explicit, what especially distinguishes him from all other outlaws was his 'curtesye'. Like King Arthur, Robin Hood has 'noo lust to dyne' until something strange and wonderful happens, until he is provided with an appropriately distinguished or unusual guest. An unprejudiced reading of the *Gest* leads one to the inescapable conclusion that the outlaw leader's famous acts of liberality derive less from any notion of the social redistribution of wealth than from the aristocratic virtues of largesse and display. Thanks to Dr Keen's excellent survey of the subject, it is now well known that the adventures of Robin Hood and his men echo those of the well-born outlaws of earlier medieval legend: in particular, analogues for various sections of the *Gest* may be found in the stories about

[1] *The Peasants' Revolt of 1381*, ed. R. B. Dobson (London, 1970), pp. 379–85; Scattergood, pp. 354–62.

[2] Holt, 'Robin Hood: Some Comments', pp. 17–18.   [3] See below, pp. 38, 204.

Hereward the Wake, the romances of Eustace the Monk and Fulk Fitzwarin, Blind Harry's *Scyr William Wallace* and the anonymous *Tale of Gameleyn*.[1] It seems clear that most of these works owe their survival in their present form to the interest taken in such heroes by the lords and knights of medieval England. Did the fourteenth-century English gentleman see the Robin Hood legend merely as a socially deviant variation on a traditional theme?

If so, it seems to us that he would certainly have been mistaken. Recent attempts to relate Robin Hood to other literary outlaw heroes of the middle ages have undoubtedly thrown much new light on the formation of the greenwood legend. But in the last resort it is the differences between Robin Hood and his counterparts rather than their similarities which deserve most attention. The adventures of Robin Hood may have their parallels; but the tone with which those adventures are presented in the *Gest* and the ballads has no real equivalent. High aristocratic birth, as the phenomenally popular examples of Bevis of Hampton and Sir Guy of Warwick will always remind us, was in itself no obstacle to the appeal of a hero of romance at all levels of society. But the fact remains that the medieval Robin Hood was not of noble birth nor ever expressed any desire to be so. In particular the Robin Hood of the *Gest*, *Robin Hood and the Monk* and *Robin Hood and the Potter* lacks land, a deficiency which at a stroke removes him from the company of his fellow legendary outlaws. Unlike Gamelyn, that younger son of 'sire Iohan of Boundys', the medieval Robin Hood was never portrayed as the victim of an evil kinsman who had deprived him of his rightful inheritance: even when pardoned by the king at the end of the *Gest* he was offered not a landed estate but a place and fee at the royal court. Only from the sixteenth century onwards is there evidence of a real attempt (never completely successful as long as the ballad tradition survived) to assimilate the forest outlaw to the conventional pattern of an unjustly dispossessed knight or nobleman.[2] Nor can this be coincidental. In many ways the most remarkable feature of the hero of the *Gest* is the self-assured way in which he accepts his non-aristocratic social status with equanimity and even pride. He may imitate the behaviour of a courteous knight but he does so in a spirit of self-confidence that suggests an awareness of his quite separate place in the social hierarchy. Indeed the authors of the early ballads often presented Robin Hood as a low-born hero who deliberately parodied the activities of chivalric lord and even king.[3] The

---

[1] Keen, *Outlaws*, passim and especially pp. 44–8, 57–8, 73–9. For the most detailed analysis of the analogues of the *Gest*, see Clawson, *Gest of Robin Hood*, pp. 125–7.

[2] *The Tale of Gamelyn*, ed. W. W. Skeat in *The Complete Works of Geoffrey Chaucer* (Oxford, 1894–7), IV, 645–7; Dobson and Taylor, 'Medieval Origins of the Robin Hood Legend', pp. 24–5.

[3] See, in particular, the reference to the 'pavage' or toll to which Robin Hood subjected travellers through Barnsdale in the opening stanzas of *Robin Hood and the Potter*. The deliberate parodying of the formal processes of Plantagenet government was by no means confined to fictional outlaws: perhaps the most famous example is the threatening

greenwood hero had his grievances but these never tempted him into wishing to change his social status. And of what that status was the early audience for the Robin Hood ballads was never left in doubt.

> 'Herkens, god yemen,
>   Comley, cortessey, and god,
> On of the best that yever bare bou',
>   Hes name was Roben Hode.'[1]

From the moment he first steps on to the historical stage Robin Hood is presented as a yeoman hero for a yeoman audience. The compiler of the *Gest*, for example, not only identifies his hero as 'a gode yeman' in the first stanza of his poem but makes it clear that Robin was absolutely aware of the social niceties of his status: 'It was never the maner, by dere worthi God, / A yoman to pay for a knyhht' (stanza 37).[2] Similarly both Little John and Robin Hood are described as yeomen within the opening verses of both *Robin Hood and the Monk* and *Robin Hood and Guy of Gisborne*. Even more explicit is *Robin Hood and the Potter*, a work in which both the hero and the narrator go out of their way to invoke the spirit of 'god yemanrey' (stanzas 23 and 83).[3] It is self-evident that the late medieval audience for the ballads of Robin Hood was being consistently asked to identify with a hero who was neither a knight nor a peasant or 'husbonde' but something in between. The historical significance of these allusions to yeomanry can only be discounted if one believes, with Professor Holt, that 'A yeoman was as yet in an official status not a social rank'.[4] Now it is certainly true that the term yeoman, like so many other elusive English words (*gesith*, thegn, esquire) which came to designate social status, originated as a name implying attendance on a lord: it seems to have arisen as a reduced form of the Middle English 'yongman' or 'yonge-man', the 'young man' who serves in the household of a master.[5] And it is equally certain that the word continued to be used until and indeed beyond the sixteenth century to designate the middle grade of the three well-known ranks of a medieval magnate's household—the esquires or *generosi*, the yeo-

---

letter sent in 1336 by 'Lionel king of the rout of raveners' from 'our Castle of the North Wind, in the Green Tower, in the first year of our reign': *Select Cases in the Court of the King's Bench, Edward III* (Selden Society, LXXVI, 1957), p. 93; Keen, *Outlaws*, p. 200. Compare the calling of a mock-official court or parliament, the 'Dodelowe', by William Beckwith and his gang of robbers in 1388 (Bellamy, *Crime and Public Order*, pp. 76–7).

[1] See below, p. 125.
[2] Cf. stanza 269 of the *Gest* ('What man that helpeth a good yeman, / His frende than wyll I be.')
[3] Cf. Chambers, *English Literature at the Close of the Middle Ages*, pp. 136–7.
[4] Holt, 'Origins and Audience of Ballads of Robin Hood', p. 100.
[5] The heroes of *Adam Bell* (No. 28 below) are still being described as 'yongemen' as well as 'yeman' in that sixteenth-century poem (stanzas 4, 97); cf. *Oxford English Dictionary*, *sub* 'Yeoman'.

men or *valecti*, and the grooms.[1] It is in the sense of someone giving honourable service that the term is customarily used in royal and private records of the fifteenth century. That said, there can be no doubt that by the date of the first surviving Robin Hood ballads, the term yeoman had by extension come to be applied to gradations in society at large and not just within the confines of the household. According to a famous sumptuary law of 1363, yeomen throughout England were socially equivalent to 'people of handicraft' (*genz de mestre et d'artifice*), both groups being technically debarred from spending more than 40s. od. a cloth on their costume.[2] In the late 1380s the Cornish clerk, John Trevisa, expressed general contemporary alarm 'that a yeman arraieth hym as a squyer'; and at about the same date the miller of Chaucer's *Reeve's Tale* (certainly in no one's service) was inordinately conscious of the need 'To saven his estaat of yomanrye'.[3] The famous 'Yeman' of the General Prologue to the *Canterbury Tales* may have been the Knight's servant on the ride to Becket's shrine; but as a forester with 'a myghty bowe' he was certainly no servile or even deferential figure—not surprisingly when one remembers that this may have been Chaucer's own portrait of Robin Hood.[4]

The self-confidence of Chaucer's Yeoman, like that of Robin Hood himself, can of course be readily related to the enhanced social and economic position of large numbers of the English peasantry in the century after the Black Death. During a period of labour shortage and higher wages, of the 'withering away' of villeinage and of a rapid expansion in personal mobility, the greenwood legend can and should be seen as an expression of social aspiration based on the real economic progress achieved by many Englishmen in the years before and after 1400.[5] Such an explanation of the appeal of the

---

[1] Compare Robin Hood's own belief that 'squyre, yoman, or page' should walk beside a mounted knight (*Gest*, stanza 80). For a discussion of the meaning of the term in the sixteenth century, see especially M. Campbell, *The English Yeoman* (London, 1960), *passim* and pp. 7–20.

[2] *Statutes of the Realm*, I, 380; cf. M. Keen, 'Robin Hood—Peasant or Gentleman?', *Past and Present*, 19 (1961), p. 12.

[3] *Polychronicon Ranulphi Higden* (Rolls Series, 41, 1865–86), II, 171; *Complete Works of Geoffrey Chaucer*, ed. Robinson, p. 56. A dramatic expansion in the use of the word yeoman (to imply social status as well as official function) clearly took place in the early fifteenth century. Thus the first individual to be recorded as 'yoman' in the York Freeman's Register entered the city's franchise in 1418–19. Between that date and 1509, 62 yeomen are recorded in the register: *Register of the Freemen of the City of York* I (Surtees Society, XCVI, 1897), p. 126; V.C.H., *City of York* (1961), p. 116.

[4] *The Complete Works of Chaucer*, ed. Skeat, V, 11; Holt, 'Origins and Audience of Ballads of Robin Hood', p. 109 n. 43. For Chaucer's often very general use of the word 'yeoman', see the references collected in J. S. P. Tatlock and A. G. Kennedy, *A Concordance to the Complete Works of Geoffrey Chaucer* (Gloucester, Mass., 1963), p. 1106.

[5] For a recent summary of the prevailing orthodoxy on these matters by the most influential English medieval economic historian of this century see M. M. Postan, *The Medieval Economy and Society* (London, 1972), pp. 143–55; cf. R. H. Hilton's excellent survey of *The Decline of Serfdom in Medieval England* (Economic History Society, 1969).

early Robin Hood ballads and the *Gest* should not be pushed to extremes;
but in the last resort it seems more convincing than either of the alternatives
—that Robin Hood was the product of peasant protest or of gentlemanly
escapism. The thesis that Robin Hood was a new type of hero for a new social
group, the yeomen of England, is bound to beg (as all interpretations of
Robin Hood inevitably must) the vexed question of his origins. But even if
one were to concede (what still remains controversial) that on their first
appearance 'the Robin Hood stories were designed primarily for a gentle
audience',[1] most of the available evidence suggests that in the fifteenth
century it was Robin's appeal to a popular rather than aristocratic or gentle
audience which ensured his survival. To contemporaries he may well have
presented a 'double image' as a figure who could appeal both to the lesser
gentry and to the yeomen. As the fifteenth century progressed his appeal
became wider still. The jocular and mock-heroic elements within the greenwood legend, already implicit in parts of the *Gest* and *Robin Hood and the
Monk*, come to dominate the conclusion of *Robin Hood and the Potter*—a
poem which ends to the accompaniment of 'a lowde lawhyng' on the part of
the sheriff of Nottingham's wife. In other words the texts of the early ballads
themselves, like the stream of contemporary comment on the ribald nature
of the legend with which our enquiry began, confirm that the farcical elements
of the later forest outlaw myth were present within the medieval tradition.
The medieval ballads, few though they are, make it clear enough that Robin
Hood was already a figure around whom, despite his heroism and 'courtesy',
comic situations could be readily created. No aspect of the legend did more to
ensure Robin Hood's enduring popularity throughout the Tudor and the
Stuart periods.

III. *The Legend since the Middle Ages*

'The personal courage of this celebrated outlaw, his skill in archery, his
humanity, and especially his levelling principle of taking from the rich
and giving to the poor, have in all ages rendered him the favourite of
the common people'[2]

(i)

The perennial appeal of the Robin Hood legend throughout the last five
centuries is by any standards one of the most extraordinary phenomena in the
social as well as literary history of England. As yet, and somewhat regrettably,
the development of that legend since the end of the middle ages has received

---

[1] Holt, 'Origins and Audience of Ballads of Robin Hood', p. 99.
[2] *Percy's Reliques of Ancient Poetry* (Everyman edition, 1906), I, 116.

much less attention than its medieval origins.[1] Robin Hood's continuing hold over popular affections is, however, in many ways even more remarkable than the emergence of his cult in the fourteenth and fifteenth centuries. It is true that since the Tudor period the large audience for adventures of Robin Hood has normally re-formulated what it found most attractive in the medieval saga without finding it necessary to destroy its original foundations. There have, nevertheless, been at least two periods when the myth of the English greenwood has been permanently modified, firstly at the hands of Elizabethan and Jacobean playwrights, and then again by the Romantic poets and novelists of the early nineteenth century. No attempt can be made here to provide more than a brief and impressionistic account of the fortunes of the Robin Hood myth since the late middle ages. But as a 'purely' medieval Robin Hood, like a 'purely' medieval King Arthur, no longer exists, the following cursory survey of the legend's later development—to be read in conjunction with some of the texts printed in this anthology—may serve to sketch in the broad outlines of a complicated and as yet largely uncharted evolution.

In the first place it is clear that by the end of the fifteenth century the Robin Hood legend had already ceased to be diffused exclusively by 'ballads', 'talkings' or recited tales. The stories of Robin Hood would not have gained the hold which they subsequently obtained over all sections of the English community had they not shown themselves to be highly adaptable to other forms of entertainment. The most obvious of these was of course dramatic representation, ranging from the primitive and almost inarticulate mummers' plays to the sophisticated achievements of Anthony Munday and Ben Jonson. So intractable are the problems of pre-Elizabethan English drama that the precise role of Robin Hood and his men in the early history of the English stage will probably always remain controversial; but at least there can be no doubt that Robin entered the world of the play from that of the medieval tale or ballad. The texts of only three popular Robin Hood plays survive (Nos. 19–21 below) and in every case their derivation from a pre-existing 'ballad' is unquestionable. Thus *'Robin Hood and the Sheriff'*, which survives in a manuscript fragment written circa 1475, never mentions Guy of Gisborne but is clearly adapted from the ballad now known by that name (No. 5). Similarly the two plays of *'Robin Hood and the Friar'* and *'Robin Hood and the Potter'* printed at the close of William Copland's edition of *A Mery Geste* (*c.* 1560), are based on the two ballads readily identifiable by those titles. As the ballads themselves possess many intrinsic dramatic qualities—abundance

---

[1] Joseph Ritson's notes to his *Robin Hood* (1795 and later editions) still remain unsurpassed as a guide to the Robin Hood legend in the early modern period. Also useful, especially for the Elizabethan period, is M. A. Nelson, *The Robin Hood Tradition in the English Renaissance* (Salzburg Studies in English Literature; Elizabethan Studies No.14; Salzburg, 1973).

of dialogue, speed of action, frequency of disguises and numerous fights—
'the transition from recital to dramatic representation' is readily understandable.[1]

The date of Robin Hood's first appearance on the 'stage' is far from certain.
The earliest allusion to the outlaw as a dramatic character occurs in the
famous letter of Sir John Paston to his brother John (16 April 1473) in which
he complained that he had been deserted by the servant employed 'to pleye
Seynt Jorge and Robyn Hod and the Shryff off Nottyngham'.[2] It seems unlikely that Robin Hood plays of any sophistication had enjoyed a long history
before that date. On the other hand, the impulse to re-enact the deeds of a
familiar folk-hero must have taken many unrecorded forms, and it would be
wise to be cautious in suggesting a precise point of origin. Most baffling of all
is Robin Hood's role in the so-called mummers' plays, a form of popular
drama characterized by its strong elements of dumb-show and primitive
mimesis. Like St George, Robin Hood was well qualified, thanks to his
association with the concept of single-handed combat, to take his place as a
major protagonist in these plays. Yet he appears in such different situations
(as a supernumerary character at Bampton, but as a leading figure in a
corrupt version of the ballad of *Robin Hood and the Tanner* at Shipton-under-
Wychwood in Oxfordshire) that no one single hypothesis can account for his
participation in such mummings. Even if we accept that the folk *ludi* of the
fifteenth and sixteenth centuries incorporated a high degree of conscious
ritualism, deliberately designed to promote agricultural and human fertility
within a primitive community, it by no means follows that Robin Hood himself was seen in terms of mythological divinity. Like Little John, St George,
Father Christmas and even 'Bold Bonaparte' in later years, he found his way
into the mummers' plays because his adventures were already famous in
village and town.[3]

It was no doubt for the same reason that Robin Hood came to play such a
dominant role in the May Games of sixteenth-century England, with profound consequences for the development of his legend. The origins of the
May festivities are lost beyond recovery; but by the early Tudor period an
abundance of allusions to their popularity makes it clear that they had become the vehicle for an unusually complex series of popular entertainments.
Precisely because the May Games were organized at the local parish or
municipality level, it is impossible to generalize with confidence about them.
Although local variation was infinite, nearly everywhere these games com-

---

[1] W. E. Simeone, 'The May Games and the Robin Hood Legend', *Journal of American Folk-Lore*, LXIV (1951), p. 266. For further discussion of these plays, see below, pp. 203–4, 208–9, 215–16.

[2] *The Paston Letters*, ed. J. Gairdner (London, 1904), V, 185; see below, p. 204.

[3] E. K. Chambers, *The English Folk-Play* (Oxford, 1933), pp. 11, 89, 152–6, 173; cf. R. J. E. Tiddy, *The Mummers' Play* (Oxford, 1923), *passim*.

prised a variety of pastimes, ranging from processional and round dances to competitive sports and pageants as well as plays. Robin Hood's participation in the May Games therefore took a bewildering variety of forms, best illustrated by a few examples. The earliest known references to the impersonation of Robin Hood in village plays occur from 1476 onwards at Croscombe in North Somerset where 'Roben Hode's recones' were regularly paid to those (including a Richard Willes) who took the part of the outlaw hero.[1] By 1498, at the borough of Wells in the same county, the *'tempus de Robynhode'*, apparently accompanied by exhibitions of dancing girls and by church ales, was being subsidized by the corporation.[2] Church ales were also associated with the spring festival (usually of five days' duration) in the parish of St Lawrence, Reading, whose churchwardens are to be discovered collecting 'the gaderyngs of Robyn Hod' after 1498–99.[3]

Much more informative are the churchwardens' accounts of Kingston-on-Thames between 1507 and 1529: these not only recorded regular expenditure on the costumes and appurtenances ('bannar', 'cote', gloves and shoes) of 'Robyn Hode' but also associate him closely with 'the mores daunsais, the frere (not yet called Tuck) and mayde Maryan' as well as 'little John'.[4] In a well-known passage from a sermon which he delivered before Edward VI on 12 April 1549, Bishop Hugh Latimer complained about his inability to preach in a certain town church: he had met with the response that 'Syr thys is a busye daye wyth us, we can not heare you, it is Robyn hoodes day. The parishe are gone a brode to gather for Robyn hoode.'[5] Parishioners, in towns as well as villages, continued to 'go abroad' on Robin Hood's behalf for many years to come. In the larger cities they were of course more likely to go to watch than to participate in the festivities. What they might encounter is perhaps best suggested by Henry Machyn's famous description of the no doubt exceptionally elaborate procession held in London on 24 June 1559: 'a May-game . . . and sant John Sacerys, with a gyant, and drumes and gunes

---

[1] *Church-Wardens' Accounts of Croscombe, etc., 1349–1560*, ed. E. Hobhouse (Somerset Record Society, IV, 1890), pp. 4, 10, 11, 14, 20. For a 'Robine Hood's All' or ale at the neighbouring village of Tintinhull in 1513, see ibid. p. 200; and for the impersonation of 'Robin Whod and little John' by tenants of the prior of Worcester in the years after 1518, see *Journal of Prior William More* (Worcestershire Historical Society, XXX, 1913–14), pp. 87, 293, 309, 332, 405.

[2] *First Report of the Royal Commission on Historical Manuscripts* (London, 1874), p. 107.

[3] C. Kerry, *A History of the Municipal Church of St. Lawrence, Reading* (London, 1883), pp. 226–30. Similarly, in 1497 Willenhall Fair in Staffordshire was attended by the inhabitants of neighbouring townships 'with the capitanns called the Abbot of Marham or Robyn Hodys to the intent to gether money with ther disportes to the profight of the chirches of the seid lordshippes' (see above, p. 4).

[4] D. Lysons, *The Environs of London*, Vol. I, *The County of Surrey* (London, 1792), pp. 226–9.

[5] Hugh Latimer, *Seven Sermons before Edward VI*, ed. E. Arber (London, 1869), pp. 173–4.

. . . and then sant Gorge and the dragon, the mores dansse, and after Robyn Hode and lytull John, and Maid Marian and frere Tuke, and they had spechys rond a-bowt London.'[1]

An even more remarkable tribute to the universality of Robin Hood's appeal is the prominent part he played in the springtime festivities (not necessarily always in May) of Scotland. Precisely how and why the Robin Hood legend should have struck such deep roots north of the Border has never been satisfactorily explained.[2] But the interest already displayed in the English outlaw hero by the Scottish chronicler Walter Bower, together with the appearance of a ship called 'Robyne Hude' or 'ly Robert Hude' at Aberdeen as early as 1438, help to make it a little less surprising that he should have come to dominate the Scottish May Games even more than their English counterparts.[3] 'Robertus Hod' is first recorded at Edinburgh in 1492; and within a very few years he had displaced his rivals, the abbots of Bonacord and Unreason, as 'lord of the May Game' not only there but also in Aberdeen and Perth. Even more than in most English communities, Robin Hood seems to have presided over a variety of 'danssis, farsiis, playis, and gamis', in which however neither the morris dances nor Maid Marian played a part. Official opposition to 'ryetouss and sumpteous banketing' on these occasions led to the Scottish parliamentary statute of 1555 which 'ordanit that in all tymes cummyng na maner of persoun be chosin Robert Hude nor Lytill Johne, Abbot of unressoun, Quenis of Maii, nor otherwise, nouther in Burgh nor to landwart in ony tyme to cum'.[4] In the face of religious disapproval and, perhaps equally important, of changes in popular taste, Robin Hood's role in the English May Games was also in decline by the end of the sixteenth century. Although he continued to figure in village plays and morris dances for centuries to come, he clearly ceased to dominate popular pastimes to quite the extraordinary degree that he had done so throughout most of the Tudor period.

Although only a transitory phase in the history of Robin Hood's post-medieval reputation, his appearance in the May Games is undoubtedly one of the most important episodes in the history of the legend. In particular, by putting Robin Hood to dance, the May Games introduced him to a world

---

[1] *The Diary of Henry Machyn, citizen and merchant-taylor of London, 1550–63* (Camden Society, Old Series, 42, 1848), p. 201.

[2] For the suggestion that the Robin Hood legend was introduced into Scotland by monarchs and nobles returning from exile or imprisonment in England, see L. Spencer, 'Robin Hood in Scotland', *Chambers's Journal*, 9th. series, XVIII (1928), pp. 94–6. It is possibly no coincidence that the title of Earl of Huntingdon assigned to Robin Hood by the late sixteenth century was one held by various twelfth-century Scottish kings.

[3] A. J. Mill, *Mediaeval Plays in Scotland* (Edinburgh, 1927), pp. 23–6.

[4] Most of the Scottish references are collected in Chambers, *Mediaeval Stage*, II, 330–6; but also see *Accounts of the Lord High Treasurer of Scotland* (Scottish Record Office, 1877–1916), II, 377; V, 432–3; VIII, 282; IX, 73–4, 316, 393; X, p. lxxxii.

very different from that of the late medieval ballads. As soon as the forest outlaw began to appear in the May festivities it was probably inevitable that he should participate not only in his own formalized dances but in the already well-established morris dances. It was here that he encountered and later assimilated into his own legend the jolly friar and Maid Marian, almost invariably among the performers in the early sixteenth-century morris dance. They appear together, for example, among the eleven dancers depicted in the so-called Tollet's window, now preserved at Minsterley, Shropshire; and it was with a 'daunce in the myre for veri pure joye' that William Copland's play of '*Robin Hood and the Friar*' ('verye proper to be played in Maye Games') came to a close.[1] Many ingenious attempts to trace the origins of the Friar Tuck of the Robin Hood legend seem to have foundered on a failure to appreciate that he was the product of a fusion between two very different friars. As a renegade outlaw he is recorded as early as 1417, when the name of 'Frere Tuk' was said to have been assumed by the leader of a gang of robbers in south-east England;[2] and it was apparently in the capacity of bellicose outlaw that he played a part in the earliest known Robin Hood play of the 1470s. The almost always anonymous 'frere' of the morris dances was an altogether more jovial and buffoon-like character, at first unconnected with the greenwood legend at all; but by a natural process of conflation he gradually became inextricably involved with Robin Hood and took a modest place among his leader's 'merry men'.[3] Only in the nineteenth century, and particularly as a result of Sir Walter Scott's brilliant portrait of the Clerk of Copmanhurst as Friar Tuck in Chapters XVI and XVII of *Ivanhoe*, did he become an indispensable character in the Robin Hood saga.

Much the most important legacy of the Tudor May Games to the Robin Hood legend was however not a fat friar but a beautiful girl. Unlike Friar Tuck, Maid Marian makes no appearance in the dramatic fragment of *c.* 1475 and clearly owes her association with Robin Hood entirely to their joint participation in the May festivities and the morris dances. The first known mention of her is by Alexander Barclay in an eclogue written not long after 1500, in which one of the characters wishes to hear 'some mery fit of Maide Marian or els of Robin Hood'.[4] As Child pointed out, this reference could suggest that the two characters were still alternatives rather than associates.

---

[1] See below, p. 214; Gutch, I, 337–65.

[2] The real name of this bandit (it is conceivable that he may have been the historical original of Friar Tuck) was Robert Stafford, a chaplain of Lindfield in east Sussex pardoned in November 1429 (*C.P.R.*, *1416–22*, pp. 84, 141; *1429–36*, p. 10).

[3] He sometimes appears as Tuck in the records of the May Day festivities, but more often as a plain friar. Friar Tuck, *eo nomine*, is mentioned in only two of the broadsides, *Robin Hood and Queen Katherine* (Child 145), and *Robin Hood's Golden Prize* (147), (Child, III, 122).

[4] Child, III, 46, 218.

Marian's own literary ancestry remains extremely controversial, but it is virtually certain that by origin she was the shepherdess Marion of the medieval French *pastourelles*, where she was partnered by the shepherd Robin.[1] In the French *fêtes du mai*, only a little less mysterious than their English counterparts, Robin and Marion tended to preside, in the intervals of the attempted seduction of the latter by a series of knights, over a variety of rustic pastimes: it is therefore highly probable that their names and functions were later transferred to the English May Games, where they became confused with the indigenous medieval outlaw characters. Here Marian, played by a boy, developed into a by-word for sexual impropriety, 'a smurkynge wenche indeede . . . none of these coy dames'.[2] The consequent liaison between Robin Hood and his Maid Marian gradually introduced a more romantically sexual element into the greenwood myth, an element completely absent in medieval tradition but absolutely essential for the later elaboration and survival of the legend. Admittedly Maid Marian made remarkably little impact, except in the case of the one jejune ballad that goes by her name (No. 11 below), on the later popular tradition of Robin Hood broadsides and garlands. But her relationship with Robin Hood was a necessary precondition for the next important stage in the evolution of the legend—its transformation into a subject suitable for literary treatment at the hands of Tudor poets and playwrights. Robin Hood had taken the decisive step of finding his way from the village festival to the royal court.

It is to the chronicler Edward Hall's well-known account of the court festivities of the young King Henry VIII that we owe what little information we possess about the origins of royal interest in Robin Hood. Once again the May Games seem to have been the critical link in the diffusion of the legend. In 1510 Henry VIII's 'Maying' took the form of entering his queen's chamber with eleven of his nobles, 'all appareled in short cotes of Kentish Kendal, with hodes on their heddes, and hosen of the same, every one of them his bowe and arrowes, and a sworde and a bucklar, like outlawes, or Robyn Hodes men'. Five years later (in May 1515) the king and queen were entertained at Shooters Hill on the way to Greenwich by two hundred yeomen, 'clothed all in grene' under the leadership of a 'Robyn Hood', who invited them 'into the grene wood, and to se how the outlawes lyve.' After a venison breakfast in a bower served by the outlaws (in reality the king's own yeomen), the royal party was met by the Ladies May and Flora together with their companions Ladies Humidity, Vert, Vegetave, Pleasaunce and Sweet Odour. It is clear enough that by this time the legend 'has become learned, alle-

---

[1] Adam de la Halle's *Jeu de Robin et Marion* of *c.* 1280, possibly written for the Neapolitan court, is a gaily dramatized version of such pastourelles: see Chambers, *Mediaeval Stage*, I, 171.

[2] See the references collected in A. R. Humphrey's Arden edition of *King Henry IV, Part I* (1966), p. 115.

gorical, and pseudo-classic'.[1] How far this highly artificial courtly patronage of Robin Hood survived the Reformation and the renewed condemnation of the outlaw cult by sixteenth-century 'puritans' is impossible to know. Precisely because Robin Hood was regarded as a more suitable subject for spectacle and pageantry than carefully composed dramatic pieces, he is inevitably inadequately represented in surviving Tudor literary texts. It would be surprising if Robin Hood did not figure in the lavish entertainments, often in a processional or allegorical form, which are known to have been a prominent feature of the English court until replaced by the highly successful masques of James I's reign. But such material has rarely survived in the form of complete play texts, and it must remain uncertain whether or not (as has sometimes been suggested)[2] there was a genuine tradition of courtly interludes and other pieces about Robin Hood throughout the sixteenth century.

It was of course the late Elizabethan dramatists who, in the case of the Robin Hood stories as of so many other traditional themes, transformed the legend by articulating and elaborating it at length. Although Shakespeare himself never wrote a Robin Hood play, his many allusions to the ballads make it clear that he was familiar with the *topos* of the English greenwood, to which indeed *As You Like It* in particular owes an obvious debt.[3] What may have been the most interesting of all Elizabethan plays on the subject, 'a pastorall plesant commedie of Robin Hood and Little John' entered in the Stationers' Register on 14 May 1594 is now unfortunately lost; and a similar fate has befallen the mysterious '*Robin Hood's Penn'orths*' (apparently a play title) mentioned in Henslowe's diary at the end of the century.[4] However George Peele's loosely structured but highly popular *Edward the First, sirnamed Edward Longshanks* (first printed in 1593) actually incorporates a Robin Hood game and borrows heavily from the ballad of the outlaw's

---

[1] Chambers, *Mediaeval Stage*, I, 180; *Hall's Chronicle* (London, 1809 edn.), pp. 520, 582; Ritson, 1846, p. 29. Cf. S. Anglo, *Spectacle, Pageantry and Early Tudor Policy* (Oxford, 1969), p. 119; S. E. Lehmberg, *The Reformation Parliament, 1529-36* (Cambridge, 1970), p. 14.

[2] For the unsubstantiated theory of H. L. D. Ward that John Skelton may have written a now lost Robin Hood interlude, see Child, III, 519, and below, p. 223.

[3] A. H. Thorndike, 'The Relation of *As You Like It* to the *Robin Hood* Plays' (*Journal of English and German Philology* IV (1902), 59-69). In *As You Like It* (I, 1), the old Duke and his 'merry men . . . live like the old Robin Hood of England . . . as they did in the golden world'; in *King Henry IV, Part I* (III, 3) Falstaff tells Mistress Quickly that 'Maid Marian may be the deputy's wife of the ward to thee'; and in *King Henry IV, Part II* (V, 3), he hears 'And Robin Hood, Scarlet and John', the refrain of *The Jolly Pinder of Wakefield* (below, p. 147); in *The Two Gentlemen of Verona* (IV, 1) there is an allusion to 'the bare scalp of Robin Hood's fat friar'; and in *The Two Noble Kinsmen* (Prologue) Shakespeare and Fletcher fear that their treatment of Chaucer's 'famed works' may prove 'lighter than Robin Hood'.

[4] E. K. Chambers, *The Elizabethan Stage* (London, 1923), III, 446-7; *Henslowe's Diary*, ed. W. Greg (London, 1904), II, 215.

contest with the potter. Another ballad (No. 6 below) provides the basis for much of the action in *George a Green, the Pinner of Wakefield* (1599), a comedy in which the hero, located in the reign of Edward IV, fights Scarlet, Much and Robin Hood in turn before inviting the latter to a banquet at his home.[1] Much more ambitious was the almost exactly contemporaneous *A Pleasant Commodie called Looke About You* (1600) which actually begins with the entry on to the stage of 'a gallant youth, a proper gentleman' in the person of Robin Hood, the young Earl of Huntington.[2]

The anonymous *Looke About You* owes an obvious debt to the recently completed pair of plays written by Anthony Munday, unquestionably the most influential of all pieces of dramatic writing about Robin Hood and the only extant Elizabethan plays in which the outlaw hero's career is treated at length. Munday's elaborately high-spirited 'two partes of Robart Hoode' left a permanent impression on the greenwood saga, firstly by identifying Maid Marian with one of the semi-mythical Matildas persecuted by King John, and secondly by elevating the outlaw leader himself to the peerage (probably if not certainly for the first time) as Robert, Earl of Huntington.[3] It is unlikely that Munday knew, or particularly cared, what effect he was making on the legend. In 1615 he introduced Robin Hood into another of his works, the *Metropolis Coronata, The Triumphes of Ancient Drapery*, a pageant prepared for the London Lord Mayor's Day: on this occasion Munday completely ignored his previous identification of Robin Hood as the son-in-law of Lord Fitzwater in favour of the startlingly new hypothesis that his father-in-law was no less a person than Henry Fitz-Aylwin, the first mayor of London.[4]

No English writer has ever handled the Robin Hood legend in a more high-handed and cavalier fashion than Anthony Munday. Possibly the view that the forest outlaw was in reality an unjustly dispossessed nobleman had already gained some currency;[5] but it was Munday who first made Robin Hood socially respectable and laid the foundations for what has since become one of the most familiar features of the myth. In the short term however he was only partially successful in imposing an aristocratic strain on what long

---

[1] George Peele, *The Famous Chronicle of King Edward the First, etc.* (Malone Society Reprints, Oxford, 1911); *The Comedy of George a Green* (Malone Society Reprints, 1911); Ritson, 1846, p. 14; Child, III, 129–30.

[2] *Looke About You* (Malone Society Reprints, 1913); Ritson, 1846, p. 6; Chambers, *Elizabethan Stage*, IV, 28.

[3] For a more detailed discussion of Munday's two Robin Hood plays, see below, pp. 220–3.

[4] *Metropolis Coronata* (London, 1615); Ritson, 1846, pp. 19–20; D. M. Bergeron, *English Civic Pageantry, 1558–1642* (London, 1971), pp. 152–5.

[5] Munday may have himself been influenced by the chronicler Grafton's belief that Robin Hood 'was for his manhood and chiualry aduanced to the noble dignitie of an Erle': *Chronicle or History of England* (London, 1809 edn.), I, 221; cf. Leland's desscription of Robin Hood as 'nobilis': Leland's *Collectanea*, ed. T. Hearne (London, 1774), I, 54.

remained an essentially plebeian legend. Admittedly the English greenwood became the object of much madrigal verse and of somewhat self-conscious literary fashion during the first forty years of the seventeenth century. Ben Jonson gave the title of *The Forrest* to his most famous collection of short poems (1616); while Michael Drayton and several of his contemporaries were eager to invite their readers to 'talke of Robin Hoode, And little John in merry Shirewoode'. But this literary addiction to the outlaw legend was apparently too artificial and too short-lived to produce any significant effect on its immediate development. Ben Jonson's own ambitious and uncompleted attempt to convert the English greenwood into a pastoral Arcady (*The Sad Shepherd*, written in the 1630s) produced what many would consider to be the best poetry ever occasioned by Robin Hood but had even less influence on his cult than Munday's plays.[1]

How far the Robin Hood legend might have been permanently transfigured by its adaption to the stage had it not been for the sudden extinction of the Elizabethan and Jacobean dramatic tradition in the 1640s must remain a matter for speculation. As it was, many years were to elapse before Robin Hood played a thoroughly *serious* role on the stage again. The curious *pièce d'occasion* presented at Nottingham on the day of Charles II's coronation (No. 24 below) is clearly no exception to the rule that Robin Hood could adapt to many milieus but not to that of Restoration drama. Only in the eighteenth century did the forest outlaw find his way back on to the stage in a series of comic operas and farces whose entertainment value, to judge from surviving texts, must have depended on the bravura performances of the actors rather than the words they spoke or the songs they sang. Thus the highlight of the 1730 version of *Robin Hood* ('An Opera, As it is Perform'd at Lee's and Harper's Great Theatrical Booth In Bartholomew-Fair') was the farcical scene in which the cuckolded Pinner of Wakefield chased Little John under the table and into a cradle for seducing his wife. Twenty years later Robin Hood made regular appearances in a 'musical entertainment' at Drury Lane, where he was presented in a much more sentimental vein as the benevolent promoter of the love-affair between Leander and Clorinda as well as the singer of a popular song entitled 'As blithe as the linnet sings in the green wood'.[2] Most popular of all was Leonard MacNally's comic opera *Robin Hood or Sherwood Forest*, which in a shortened form was performed two or three times a season at the Theatre Royal, Covent Garden, throughout the last decade of the eighteenth century.[3] One can only regret, like Joseph

---

[1] See below, pp. 231–6.

[2] *Robin Hood, An Opera* (printed for J. Watts, London, 1730); *Robin Hood, A New Musical Entertainment* (printed by M. Cooper, London, 1751).

[3] Leonard MacNally, *Robin Hood, or Sherwood Forest: A Comic Opera* (London, 1784); *The London Stage, Part 5, 1776–1800*, ed. C. B. Hogan (Southern Illinois University Press, 1968), III, pp. 1481, 1555, 1583, 1597, 1693.

Ritson in 1795, that 'the elegant author of *The School for Scandal*' never wrote more than one unpublished act of his projected drama on Robin Hood.[1]

(ii)

Much more important than such now forgotten musical dramas in preserving the Robin Hood legend between the age of Munday and Jonson and that of Sheridan and Ritson was the printed popular ballad. The extent to which 'Robin Hood is absolutely a *creation* of the ballad-muse' will always remain controversial; but there can be no doubt that the singing of ballads about him was the primary reason for his continuous popularity and eventual survival into modern industrial society. As the patron saint of English archery during its most flourishing period, and as a hero who lent his name to innumerable inns throughout the country, Robin Hood's immortality was already assured.[2] But it is, after all, remarkable how little attention the medieval greenwood saga received from the familiar names of English literary history between the early seventeenth and late eighteenth centuries. The major and highly eccentric exception was the antiquary William Stukeley (1687–1765), whose bizarre opinions on the Robin Hood legend are indeed displayed to best advantage in the annotations he made to his own copy of the Robin Hood Garland.[3] During this long period, one in which the Robin Hood *persona* became more plebeian than ever before or since, the diffusion of his reputation rested almost entirely on the popularity of the so-called street ballad, first in its simple broadside and then in chapbook form.

'Street balladry', best defined as the commercial production of songs for sale in the fair or market-place by itinerant hawkers and pedlars, may well have preceded the introduction of printing into England; but it was the ability of the cheap press to produce large quantities of one-sheet printed broadsides from the early sixteenth century onwards which completely transformed the situation. In this field, as in so many others, the transition from script to print created a series of important qualitative as well as quantitative changes—not the least confusing of which was the application of the term 'ballad', originally confined to songs designed to accompany dances, to *any* popular verse-forms disseminated by broadside texts. 'To Shakespeare, Jonson, Beaumont, Fletcher, Dryden, and Pepys the word *ballad* had in general one meaning only: namely a song (usually written by a hack-poet) that was printed on a broadside and sold in the streets by professional

---

[1] 'The first act, said to have been written many years ago, is, by those who have seen or heard it, spoken of with admiration' (Ritson, 1846, p. 21).
[2] For the most famous of all Robin Hood Inns, that in Butcher's Row, London, which after 1747 enjoyed much notoriety as 'a Receptacle for the Illiterate and the Impious', see the anonymous *History of the Robinhood Society* (London, 1764). Also see below, p. 293.
[3] Folger Shakespeare Library, Washington D.C., PR 2125 R6; and see below, p. 59 n.1.

singers'.[1] The oldest surviving broadside ballad of this type is usually held to be John Skelton's *A Ballade of the Scottyshe Kynge*, printed by Richard Fawkes soon after the battle of Flodden in 1513; and there can be no doubt of the popularity of broadsides by the end of Henry VIII's reign. Compulsory registration of printed ballads with the London Stationers' Company from the 1550s onwards has enabled H. E. Rollins and others to trace the progress of this flourishing industry in great detail. After the 1580s, and thanks to the later enthusiasm for the genre of a famous series of collectors from John Selden to the third Duke of Roxburghe, broadside texts themselves (notoriously difficult to date at all precisely) survive in very large numbers. Only with the legal prohibition of ballad-singing under the Commonwealth can the first and golden age of the English broadside ballad be said to have come to a close.[2]

The exact role and status of the Robin Hood ballad within the context of this remarkable efflorescence of the broadside remain largely uncharted and often obscure. Not a single extant Robin Hood printed ballad text can be dated to the sixteenth century; and it may well be that only in the reigns of James I and Charles I did the outlaw legend completely succumb to the commercial pressures inherent in the production and marketing of broadsides. That songs of Robin Hood were circulating widely throughout late Elizabethan England is not of course in doubt: their popularity is vouched for by a great host of Shakespeare's contemporaries. But how large a proportion of such songs were yet being disseminated by means of the printed broadside ballad remains difficult to estimate. Of the only two ballad entries relating to Robin Hood in the Stationers' Registers before 1600, the 'ballett of Wakefylde and a grene' (1557–8) certainly sounds like an early version of *The Jolly Pinder of Wakefield* (No. 6 below); but it has been suggested that the second item, an unidentifiable 'ballett of Robyn Hod' registered with the Stationers in 1562–3, was actually an edition of the long *Gest*.[3] Nor does it seem at all certain that the famous 'stories' of Robin Hood, Bevis of Hampton, Adam Bell and other medieval heroes owned by Captain Cox in 1575 were in printed broadside form.[4] But in the course of the next two generations the commercial broadside undoubtedly did begin to carry all before it and soon became the main vehicle for the transmission of the Robin Hood legend. During the thirty years after the appearance of a 'Robin Hood and Little

[1] H. E. Rollins, *A Pepysian Garland* (Cambridge, 1922), p. ix; A. B. Friedman, *The Ballad Revival* (Chicago, 1961), pp. 35–83.

[2] C. H. Firth, 'Ballads and Broadsides', *Shakespeare's England*, ed. S. Lee (London, 1917), II, 511–38; *The Common Muse*, ed. V. de Sola Pinto and A. E. Rodway (1965 edn.), pp. 31–9; Rollins, *Pepysian Garland*, p. ix.

[3] H. E. Rollins, 'Analytical Index to the Ballad Entries in the Registers of the Company of Stationers', *Studies in Philology*, XXI (1924), p. 199; Arber, I, 76.

[4] *Captain Cox, His Ballads and Books; or, Robert Laneham's Letter*, ed. F. J. Furnivall (Ballad Society, London, 1871), pp. xii–xiii, li–liv.

John' in June 1624, the titles of Robin Hood ballads figure frequently in the Stationers' Registers: moreover they can now be confidently associated with surviving broadside texts. Thus 'The Noble Ffisherman, or, Robin Hood's great Prize' entered to the London publisher Francis Coles on 13 June 1631 is almost certainly represented by a contemporary broadside copy of that ballad now preserved among Antony Wood's volumes in the Bodleian Library, Oxford (No. 12 below).[1] None of the earliest surviving Robin Hood broadside ballads is exactly dated, but a very large number of those preserved in the great collections of Wood, Pepys and Roxburghe were undoubtedly printed by Francis Coles and his London rivals during the middle years of the seventeenth century. By that period, indeed, the repertory of Robin Hood broadsides was already very extensive and its major themes had all been fully articulated. Not only did the greatest ballad-monger of them all, Martin Parker (*c*. 1600–56) find it desirable to turn his attention to the outlaw hero in 1631–2; in his *A True Tale of Robin Hood* (No. 14 below), he provided a résumé of what was obviously an already voluminous broadside literature.[2]

The important consequences of the triumph of the broadside on the development of the Robin Hood legend will be obvious to all readers of this anthology. With a very few exceptions, almost all the supposedly 'traditional' Robin Hood ballads collected by Child under 38 different titles are themselves printed broadside texts. In several cases, like those of *Robin Hood and the Tanner* (Child 126) and *Robin Hood and the Tinker* (Child 127), such ballads may actually have begun their careers as entirely new stories fabricated for a flourishing market by the ballad-mongers of the seventeenth century. The best example of the creation of a new Robin Hood tale by a professional ballad-writer is however *Robin Hood's Golden Prize* (Child 147), registered with the Stationers in June 1656 and interesting as the only work of its kind which can be ascribed to an identified author, Laurence Price (*c*. 1625–80).[3] Nor would such blatantly commercial origins necessarily prevent the ballads in question from enjoying favour with later 'folk-singers'; as G. H. Gerould has pointed out, 'Sometimes, however, one or another of the various new ballads written to a single old tune must have sunk deep into popular memory and quite ousted the traditional narrative.'[4]

However, most of the Robin Hood broadside ballads were undoubtedly adaptations of existing verse-narratives rather than completely new stories. Just because the printed broadside versions of Robin Hood tales supplanted their earlier predecessors so completely, it is rarely possible to trace in any detail the process of transformation. Only in the case of the early Robin Hood

[1] Wood 402, p. 18; cf. Arber, IV, 254; Child, III, 211.

[2] H. E. Rollins, 'Martin Parker, Ballad-Monger', *Modern Philology* XVI (1919), 113–38.

[3] *Roxburghe Ballads*, VI, 64; Rollins, 'Analytical Index to Ballad Entries', p. 200; Child, III, 208, 519.

[4] G. H. Gerould, *The Ballad of Tradition*, p. 240.

ballads entered into the famous Percy Folio, and in particular of *Robin Hood and the Butcher* (see below, pp. 150–7), do we have much opportunity of appreciating the manner in which the comparatively informal and un-structured outlaw songs of the sixteenth century were brought within the rigid and stereotyped conventions of the typical broadside. The wide circula-tion of a particular Robin Hood ballad in a printed text itself tended to set or fix that text more permanently than its manuscript or memorized predeces-sors. Even more important was the effect of the practice of producing new Robin Hood songs to old tunes, of re-writing the words of a traditional Robin Hood ballad to conform to one of a small repertoire of familiar melodies.[1] As a result many of the Robin Hood ballads, and especially the most popular ones, were brought into a series of common and remarkably frozen musical and metrical patterns. Among the resulting literary characteristics of the Robin Hood broadside (see Nos. 6–14 below), perhaps the most obvious is the increase in the use of circumlocutory dialogue and of stock formulaic phrases, clearly the consequence of the need to make the written line match the musical one. Whereas the *Gest, Robin Hood and the Monk* and *Robin Hood and the Potter* derive much of their impact on the modern reader from their extreme concision and a sometimes cryptic quality, the later broadsides are so repetitive and verbose that (like the modern popular song) they can only hope to succeed when heard rather than seen on the printed page. Most of the aesthetic effects of the Robin Hood broadsides are, in other words, likely to be musical rather than literary, a conclusion confirmed by Professor Fowler's recent analysis of *Robin Hood Rescuing Three Squires* (Child 140) as an example of 'baroque minstrelsy of the eighteenth century'.[2] It might be pointed out however that most of the hallmarks of the genre, including fre-quent uses of verbal parallelism and sudden transitions to a new theme, were already in full being before the Restoration. Few features of the Robin Hood legend are more intriguing than the fact that the great majority of the outlaw ballads to be heard in the early nineteenth-century English countryside were still being sung to the words and tunes of the London ballad-mongers of two hundred years earlier.

It follows that the broadside ballad of the early and mid-seventeenth century perpetuated the Robin Hood legend at the cost of fossilizing not only its literary and musical forms but also its subject-matter. Within the simple and limited framework of the genre popularized by Martin Parker and his contemporaries, there was little room for any development in the character of

---

[1] W. Chappell, *The Ballad Literature and Popular Music of the Olden Time* (London, 1859), II, 387–400; Gutch, II, 433–47; B. H. Bronson, *The Traditional Tunes of the Child Ballads* (Princeton, 1959–72, in progress), III, 13–71, the indispensable treatment of the tunes of the Robin Hood ballads and highly critical of Chappell's and Rimbault's conclusions.

[2] Fowler, *Literary History of the Popular Ballad*, pp. 165–7.

Robin Hood and his men—or indeed of the social or political situations within which they found themselves. As might be expected, the Robin Hood created by the ballad-mongers was an adaptation of the medieval outlaw figure to conform to the general conventions of the street ballad. In particular, he was recast in the mould of the independent artisan, that heroic figure of Elizabethan 'low life' immortalized by Thomas Delaney in the persons of *Jack of Newbury* and *Thomas of Reading*. Nor can there be any doubt that the concept of sylvan liberty was a deliberate idealization of the criminal life actually led by masterless men in the English forests on the part of town-dwellers who never went there.[1] Part of Robin Hood's appeal to early seventeenth-century audiences arose from the paradox that he was converted into an urban hero, not too dissimilar from George a Green, the pinner of Wakefield. To judge from surviving broadsides, no part of the Robin Hood legend was more popular than his contests with tanners, tinkers and butchers; nor is it without significance that such artisan figures displayed an increasing ability to out-wit or out-fight Robin himself.

More generally, the Robin of the broadsides is a much less tragic, less heroic and in the last resort less mature figure than his medieval predecessor. His exploits are made much more ingeniously, if light-heartedly, fantastic (see *The Noble Fisherman* and *Robin Hood and the Valiant Knight*, Nos. 12 and 13 below); and the 'courtly' elements which play such a distinctive part in the *Gest* and the two medieval ballads are either completely suppressed or subjected to crude burlesque. The theme of romantic love rarely enters the world of the broadside ballad, and when it does (as in *Robin Hood and Allen A Dale* and *Robin Hood and Maid Marian*, Nos. 10 and 11 below) it is the object of merriment rather than sentiment. The Robin Hood broadside of the seventeenth and eighteenth centuries, like other products of the 'Common Muse', 'is less akin (than the traditional ballad) to myth and primitive ritual and it rarely taps the deeper springs of the psyche'.[2] To many ballad enthusiasts the Robin Hood broadsides therefore share the undoubted limitations of their commercialized type, 'frequently mawkish, sentimental, vulgar—the kind of poetry that skilful versifiers of little taste would write'.[3] But it must always be remembered that the very simplicity, repetitiveness and banality of the broadside—like 'the extraordinary amount of tautology' which George Orwell analysed in the often analogous case of 'Boys' Weeklies'[4]—are exactly those qualities most needed to create a continuously appealing popular fictional world.

---

[1] C. Hill, *The World Turned Upside Down: Radical Ideas during the English Revolution* (London, 1972), pp. 35–6, 40–1, 62.

[2] *The Common Muse*, p. 20.

[3] *The Ballad Book*, ed. MacEdward Leach (New York, 1964), p. 33.

[4] *Collected Essays, Journalism and Letters of George Orwell*, ed. S. Orwell and I. Angus (1970 edn.), I, 508.

The primitive black-letter broadside therefore left a permanent impress on the development of the Robin Hood legend; but by the end of the seventeenth century the broadside itself was in decline. As Ritson pointed out long ago, most surviving 'common broad-sheet ballads' were printed between the Restoration of 1660 and the Revolution of 1688.[1] After that date the production of single Robin Hood ballads in broadsheet form certainly continued; but of the remarkably few surviving examples, most were in white-letter and apparently had a limited circulation. The broadside had ceased to be the main vehicle for the diffusion of the outlaw songs. Thus the splendid series of single-sheet Robin Hood ballads published by C. Sheppard of Lambert Hill, Doctors Commons, London, in 1791 (the most handsomely illustrated Robin Hood broadsides ever printed) were clearly directed at a 'prestige' rather than popular market.[2] Throughout the eighteenth and early nineteenth centuries the great majority of those who wished to own songs of Robin Hood no longer bought copies of individual ballads but one of the innumerable cheap anthologies or Robin Hood Garlands instead. These Garlands were one of the most popular as well as most specialized varieties of the chapbooks of the age, those little books which 'more than any other evidence we have open a window on the world of the eighteenth-century poor'.[3] During a period when such 'penny histories' provided most of the reading matter of the deprived sections of the community, the importance of the Garlands in popularizing the Robin Hood legend needs no particular urging. Like most chapbooks they were usually crudely printed on coarse rag-paper. However as nearly all Garlands contained between sixteen and twenty-seven separate Robin Hood songs, they tended to be considerably larger—and therefore more expensive —than the ordinary chapbook. By the late eighteenth century a Robin Hood Garland usually ran to eighty or a hundred pages as compared to the chapbook's customary twenty-four; and it normally sold at fourpence, sixpence or even a shilling a copy as opposed to the penny of the small chapbook. The catalogue issued in 1764 by Cluer Dicey and Richard Marshall, partners who dominated the entire English chapbook trade from their premises in Bow Churchyard at the time, offered Robin Hood's Garlands, with 29 illustrations, at sixteen shillings a hundred to running stationers—who in turn sold them retail at sixpence each.[4]

The long recorded history of the Robin Hood Garlands begins with the publication in 1663 ('for W. Gilbertson, at the Bible in Giltspur-street without Newgate') of *Robin Hood's Garland or Delightful Songs shewing the noble exploits of Robin Hood, and his yeomandrie*.[5] Although the earliest known copy

---

[1] Ritson, 1846, p. 25. [2] Bodleian Library, Oxford, Douce F. F. 71, nos. 11–15.
[3] J. Ashton, *Chap-Books of the Eighteenth Century* (London, 1882), p. 6; cf. V. E. Neuburg, *The Penny Histories* (Oxford, 1968), pp. 1–20.
[4] Neuburg, *Penny Histories*, p. 31.
[5] Bodleian Library, Oxford, Wood 79; cf. Child, III, 42.

of the Garland, this collection of seventeen different songs—with 'new edditions and emendations'—cannot have been the first. In the previous year (1662) the same publisher had helped to print a prose version of the Garland 'in twelve several stories'.[1] It therefore seems probable that the Robin Hood Garland originated in the 1650s as a collection of a dozen ballads. Within a few years, however, the number of Robin Hood songs in the common Garland had increased to sixteen, namely *Robin Hood's Progress to Nottingham* (Child 139), *Robin Hood Newly Revived* (128), *The Pinder of Wakefield* (124), *Robin Hood and the Bishop* (143), *Robin Hood and the Butcher* (122), *Robin Hood Rescuing William Stutely* (141), *Robin Hood and the Beggar* (133), *Robin Hood and Queen Katherine* (145), *Robin Hood and the Tanner* (126), *Robin Hood and the Curtal Friar* (123), *The Noble Fisherman* (148), *Robin Hood and the Shepherd* (135), *Robin Hood's Golden Prize* (147), *Robin Hood's Chase* (146), *Little John and the Four Beggars* (142), and *Robin Hood's Delight* (136).[2] All these ballads could still of course be bought in their original single-sheet broadside form: indeed every one of the sixteen titles listed above figured among the broadsides available for purchase in 1685 from William Thackeray at the Angel in Duck Lane, London.[3] The Garlands, in other words, were essentially collections of Robin Hood broadside ballads and little more. They added nothing of substance to the development of the legend in their own right, but were nevertheless of outstanding importance in perpetuating the ballads current in the 1660s and 1670s into the next century and beyond, long after the decline in popularity of the black-letter broadside.

Indeed the most remarkable feature of the innumerable Robin Hood Garlands between the 1660s and 1830s is their sustained conservatism. Although the indispensable stock-in-trade of a bewildering variety of London and provincial printers, little attempt was ever made to change the words of any ballad during this long period. Textual variations between the countless different editions of the Garland are nearly always due to misprinting by a cheap and inadequately supervised press rather than any effort to 'improve' a particular Robin Hood song or to bring it up to date.[4] Although

---

[1] *The Noble Birth and Gallant Atchievements of that remarkable outlaw Robin Hood* (London, for Thomas Vere and William Gilbertson, 1662): a copy of the second edition (1678) of this work is printed in W. J. Thoms, *Early English Prose Romances* (2nd edn., London, 1858), II, 90–124.

[2] These are the songs, in order, collected in the second oldest surviving Robin Hood Garland, that printed at London for F. Coles, T. Vere and J. Wright in 1670 (Bodleian Library, Oxford, Douce H. 80).

[3] *The Bagford Ballads*, ed. J. W. Ebsworth (Ballad Society, Hertford, 1878), I, pp. lx–lxxvi; Gable, p. 13.

[4] This conclusion emerges very clearly from a comparison of the successive editions of the Garland produced by three York printers, Thomas Gent in *c.* 1760, Thomas Wilson in 1811, and James Kendrew *c.* 1825 (York Minster Library, B. 8, B. 9; York City Reference Library, Y. 920). For the popularity of outlaw chapbooks in the north at this period, see C. A. Federer, *Yorkshire Chap-Books* (London, 1889), pp. 7–9.

the title of the Garland might change (*The History and Famous Exploits of Robin Hood* and *The English Archer* were the most common alternatives), its contents rarely did so. The only important development was the addition, apparently during the course of the first half of the eighteenth century, of new items to the common Garland repertory of songs: 'For now at last, by true industrious care, The *sixteen* songs to twenty-seven we mount'.[1] By the time Joseph Ritson produced the first scholarly anthology of Robin Hood ballads in 1795, the standard Garland contained in addition to the original sixteen songs the following eleven: *Robin Hood's Birth, Breeding, Valor and Marriage* (Child 149), *Robin Hood and the Tinker* (127), *Robin Hood and Allen A Dale* (138), *Robin Hood and the Prince of Aragon* (129), *Robin Hood and the Ranger* (131), *Robin Hood and Little John* (125), *Robin Hood and the Bishop of Hereford* (144), *Robin Hood and the Three Squires* (140), *The King's Disguise* (151), *Robin Hood and the Golden Arrow* (152), and *Robin Hood and the Valiant Knight* (153).[2] Although *Robin Hood's Birth* (more usually known as *The Pedigree, Education and Marriage of Robin Hood*) was normally placed first in the collection and *Robin Hood and the Valiant Knight* ('*with an Account of his Death and Burial, etc.*') usually closed the later Garlands, no other attempt was made to provide these anthologies with a thematic or chronological structure. To the very end of their existence—as late as the 1830s and 1840s in the case of some of the smaller provincial presses[3]—the Robin Hood Garlands continued to preserve and indeed fossilize the outlaw songs as well as the outlaw *persona* of the mid-seventeenth century.

(iii)

The first step in the liberation of Robin Hood from the dead weight of the tradition of the broadsides and the Garlands can be said to be the publication of Thomas Percy's *Reliques of Ancient English Poetry* in 1765.[4] In providing his readers with the opportunity to read *Robin Hood and Guy of Gisborne* (No. 5 below), Percy made available the first printed text of a ballad 'of much greater antiquity than any of the common popular songs on this subject'. Much more important was the general stimulus of the *Reliques* in creating the ballad mania of the late eighteenth century, a mania out of which a substantially new and recognizably 'modern' Robin Hood eventually came to be born. In the course of their search for poetry that would be popular rather

---

[1] Quoted from the verse address 'To all gentlemen archers' which is prefixed to the great majority of late editions of the Robin Hood's Garland; cf. Ritson, 1846, p. 25.

[2] See, for a representative and apparently often pirated Robin Hood's Garland, the edition of *c.* 1753 printed by the Diceys 'in St Mary Aldermary Church Yard, Bow Lane, Cheapside, and sold at the Warehouse at Northampton' (Bodleian Library, Oxford, Douce F. F. 71).

[3] Gable, pp. 120–5.

[4] For an interesting discussion of this 'pivotal document of the ballad revival', see especially Friedman, *Ballad Revival*, pp. 185–232.

than aristocratic, and 'natural' rather than artificial, the poets and scholars of the period developed a much greater interest in Robin Hood ballads than any of their predecessors. One sign of changing attitudes to the outlaw legend was the inclusion of large numbers of ballads from the Garlands in Thomas Evans's popular collection of *Old Ballads, Historical and Narrative* (1777). Nevertheless literary as well as social prejudice against 'foolish tales of Robin Hood' died hard: for a contributor to the *Critical Review* in January 1792, Robin Hood ballads were still by definition 'the refuse of a stall'.[1]

The rehabilitation of Robin Hood was essentially the work of one man, the eccentrically indefatigable Joseph Ritson (1752–1803), whose *Robin Hood: A Collection of all the Ancient Poems, Songs and Ballads, now extant, relative to that celebrated Outlaw* appeared in 1795. As an already well-established collector of local verse noted for the rigour of his critical standards, as the acquaintance of Dr Johnson as well as the friend of Sir Walter Scott, Ritson had the best possible credentials for his task. He was triumphantly successful. With the single important exception of the ballad of *Robin Hood and the Monk* (No. 2 below), the first edition of Ritson's comprehensive anthology made available reliable texts of all the major works in the Robin Hood canon. Frequently reprinted in revised and extended form during the course of the nineteenth century, Ritson's *Robin Hood* remains an indispensable handbook to the outlaw legend even now. Perhaps the greatest tribute to its value is that it has only had two successors. John Mathew Gutch's two-volumed collection of 1847 is largely based on Ritson's and displays considerably less critical acumen than its model. Nor did it ever attain the commercial success of Ritson's work.[2] Only in 1888 with the appearance of Francis Child's edition of the *Gest* and the Robin Hood ballads was Ritson's achievement surpassed by a scholar whose learning was even greater than his own.[3]

One of the greatest of Child's many virtues was his ability, as an American, to approach the study of England's greatest outlaw myth in a spirit of critical detachment, a quality which Ritson and his many disciples inevitably found it hard to achieve. Nevertheless it is salutary to remember that Child's formidable scholarship has exercised comparatively little influence outside the world of learning. Ritson's *Robin Hood*, on the other hand, is itself a critical document in the history of the legend. By providing the English poets and novelists of the Romantic and Victorian periods with a convenient source-book, Ritson gave them the opportunity to re-create Robin Hood in their own imagination. So extensive was the effect of his anthology that it

---

[1] Ritson, 1846, p. 1.

[2] Whereas Gutch's *A Lytell Geste of Robin Hode, with other Ancient and Modern Ballads and Songs* only appeared in two editions (1847 and 1850), Ritson's *Robin Hood* was reprinted in 1820, 1823, 1826, 1827, 1832, 1840, 1846, 1853, 1862, 1865, 1866, 1867, 1884, 1885 and 1887 (Gable, pp. 96–100).

[3] Child, III, 39–233.

may even have influenced the 'folk' traditions dear to the hearts of the lovers of popular ballads. Is it altogether a coincidence that the famous Mrs Brown of Falkland provided Robert Jamieson with a song on *The Birth of Robin Hood* (No. 16 below) in 1800, only five years after the publication of Ritson's *Robin Hood* revealed a surprising absence of any existing ballad on that important theme?[1] More important still, it was Ritson who gave pride of place in his collection of Robin Hood songs to the *Gest* and established that poem as the central work in the outlaw saga, a position it has held ever since. Above all perhaps, the sheer weight of learning Ritson brought to his self-imposed task of rehabilitating Robin Hood (most evident in his prefatory 'Life' with accompanying 'Notes and Illustrations') made Robin Hood intellectually as well as socially respectable for the first time in his long history. As Sir Walter Scott wrote, with his usual perspicacity, Ritson 'had an honesty of principle about him, which, if it went to ridiculous extremities, was still respectable from the soundness of the foundation'.[2]

However, Joseph Ritson's contribution to the development of the green-wood legend went further still. Not only did he popularize and legitimize the study of Robin Hood, he also produced a highly influential interpretation of the hero. In the first place the fact that Ritson himself actually believed in the existence of a historical Robin Hood ('just, generous, benevolent, faithful, and beloved or revered by his followers or adherents for his excellent and amiable qualities')[3] had an incalculable effect in promoting the still continuing quest for the man behind the myth. More specifically, Ritson was the first writer to convert Robin Hood into a thoroughgoing ideological hero, a repository for his own extremely complex and at times idiosyncratic revolutionary opinions. For Ritson Robin Hood was 'a man who, in a barbarous age, and under a complicated tyranny, displayed a spirit of freedom and independence, which has endeared him to the common people, whose cause he maintained (for all opposition to tyranny is the cause of the people); and, in spite of the malicious endeavours of pitiful monks, by whom history was consecrated to the crimes and follies of titled ruffians and sainted idiots, to suppress all record of his patriotic exertions and virtuous acts, will render his name immortal'.[4] The sentiments here are of course those of the French Revolution (Ritson was one of the few Englishmen to adopt the French revolutionary calendar) and, more specifically, of Tom Paine. Only three years before the publication of Ritson's *Robin Hood*, Paine had converted another famous medieval English rebel, Wat Tyler, into a revolutionary hero in

[1] Fowler, *Literary History of the Popular Ballad*, p. 304.
[2] Gutch, II, p. xix. Cf. C. C. Moreland, 'Ritson's Life of Robin Hood' *Publications of the Modern Language Association of America*, L (1935), pp. 522–36.
[3] Ritson, 1846, p. 4.
[4] Ibid., pp. 3–4. Ritson's unusual political attitudes (he was a Jacobite who became a Jacobin) are discussed in B. Bronson, *Joseph Ritson, Scholar at Arms* (Berkeley, California, 1938). See also *The Letters of Joseph Ritson, Esq.* (2 vols., London, 1833), II, 30.

exactly the same manner ('his fame will outlive their falsehood').[1] The relevance of Robin Hood, like that of Wat Tyler, to modern revolutionary movements is perhaps questionable and certainly ambiguous; but the long and still continuing interpretation of the forest outlaw as an apostle of popular liberty only seriously began with Joseph Ritson. 'What better title king Richard could pretend to the territory and the people of England, than Robin Hood had to the dominion of Barnsdale or Sherwood, is a question humbly submitted to the political philosopher'.[2]

That particular question remains a relevant one. Interestingly enough it was taken up, in very different ways, by the two greatest 'Robin Hood novels' both written in 1818. Although Thomas Peacock's *Maid Marian* was not published until 1822, three years after the appearance of Walter Scott's *Ivanhoe*, each book was based on an independent reading of Ritson's Robin Hood anthology.[3] The two most forceful and imaginative contributions of early-nineteenth century Romanticism to the Robin Hood legend, *Maid Marian* and *Ivanhoe* illustrate to perfection the complexities and ambiguities of the Romantic movement. Of the two novels *Maid Marian* is at the same time much more subtle and much the less successful. Peacock's light-hearted and astonishingly cavalier re-telling of the Robin Hood story has been rightly categorized as 'an in-between book: half comic opera, half novelistic idyll; or half social satire, half genuine, if humorous, romance'.[4] When compared with his famous 'conversation novels', *Maid Marian* seems a disappointing commentary on Peacock's inability to handle the material he had pillaged from Ritson. Yet this is perhaps to miss the important point that Peacock's failure is as much symptomatic as personal: *Maid Marian* reveals, better than any other work in Robin Hood literature, the impossibility of reconciling the medieval outlaw legend with a modern literary sensibility. To put the problem in its simplest possible terms, Peacock could never decide exactly how seriously to regard Robin Hood; and it is this uncertainty which accounts for his novel's inconsistency of tone and discontinuity of structure. *Maid Marian*'s most obvious feature to the modern reader is its mock-violent buffoonery, a quality so apparent that it ensured the work's commercial success at Covent Garden when converted into a comic opera for Christmas entertainment at the end of 1822.[5] Yet what Peacock thought he was writing, as he remarked in a letter to

---

[1] R. B. Dobson, ed., *The Peasants' Revolt of 1381*, pp. 394–6. [2] Ritson, 1846, p. 2.

[3] In the prefatory note to *Maid Marian*, Peacock claimed that 'This little work, with the exception of the last three chapters, was written in the autumn of 1818'. For the view that, despite this disclaimer, Scott's *Ivanhoe* was one of the objects of Peacock's satire, see Henry Newbolt, *The Greenwood: A collection of literary readings relating to Robin Hood* (London, 1925), pp. 123–32.

[4] C. Dawson, *His Fine Wit: A Study of Thomas Love Peacock* (London, 1950), pp. 223–4.

[5] This opera, *Maid Marian: or, The Huntress of Arlingford*, proved 'all the rage' in the 1820s and was translated into German and French as well as being produced in New York: see J. B. Priestley, *Thomas Love Peacock* (London, 1966 edn.), pp. 59–61.

Shelley, was 'a comic Romance of the Twelfth Century, which I shall make the vehicle of much oblique satire on all the oppressions that are done under the sun'. Peacock's satire failed because it had too many targets, not only the reactionary political forces of the day but also Ritson's Cobbett-like radical agrarianism, caricatured as the view that 'Robin Hood is king of the forest both by dignity of birth and by virtue of his standing army'. In the last resort Peacock was content to present the forest outlaw as a figure of nostalgic and idyllic 'romance', to be remembered (as he remembered Old Windsor Forest itself) with resigned regret.[1]

Sir Walter Scott approached the Robin Hood legend in a much more positive and less qualified spirit. Robin Hood had long been 'no small favourite of mine' when in *Ivanhoe* he triumphantly fulfilled his promise 'to excite an interest for the traditions and manners of old England, similar to that which has been obtained in behalf of those of our poorer and less celebrated neighbours'.[2] The correctness of Scott's belief that 'the name of Robin Hood, if duly conjured with, should raise a spirit as soon as that of Rob Roy' is vouched for by the phenomenal popularity of this first venture into medieval English history on the part of the author of the Waverley Novels. Scott's *Ivanhoe* can fairly be said to have re-created the world of the English middle ages. The appearance, as important if subsidiary characters, of Robin Hood and Friar Tuck (alias Locksley and the Hermit of Copmanhurst) consequently did more than anything else to ensure their continued fame throughout the rest of the nineteenth century. As recent reassessments of Scott have revealed, his historical novels are more complex than most of his contemporary readers were aware. The Robin Hood of *Ivanhoe*, like Cedric the Saxon and even Ivanhoe himself, is a character compelled to sacrifice at least part of his idyllic freedom in the cause of order and strong government. Despite his personal bravery and the loyalty of his men, Scott's Robin Hood is a figure condemned to extinction by the inexorable laws of the historical process. This is the chord, sounded by both Peacock and Scott, which continued to reverberate throughout the Robin Hood literature of the nineteenth century. In 1818, the very year in which *Maid Marian* and *Ivanhoe* were being written, John Keats had produced his own slight 'dirge of a national legend' in the form of a Robin Hood poem (No. 17 below). At the very time when the long tradition of the popular Robin Hood Garland was finally coming to its end, the outlaw hero had been rescued from oblivion by the professional novelist and poet. For this survival he has admittedly had to pay a heavy price. Of the many Victorian and Edwardian men of letters to have taken up the outlaw's

[1] T. L. Peacock, *Memoirs of Shelley and other Essays and Reviews*, ed. H. Mills (London, 1970), pp. 233–40, reprints the author's moving lament for 'The Last Day of Windsor Forest'.

[2] J. G. Lockhart's *Life of Scott* (London, 1893 edn.), p. 229; the other quotations are from the original 'Dedicatory Epistle' to the first edition (1819) of *Ivanhoe*.

bow, from Leigh Hunt to Alfred Tennyson (No. 25) and from John Drinkwater to Alfred Noyes (No. 18), not one proved able to make Robin Hood
seem relevant to the issues of his own day. The writers of the Romantic
period and after popularized Robin Hood only at the cost of converting him
from a real outlaw into a literary symbol of a vanished and largely illusory
medieval Arcadia. 'Playing Robin Hood and Maid Marian' became an
appropriately light diversion for the leisured classes of Victorian society—in
fact as well as fiction.[1]

(iv)

Much more significant than the sporadic and nostalgic interest in Robin Hood
displayed by various English men of letters during the last century and a half
has been the growth of a vast juvenile audience for the greenwood legend.
Indeed many of the features of the traditional Robin Hood saga which have
made it irresponsive to sophisticated literary treatment—its loose and episodic
structure, its lack of pronounced characterization, the absence of any strong
sexual connotations—are exactly those guaranteed to ensure its appeal to the
young. The ability of children throughout the world to identify with the forest
outlaw hero-figure is now, as it has been for many years, the most important
single reason for his immortality. It is clear enough that a series of short adventure stories which are linked together by readily identifiable heroes and
villains can readily mirror the fantasies of the child. In particular, the concept of a gang or fellowship which triumphantly undergoes different tests or
ordeals on successive appearances provides the standard framework for much
conscious 'day-dreaming' experienced by children now and presumably at
all times in the past. The juvenile audience for Robin Hood certainly
existed long before *Ivanhoe*. As early as the seventeenth century it is evident
that a taste for the heroes of medieval romance, King Arthur and Guy of
Warwick, Bevis of Hampton and Robin Hood, was regarded as a characteristic of old women, the servant classes and children.[2] Despite the advice provided by such manuals as Thomas White's *A Little Book for Little Children*
('When thou canst read, read no Ballads and foolish Books, but the Bible'),
there is similarly no doubt that children were amongst the most avid readers
of, or listeners to, the Robin Hood Garlands of the eighteenth century.[3] It was

---

[1] See, e.g., George Eliot, *Daniel Deronda* (Penguin English Library, 1967), p. 157. Real
archery contests had of course been a popular feature of pre-industrial English social
life for many centuries and contributed in no small way to the continuous vogue for
Robin Hood. The Earls of Essex and Cumberland organized such an event at York as
early as 1584 when it was the subject of a ballad by William Elderton (*Roxburghe
Ballads*, I, 1).

[2] Cf. R. S. Crane, 'The Vogue of *Guy of Warwick* from the Close of the Middle Ages to
the Romantic Revival', *Publications of Modern Language Association of America* XXX
(1915), p. 167.

[3] Neuburg, *The Penny Histories*, pp. 10–20.

as a young boy that William Stukeley, later the ingenious fabricator of Robin Hood's most fraudulent pedigree, listened 'enraptured to an old man who remembered the traditional ballads of Robin Hood';[1] and as a boy too that William Wordsworth first encountered in the chapbooks those nostalgically remembered joys of 'the Wishing-Cap / of Fortunatus, and the invisible Coat / Of Jack the Giant-Killer, Robin Hood / And Sabra in the forest with St George!'[2]

Nevertheless it was during Wordsworth's own life-time that a decisive change occurred—less perhaps in the history of juvenile enthusiasm for Robin Hood than in the readiness and ability of writers and publishers to produce versions of the Robin Hood tales addressed specifically to young readers. The innumerable Robin Hood Garlands of the late eighteenth century may have been read by more children than adults; but with their traditionally coarse humour, they were clearly not written specifically for children. Not long after 1800, partly in response to an extension of literacy as well as to improvements in the production and distribution of printed matter, the situation began to alter. The emergence of a Robin Hood ballad anthology in folding toy-book form, the appearance of more and bigger illustrations, and (above all) the increased popularity of connected prose narratives rather than the traditional verse garlands were the harbingers of the impending revolution in book-production for children.[3] One indication of the change was the appearance in 1820 of the second edition of Ritson's *Robin Hood* collection, now abridged into a single volume 'which could with propriety be put into the hands of young persons'.[4] Children's editions of the traditional chapbooks were still produced here and there in the 1840s;[5] but by that decade they were being rapidly replaced in popularity by a new genre of Robin Hood literature—the children's novel, often appearing in weekly penny serial instalments, which handled the characteristic themes of the Robin Hood tales with an unprecedented freedom and made a deliberate appeal to middle-class Victorian juvenile taste. It could be argued that Pierce Egan the younger's *Robin Hood and Little John; or, The Merry Men of Sherwood Forest* (first published in 1840) has exercised more influence on the development of the

---

[1] S. Piggott, *William Stukeley, an eighteenth-century Antiquary* (Oxford, 1950), p. 20; Stukeley's much copied 'pedigree of Robin Hood earl of Huntingdon' first appeared in the author's *Palaeographia Britannica, Origines Roystoniae*, Part 2 (Stamford, 1746), p. 115. Cf. the even more preposterous version in Folger Library, PR 2125 R6.

[2] Wordsworth's *The Prelude*, V, lines 341-4 (ed. E. de Selincourt, Oxford, 1933, p. 77).

[3] So too was the omission of the death scene at Kirklees Priory: see, e.g., *The History of Robin Hood* (Lumsden and Son, Glasgow, *c.* 1810); *Robin Hood*, with engraved pictures by William Darton Jr. (London, 1818).

[4] Ritson, 1820, 1823, Preface.

[5] Thus *Gammer Gurton's famous histories of Sir Guy of Warwick . . . Robin Hood, newly revised and amended by Ambrose Merton* (Joseph Cundall, Westminster, 1846) followed the texts of the Aldermary chapbooks very closely indeed.

outlaw legend than any other work since *Ivanhoe*. Like his father of the same name, Pierce Egan (1814–80) was a leading pioneer in the development of cheap literature for the Victorian public; and it is characteristic of his approach as well as of the predilections of his audience that his book begins with Robin Hood as an abandoned baby in the cottage of a humble forester named Gilbert Head or Hood. Egan introduced new characters into the story such as Roland Ritson of Mansfield, the brother of Gilbert Head's wife. As he confessed in his introduction, 'the Author had no material for the early portions of Robin Hood's life but such as his imagination supplied him with'!

Perhaps the greatest tribute to the exceptional popularity of Egan's *Robin Hood and Little John* was its use by Alexandre Dumas as the basis for his own two Robin Hood novels, *Le Prince des Voleurs* (1872) and *Robin Hood Le Proscrit* (1873), themselves later to be widely read in English translation as well as in France itself. The popular French cult of *Robin des Bois*, now nearly always naturalized as a hero of the medieval French maquis, derives in all its essentials from Dumas's adaptation of the legend.[1] Much more spectacular was Robin Hood's conquest of late nineteenth-century America, a conquest which reached its climax with Howard Pyle's superbly illustrated *The Merry Adventures of Robin Hood of Great Renown in Nottinghamshire*, first published by Charles Scribner's Sons of New York in 1883. The quality of Pyle's illustrations, and the genuine literary skill with which he forged an integrated story out of the traditional ballad episodes, account for that work's enduring success. Although Pyle's deliberate archaisms now often strike a jarring note, his refusal to write down to his audience could well have been emulated to advantage by his countless successors in this country as well as the United States. Much the most popular prose re-tellings of the Robin Hood stories in the first half of this century were Henry Gilbert's *Robin Hood and the Men of the Greenwood* (various editions since 1914) and E. Charles Vivian's *The Adventures of Robin Hood* (1927), neither of particular distinction despite their laudable attempt to stir 'the hearts of healthy boys and girls' and their common emphasis on Robin as a benevolent patron of the poor serfs. More recently still the writing of a version of the Robin Hood legend has shown unfortunate signs of becoming almost a compulsory obligation imposed by their publishers upon the writers of children's stories.[2] Despite the occasional attempt to provide a novel emphasis, for example by means of an overtly political interpretation of the story in Geoffrey Trease's *Bows Against the Barons* (1934), few of the countless modern re-tellings of the greenwood

---

[1] For unconvincing attempts to derive *Robin des Bois* from Germanic forest spirits analogous to those in Weber's *Der Freischutz*, see the lively controversy which developed in *Notes and Queries* between 1903 and 1906, and especially the contribution, 'Robin Hood in French', made by T. P. Armstrong in 9th series, XI, p. 258 (28 March 1903).

[2] E.g., Enid Blyton, *Tales of Robin Hood* (London, 1930); Carola Oman, *Robin Hood, the Prince of Outlaws* (London, 1939); Antonia Fraser, *Robin Hood* (London, 1955).

1. Robin Hood and Richard I: an illustration from the 1850 edition of Pierce Egan's *Robin Hood and Little John*

tales display any real originality or distinction. On the whole, the most successful recent versions of the Robin Hood saga for children are those, like R. L. Green's *The Adventures of Robin Hood* (London, 1956), which have treated the original ballad stories with the greatest sensitivity and respect.

The children's story may not however always continue to hold its present place as the primary vehicle for the diffusion of the Robin Hood legend. Indeed the most enterprising recent publicists of the outlaw have shown greater interest in soliciting the attentions of the film producer or television director rather than those of the book publisher. The adaptation of the medieval outlaw legend to the screen is almost as old as the history of film itself. For obvious reasons, the story of Robin Hood lent itself particularly well to the requirements of the silent cinema. At least five British or American Robin Hood screen 'spectacles' on the subject had been produced before the outbreak of the First World War. This tradition reached its greatest and most fabulously expensive climax with Douglas Fairbanks's Hollywood version of *Robin Hood* in 1922.[1] Sixteen years later, and with the added attractions of Technicolor as well as sound, Erroll Flynn and Olivia de Havilland starred in *The Adventures of Robin Hood*, perhaps the most vigorous of all twentieth-century treatments of the Robin Hood legend in any form. Although no later director has ever come close to rivalling the panache displayed by Michael Curtiz when he made that film in 1938, films based on the legend have continued to proliferate.[2] The special requirements of the film medium as well as the preconceptions determining the aims of the film industry have undoubtedly had an important influence in determining the contemporary characteristics of the legend. It is by now a convention of the genre that Robin Hood will be an unjustly dispossessed nobleman, the leader of 'free Saxons' against their oppressive Norman masters, finally restored to his title and united to his equally aristocratic Maid Marian at the hands of a grateful monarch.[3] Rather more seriously, the need to compress the action of a film into ninety or so minutes of running time has led to the replacement of the traditional episodic quality of the Robin Hood story into a more closely structured and

[1] R. Low, *The History of the British Film*, II, *1906–14* (London, 1949), p. 291; K. Brownlow, *The Parade's Gone By* . . . (London, 1968), pp. 282–92; L. Halliwell, *The Filmgoer's Companion* (London, 1970 edn.), p. 829.

[2] E.g. *The Bandit of Sherwood Forest* (U.S.A., 1946); *Prince of Thieves* (U.S.A., 1948); *Rogues of Sherwood Forest* (U.S.A., 1950); *Tales of Robin Hood* (U.S.A., 1950); *The Story of Robin Hood and his Merrie Men* (U.S.A., 1952); *Men of Sherwood Forest* (G.B., 1954); *Sword of Sherwood Forest* (G.B., 1961); *Robin Hood and the Pirates* (Italy, 1964); *A Challenge for Robin Hood* (G.B., 1967). The most curious of all films on the subject are however *The Son of Robin Hood* (U.S.A., 1958), in which the outlaw hero becomes a heroine, Robina Hood; and the recent Disney production of *Robin Hood* (U.S.A., 1973), in which Little John appears as a bear, Friar Tuck as a badger and their leader as a fox.

[3] In Erroll Flynn's words, the *reductio ad absurdum* of the 'Norman Yoke' myth, 'You know we Saxons aren't going to put up with it much longer!': *The Adventures of Robin Hood, based on the First National Pictures Technicolor Production* (London, 1938), p. 31.

tightly organized form. How far this will be a permanent legacy of the cinema
to the Robin Hood legend is altogether less certain. In recent years no treatment of the outlaw stories has proved more popular with children than a
B.B.C. television series which reverted in several ways to the episodic,
cyclical world of the traditional ballads. An even more interesting sign of the
times is the new vogue for portraying Robin Hood as a personally disillu-
sioned as well as socially alienated exile in the greenwood.

(v)

As a folk hero, portrayed successively in the medieval ballads, the May Games,
the broadsides and garlands, the Victoria penny weekly and the modern film,
Robin Hood inevitably retains the characteristics of his kind. If 'to become a
public legend a man must have simple outlines',[1] then Robin Hood was and
is ideally qualified for his role. Like other popular heroes, Robin must be
clever, brave and resourceful and can only die (if he dies at all) by treachery.[2]
Yet it is not his personality nor his physical appearance but his prowess with
the longbow which identifies him through the ages. Indeed the very absence
of any serious attempt at positive characterization of the outlaw leader in the
late medieval ballads has proved a positive advantage in allowing him to
appear a different kind of hero to different generations. With the one possible
exception of the stained glass window now at Minsterley in Shropshire, which
may date from the reign of Edward IV,[3] there survive no medieval repre-
sensations of Robin Hood. As the woodcuts which preface the Lettersnijder
printed edition of the *Gest* (No. 1 below) were derived from existing blocks
not originally intended to illustrate the outlaw legend at all, the iconography
of Robin Hood only properly begins with the broadsides and chapbooks of the
seventeenth century. For many decades the outlaw was depicted in contemporary dress of the Stuart period, for example in a long gown and a shovel
hat. By the early nineteenth century, in the various editions of Ritson's *Robin
Hood* anthology, he was usually portrayed as a woodman. Not until the high
Victorian period did a distinctive 'medieval' image emerge, the work of illus-
trators in England and America who depicted the forest hero as a bearded
figure, clad in his familiar suit of Lincoln green. The occasional attempts of
twentieth-century artists and sculptors to diverge from this tradition and to
portray Robin Hood in a more contemporary idiom (James Woodford's statue
on Castle Green in Nottingham for example) have failed to displace the
Victorian conventions. In so far as the outlaw hero is ever visualized at all
precisely, he still conforms to the stereotype originally created by Walter
Scott's *Ivanhoe*.

[1] E. J. Hobsbawm, *Bandits* (London, 1969), p. 108.   [2] See below, pp. 78–9, 133–9, 279.
[3] The figures in this window include (on the bottom row) a Queen of the May, a Friar and
an apparent Robin Hood; they are reproduced in Gutch, II, 349, together with a
detailed if outdated discussion of Tollet's window by Francis Douce.

Though he possessed qualities that appealed to a contemporary audience, Robin Hood was not of course the only medieval hero figure to survive the passing of the middle ages. To sixteenth- and seventeenth-century observers his peers were men like Guy of Warwick and Bevis of Hampton, Hereward the Wake and Fulk Fitz Warin. As a swashbuckling adventurer whose exploits could be celebrated as easily in song as prose, as a rudimentary symbol of protest against a corrupt ruler or form of government, Robin Hood's attributes were certainly not unique. The fact remains that the hero of the English greenwood has outlasted all his rivals to become the ideal standard by which all outlaws, real and imaginary, past and future, tend to be assessed. Why has an obscure highwayman earned immortality when it is the inevitable lot of most bandits to be forgotten (except by the historian) within a relatively short space of years? To this, the most important of all questions to do with Robin Hood, there can never be a simple answer. But one possible explanation can at least be put firmly out of court. To several students of the legend, admittedly more common in the late nineteenth than the twentieth century, Robin Hood was not so much a historical character as a mythological figure, one 'whose name but faintly disguises either Woden in the aspect of a vegetation deity, or a minor wood-spirit Hode, who also survives in the Hodeken of German legend'.[1] To this hypothesis have been added such modern variants as the identification of Robin with Robin Goodfellow, or Hood with a mysterious 'log cut from the sacred oak'. The last word on these ingenious notions still belongs to Francis Child: 'I cannot admit that even the shadow of a case has been made out by those who would attach a mythical character either to Robin Hood or to the outlaws of Inglewood'.[2]

While such mythological theories bear indirect witness to the immense appeal of the legend, and to its part in popular folk culture, against them all it must be said that when we first meet Robin Hood in the ballads he is firmly anchored in the historical world. Mythological characters like Woden and Balder generally belong to a much earlier period of European history. As we have seen, what evidence there is suggests that Robin Hood was, in fact, based upon the memory of one or a number of Barnsdale outlaws. The association of Robin Hood with various English place-names and natural features, often quoted in favour of his mythological origin, can only be dated to periods long after the first literary development of the legend.[3] Similarly the connection of Robin Hood with the May Games came after, and probably because of, the popular appeal of the 'rymes'. The student of Robin Hood is therefore encountering not mythology which became literature, but a literary phenome-

---

[1] Chambers, *Mediaeval Stage*, I, 175; cf. the valuable critique of such beliefs in Keen, *Outlaws*, pp. 219–22.

[2] Margaret Murray, *The God of the Witches* (London, 1933), p. 35 et seq.; Robert Graves, *The White Goddess* (London, 1948), p. 350; Child, III, 48.

[3] See Appendix IV.

non which attained exceptionally wide currency. It is clear from what we know of developments in the sixteenth century that the legend of Robin Hood was one capable of moving out of the ballad world into a broader cultural setting. At an early date Robin Hood became in fact not simply a character in literature but a folk hero, and it is this which distinguishes him most from other literary and historical figures of the middle ages and later.

As an outlaw figure who became a folk hero, Robin Hood has never completely lost the attributes of his origins in the social and economic world of late medieval England. He is the familiar archetype of the 'social bandit' found in most pre-industrial peasant societies.[1] In such societies the bonds of lordship may have weakened but gentry and popular cultures still intermingled. In his general outlines Robin Hood is therefore the product of a period when the state was relatively weak, and when local power groups could be portrayed in the form of the sheriff and the abbot. In this society the 'noble bandit' could redress social wrongs, and justice be done by one man's heroism and audacity. Like those other heroes of twentieth-century fantasy, the Westerner and the gangster, Robin Hood also poses a fundamental problem in its simplest possible outlines: he too, 'exhibits a moral ambiguity, which darkens his image and saves him from absurdity'.[2] Under what conditions is a man justified in leaving the society of his fellow men and taking the law into his own hands? That important question duly considered, the limitations of the social bandit's role must also be recognized. From the viewpoint of the inhabitants of modern industrialized societies the deeds of Robin Hood are too circumscribed to solve complex social problems, while he himself is perhaps too simplistic a hero to engage deeply the sympathies of a modern adult audience. Yet for centuries Robin Hood was a real hero to simple and unlettered people: his perennial popularity shows that, transcending its historical context, his myth had in it some element of universal appeal. This we may possibly ascribe to 'a dream of justice' latent in all peoples at all stages of historical development, allied to the fact that with the passage of time the land of Robin Hood came to hold its own particular brand of nostalgia. It became a 'spiritual Indian territory', an escape from the monotony of the urbanized present into a medieval 'Sherwood' that was itself largely the creation of the ballad writers and never really existed elsewhere.

[1] Hobsbawm, *Bandits*, pp. 26, 53–4, 127–34.
[2] R. Warshow, 'The Westerner', *Film: An Anthology*, ed. D. Talbot (Berkeley, U.S.A., 1959), p. 153.

NOTE ON THE TEXTS OF THE BALLADS

The editing of popular ballads is a notoriously difficult and hazardous under-
taking, raising a variety of problems for which no perfect solution can ever be
attained. By its very nature, a genuinely traditional ballad will have no written or printed 'original';[1] and any attempt, however meticulous, to produce a
text for the eye must be considered an unsatisfactory substitute for the primary ballad experience—the auditory impression left by hearing one singer
communicating the song in his own way. Like the improvisations of the blues
singer or the jazz musician, to take the most obvious twentieth-century analogies, the message of the ballad can never be properly transcribed for the
printed page. Awareness of this limitation is of course as old as scholarly
interest in the popular ballad itself; and it has naturally led most modern
ballad editors to regard themselves as improvisers or 'improvers' too. The
readiness of Thomas Percy, John Pinkerton, Sir Walter Scott and other early
ballad collectors to re-write ballads very extensively is well known. Much more
influential has been the survival of the once universally held belief that it was
proper (in Scott's words) 'to make the best possible set of an ancient ballad
out of several copies obtained from different quarters'. It is still perhaps in-
sufficiently appreciated that the apparently definitive texts published between 1882 and 1898 by the greatest of all ballad scholars, Francis Joseph
Child, have been subjected to a great variety of minor 'improvements' of this
latter type. Child's sometimes optimistic assumption that his textual con-
flations would serve to recapture a more authentic, more original and more
'popular' version of a ballad than any of its surviving copies still commands
our respectful attention today; and he was usually scrupulously careful to
collate his own editions of the ballads with the readings of the texts he had
consulted. Nevertheless it must now seem that the much anthologized texts
of Child's *The English and Scottish Popular Ballads* are expressions less of a
permanently valid ideal than of the editor's own inimitable but often highly
personal qualities of learning and intuition.[2]

  As the texts of the Robin Hood ballads presented in this collection are
designed for the general reader and not the textual critic or philologist, they
are based on different and simpler principles than those employed either by
Child or modern editors of full-scale editions of medieval literary texts.

---

[1] The one apparently 'original' ballad text in this selection, Martin Parker's *A True Tale
of Robin Hood* (No. 14) is not of course a 'traditional ballad' in any meaningful sense of
the expression.

[2] For a detailed account of the less subjective criteria employed by the modern editor of
early literary texts see G. Kane, ed., *Piers Plowman: The A Version*, Vol. I (London,
1960), pp. 115–72 ('Editorial Resources and Methods').

Indeed not one of the following ballad texts is exactly identical with its counterpart in Volume III of *English and Scottish Popular Ballads*, precisely because we have deliberately refrained from any attempt to construct a 'superior' text from several sources. In general our own transcriptions have been made from a single base manuscript or printed version specified at the beginning of the introduction to each ballad. As the medieval tales of *Robin Hood and the Monk* (No. 2) and *Robin Hood and the Potter* (No. 3), as well as various Robin Hood ballads preserved in the Percy Folio manuscript (Nos. 4a, 5, 6b, 7a, 8a), survive only in a unique manuscript copy, the source of our texts of these is self-evident: in such cases our variations from Child's edition are deliberate and the result of a re-reading of the manuscripts. However, in the very special case of the *Gest of Robyn Hode* (No. 1), which survives only in printed form, we present a text constructed from what appear to be the two earliest extant versions, one of which is incomplete.[1]

Almost all the other Robin Hood ballads survive in broadsides and chapbooks (Robin Hood Garlands) of the seventeenth to early nineteenth centuries: our objective here has been to provide an accurate transcription of a single printed version. Of the numerous texts of particular Robin Hood ballads printed during the course of this long period, remarkably few show signs of major textual development or even variation. On close inspection the great majority of these so-called traditional Robin Hood ballads prove to have become set in a more or less permanent literary form by the late seventeenth century—a fact which in itself makes the propriety of applying the usual qualitative criteria employed in discussing other Child ballads to those of Robin Hood somewhat questionable. In these circumstances it seemed to us unnecessary and perhaps inadvisable to print all the broadside and chapbook texts of Robin Hood ballads in this selection from the earliest known published editions: not only is the precise dating of broadsides and garlands still a highly speculative enterprise but, as is well known, 'late' versions of a ballad can be less corrupt and even sometimes closer to an oral tradition than their chronological predecessors. Our texts of the later Robin Hood ballads are therefore transcriptions of single base texts drawn from a wide range of broadsides and chapbooks. The choice of the latter has been deliberately varied as regards both date and place of publication to give the reader an impression of the large number of alternative sources available. In particular, several of our texts are derived from Robin Hood Garlands printed at York in the eighteenth and early nineteenth centuries, some never consulted by Child or other editors. For those who wish to consult a wider variety of versions of broadside and chapbook Robin Hood songs, references to major previous editions are given in the introduction to each ballad.

As regards the texts themselves, our primary aim has been to produce as

[1] For an explanation of the special methods employed in editing the *Gest of Robyn Hode*, see below, pp. 71–4.

faithful a version of the base manuscript or printed text as possible without making it inaccessible to the modern reader. Perhaps the only serious problem lay in the unfamiliar vocabulary of some of the earlier ballads, especially *Robin Hood and the Potter* and (to a lesser extent) *Robin Hood and the Monk* and the *Gest of Robyn Hode*. In these cases the original word or phrase has been retained in the text but glossed in the footnotes, which are otherwise restricted to comments on precise issues. Other conventions employed are as follows:

1. The original manuscript or printed spellings are retained, except that:
    a) Scribal abbreviations are silently expanded; printed contractions (e.g. *ta'en* for *taken*) are normally retained.
    b) The obsolete Middle English letters are replaced by their modern equivalents: þ by *th*; ƿ by *w*; ȝ by *y, i, gh*, or *s*.
    c) The scribal use of *u* and *v*, and of *i* and *j*, has been brought into conformity with modern spelling practice.
    d) Arabic and Roman numerals as well as monetary symbols (e.g. *li.*) have been converted into words.
    e) The ampersand (&) has been converted into *and*.
    f) Omitted letters, when they appear to be simple mechanical aberrations, are restored within square brackets.
    N.B. *the* (thee), *the* (they), *he* (they) and *hem* (them) are retained in their original form.

2. Metrical arrangement, paragraphing and division into stanzas, where these are not already present in the base text, are provided by the editors —wherever possible in consistency with the methods employed by Child.

3. Capitalization and punctuation (including the introduction of quotation marks) are also editorial.

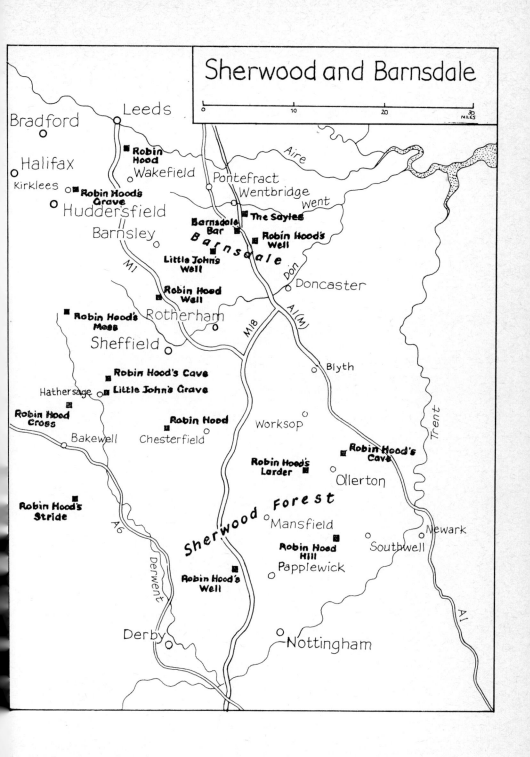

Sherwood and Barnsdale

| 0 | 10 | 20 | 30 MILES |

Bradford

Leeds

Halifax

Kirklees

■ Robin Hood

Wakefield

■ Robin Hood's Grave

Huddersfield

Barnsley

Pontefract

Wentbridge

Went

Aire

■ The Sayles

Barnsdale Bar

Barnsdale

■ Robin Hood's Well

Little John's Well

Don

Doncaster

■ Robin Hood Well

Rotherham

A1(M)

■ Robin Hood's Moss

M18

Sheffield

Blyth

■ Robin Hood's Cave

■ Little John's Grave

Hathersage

Robin Hood Cross

Worksop

■ Robin Hood

Chesterfield

■ Robin Hood's Cave

Bakewell

■ Robin Hood's Larder

Ollerton

Sherwood Forest

■ Robin Hood's Stride

Mansfield

Newark

A6

■ Robin Hood Hill

Southwell

Papplewick

Derwent

■ Robin Hood's Well

Trent

Derby

Nottingham

A1

I

A GEST OF ROBYN HODE (Child 117)

Sources:
1. Lettersnijder edition of the *Gest of Robyn Hode* (National Library, Edinburgh). David Laing printed a type facsimile in 1827 (see below). Later editions of the Lettersnijder text include (1) George Stevenson, *Pieces from the Makculloch and the Gray MSS. Together with the Chepman and Myllar Prints.* (The Scottish Text Society, Edinburgh / London, 1918), 267–90 (2) William Beattie, *The Chepman and Myllar Prints. Nine Tracts from the First Scottish Press, Edinburgh, 1508. Followed by the Two Other Tracts in the Same Volume in the National Library of Scotland. A Facsimile with a Bibliographical Note* (The Edinburgh Bibliographical Society, 1950), 197–220.

This edition has been attributed to the press of Jan van Doesborch at Antwerp, and dated 1510–1515: Robert Proctor, *Jan van Doesborch* (Bibliographical Society, 1894), p. 24, see also Nijhoff-Kronenberg, *Nederlandsche Bibliographie*, No. 3080.

2. Wynkyn de Worde edition of the *Lytell Geste of Robyn Hode* (Cambridge University Library Ms. Sel. 5. 18). The text was reprinted by Gutch, I, 145–219. The date of the Wynkyn de Worde edition is difficult to date more precisely than between 1492 and 1534.

3. William Copland's edition of the *Mery Geste of Robyn Hoode* together with a text of the May Games play of Robin Hood (see below, Nos. 20 and 21). Copland's edition was reproduced in facsimile in *Old English Drama* (*Students' Facsimile Edition*) (1914). The date of Copland's edition is *circa* 1560.

4. Douce fragments in the Bodleian Library, Oxford. These printed fragments of the text, which probably belong to the sixteenth century, are now catalogued as Douce fragments, e. 12 and f. 1. For Douce fragment f. 51 see (5).

5. An edition of the *Gest* by Richard Pynson (d. 1530) also survives in fragments. (See *A Short-Title Catalogue of Books Printed in England, Scotland and Ireland, and of English Books Printed Abroad, 1475–1640*, ed. A. Pollard, G. Redgrave, Bibliographical Society (London, 1926), No. 13688; E. Duff, *Fifteenth Century English Books* (Meisenheim, 1964), No. 362). These fragments are:

(1) A leaf, Inc. 4.J.3.6. in University Library, Cambridge.

(2) The Penrose fragment, a leaf and a half, in the Folger Shakespeare Library, Washington (PR 1400 13688).

(3) Bodleian Library, Douce fragment f. 51.

It has been suggested that this edition was the original of the text found among the Chepman and Myllar prints. See J. C. T. Oates, 'The Little Gest of Robin Hood: A Note on the Pynson and Lettersnijder Editions', *Studies in Bibliography*, XVI (1963), pp. 3–8.

Of Pynson's text, originally of 402 lines of text, there survive only the following passages:

(1) *Cambridge University Library.*

verses 220^1–227^3

319^4–327^2

(2) *Folger Shakespeare Library.*

verses 327^3–335^1

243^2–250^4

312^4–319^3

227^4–235^2

(3) *Bodleian Library, Douce Fragment* (very imperfect).

verses 435^4–443^2

443^3–451^1

N.B. Edward White's reprint of the text has not been used. There were two Edward Whites publishing in the period 1577–1624. See *Malone Society (1908)*, *Collections*, Part II.

Other Editions:

Ritson, 1795, I, 1–80; Gutch, 1847, I, 145–219; Campbell, 1853, 29–93; Child, 1888, III, 39–89; Quiller-Couch, 1910, 497–574.

The fundamental part played by the famous *Gest of Robyn Hode* in the development of the Robin Hood legend must be evident to every reader of this book and needs no urging here. The most obvious proofs of its influence are indeed the numerous sixteenth- and seventeenth-century editions of the poem which themselves provide our earliest sources for the text. The *Gest* was reprinted several times between 1500 and 1600, which was apparently and significantly not the case with other early Robin Hood Ballads.

The aim of the present edition is to give a version of the earliest text based upon the two principal editions: (1) the Lettersnijder version found in the Chepman and Myllar prints in the National Library of Scotland,[1] (2) the

---

[1] David Laing's 1827 type-facsimile of the Lettersnijder version is not an exact reproduction of the original.

Wynkyn de Worde version in C.U.L. (Ms. Sel. 5. 18). Pynson's edition survives only in small fragments, one of which (the Douce fragment) is in a very imperfect state. Where its text can be compared with that of the Lettersnijder edition (verses 314–316, 319–335), there are several differences in spelling and sense (for example, verses 319–327). The Lettersnijder version itself, though it preserves only half the narrative, contains in all probability the earlier text, and was used by Child as the basic source for his edition. The text of this version, designated as (A), has therefore been used in its entirety, and is printed in Roman type. The verses from the Wynkyn de Worde edition, designated as (B), supply the remainder of the text, and have been italicized. In certain cases readings have been supplied from Pynson's edition (P), the sixteenth-century edition of William Copland (British Museum, C.21 c.63), which is designated as (C), and the fragments of about the same date, now in the Douce Collection in the Bodleian Library, Oxford. These fragments are described as (D).

The date and provenance of the Douce fragments e.12, f.1., are unknown, but they clearly belong to a relatively early period in the history of the printed text, while their variant readings establish them as belonging to a separate textual tradition. They contain the following verses:

Douce fragment e.12 contains verses 26–60.

Douce fragment f.1. contains verses 280–350.

As regards the present text of the *Gest* certain corrupt readings and typographical errors in (A) have been corrected from (B), and in such places the readings are italicized. Where (B) is the sole authority (as it is for more than half of the text) its omissions have been supplemented from (P), (C) or (D), and these are printed in Roman type.

Although this version of the *Gest* in no way seeks to replace Child's version (which provides most major variants), it does endeavour to place before the reader a clearer picture of what probably constitutes the earliest text. Child on occasion supplied particular lines and spellings which are not to be found in any of the texts which he used.

The following table indicates how this narrative of the *Gest* is constructed from the Lettersnijder edition (A), and the Wynkyn de Worde version (B).

(A) supplies verses $1-83^3$
(B) supplies verses 83^4-118^3
(A) supplies verses 118^4-123^4
(B) supplies verses 124^1-127^3
(A) supplies verses 127^4-133^2
(B) supplies verses 133^3-136^3
(A) supplies verses 136^4-208^3
(B) supplies verses 208^4-314^1
(A) supplies verses 314^2-349^3
(B) supplies verses 349^4-456^4

(A) contains therefore only verses $1-83^3$, 118^4-123^4, 127^4-133^2, 136^4-208^3, 314^2-349^3, of the total 456.

The *Gest of Robyn Hode* is much the most complex as well as the most important and lengthy (c. 13,900 words) item in the corpus of English outlaw literature. It is therefore essential to emphasize that the narrative of the *Gest* undoubtedly derives from a number of earlier tales, put together by an un-unknown compiler, probably in the early fifteenth century.[1] Three main sections may be distinguished: 1) the story of the knight and the repayment of his debt (fyttes I, II, and IV); 2) the story of Robin Hood and the sheriff of Nottingham (fyttes III, V, VI); and 3) the story of Robin Hood and the King (fyttes VII and VIII).[2] There are in addition a number of subsidiary themes, together with a concluding section on the death of Robin Hood, which, although it does not relate directly to the preceding stories, forms a fitting conclusion to the whole. The *Gest*, *Lyttel Geste*, or *Merry Geste of Robin Hood* as it is variously described, is best regarded therefore as an attempted unity which comprises three principal stories, each constructed from a number of different tales; among these, if we accept the evidence of the sixteenth-century Wynkyn de Worde version, the tales relating to the sheriff of Nottingham were the ones which had impressed themselves most vividly on an early audience.[3]

The first main story is that of Robin and the knight, into which is woven a tale of Robin Hood and the monk. Robin is in the forest of Barnsdale and in the manner of the romances he declares that he will not eat until he has some guest to sit down with him. He sends Little John, Much the Miller, and Will Scarlock to walk 'up to the Saylis' to discover someone whom they can bring back to the outlaw feast. After encountering an unnamed Lancashire knight the outlaws take him to Robin, and they dine together. When it comes to the matter of payment, however, the knight confesses that he cannot pay, for he has only ten shillings on his person. After Little John examines his cloak and finds that this is true, Robin invites his guest to tell his story. The knight's tale in an unhappy one. His son, some twenty years old, has killed a 'knyght of Lancaster' and a squire, and to buy his son's pardon, the knight's lands have been pledged for the sum of £400 to the abbot of St Mary's, York. The time has now come to repay the loan and prevent the lands being forfeited to the

---

[1] Child, *Ballads*, III, 50. See also W. H. Clawson's analysis in *The Gest of Robin Hood* (Toronto, 1909), and above p. 8.

[2] See the interesting analysis in Joost de Lange, *The Relation and Development of English and Icelandic Outlaw-Traditions* (Haarlem, 1935), pp. 44–57.

[3] The Wynkyn de Worde version in Cambridge University Library, Sel. 5. 18 has the heading, 'Here begynneth a lytell geste of Robyn Hode and his meyne, And of the proude sheryfe of Notyngham'.

abbey. The knight has no money, and his former friends have deserted him. Robin offers to provide the necessary sum but the knight has no guarantor except Our Lady. This, however, is sufficient for Robin. At this point Little John observes that the knight's clothes are threadbare, and that he is poorly equipped. The outlaws give the knight clothes, a horse, saddle, boots, and spurs, and Little John goes with him to York to act as his squire.

In the second of the eight 'fyttes' which make up the *Gest*, the scene shifts to York and to St Mary's Abbey, where the prior of the house is urging the abbot not to stand upon the letter of the law in regard to the knight as he is probably overseas. The abbot however, supported by the cellarer and an attendant justice, declares that unless the knight repays his loan, his lands will be seized. The knight arrives at the abbey dressed, like his followers, in travel-stained clothing; he at first pretends that he has not raised the money. He begs for a delay, but the abbot and the justice are determined to seize his lands. At last the knight, to the discomfiture of his creditors, produces the whole of his debt. All that remains is for the knight to put on his new clothing and return to his home at Wyresdale in Lancashire where his wife is waiting for him. There he starts to collect the money in order to repay the loan. This done, he leaves with a retinue of a hundred men for Barnsdale. On the way to Barnsdale, however, the knight passes a wrestling match where a yeoman who is winning too many prizes is in danger of losing his life. The knight comes to his help, and is accordingly detained for some time (stanza 143 at the end of second fytte).

This particular tale is finally concluded in the fourth fytte after a preliminary episode with a monk of St Mary's Abbey. Robin, regretful that Our Lady has not secured the repayment of his loan, again asks Little John, Much, and Scarlock to find a guest. This time the outlaws meet a monk, bound with a retinue of fifty-two men for London on the business of the abbey. The monk turns out to be the high cellarer of St Mary's Abbey. After putting his followers to flight, the outlaws take the cellarer back to Robin. There the earlier scene with the knight is re-enacted, the cellarer is obliged to eat and drink, and then asked how much money he carries. This time, however, the answer is not so truthful. The cellarer replies that he has only 20 marks, yet on examination £800 is discovered in his mantle. Robin ironically professes to see in the monk the messenger of Our Lady come to repay his loan. He keeps the money, but allows the monk to go free after his expensive meal (stanza 260). When the knight at last arrives to repay his loan, with an additional twenty marks 'for courtesy', Robin tells him that Our Lady, by the agency of the cellarer, has already repaid it twice over. He then gives the knight another £400 to buy a new horse and harness (end of fourth fytte).

This first story in the *Gest* is clearly made up of two if not three narratives. These are 1) the story of the knight's interception by Robin Hood; 2) his visit to the abbey of St Mary's; and 3) the story of the monk. As it survives, the tale of Robin Hood and the knight is far from being a perfect unity and there are a number of loose ends. We are told, for example, that as the knight and his retinue approach St Mary's Abbey they put on clothing which they have brought from overseas (stanza 97), yet this allusion is never taken up elsewhere in the poem. The account of the wrestling match in the 'west country', possibly the West Riding of Yorkshire, is again not integral to the text and may be part of a lost ballad used in the construction of the *Gest*. In its setting it recalls that episode in the *Tale of Gamelyn*, where Gamelyn avenges the sons of the franklin in a country wrestling match.[1] The tale of the monk which continues the story appears originally to have referred to two monks, as seen in stanzas 213 and 214 ('Then were they ware of two blacke monkes').[2] Finally the compiler of the *Gest* appears to have known the thirteenth-century tale of Eustace the Monk, an outlaw who—like Robin with the knight—met a merchant who gave a courteous and truthful reply to a question concerning the amount of money that he carried.[3] The theme of courtesy, derived from the romances, is evident in this as in other parts of the *Gest*.[4]

The second main story in the *Gest* begins at the third fytte. This concerns Little John and the sheriff of Nottingham, and the manner in which a knight called Sir Richard is aided by the outlaws. The scene now shifts temporarily some fifty miles south from Barnsdale to Nottingham, although Sherwood Forest itself is not mentioned by name in any part of the *Gest*. Little John takes part in an archery contest and shoots so well that the sheriff of Nottingham, present at the time, wants to take him into service. Although Little John explains that he already serves a 'curteys knight', the sheriff arranges to secure his services for a year. Little John decides that he will deliberately serve the sheriff badly. When the sheriff is out hunting, Little John lies in bed and asks for a meal to be prepared. After an ensuing quarrel with the butler, he next falls to blows with the cook, who proves himself so redoubtable an adversary that Little John persuades him to join Robin Hood and the outlaws in the forest. Together they set off to meet Robin, taking with them over £300 of the sheriff's money and much of his silver and spoons. There follows (stanzas 181–204) perhaps the best of all versions of the popular theme of the sheriff's being decoyed into the greenwood. Little John goes to meet the sheriff while hunting and promises to show him a remarkable 'fair hart'; the unsuspecting sheriff is then brought before Robin. There he is compelled to eat from his own plate, and after being stripped of his fine clothes is obliged to pass a night in the outlaws' dress. The next morning, aching in every limb,

---

[1] *The Tale of Gamelyn* is best edited in *The Complete Works of Geoffrey Chaucer*, ed. Skeat (Oxford, 1894), Vol. IV, pp. 645–67. See E. K. Chambers, op. cit. p. 132; Keen, *Outlaws*, pp. 78–94.

[2] Joost de Lange, p. 50.

[3] *Roman d'Eustache le Moine*, ed. F. Michel (Paris, 1834), p. 34.

[4] E. K. Chambers, op. cit. p. 137; see above, p. 32.

he promises to leave the outlaws undisturbed in exchange for his freedom.

This episode concludes the first tale of Robin Hood, Little John, and the sheriff of Nottingham, distinct from another story about the sheriff of Nottingham which follows later. With the fourth 'fytte', however, the scene moves back to Barnsdale and concludes, as we have seen, the story of Robin Hood and the knight. Thereafter, in the fifth fytte, the narrative of the *Gest* returns to the setting of Nottingham, this time to the new subject of the sheriff's treachery at a shooting match. An archery contest is held at which Robin, the outlaws, and a character new to the stories, 'Gilbert with the white hand', all excel. Despite the sheriff's promise not to harm the outlaws, an ambush is prepared and Little John falls wounded in the knee. He begs Robin to kill him so that he will not fall alive into the sheriff's hands, but Robin carries him to the castle of Sir Richard which is situated near Nottingham. Here the outlaw leader and his 'merry men' take shelter (stanza 316). As the sheriff hastens to London to inform the king, Robin goes back to the forest to learn that Sir Richard has been captured while out hawking. Sir Richard's wife tells Robin of these events and the outlaw leader sets out for Nottingham, kills the sheriff, and releases Sir Richard. Together they set off for the forest to await King Edward's pardon. This concludes the sixth fytte and second main section of the *Gest*.

It is evident that this second section, extending from the third to the end of the sixth fytte and having as its main subject the sheriff of Nottingham and his relations with the outlaws, was constructed from a number of different tales. The story of Little John's fight with the cook, in which the cook gets the better of him, is in the pattern of earlier and later outlaw stories where the hero meets his match: the theme is found, for example, in the *Gesta Herewardi*. Similarly, the motif of the sheriff of Nottingham being enticed to the outlaws' camp is encountered in later ballads such as *Robin Hood and the Potter* (below, No. 3). The story of the siege of Sir Richard's castle, and the knight's rescue by the outlaws, is reminiscent of *Robin Hood and the Monk* (below, No. 2), the rescue theme in *Adam Bell*, and the *Tale of Gamelyn*. Skilfully as the compiler put his stories together, however, a number of inconsistencies remain. It has been suggested that stanza 333 is an interpolation, and does not properly fit into the narrative.[1] There is also the problem of the identity of Sir Richard and the unnamed knight of the first section. One commentator has suggested that the two knights are not the same person and that 'for the sake of unity the compiler identified Sir Richard with the unnamed knight of the first section.'[2]

The third main story of the *Gest* opens at the seventh fytte (stanza 354) with the king's arrival at Nottingham in order to capture Robin and Sir

[1] R. Fricke, *Die Robin Hood Balladen* (Braunschweig, 1883), among others, drew attention to stanza 333, 'The sheref sware a full grete othe . . .' etc.

[2] Joost de Lange, pp. 52–3.

Richard. This story is a lively variation on the familiar medieval theme (best represented by the poem *The King and the Miller*) of the disguised monarch among his subjects. After the king has made several fruitless enquiries and seen the damage done by the outlaws,[1] a forester advises him to disguise himself as a monk and, with five of his best knights, take a route to Nottingham which the forester will indicate. There, as the forester has predicted, Robin waylays the king and asks him how much money he carries. Half of the £40 which the king produces is divided between the outlaws, and half is handed back to the king. The king, in his role as abbot, now tells Robin that he bears a message from the king at Nottingham; and this provides Robin with a splendid opportunity to declare his loyalty to his sovereign, who, to the outlaw, is the fount of all justice. After a dinner of venison, wine and ale, the company hold an archery contest in which Robin shoots well. Eventually, however, he misses the target, and picking himself up after the blow which the king has given him as a penalty, Robin recognizes his monarch. The outlaw and Sir Richard kneel down and beg the king's forgiveness, which the latter grants on condition that they leave the forest and go to court. Robin agrees and takes with him a great many of his men. The theme of the medieval outlaw making his peace with the king is found in many other ballads, including *Adam Bell* (below, No. 28) and the *Tale of Gamelyn*. In so doing, Robin is in fact following a well marked path, trodden before him by heroes such as Hereward the Wake and Eustace the Monk.

The eighth and last fytte of the *Gest* sees the outlaws returning to Nottingham accompanied by the king. There is a holiday atmosphere, and they play pluck-buffet with the king. Yet in spite of this gaiety Robin feels that he can no longer stay at the king's court after he has lived there for a year and three months. His money is gone, and his followers have drifted back to the forest, with the solitary exceptions of Little John and Will Scarlock (stanza 435). Robin tells the king that he wishes to return to Barnsdale, and to the chapel which he has built there. The king grants him leave to return for a week, but once Robin is back in his old haunts, he cannot bring himself to go back to court. According to this section of the *Gest*, Robin lived for twenty-two years in the forest until he was finally done to death by the treachery of his kinswoman, the prioress of Kirklees, a religious house near Huddersfield. With the help of Sir Roger of Doncaster, the prioress conspired to kill Robin after he had gone to the priory to be bled. Her motives are not, however, disclosed in the *Gest* which ends abruptly at this point. Yet even this cryptic account of Robin Hood's death is in the best tradition of later outlaw legend.[2] The unknown compiler of this story stands in fact near the beginning of the literary convention that the true outlaw hero dies by treachery; and that death by

---

[1] This is said to be in Plumpton Park, usually located in Cumberland. It could be a reference to Plumpton Park, near Harrogate. See stanza 357.

[2] For more detailed ballad accounts of Robin Hood's death, see below, pp. 133–9.

betrayal is the necessary, fitting, and final climax to the outlaw's career. Here, as elsewhere, the *Gest* broaches themes which will continue to reverberate through the later history of the Robin Hood legend and the later items in this collection.

The First Fytte

1

Lythe[1] and listin, gentilmen,
   That be of frebore[2] blode;
I shall you tel of a gode yeman,
   His name was Robyn Hode.

2

Robyn was a prude outlaw,
   Whyles he walked on grounde;
So curteyse an outlawe as he was one
   Was never non founde.

3

Robyn stode in Bernesdale,[3]
   And lenyd hym to a tre;
And bi hym stode Litell Johnn,
   A gode yeman was he.

4

And alsoo dyd good Scarlok,
   And Much, the myller's son;
There was non ynche of his bodi,
   But it was worth a grome.[4]

5

Than bespake Lytell Johnn
   All untoo Robyn Hode:
'Maister, and ye wolde dyne betyme
   It wolde doo you moche gode.'

6

Than bespake hym gode Robyn:
   'To dyne have I noo lust,[5]
Till that I have som bolde baron,
   Or some *unketh*[6] gest.

7

Till that I have som bolde baron,[7]
   That may pay for the best,
Or som knyght, or *some* squyer
   That dwelleth here bi west.'

8

A gode maner than had Robyn;
   In londe where that he were,
Euery day or[8] he wold dyne
   Thre messis wolde he here:

9

The one in the worship of the Fader,
   And another of the Holy Ghost,
The thirde of Our dere Lady
   That he loved allther[9] moste.

10

Robyn loved Oure dere Lady;
   For dout of dydly synne
Wolde he never do compani harme
   That any woman was in.

11

'Maistar,' than sayde Lytil Johnn,
   'And we our borde shal sprede,
Tell us wheder that we shal go
   And what life that we shall lede;

12

'Where we shall take, where we shall leve,
   Where we shall abide behynde,
Where we shall robbe, where we shal reve,[10]
   Where we shal bete and bynde.'

---

[1] Lythe: *attend*   [2] frebore: *freeborn*   [3] See Introduction, p. 19.   [4] grome: *man*
[5] lust: *inclination*   [6] unketh: *unknown*   [7] Missing in A, B and C   [8] or: *before*
[9] allther: *of all*   [10] reve: *despoil*

13

'Thereof no force,'[1] than sayde Robyn;
  'We shall do well inowe;
But loke ye do no husbonde[2] harme
  That *tylleth* with his ploughe.

14

'No more ye shall no gode yeman
  That walketh by grene wode shawe;[3]
Ne no knyght ne no squyer
  That wol be a gode felawe.

15

'These bisshoppes and these arche-
  bishoppes,
  Ye shall them bete and bynde;
The hye sherif of Notyingham,
  Hym holde ye in your *mynde*.'

16

'This worde shalbe holde,' sayde Lytell
  Johnn,
  'And this lesson we shall lere;[4]
It is fer dayes;[5] God sende us a gest,
  That we were at oure dynere.'

17

'Take thy gode bowe in thy honde,'
  sayde Rob*yn*,
  'Late Much wende with the,
And so shal Willyam Scarlo*ke*
  And no man abyde with me;

18

'And walke up to the Saylis,[6]
  And so to Watli*n*ge Stret*e*
And wayte after some *unketh* gest;[7]
  Up chaunce ye may them mete.

19

'Be he erle, or ani baron,
  Abbot, or ani knyght,
Bringhe hym to lodge to me;
  His dyner shall be dight.'[8]

20

They wente up to the Saylis,
  These yeman all thre;
They loked est, they lok*e*d weest,
  They myght no man see.

21

But as they loked in to Bernysdale,
  Bi a derne strete,[9]
Then came a knyght ridinghe;
  Full sone they gan hym mete.[10]

22

All dreri was his semblaunce,[11]
  And lytell was his pryde;
His one fote in the styrop stode,
  That othere wavyd beside.

23

His hode hanged in his iyn two;
  He rode in symple aray;
A soriar man than he was one
  Rode never in somer day.

24

Litell Johnn was full curteyes,
  And sette hym[12] on his kne;
'Welcom be ye, gentyll knyght,
  Welcom ar ye to me.

25

'Welcom be thou to grene wode.
  Hende[13] knyght and fre;[14]
My maister hath abiden you[15] fastinge
  Syr, al these oures thre.'

26

'Who is thy maister?' sayde the knyght.
  Johnn sayde, 'Robyn Hode'.
'He is *a* gode yoman,' sayde the knyght,
  'Of hym I have herde moche gode.

---

[1] no force: *no matter*   [2] husbonde: *husbandman, small farmer*
[3] shawe: *thicket (of the green wood)*   [4] lere: *learn*   [5] fer dayes: *far on in the day*
[6] See Introduction, p. 22.   [7] unketh: *unknown*   [8] dight: *prepared*
[9] derne strete: *secret way*   [10] gan . . . mete: *(did) meet*   [11] semblaunce: *appearance*
[12] sette hym: *went down*   [13] hende: *gracious*   [14] fre: *noble*   [15] abiden you: *waited for you*

27
'I graunte,' he sayde, 'with you to wende,
    My bretherne, all in fere;[1]
My purpos was to have dyned to day
    At Blith[2] or Dancastere.'

28
Furth than went this gentyl knight,
    With a carefull chere;[3]
The teris oute of his iyen ran,
    And fell downe by his lere.[4]

29
They brought hym to the lodge dore;
    Whan Robyn hym gan see,
Full curtesly dyd of his hode,
    And sette hym on his knee.

30
'Welcome, sir knight,' than sayde
    Robyn,
    'Welcome art thou to me;
I have abyden you fastinge, sir,
    All these ouris thre.'

31
Than answered the gentyll knight,
    With wordes fayre and fre;
'God the save, goode Robyn,
    And all thy fayre meyne.'[5]

32
They wasshed togeder and wyped bothe,
    And sette to theyr dynere;
Brede and wyne they had right *ynough*,
    And noumbles[6] of the dere.

33
Swannes and *fesauntes* they had full
    gode,
    And foules of the ryvere;
There fayled none so litell a birde
    That ever was bred on bryre.[7]

34
'Do gladly, sir knight,' sayde Robyn.
    'Gramarcy, sir,' sayde he;
'Suche a dinere had I nat
    Of all these wekys thre.

35
'If I come ageyne, Robyn,
    Here by thys contre,
As gode a dyner I shall the make
    As that thou haest made to me.'

36
'Gramarcy, knyght,' sayde Robyn;
    'My dyner whan that I it have,
I was never so gredy, bi dere worthy
        God,
    My dyner for to crave.

37
'But pay or ye *wende*,' sayde Robyn;
    'Me thynketh it is gode ryght;
It was never the maner, by dere worthi
        God,
    A yoman to pay for a knyhht.'

38
'I have nought in my coffers,' saide the
        knyght,
    'That I may profer for shame:'
'*Lytell* Johnn, go loke,' sayde Robyn,
    'Ne let[8] nat for no blame.

39
'Tel me truth,' than saide Robyn,
    'So God *have* parte of *the*:'
'I have no more but ten shelynges,'
        sayde the knyght,
    'So God have parte of me.'

40
'If thou hast no more,' sayde Robyn,
    'I woll nat one peny;
And yf thou have nede of any more,
    More shall I lend the.

[1] in fere: *in company*   [2] Blith: *Blyth* (*Notts.*)   [3] carefull chere: *troubled look*
[4] lere: *face*   [5] meyne: *company*   [6] noumbles: *entrails*   [7] bryre: *branch, twig*   [8] let: *delay*

41

'Go *now* furth, Litell Johnn,
    The truth tell thou me;
If there be no more but *ten shelinges*,
    No peny that I se.'

42

Lytell Johnn sprede downe hys mantell
    Full fayre upon the grounde,
And there he fonde in the knyghtes
        cofer[1]
    But even halfe *a* pounde.

43

Litell Johnn let it lye full styll,
    And went to hys maysteer *full* lowe;
'What tidynges, Johnn?' sayde Robyn;
    'Sir, the knyght is true inowe.'

44

'Fyll of the best wine,' sayde Robyn,
    'The knyght shall begynne;
Moche wonder thinketh me
    Thy clot*h*ynge is so thin*n*e.

45

'Tell me *one* worde,' sayde Robyn,
    'And counsel shal it be;
I trowe thou warte made a knyght of
        force,[2]
    Or ellys of yemanry.

46

'Or ellys thou hast bene a sori husbande,
    And lyved in *stroke* and stryfe;
An[3] okerer,[4] or ellis a lechoure,' sayde
        Robyn,
    'Wyth wronge hast led thy lyfe.'

47

'I am none of those,' sayde the knyght,
    'By God that made me;
An hundred wynter here before
    Myn auncetres knyghtes have *be*.

48

'But oft it hath befal, Robyn,
    A man hath be disgrate;[5]
But God that sitteth in heven above,
    May amende his state.

49

'Withyn this two yere, Robyne,' he
        sayde,
    'My neghbours well it knowe,
Foure hundred pounde of gode money
    Ful well than myght I spende.

50

'Nowe have I no gode,' saide the knyght,
    '*God hath shaped such an ende,*
But my chyldren and my wyfe,
    Tyll God yt may amende.'

51

'In what manner,' than sayde Robyn,
    'Hast thou lorne[6] thy rychesse?'
'For my greate foly,' he sayde,
    'And for my kyndnesse.

52

'I hade a sone, forsoth, Robyn,
    That shulde hav*e* ben myn ayre;
Whanne he was twenty wynter olde
    In felde wolde iust[7] full fayre.

53

'He slewe a knyght of Lancaster,
    And a squyer bolde;
For to save hym in his ryght
    My godes both sette and solde.

54

'My londes both sette to wedde,[8] Robyn,
    Untyll a certayn day,
To a ryche abbot here besyde
    Of Seynt Mari Abbey.'

---

[1] cofer: *strongbox*

[2] a knight of force: *by distraint of knighthood* (*by compulsion*): see above, p. 14.

[3] 'And': A, B and D. Supplied from C   [4] okerer: *usurer*   [5] disgrate: *deprived of status*

[6] lorne: *lost*   [7] iust: *joust*   [8] sette to wedde: *pledged as security*

55

'What is the som?' sayde Robyn;
  'Trouth than tell thou me;'
'Sir,' he sayde, 'foure hundred pounde;
  The abbot told it to me.'

56

'Nowe and thou lese thy lond,' sayde
  Robyn,
  'What woll fall of the?'
'Hastely I wol me buske,'[1] sayd the
  knyght,
  'Over the salte see,

57

'And se *w*here Criste was quyke and
  dede,
  On the mount of Calvere;
Fare wel, frende, and have gode day;
  It may no better be.'

58

Teris fell out of hys iyen two;
  He wolde have gone hys way:
'Farewel, frende, and have gode day,
  I ne have no more to pay.'

59

'Where be thy frendes?' sayde Robyn:
  'Syr, never one wol me knowe;
While I was ryche ynowe at home
  Great boste than wolde they blowe.

60

'And nowe they renne[2] away fro me,
  As bestis on a rowe;
They take no more hede of me
  Thanne they had me never sawe.'

61

For ruthe[3] thanne wept Litell Johnn,
  Scarlok and Muche in fere;
'Fyl of the best wyne,' sayde Robyn,
  'For here is a symple chere.[4]

62

'Hast thou any frende,' sayde Robyn,
  'Thy borowe[5] that wolde be?'
'I have none,' than sayde the knyght,
  'But God that dyed on tree.'

63

'Do away thy iapis,'[6] than sayde Robyn,
  'Thereof wol I right none;
Wenest thou I wolde have God to
  borowe,
  Peter, Poule, or Johnn?

64

'Nay, by hym that me made,
  And shope[7] both sonne and mone,
Fynde me a better borowe,' sayde
  Robyn,
  'Or money getest thou none.'

65

'I have none other,' sayde the knyght,
  'The sothe for to say,
But yf yt be Our dere Lady;
  She fayled me never or thys day.'

66

'By dere worthy God,' sayde Robyn,
  'To seche all Englonde thorowe,
Yet fonde I never to *my* pay[8]
  A moche better borowe.

67

'Come nowe furth, Litell Johnn,
  And go to my tresoure,
And bringe me foure hundered pound,
  And loke well tolde[9] it be.'

68

Furth than went Litell Johnn,
  And Scarlok went before;
He tolde oute foure hundred pounde
  By eight *and*[10] twenty score.

---

[1] buske: *prepare to go*   [2] renne: *run*   [3] ruthe: *pity*   [4] chere: *repast*
[5] borowe: *security*   [6] iapis: *tricks*   [7] shope: *created*   [8] pay: *satisfaction, liking*
[9] tolde: *counted*   [10] B: eyghtene score

69

'Is thys well tolde?' sayde *lytell* Much;
  Johnn sayde, 'What greveth the?
It is almus[1] to helpe a gentyll knyght
  That is fal in poverte.

70

'Master,' than sayde Lityll John,
  'His clothinge is full thynne;
Ye must gyve the knight a lyveray
  To helpe his body therein.

71

'For ye have scarlet and grene, mayster,
  And many a riche aray;
There is no marchaunt in mery Englond
  So ryche, I dare well say.'

72

'Take hym thre yerdes of every colour,
  And loke well mete[2] that it be.'
Lytell Johnn toke none other mesure
  But his bowe tree.

73

And at every handfull that he met[3]
  He leped footes three;
'What devylles drapar,' sayid litell
    Muche,
  'Thynkest thou for to be?'

74

Scarlok stode full stil and loughe,[4]
  And sayd, 'By God Almyght,
Johnn may gyve hym gode mesure,
  For it costeth hym but lyght.'

75

'Mayster,' than said Litell Johnn
  To gentill Robyn Hode,
'Ye must give the kni*gh*t a hors
  To lede home this gode.'

76

'Take hym a gray coursar,' sayde
    Robyn,
  'And a saydle newe;
He is Oure Ladye's messangere;
  God graunt that he be true.'

77

'And a gode palfray,[5]' sayde lytell Much,
  'To mayntene hym in his right;'
'And a peyre of *botes*,' sayde Scarlock,
  'For he is a gentyll knight.'

78

'What shalt thou gyve hym, Litell John?'
    said Robyn;
  'Sir, a peyre of gilt sporis clere,
To pray for all this company;
  God bringe hym oute of tene.'[6]

79

'Whan shal mi day be,' said the knight,
  'Sir, and your wyll be?'
'This day twelve moneth,' saide Robyn,
  'Under this grene wode tre.

80

'It were greate shame,' sayde Robyn,
  'A knight alone to ryde,
Withoute squyre, yoman, or page,
  To walke by his syde.

81

'I shall the lende Litell John, my man,
  For he shalbe thy knave;[7]
In a yeman's stede he may the stande,
  If thou greate nede have.'

---

[1] almus: *alms*   [2] mete: *measured*   [3] met: *measured*   [4] loughe: *laughed*
[5] palfray: *saddle-horse*   [6] tene: *sorrow*   [7] knave: *servant*

The Second Fytte

82

Now is the knight gone on his way;
  This game hym thought full gode;
Whanne he loked on *Bernysdale*,
  He blessyd Robyn Hode.

83

And whanne he thought on Bernysdale,
  On Scarlok, Much, and Johnn,
He blyssyd them for the best company
  That ever he in come.[1]

84

Then spake that gentyll knyght,
  To Lytel Johnn gan he saye,
To-morowe I must to Yorke toune
  To Saynt Mary abbay.

85

And to the abbot of that place
  Foure hondred pounde I must pay;
And but I be there upon this nyght
  My londe is lost for ay.

86

The abbot sayd to his covent,
  There he stode on grounde,
This day twelfe moneth came there a
  knyght,
  And borrowed foure hondred pounde.

87

He borowed foure hondred pounde,[2]
  Upon all his londe fre;
But[3] *he come this ylke*[4] *day*
  Dysheryte shall he be.

88

'*It is full erely,*' *sayd the pryoure,*
  '*The daye is not yet ferre gone;*
I had lever[5] *to pay an hondred pounde,*
  And lay downe anone.

89

'*The knyght is ferre beyonde the see,*
  In Englonde he is[6] *ryght,*
And suffreth honger and colde
  And many a sory nyght.

90

'*It were grete pyte,*' *sayd the pryoure,*
  '*So to have his londe;*
And ye be so lyght of your consyence,
  Ye do to hym moch wronge.'

91

'*Thou arte ever in my berde,*' *sayd the*
  abbot,
  '*By God and Saynt Rycharde;*'[7]
With that cam in a fat heded monke,
  The heygh selerer.[8]

92

'*He is dede or hanged,*' *sayd the monke,*
  '*By God that bought me dere,*
And we shall have to spende in this place
  Foure hondred pounde by yere.'

93

The abbot and the hy selerer
  Sterte[9] *forthe full bolde,*
The justyce of Englonde
  The abbot there dyde holde.

94

The hye iustyce and many mo
  Had take in to they honde
Holy all the knyghtes det,
  To put that knyght to wronge.

95

They demed[10] *the knyght wonder sore,*
  The abbot and his meyne:
'*But he come this ylke day,*
  Dysheryte shall he be.'

---

[1] come: *came* [2] Missing in A, B, C [3] But: *Unless* [4] ylke: *same*
[5] had lever: *would rather* [6] he is: presumably an error for 'is his'
[7] Possibly St. Richard of Chichester (*canonized 1262*) [8] heygh selerer: *chief cellarer*
[9] sterte: *leapt* [10] demed: *judged*

96

'He wyll not come yet,' sayd the iustyce,
 'I dare well undertake'.
But in sorowe tyme for them all
 The knyght came to the gate.

97

Than bespake that gentyll knyght
 Untyll[1] his meyne :
Now put on your symple wedes[2]
 That ye brought fro the see.

98

They put on their symple wedes[3]
 They came to the gates anone ;
The Porter was redy hymselfe,
 And welcomed them everychone.

99

'Welcome, syr knyght,' sayd the porter,
 'My lorde to mete[4] is he,
And so is many a gentyll man,
 For the love of the.'

100

The porter swore a full grete othe ;
 'By God that made me,
Here be the best coresed[5] hors
 That ever yet sawe I me.

101

'Lede them in to the stable,' he sayd,
 'That eased myght they be' ;
'They shall not come therein', sayd the
  knyght,
 'By God that dyed on a tre'.

102

Lordes were to mete isette[6]
 In that abbotes hall ;
The knyght went forth and kneled downe
 And salued them grete and small.

103

'Do gladly, syr abbot,' sayd the knyght,
 'I am come to holde my day'.
The fyrst word the abbot spake,
 'Hast thou brought my pay ?'

104

'Not one peny', sayd the knyght,
 'By God that maked me ;'
'Thou art a shrewed[7] dettour,' sayd the
  abbot ;
 'Syr iustyce, drynke to me.'

105

'What doost thou here,' sayd the abbot,
 'But thou haddest brought thy pay ?'
'For God,' than sayd the knyght,
 'To pray of a lenger daye.'

106

'Thy daye is broke,' sayd the iustyce,
 'Londe getest thou none.'
'Now, good syr iustyce, be my frende,
 And fende me of my fone.'[8]

107

'I am holde with the abbot,' sayd the
  iustyce,
 'Both with cloth and fee' :
'Now, good syr sheryf, be my frende.'
 'Nay, for God,' sayd he.

108

'Now, good syr abbot, be my frende,
 For the curteyse,
And holde my londes in thy honde
 Tyll I have made the gree[9]

109

'And I wyll be thy true servaunte
 And trewely serve the,
Tyl ye have foure hondred pounde
 Of money good and free.'

---

[1] untyll: *to* [2] wedes: *garments* [3] This line is not in B. C [4] to mete: *at dinner*
[5] coresed: *built* [6] to mete isette: *seated to dine* [7] shrewed: *cursed*
[8] fend me of my fone: *defend me from my enemies* [9] gree: *satisfaction*

110

The abbot sware a full grete othe,
 'By God that dyed on a tree,
Get the londe where thou may,
 For thou getest none of me.'

111

'By dere worthy God,' then sayd the
 knyght,
 'That all this worlde wrought,
But[1] I have my londe agayne,
 Full dere it shall be bought.[2]

112

'God, that was of a mayden borne,
 Leve[3] us well to spede.[4]
For it is good to assay a frende
 Or that[5] a man have nede.'

113

The abbot lothely on hym gan loke,
 And vylaynesly hym gan call ;[6]
'Out,' he sayd, 'thou false knyght,
 Spede the[7] out of my hall !'

114

'Thou lyest,' then sayd the gentyll knyght,
 'Abbot, in thy hal ;
False knyght was I never,
 By God that made us all.'

115

Up then stode that gentyll knyght,
 To the abbot sayd he,
'To suffre a knyght to knele so longe,
 Thou canst no curteysye.[8]

116

In ioustes and in tournement
 Full ferre than have I be,
And put my selfe as ferre in prees[9]
 As ony that ever I se'.

117

'What wyll ye gyve more,' sayd the iustice,
 'And the knyght shall make a releyse ?[10]
And elles I dare safly swere
 Ye holde never your londe in pees'.

118

'An hondred pounde,' sayd the abbot ;
 The justice sayd, 'Gyve hym two ;
'Nay, be God,' sayd the knyght,
 'Yit gete ye it not so.

119

'Though ye wolde gyve a thousand more,
 Yet were ye never the nere ;
Shall there never be myn heyre
 Abbot, iustice, ne frere.'

120

He stert hym to a borde anone,
 Tyll a table rounde,
And there he shoke oute of a bagge
 Even[11] four hundred pound.

121

'Have here thi golde, sir abbot,' saide
 the knight,
 'Which that *thou* lentest me ;
Had thou ben curtes at my comynge,
 Rewarded shuldest thou have be.'[12]

---

[1] but: *unless*   [2] i.e. somebody will surely suffer for it   [3] leve: *grant*   [4] spede: *succeed*
[5] or that: *before*   [6] This line is missing in C   [7] spede the: *take yourself quickly*
[8] canst no curteysye: *thou art unacquainted with good manners*
[9] and put myselfe as ferre in prees: *and have put myself in as great danger*
[10] i.e. so that the knight will release his claim on the land   [11] even: *exactly*
[12] 'The knight would have given something for the use of the four hundred pound had the
   abbot been civil, though under no obligation to pay interest' (Child, III, 52); cf.
   stanza 270

122

The abbot sat styll, and ete no more,
  For all his ryall fare;
He cast his hede on his shulder,
  And fast began to stare.

123

'Take me my golde agayne,' saide the
    abbot,
  'Sir iustice, that I toke the.'
'Not a peni,' said the iustice,
  'Bi God, *that dy*ed on tree.'

124

'Sir *abbot, and ye men* of lawe,[1]
  Now have I holde my daye ;
Now shall I have my londe agayne,
  For ought that you can saye.'

125

The knyght stert out of the dore,
  Awaye was all his care,
And on he put his good clothynge,
  The other he lefte there.

126

He wente hym forth full mery syngynge,
  As men have tolde in tale ;
His lady met hym at the gate,
  At home in Verysdale.[2]

127

'*Welcome, my lorde,*' *sayd his lady ;*
  '*Syr, lost is all your good ?*[3]'
'*Be mery, dame,*' *sayd the knyght,*
  '*And pray for Robyn Hode,*

128

'That ever his soule be in blysse:
  He holpe me out of tene;
Ne had he his kyndenesse,
  Beggers had we bene.

129

'The abbot and I accorded ben,
  He is served of his pay;
The god yoman lent it me,
  As I cam by the way.'

130

This knight than dwelled fayre at home,
  The sothe for to saye,
Tyll he had gete four hundred pound,
  Al redy for to pay.

131

He purveyed him an hundred bowes,
  The strynges well ydyght,[4]
An hundred shefe of *arowes* gode,
  The hedys burneshed full bryght;

132

And every arowe an *elle*[5] longe,
  With pecok wel idyght,[6]
Worked all with whyte silver;
  It was a semely syght.

133

He purveyed hym an *hondreth men,*
  Well harness*ed*[7] in that stede,
And hym selfe in that same sete,
  And clothed in whyte and rede.

134

He bare a launsgay[8] *in his honde,*
  And a man ledde his male,[9]
And reden with a lyght songe
  Unto Bernysdale.

135

But as he went at a brydge[10] *ther was a*
    wraste-lyng,
  And there taryed was he,
And there was all the best yemen
  Of all the west countree.

---

[1] The end of a fragment (stanzas 118–24) in the Lettersnijder version
[2] Verysdale: probably a reference to Wyresdale in northern Lancs
[3] good: *possessions*   [4] ydyght: *fitted*   [5] elle: *ell (45 inches)*
[6] Goose feathers were cheaper and more usual. For the 'sheef of pecok arwes' carried by
  the Yeoman in the *Canterbury Tales*, see *Works of Geoffrey Chaucer*, ed. Robinson, p. 18
[7] The end of the third fragment (stanzas 128–33) in the Lettersnijder version
[8] launsgay: *lance*   [9] male: *trunk*
[10] A possible play on the place-name Wentbridge, in northern Barnsdale (see above, p. 21)

136

A full fayre game there was up set,
A whyte bulle i up pyght,[1]
A grete courser, with sadle and brydil,
  With golde burnyssht full bryght.

137

A payre of gloves, a rede golde rynge,
  A pype of wyne, in fay:[2]
What man that bereth hym best i wys
  The pryce shall bere away.

138

There was a yoman in that place,
  And best worthy was he,
And for he was ferre and frembde
    bested,[3]
  Slayne he shulde have be.

139

The knight had ruthe[4] of this yoman,
  In place where he stode,
He sayde that yoman shulde have no
    harme,
  For love of Robyn Hode.

140

The knyght presed in to the place,
  An hundreth folowed hym *free*,
With bowes bent and arowes sharpe,
  For to shende[5] that companye.

141

They shulderd all and made hym rome,
  To wete[6] what he wolde say;
He toke the yeman bi the hande,
  And gave hym al the play.

142

He gave hym fyve marke for his wyne,[7]
  There it lay on the molde,[8]
And bad it shulde be set a broche,[9]
  Drynke who so wolde.

143

Thus *longe* taried this gentyll knyght,
  Tyll that play was *done*;
So longe abode Robyn fastinge,
  Thre houres after the none.

The Third Fytte

144

Lyth and lystyn, gentilmen,
  All that nowe be here,
Of Litell Johnn, that was the knightes
    man,
  Goode myrth ye shall here.

145

It was upon a mery day
  That yonge men wolde go shete;[10]
Lytell Johnn fet[11] his bowe anone,
  And sayde he wolde them mete.

146

Thre tymes Litell Johnn shet aboute,
  And alwey he slet the wande,
The proude sherif of Notingham
  By the markes can stande.[12]

147

The sherif swore a full great othe,
  'By hym that dyede on a tre,
This man is the best arschere
  That ever yet sa we.

---

[1] up pyght: *placed*. A ram was the usual prize for a wrestling-match rather than the splendid ones offered here.   [2] fay: *truth*
[3] And for he was ferre and frembde bested: *and because he was a stranger and in the predicament of being a foreigner*   [4] ruthe: *pity*   [5] shende: *put to shame*   [6] wete: *know*
[7] 5 marks (£3 6s. 8d.) was a common selling price for a pipe of wine in northern England during the decades before and after 1400 (see, e.g., R. B. Dobson, *Durham Priory, 1400–1450,* Cambridge 1973, p. 265).
[8] molde: *ground*   [9] set a broche: *tapped and set running*   [10] shete: *shooting*
[11] fet: *fetched*   [12] can stande: *stood*

148

'Say me nowe, wight[1] yonge man,
    What is nowe thy name?
In what countre were thou borne,
    And where is thy wonynge wane?'[2]

149

'In Holdernes,[3] sir, I was borne,
    I wys al of my dame;
Men cal me Reynolde Grenelef[4]
    Whan I am at home.'

150

'Sey me, *Reynaud* Grenelefe,
    Wolde thou dwell with me?
And every yere I woll the gyve
    Twenty marke *to* thy fee.'

151

'I have a maister,' sayde Litell Johnn,
    'A curteys knight is he;
May ye leve gete of hym,
    The better may it be.'

152

The sherif gate Litell John
    Twelve monethes of the knight,
Therfore he gave him right anone
    A gode hors and a wight.

153

Nowe is Litell John the sherifes man,
    God lende us well to spede,
But alwey thought Lytell John
    To quyte hym wele his mede.[5]

154

'Nowe so God me helpe,' sayde Litell
    John,
    'And by my true leutye,[6]
I shall be the worst servaunt to hym
    That ever yet had he.'

155

It fell upon a Wednesday,
    The sherif on huntynge was gone,
And Litel John lay in his bed,
    And was foriete[7] at home.

156

Therfore he was fastinge
    Til it was past the none.
'Gode sir stuarde, I pray to the,
    Gyve me my dynere,' saide Litell John.

157

'It is longe for Grenelefe,
    Fastinge thus for to be;
Therfor I pray the, sir stuarde,
    Mi dyner gif me.'

158

'Shalt thou never ete ne drynke,' said
    the stuarde,
    'Tyll my lorde be come to towne.'
'I make myn avowe to God,' saide Litell
    John,
    'I had lever to crake thy crowne.'

159

The boteler[8] was full uncurteys,
    There he stode on flore,
He start to the botery
    And shet fast the dore.

160

Lytell Johnn gave the boteler such a tap
    His backe went nere in two;
Tho he lived an hundred ier,[9]
    The wors *he shuld* go.

161

He sporned the dore with his fote,
    It went open wel and fyne,
And therefore he made large lyveray[10]
    Bothe of ale and of wyne.

---

[1] wight: *brave*   [2] wonynge wane: *dwelling place*
[3] Holderness, in the south-east of E. Yorks
[4] Perhaps the most obscure of all the names in the Robin Hood legend: 'Reynolde' appears as a character distinct from Little John in stanza 293 below. Also see below p. 225, and Child, III, 54.
[5] to quyte . . . his mede: *to pay him out*   [6] leuyte: *fidelity*   [7] foriete: *forgotten*
[8] boteler: *butler*   [9] ier: *years*   [10] made large lyveray: *took a good allowance*

162

'Sith ye wol nat dyne,' sayde Litell John,
  'I shall *gyve* you to drinke,
And though ye lyve an hundred wynter,
  On Lytel Johnn ye shall thinke.'

163

Litell John ete, and Litel John drank,
  The while that he wol be.
The sherife had in his kechyn a coke,
  A stoute man and a bolde.

164

'I make myn avowe to God,' saide the
  coke,
  'Thou arte a shrewde hynde,[1]
In ani hous for to dwel,
  For to aske thus to dyne.'

165

And there he lent Litell John
  Good strokis thre,
'I make myn *avowe* to God,' sayde
  Lytell John,
  'These strokis lyked well me.

166

'Thou arte a bolde man and hardy,
  And so thinketh me;
And or I pas fro this place,
  Assayed better shalt thou be.'

167

Lytell Johnn drew a ful gode sworde,
  The coke toke another in hande;
They thought no thynge for to fle,
  But stifly[2] for to stande.

168

There they faught sore[3] togedere
  Two myle way and well more,
Myght neyther other harme done,
  The mountnaunce of an owre.[4]

169

'I make myn avowe to God,' sayde Litell
  Johnn,
  'And by my true lewte,
Thou art one of the best sworde men
  That ever yit sa we.

170

'Cowdest thou shote as well in a bowe,
  To grene wode thou shuldest with
  me,
And two times in the yere thy clothinge
  Chaunged shulde be;

171

'And every yere of Robyn Hode
  Twenty merke to thy fe.'
'Put up thy swerde,' saide the coke,
  'And felowes woll we be.'

172

Thanne he fet to Lytell Johnn
  The nowmbles of a do,[5]
Gode brede, and full gode wyne,
  They ete and drank theretoo.

173

And when they had dronkyn well,
  Theyre trouthes togeder they plight,
That they wolde be with Robyn
  That ylke same nyght.

174

They dyd them to the tresoure hows,
  As fast as they myght gone,
The lokkes, that were of full gode stele
  They brake them everichone.

175

They toke away the silver vessell,
  And all that thei might get,
Pecis,[6] *masars*,[7] ne sponis,
  Wolde thei not forget.

---

[1] shrewde hynde: *cursed servant*   [2] stifly: *unyielding*   [3] sore: *bitterly*
[4] i.e. the amount of an hour   [5] do: *doe*   [6] pecis: *pieces*
[7] masars: *drinking cups*

176

Also *they* toke the gode pens,
  Thre hundred pounde and more;
And did them streyte to Robyn Hode,
  Under the grene wode hore.

177

'God the save, my dere mayster,
  And Criste the save and se!'
And thanne sayde Robyn to Litell
    Johnn,
  'Welcome myght thou be.

178

'Also be that fayre yeman
  Thou bryngest there with the:
What tydynges fro Notyngham?
  Lytill Johnn, tell thou me.'

179

'Well the gretith the proude sheryf,
  And sende the here by me
His coke and his silver vessel,
  And thre hundred pounde and thre.'

180

'I make myne *avowe* to God,' sayde
    Robyn,
  'And to the Trenyte,
It was never by his gode wyll
  This gode is come to me.'

181

Lytell Johnn there hym bethought
  On a shrewde wyle,
Fyve myle in the forest he ran,
  Hym happed all his wyll.[1]

182

Than he met the proude sheref,
  Huntynge with houndes and horne,
Lytell Johnn coude[2] of curtesye,
  And knelyd hym beforne.

183

'God the save, my dere mayster,
  And Criste the save and se!'
'*Raynolde* Grenelefe,' sayde the shryef,
  'Where hast thou nowe be?'

184

'I have be in this forest,
  A fayre syght can I se,
It was one of the fayrest syghtes
  That ever yet sawe I me.

185

'Yonder I sawe a ryght fayre harte,
  His coloure is of grene,
Seven score of dere upon a herde
  Be with hym all bydene.[3]

186

'Their tyndes[4] are so sharpe, maister,
  Of sexty, and well mo,
That I durst not shote for drede
  Lest they wolde me slo.'

187

'I make myn avowe to God,' sayde the
    sheryf,
  'That syght wolde I fayne se.'
'Buske you thyderwarde, mi dere may-
    ster,
  Anone, and wende with me.'

188

The sherif rode, and Litell Johnn
  Of fote he was full smerte,
And whane they came before Robyn;
  'Lo, sir, here is the mayster herte!'

189

Still stode the proude sherief,
  A sory man was he;
'Wo the worthe,[5] Raynolde Grenelefe,
  Thou hast betrayed nowe me.'

---

[1] i.e. all his wish came to pass   [2] coude: *knew*   [3] bydene: *together*
[4] tyndes: *antlers*   [5] wo the worthe: *a plague on you*

190

'I make myn avowe to God,' sayde
    Litell Johnn,
'Mayster, ye be to blame,
I was mysserved of my dynere
    Whan I was with you at home.'

191

Sone he was to souper sette,
    And served well with silver white,
And whan the sherif sawe his vessell,
    For sorowe he myght nat ete.

192

'Make glad chere,' sayde Robyn Hode,
    'Sherif, for charite!
And for the love of Litill Johnn,
    Thy lyfe I graunt to the.'

193

Whan they had souped well,
    The day was al gone;
Robyn commaundyd Litell Johnn
    To drawe of his hosen and his shone,[1]

194

His kirtell, and his cote of pie,[2]
    That was fured well and fine,
And toke hym a grene mantel,
    To lap[3] his body therein.

195

Robyn commaundyd his wight yonge
    men,
    Under the grene wood tree,
They shulde lye in that same sute;
    That the sherif myght them see.

196

All nyght lay the proude sherif,
    In his breche and in his schert,
No wonder it was, in grene wode,
    Though his sydes gan to smerte.

197

'Make glade chere,' sayde Robyn Hode,
    'Sheref, for charite!

For this is our ordre i wys,
    Under the grene wode tree.'

198

'This is harder order,' sayde the sherief,
    'Than any ankir or frere;[4]
For all the golde in mery Englonde
    I wolde nat longe dwell her.'

199

'All this twelve monthes,' sayde Robin,
    'Thou shalt dwell with me;
I shall the teche, proude sherif,
    An outlawe for to be.'

200

'Or I be here another nyght,' sayde the
    sherif,
    'Robyn, nowe pray I the,
Smyte of mijn hede rather to-morowe,
    And I forgyve it the.

201

'Lat me go,' than sayde the sherif,
    'For saynte charite!
And I woll be thy best frende
    That ever yet had ye.'

202

'Thou shalt swere me an othe,' sayde
    Robyn,
    'On my bright bronde,[5]
Shalt thou never awayte me *scathe*,[6]
    By water ne by lande.

203

'And if thou fynde any of my men,
    By nyght or day,
Upon thyn othe[7] thou shalt swere,
    To helpe them that thou may.'

204

Nowe hathe the sherif sworne his othe,
    And home he began to gone;
He was as full of grene wode
    As ever was hepe[8] of stone.

---

[1] shone: *shoes*   [2] cote of pie: *possibly a corruption of 'courtepi', meaning a short jacket*
[3] to lap: *to wrap up*   [4] ankir or frere: *hermit or friar*   [5] bronde: *sword*
[6] awayte me scathe: *contrive harm to me*   [7] othe: *oath*
[8] hepe: *rose hip, or (more probably, because it contains little 'stones') the hip or haw of the white thorn (Ritson, 1846, p. 43)*

The Fourth Fytte

205

The sherif dwelled in Notingham;
 He was fayne he was agone;
And Robyn and his mery men
 Went to wode anone.

206

'Go we to dyner,' sayde Litell Johnn,
 Robyn Hode sayde, 'Nay;
For I drede Our Lady be wroth with me,
 For she sent me nat my *pay*.

207

'Have no doute, maister,' sayde Litell
 Johnn;
 'Yet is nat the sonne at rest;
For I dare say, and savely swere,
 The knight is true and truste.'

208

Take thy bowe in thy hande,' sayde
 Robyn,
 Late Much wende with the,
And so shal Wyllyam Scarlok,
 And no man abyde with me.[1]

209

'*And walke up under the Sayles,*
 And to Watlynge strete,[2]
And wayte after such unketh gest;
 Up-chaunce ye may them mete.

210

Whether he be messengere,
 Or a man that myrthes can,[3]
Or yf he be a pore man
 Of my good he shall have some.

211

Forth then stert Lytel Johan,
 Half in tray and tene,[4]
And gyrde hym with a full good swerde,
 Under a mantel of grene.

212

They went up to the Sayles,
 These yemen all thre;
They loked est, they loked west,
 They myght no man se.

213

But as they loked in Bernysdale,
 By the hye waye,
Than were they ware of two blacke monkes,
 Eche on a good palferay.

214

Then bespake Lytell Johan,
 To Much he gan say,
'*I dare lay my lyfe to wedde,*[5]
 That these *monkes have brought our*
 pay.

215

'*Make glad chere', sayd Lytell Johan,*
 '*And frese*[6] *our bowes of ewe,*
And loke your hertes be seker and sad,[7]
 Your strynges trusty and trewe.

216

'*The monke hath two and fifty* men,
 And seven somers[8] *full stronge;*
There rydeth no bysshop in this londe
 So ryally, I understond.

---

[1] This, and several of the following stanzas, deliberately repeat the words on p. 80 above.
[2] See Introduction, p. 22   [3] i.e. a minstrel or other type of entertainer
[4] tray and tene: *anger and annoyance.* Cf. Little John's quarrel with Robin in No. 5 (p. 142) below
[5] wedde: *pledge*   [6] frese: possibly *free, make ready?*
[7] seker and sad: *sure and steadfast*
[8] somers: *pack-horses.* Note that the two Benedictine monks of stanza 213 have been reduced to one.

217

'Brethern,' sayd Lytell Johan,
  'Here are no more but we thre ;
But we brynge them to dyner,
  Our mayster dare we not se.

218

'Bende your bowes,' sayd Lytell Johan,
  'Make all yon prese[1] to stonde ;
The formost monke, his lyfe and his deth
  Is closed in my honde.

219

'Abyde, chorle monke,' sayd Lytell Johan,
  'No ferther that thou gone ;
Yf thou doost, by dere worthy God,
  Thy deth is in my honde.

220

'And evyll thryfte[2] on thy hede,' sayd
  Lytell Johan,
  'Ryght under thy hattes bonde !
For thou hast made our mayster wroth,
  He is fastynge so longe.'

221

'Who is your mayster ?' sayd the monke
  Lytell Johan sayd, 'Robyn Hode',
'He is a stronge thefe,' said the monke,
  'Of hym herd I never good.'

222

'Thou lyest,' than sayd Lytell Johan,
  'And that shall rewe the ;
He is a yeman of the forest,
  To dyne he hath bode the.'

223

Much was redy with a bolte,[3]
  Redly[4] and anone,
He set the monke to fore the brest,
  To the grounde that he can gone.

224

Of two and fyfty wyght yonge yemen
  There abode not one,
Saf a lytell page and a grome,
  To lede the somers with Lytel Johan.

225

They brought the monke to the lodge dore,
  Whether he were loth or lefe,[5]
For to speke with Robyn Hode,
  Maugre in theyr tethe.[6]

226

Robyn dyde adowne his hode,
  The monke whan that he se ;
The monke was not so curteyse,
  His hode then let he be.

227

'He is a chorle, mayster, by dere worthy
  God,'
  Than sayd Lytell Johan,
'Thereof no force,'[7] sayd Robyn,
  'For curteyse can he none.

228

'How many men,'[8] sayd Robyn,
  'Had[9] this monke, Johan ?'
'Fyfty and two whan that we met,
  But many of them be gone.'

229

'Let blowe a horne,' sayd Robyn,
  'That felaushyp may us knowe.'
Seven score of wyght yemen
  Came pryckynge[10] on a rowe.

230

And everych of them a good mantell
  Of scarlet and of raye ;[11]
All they came to good Robyn,
  To wyte what he wolde say.

---

[1] prese: *crowd*   [2] evyll thryfte: *bad fortune*   [3] bolte: *short arrow*
[4] redly: *promptly.* P reads 'rapely'   [5] lefe: *glad*
[6] maugre in theyr tethe: *in spite of their resistance*   [7] no force: *no matter*
[8] P. adds 'than'   [9] P. adds 'nowe'   [10] pryckynge: *riding*   [11] raye: *striped cloth*

231

They made the monke to wasshe and wype,
  And syt at his denere,
Robyn Hode and Lytell Johan
  They served him both in fere.[1]

232

'Do gladly, monke,' sayd Robyn,
  'Gramercy, syr,' sayd he.
'Where is your abbay, whan ye are at
    home,
  And who is your avowe?'[2]

233

'Saynt Mary abbay,' sayd the monke,
  'Though I be symple[3] here.'
'In what offyce?' sayd Robin:
  'Syr, the hye selerer.'

234

'Ye be the more welcome,' sayd Robyn,
  'So ever mote I the[4]:
Fyll of the best wyne,' sayd Robyn,
  'This monke shall drynke to me.

235

'But I have grete mervayle,' sayd Robyn,
  'Of all this longe day;
I drede Our Lady be wroth with me,
  She sent me not my pay.'

236

'Have no doute, mayster,' sayd Lytell
    Johan,
  'Ye have no nede, I saye
This monke it hath brought, I dare well
    swere,
  For he is of her abbay.'

237

'And she was a borowe,[5]' sayd Robyn,
  'Betwene a knyght and me,
Of a lytell money that I hym lent,
  Under the grene wode tree.

238

And yf thou hast that sylver ibrought,
  I pray the let me se;
And I shall helpe the eftsones,
  Yf thou have nede to me.'

239

The monke swore a full grete othe,
  With a sory chere,
'Of the borowehode thou spekest to me
  Herde I never ere.'

240

'I make myn avowe to God,' sayd Robyn,
  'Monke, thou art to blame;
For God is holde a ryghtwys man,
  And so is his dame.[6]

241

'Thou toldest with thyn owne tonge,
  Thou may not say nay,
How thou arte her servaunt,
  And servest her every day.

242

'And thou art made her messengere,
  My money for to pay;
Therefore I cun the more thanke[7]
  Thou art come at thy day.

243

'What is in your cofers?' sayd Robyn,
  'Trewe[8] than tell thou me.'
'Syr,' he sayd, 'twenty marke,
  Al so mote I the.'

244

'Yf there be no more,' sayd Robyn,
  'I wyll not one peny;
Yf thou hast myster[9] of ony more,
  Syr, more I shall lende to the.

---

[1] in fere: *in company*   [2] avowe: *patron, protector*   [3] symple: *humble, insignificant*
[4] i.e. so may I always prosper   [5] borowe: *guarantor*   [6] dame: *mother* (i.e. Our Lady)
[7] i.e. I am the more grateful   [8] P. reads 'The truthe'   [9] myster: *need*

245
'And yf I fynde more,' sayd *Robyn*,
  'I wys thou shalte it for gone ;[1]
For of thy spendynge sylver, monke,
  Thereof wyll I ryght none.

246
'Go nowe forthe, Lytell Johan,
  And the trouth tell thou me;
If there be no more but twenty marke,
  No peny that I se.'

247
Lytell Johan spred his mantell downe,
  As he had done before,
And he tolde out of the monkes male[2]
  Eyght hondred pounde and more.

248
Lytell Johan let it lye full styll,
  And went to his mayster in hast ;
'Syr,' he sayd, 'the monke[3] is trewe
      ynowe,
  Our Lady hath doubled your cast.[4]

249
'I make myn avowe to God,' sayd *Robyn*,
  'Monke, what[5] tolde I the ?
Our Lady is the trewest woman
  That ever yet founde I me.

250
'By dere worthy God,' sayd *Robyn*,
  'To seche all Englond thorowe,
Yet founde I never to my pay
  A moche better borowe.

251
'Fyll of the best wyne, and do hym
      drynke,' sayd *Robyn*,
  'And grete well thy lady hende,[6]
And yf she have nede to Robyn Hode,
  A frende she shall hym fynde.

252
'And yf she nedeth ony more sylver,
  Come thou agayne to me,
And, by this token she hath me sent,
  She shall have such thre.'

253
The monke was goynge to London ward,
  There to holde grete mote,[7]
The knyght that rode so hye on hors,
  To brynge hym under fote.

254
'Whether be ye away ?' sayd *Robyn*
  'Syr, to maners in this londe,
Too reken with our reves,
  That have done moch wronge.'

255
'Come now forth, Lytell Johan,
  And harken to my tale,
A better yemen I knowe none,
  To seke[8] a monkes male.'

256
'How much is in yonder other corser ?[9]
  The soth must we see.'
'By Our Lady,' than sayd the monke,
  'That were no curteysye,

257
'To bydde a man to dyner,
  And syth[10] hym bete and bynde,'
'It is our olde maner', sayd *Robyn*,
  'To leve but lytell behynde.'

258
The monke toke the hors with spore,
  No lenger wolde he abyde ;
'Aske to drynke,' than sayd *Robyn*,
  'Or that ye forther ryde.'

---

[1] for gone: *forgo*   [2] male: *trunk*   [3] P. reads 'knyght' incorrectly
[4] i.e. has doubled Robin's outlay to the knight of £400 (stanza 67 above)   [5] P. 'that'
[6] hende: *gracious*   [7] mote: *assembly*   [8] seke: *search*
[9] corser (courser): *horse* (i.e. is on the other horse)   [10] syth: *afterwards*

259

Nay, for God,' than sayd the monke,
  'Me reweth I cam so nere ;
For better chepe[1] I myght have dyned
  In Blythe or in Dankestere.'[2]

260

'Grete well your abbot,' sayd Robyn,
  'And your pryour, I you pray,
And byd hym send me such a monke
  To dyner every day.'

261

Now lete we that monke be styll,
  And speke we of that knyght :
Yet he came to holde his day,
  Whyle that it was lyght.[3]

262

He dyed him[4] streyt to Bernysdale,
  Under the grene wode tre,
And he founde there Robyn Hode,
  And all his merry meyne.

263

The knyght lyght doune[5] of his good
    palfray ;
Robyn whan he gan see,
So curteysly he dyde adoune his hode,
  And set hym on his knee.

264

'God the save, Robyn Hode,
  And all this company.'
'Welcome be thou, gentyll knyght,
  And ryght welcome to me.'

265

Than bespake hym Robyn Hode,
  To that knyght so fre :
'What nede dryveth the to grene wode ?
  I praye the, syr knyght, tell me.

266

'And welcome be thou, gentyll knyght,
  Why hast thou be so longe ?'
'For the abbot and the hye iustyce
  Wolde have had my londe.'

267

'Hast thou thy londe a gayne ?' sayd Robyn
  'Treuth than tell thou me.'
'Ye, for God,' sayd the knyght,
  'And that thanke I God and the.

268

'But take not a grefe,' sayd the knyght,
  That I have be so longe
I came by a wrastelynge,
  And there I holpe a pore yeman,
    With wronge was put behynde.'

269

'Nay, for God,' sayd Robyn,
  'Syr knyght, that thanke I the ;
What man that helpeth a good yeman,
  His frende than wyll I be.'

270

'Have here foure hondred pounde,' than
    sayd the knyght,
  'The whiche ye lent to me ;
And here is also twenty marke
  For your curteysy.'

271

'Nay, for God,' than sayd Robyn,
  'Thou broke[6] it well for ay ;
For Our Lady, by her high selerer,
  Hath sent to me my pay.

272

'And yf I toke it i twyse,
  A shame it were to me ;
But trewely, gentyll knyght,
  Welcom arte thou to me.'

---

[1] chepe: *bargain*

[2] Blyth (Notts.) is ten miles south of Doncaster by the great north road and so an entirely appropriate stopping-point for a monk of York travelling through Barnsdale to London

[3] This stanza takes up the story of the knight from stanza 143   [4] dyed him: *betook himself*

[5] lyght doune: *dismounted*   [6] broke: *enjoy the use of*

273
Whan Robyn had tolde his tale,
He leugh[1] and had good chere ;
'By my trouthe,' then sayd the kynght,
Your money is redy here.'

274
'Broke it well,' sayd Robyn,
'Thou gentyll knyght so fre ;
And welcome be thou, gentyll knyght,
Under my trystell tre.[2]

275
'But what shall these bowes do ?' sayd
Robyn,
And these arowes fethered fre ?'[3]
'By God,' than sayd the knyght,
'A pore present to the.'

276
'Come now forth, Lytell Johan,
And go to my treasure,
And brynge me there foure hondred pounde ;
The monke over tolde it me.

277
'Have here foure hondred pounde,
Thou gentyll knyght and trewe,
And bye hors and harnes good,
And gylte thy spores all newe.

278
'And yf thou fayle[4] ony spendynge,
Com to Robyn Hode,
And by my trouth thou shalt none fayle,
The whyles I have any good.

279
'And broke well thy foure hondred pound,
Whiche I lent to the,
And make thy selfe no more so bare,
By the counsell of me.'

280
Thus than holpe hym good Robyn,
The knyght all of his care :
God, that syt in heven hye,
Graunte us well to fare.

The Fifth Fytte

281
Now hath the knight his leve i take,
And wente hym on his way ;
Robyn Hode and his mery men
Dwelled styll full many a day.

282
Lyth and lysten, gentil men,
And herken what I shall say,
How the proud sheryfe of Notyngham,
Dyde crye a full fayre play.

283
That all the best archers of the north
Sholde come upon a day,
And they that shoteth allther best[5]
The game shall bere a way.

284
He that shoteth allther best,
Furthest fayre and lowe,
At a pair of fynly[6] buttes,
Under the grene wode shawe,

285
A ryght good arowe he shall have,
The shaft of sylver whyte,
The hede and the feders of ryche rede golde,
In Englond is none lyke.

286
This than herde good Robyn,
Under his trystell tre :
'Make you redy, you wyght yonge men
That shotynge wyll I se.'

---

[1] leugh: *laughed*
[2] trystell tre: *tree fixed upon for a rendezvous (see stanza 79, and below stanzas 387, 412 and pp. 118, 141).*
[3] For the knight's presents to Robin Hood, see stanzas 131–2 above   [4] fayle: *lack*
[5] allther best: *best of all*   [6] fynly: *goodly*

287

'Buske you, my mery yonge men,
    Ye shall go with me;
And I wyll wete[1] the shryves fayth,
    Trewe and yf he be.'

288

Whan they had theyr bowes i bent,
    Theyr takles[2] fedred fre,
Seven score of wyght yonge men[3]
    Stode by Robyns kne.

289

Whan they came to Notyngham,
    The buttes were fayre and longe;
Many was the bold archere
    That shoted with bowes stronge.

290

'There shall but syx shote with me;
    The other shal kepe my hede,
And stande with good bowes bent,
    That I be not desceyved.'

291

The fourth outlawe his bowe gan bende.
    And that was Robyn Hode,
And that behelde the proud sheryfe,
    All by the but he stode.

292

Thryes Robyn shot about,
    And alway he slist[4] the wand,
And so dyde good Gylberte
    Wyth the whyte hande.[5]

293

Lytell Johan and good Scatheloke[6]
    Were archers good and fre;
Lytell Much and good Reynolde,[7]
    The worste wolde they not be.

294

Whan they had shot aboute,
    These archours fayre and good,
Evermore was the best,
    For soth, Robyn Hode.

295

Hym was delyvered the good arowe,
    For best worthy was he;
He toke the yeft[8] so curteysly,
    To grene wode wolde he.

296

They cryed out on Robyn Hode
    And grete hornes gan they blowe:
'Wo worth the, treason!' sayd Robyn,
    'Full evyl thou art to knowe.

297

'And wo be thou, thou proude sheryf,
    Thus gladdynge thy gest;[9]
Other wyse thou behote me[10]
    In yonder wylde forest.

298

'But had I the in grene wode,
    Under my trystell tre,
Thou sholdest leve me a better wedde[11]
    Than thy trewe lewte.'

299

Full many a bowe there was bent,
    And arrowes let they glyde;
Many a kyrtell there was rent,
    And hurt many a syde.

300

The outlawes shot was so stronge
    That no man myght them dryve,
And the proud sheryfes men
    They fled away full blyve.[12]

---

[1] wete: *know*   [2] takles: *arrows*
[3] 'the right number for a band of outlaws' (Child, III, 53); cf. stanzas 229, 342, 389, 448 and below, p. 185.
[4] slist: *slit*   [5] See Introduction, p. 5.
[6] Presumably the William Scarlok of stanzas 17 and 208
[7] For 'Reynolde Grenelef' see stanzas 149–50   [8] yeft: *gift*
[9] i.e. so making light of your word (at stanza 204 above)   [10] behote: *promised, vowed*
[11] wedde: *pledge*   [12] blyve: *quickly*

301
Robyn sawe the busshement¹ to broke,
    In grene wode he wolde have be ;
Many an arowe there was shot
    Amonge that company.

302
Lytell Johan was hurte full sore,
    With an arowe in his kne,
That he myght neyther go nor ryde
    It was full grete pyte.

303
'Mayster,' then sayd Lytell Johan,
    'If ever thou lovest me,
And for that ylke lordes love,
    That dyed upon a tre,

304
'And for the medes² of my servyce,
    That I have served the,
Lete never the proude sheryf
    Alyve now fynde me ;

305
'But take out thy browne³ swerde,
    And smyte all of my hede
And gyve me woundes depe and wyde,
    No lyfe on me be lefte.'

306
'I wolde not that,' sayd Robyn,
    'Johan, that thou were slawe,
For all the golde in mery Englonde,
    Though it lay now on a rawe.'⁴

307
'God forbede,' said Lytell Much,
    'That dyed on a tre,
That thou sholdest, Lytell Johan,
    Parte our company.'

308
Up he toke hym on his backe,
    And bare hym well a myle
Many a tyme he layd hym downe,
    And shot another whyle.

309
Then was there a fayre castell,
    A lytell within the wode;
Double dyched it was about,
    And walled, by the rode.⁵

310
And there dwelled that gentyll knyght,
    Syr Rychard at the Lee,⁶
That Robyn had lent his good,
    Under the grene wode tree.

311
In he toke good Robyn,
    And all his company :
'Welcome be thou, Robyn Hode,
    Welcome arte thou to me,

312
'And moche I thanke the of thy confort,
    And of thy curteysye,
And of thy grete kyndenesse,
    Under the grene wode tre ;

313
'I love no man in all this worlde
    So much as I do the ;
For all the proud sheryf of Notyngham,
    Ryght here shalt thou be.

314
'Shyt the gates, and drawe the brydge,
    And let no man come in,
And arme you well, and make you redy,
    And to the walles ye wynne.

---

¹ busshement: *ambushment*   ² medes: *rewards*
³ browne: *bright, shining*   ⁴ rawe: *row, line*   ⁵ by the rode: *by the Cross* (an expletive)
⁶ The first time this name occurs in the *Gest* (see above, p. 77)

315

'For one thynge, Robyn, I the behote,[1]
  I swere by Saynt Quyntyne,
These forty dayes thou wonnest[2] with
    me,
    To soupe, ete, and dyne.'

316

Bordes were layde, and clothes were
    spredde,
  Redely and anone;
Robyn Hode and his merry men
    To mete can they gone.

The Sixth Fytte

317

Lythe and lysten, gentylmen,
  And herkyn to your songe;
Howe the proude shyref of Notyngham
  And men of armys stronge,

318

Full fast cam to the hye shyref,
  The contre up to route,[3]
And they besette the knyghtes castell,
  The walles all aboute.

319

The proude shyref loude gan crye,
  And sayde, 'Thou traytour knight,
Thou keepest here the kynges enemys,
  Agaynst the lawe[4] and ryght.'

320

'Syr, I wyll avowe that I haue done,
  The dedys that here be dyght,[5]
Upon all the landes that I have,
  As I am a trewe knyght.

321

'Wende furth, sirs, on your way,
  And do no more to me
Tyll ye wyt oure kynges *wyll*,[6]
  What he wyll say to the.'

322

The shyref thus had his answere,
  Without any lesynge;[7]
Furth[8] he yede to London towne,
  All for to tel our kinge.

323

Ther he telde him of that knight,
  And eke of Robyn Hode,
And also of the bolde archars
  That were soo noble and gode.

324

'He wyll avowe that he hath done,
  To mayntene the outlawes stronge,
He wyll be lorde, and set you at nought,
  In all the northe londe.'

325

'I wil be at Notyngham,' saide our kynge,
  'Within this fourteenyght,
And take I wyll Robyn Hode,
  And so I wyll that knight.

326

'Go nowe home, shyref,' sayde our
    kynge,
  'And do as I byd the,
And ordeyn[9] gode archers ynowe,[10]
  Of all the wyde contre.'

327

The shyref had his leve i take,
  And went hym on his way;
And Robyn Hode[11] to grene wode
  Upon a certen day.

328

And Lytel John was hole of the arowe
  That shot was in his kne,
And dyd hym streyght to Robyn Hode,
  Under the grene wode tree.

---

[1] behote: *request*   [2] wonnest: *dwell*   [3] up to route: *to stir up*   [4] P. reads 'lawes'
[5] dyght: *done*   [6] P. reads 'welle'   [7] lesynge: *falsehood*   [8] Supplied from P.
[9] ordeyn: *array*   [10] ynowe: *in plenty*   [11] P. adds 'wente'

329
Robyn Hode walked in the forest
  Under the levys grene;
The proude shyref of Notyngham
  Thereof he had grete tene.[1]

330
The shyref there fayled of[2] Robyn Hode,
  He myght not have his pray;
Than he awayted this gentyll knyght,
  Bothe by nyght and day.

331
Ever he wayted the[3] gentyll knyght,
  Syr Richarde at the Lee,
As he went on haukynge by the ryver-
      syde,
  And lete *his* haukes flee.[4]

332
Toke he there this gentyll knight,
  With men of armys stronge,
And led hym to Notyngham warde,
  Bounde bothe fote and hande.

333
The sheref sware a full grete othe,
  Bi hym that dyed on rode,
He had lever than an hundred pound
  That he had Robyn Hode.

334
This harde the knyghtes wyfe,
  A fayr lady and a free;
She set hir on a gode palfrey,
  To grene wode anone rode she.

335
Whanne she cam in the forest,
  Under the grene wode tree,
Fonde she there Robyn Hode
  And al his fayre mene.

336
'God the save, gode Robyn,
  And all thy company;
For Our dere Ladyes sake,
  A bone graunte thou me.

337
'Late never my wedded lorde
  Shamefully slayne be;
He is fast bowne to Notingham warde,
  For the love of the.'

338
Anone than saide goode Robyn,
  To that lady so fre,
'What man hath your lorde take?'
  '*The proude shirife,*' *than sayd she.*[5]

339
'*The proude shirife*', *than sayd she,*[5]
  'For soth as I the say;
He is not yet thre *myles*
  Passed on his way.'

340
Up than sterte gode Robyn
  As man that had ben wode:[6]
'Buske you, my mery men,
  For hym that dyed on rode.

341
'And he that this sorowe forsaketh,
  By hym that dyed on tre,
Shall he never in grene wode
  No lenger dwel with me.'

342
Sone there were gode bowes bent,
  Mo than seven score;
Hedge ne dyche spared they none
  That was them before.

---

[1] tene: *vexation*   [2] fayled of: *missed*   [3] P. 'this'   [4] P. 'flye'   [5] Supplied from C.
[6] wode: *insane, furious*

343

'I make myn avowe to God,' sayde
　Robyn,
'The sherif wolde I fayne see,
And if I may hym take,
　I-quyte shall it be.'

344

And whan they came to Notingham,
　They walked in the strete;
And with the proude sherif i-wys
　Sone can they mete.

345

'Abyde, thou proude sherif,' he sayde,
　'Abyde, and speke with me;
Of some tidinges of oure kinge
　I wolde fayne here of the.

346

'This seven yere, by dere worthy God,
　Ne yede[1] I this fast on fote,
I make myn avowe to God, thou proude
　sherif,
　It is nat for thy gode.'

347

Robyn bent a full goode bowe,
　An arrowe he drowe at wyll;
He hit so the proude sherife,
　Upon the grounde he lay full still.

348

And or he myght up aryse,
　On his fete to stonde,

He smote of the sherifs hede,
　With his bright bronde.

349

'Lye thou there, thou proude sherife,
　Evyll mote thou cheve:[2]
There myght no man to the truste
　The whyles thou were a lyve.'

350

His men drewe out theyr bryght swerdes,
　That were so sharpe and kene,
And layde on the sheryves men,
　And dryved them downe bydene.[3]

351

Robyn stert to that knyght,
　And cut a two his hoode,
And toke hym in his hand a bowe,
　And bad hym by hym stonde.

352

'Leve thy hors the behynde,
　And lerne for to renne;[4]
Thou shalt with me to grene wode,
　Through myre, mosse, and fenne.

353

'Thou shalt with me to grene wode,
　Without ony leasynge,
Tyll that I have gete us grace
　Of Edwarde, our comly kynge.'

The Seventh Fytte

354

The kynge came to Notynghame,
　With knyghtes in grete araye,
For to take that gentyll knyght
　And Robin Hode, and yf he may.

355

He asked men of that countre
　After Robyn Hode,
And after that gentyll knyght,
　That was so bolde and stout.

---

[1] yede: *went*　　[2] evyll mote thou cheve: *evilly must you end*　　[3] bydene: *forthwith*
[4] renne: *run*

356

Whan they had tolde hym the case
  Our kynge understonde ther tale,
And seased in his honde
  The knyghtes londes all.

357

All the passe of Lancasshyre
  He went both ferre and nere,
Tyll he came to Plomton Parke,[1]
  He faylyd[2] many of his dere.

358

There our kynge was wont to se
  Herdes many one,
He coud unneth[3] fynde one dere,
  That bare ony good horne.

359

The kynge was wonder wroth withall,
  And swore by the Trynyte,
'I wolde I had Robyn Hode,
  With eyen I myght hym se.

360

'And he that wolde smyte of the knyghtes
      hede,
  And brynge it to me,
He shall have the knyghtes londes,
  Syr Rycharde at the Le.

361

'I gyve it hym with my charter,
  And sele it with my honde,
To have and holde for ever more,
  In all mery Englonde.'

362

Than bespake a fayre olde knyght
  That was treue in his fay :[4]
'A, my leege lorde the kynge,
  One worde I shall you say.

363

'There is no man in this countre
  May have the knyghtes londes,
Whyle Robyn Hode may ryde or gone,
  And bere a bowe in his hondes,

364

'That he ne shall lese his hede,
  That is the best ball in his hode,
Give it no man, my lorde the kynge,
  That ye wyll any good.'

365

Half a yere dwelled our comly kynge
  In Notyngham, and well more ;
Coude he not here of Robyn Hode,
  In what countre that he were.

366

But alway went good Robyn
  By halke[5] and eke by hyll,
And alway slewe the kynges dere,
  And welt them at his wyll.[6]

367

Than bespake a proude fostere,[7]
  That stode by our kynges kne :
'Yf ye wyll se good Robyn,
  Ye must do after me.

368

'Take fyve of the best knyghtes
  That be in your lede,[8]
And walke downe by yon abbay,
  And gete you monkes wede.

369

'And I wyll be your ledes-man,
  And lede you the way,
And or ye come to Notyngham,
  Myn hede then dare I lay,

---

[1] Possibly Plumpton Park near Knaresborough in the West Riding of Yorkshire
  rather than in Cumberland as is often assumed (Child, III, 54–5)
[2] faylyd: *missed*   [3] unneth: *scarcely*   [4] fay: *faith*   [5] halke: *hiding place*
[6] welt them at his wyll: *did with them as he liked*   [7] fostere: *forester*
[8] lede: *company*

370

'That ye shall mete with good Robyn,
   On lyve yf that he be ;
Or ye come to Notyngham
   With eyen ye shall hym se'.

371

Full hastly our kynge was dyght,
   So were his knyghtes fyve,
Everych of them in monkes wede,
   And hasted them thyder blyve.[1]

373

Our kynge was grete aboue his cole,[2]
   A brode hat on his crowne,
Ryght as he were abbot-lyke,
   They rode up into the towne.

373

Styf botes our kynge had on,
   Forsoth as I you say ;
He rode syngynge to grene wode,
   The covent was clothed in graye.

374

His male hors[3] and his grete somers
   Folowed our kynge behynde,
Tyll they came to grene wode,
   A myle under the lynde.[4]

375

There they met with good Robyn,
   Stondynge on the waye,
And so dyde many a bolde archere,
   For soth as I you say.

376

Robyn toke the kynges hors,
   Hastely in that stede,[5]
And sayd, 'Syr abbot, by your leve,
   A whyle ye must abyde.

377

'We be yemen of this foreste,
   Under the grene wode tre ;
We lyve by our kynges dere,
   Other shyft have not we,[6]

378

'And ye have chyrches and rentes both,
   And gold full grete plente,
Gyve us some of your spendynge,
   For saynt charyte.'

379

Than bespake our cumly kynge,
   Anone than sayd he,
'I brought no more to grene wode
   But forty pounde with me.

380

'I have layne at Notyngham
   This fourtynyght with our kynge,
And spent I have full moche good
   On many a grete lordynge.

381

'And I have but forty pounde,
   No more than have I me :
But yf I had an hondred pounde,
   I wolde vouch it safe on the'.

382

Robyn toke the forty pounde,
   And departed it in two partye ;
Halfendell he gave his mery men,
   And bad them mery to be.

383

Full curteysly Robyn gan say,
   'Syr, have this for your spendyng :
We shall mete another day'.
   'Gramercy', than sayd our kynge.

---

[1] blyve: *quickly*   [2] cole: *cowl*   [3] male hors: *baggage horse*   [4] lynde: *trees*
[5] stede: *place*   [6] Supplied from C.

384
'But well the greteth Edwarde, our kynge,
  And sent to the his seale,
And byddeth the com to Notyngham,
  Both to mete and mele.'[1]

385
He toke out the brode targe,[2]
  And sone he lete hym se ;
Robyn coud his courteysy,
  And set hym on his kne.

386
'I love no man in all the worlde
  So well as I do my kynge ;
Welcome is my lordes seale ;
  And, monke, for thy tydynge.

387
'Syr abbot, for thy tydynges,
  To day thou shalt dyne with me,
For the love of my kynge,
  Under my trystell tre.'

388
Forth he lad our comly kynge
  Full fayre by the honde ;
Many a dere there was slayne,
  And full fast dyghtande.[3]

389
Robyn toke a full grete horne,
  And loude he gan blowe ;
Seven score of wyght yonge men
  Came redy on a rowe.

390
All they kneled on theyr kne,
  Full fayre before Robyn ;
The kynge sayd hym selfe untyll,
  And swore by Saynt Austyn,[4]

391
'Here is a wonder semely syght
  Me thynketh, by Goddes pyne,[5]
His men are more at his byddynge
  Then my men be at myn.'

392
Full hastly was theyr dyner idyght,
  And thereto gan they gone ;
They served our kynge with al theyr myght,
  Both Robyn and Lytell Johan.

393
Anone before our kynge was set
  The fatte venyson,
The good whyte brede, the good rede wyne,
  And thereto the fyne ale and browne.

394
'Make good chere,' said Robyn,
  'Abbot, for charyte,
And for this ylke tydynge,
  Blyssed mote thou be.

395
'Now shalte thou se what lyfe we lede,
  Or thou hens wende ;
Than thou may enfourme our kynge,
  Whan ye togyder lende.'[6]

396
Up they sterte all in hast,
  Theyr bowes were smartly bent ;
Our kynge was never so sore agast,
  He wende to have be shent.[7]

397
Two yerdes[8] there were up set,
  Thereto gan they gange ;
By fyfty pase, our kynge sayd,
  The merkes were to longe.

---

[1] i.e. to unstinted hospitality (Ritson, 1846, p. 51)
[2] targe: *seal*. The usual meaning is a shield.
[3] dyghtande: *prepared*   [4] Saynt Austyn: *St Augustine*   [5] pyne: *pain*
[6] lende: *dwell*   [7] shent: *hurt*   [8] yerdes: *rods*

398

On every syde a rose garlonde,[1]
  They shot under the lyne :
'Who so fayleth of the rose garlonde,' sayd
    Robyn,
  'His takyll he shall tyne,[2]

399

'And yelde it to his mayster,
  Be it never so fyne ;
For no man wyll I spare,
  So drynke I ale or wyne,

400

'And bere a buffet on his hede
  I wys ryght all bare' ;
And all that fell in Robyns lote
  He smote them wonder sare.

401

Twyse Robyn shot aboute,
  And ever he cleved the wande,
And so dyde good Gylberte
  With the good Whyte Hande.[3]

402

Lytell Johan and good Scathelocke,
  For nothynge wolde they spare ;
When they fayled of the garlonde
  Robyn smote them full sore.

403

At the last shot that Robyn shot,
  For all his frendes fare,
Yet he fayled of the garlonde
  Thre fyngers and mare.

404

Then bespake good Gylberte,
  And thus he gan say :
'Mayster', he sayd, 'your takyll is lost,
  Stande forth and take your pay.'

405

'If it be so,' sayd Robyn,
  'That may no better be,
Syr abbot, I delyver the myn arowe,
  I pray the, syr, serve thou me.'

406

'It falleth not for myn ordre,' sayd our
    kynge,
  'Robyn, by thy leve,
For to smyte no good yeman,
  For doute I sholde hym greve.'

407

'Smyte on boldely,' sayd Robyn,
  'I give the large leve'.
Anone our kynge, with that worde
  He folde up his sleve,

408

And sych a buffet he gave Robyn,
  To grounde he yede[4] *full nere :*
'I make myn avowe to God,' sayd Robyn,
  'Thou arte a stalworthe frere.

409

'There is pith in thyn arme,' sayd Robyn,
  'I trowe thou canst well shete'.
Thus our kynge and Robyn Hode
  Togeder gan they met.

410

Robyn behelde our comly kynge
  Wystly[5] *in the face,*
So dyde Syr Rycharde at the Le,
  And kneled downe in that place.

411

And so dyde all the wylde outlawes,
  Whan they se them knele :
'My lorde the kynge of Englonde,
  Now I knowe you well'.

---

[1] A garland (probably an extemporized ring of twigs) seems to have been attached to the two 'yerdes': arrows shot outside the garland would be reckoned failures (Child V, 370).
[2] tyne: *forfeit*
[3] See stanza 292 for an earlier reference to Gylberte. C has 'lilly' for 'good'
[4] yede: *went*   [5] wystly: *intently*

412
'Mercy then, Robyn,' sayd our kynge,
    'Under your trystyll tre,
Of thy goodnesse and thy grace,
    For my men and me!'

413
'Yes, for God,' sayd Robyn,
    'And also God me save,
I aske mercy, my lorde the kynge,
    And for my men I crave.'

414
'Yes, for God,' than sayd our kynge,
    'And thereto sent I me,
With that thou leve the grene wode,
    And all thy company;

415
'And come home, syr, to my courte,
    And there dwell with me.'
'I make myn avowe to God,' sayd Robyn,
    'And ryght so shall it be.

416
'I wyll come to your courte,
    Your servyse for to se,
And brynge with me of my men
    Seven score and thre.

417
'But me lyke well your servyse,
    I wyll come agayne full soone,
And shote at the donne[1] dere,
    As I am wonte to done.'

The Eighth Fytte

418
'Haste thou ony grene cloth,' sayd our
        kynge,
    'That thou wylte sell nowe to me?'
'Ye, for God,' sayd Robyn,
    'Thyrty yerdes and thre.'

419
'Robyn,' sayd our kynge,
    'Now pray I the,
Sell me some of that cloth,
    To me and my meyne.'[2]

420
'Yes, for God,' then sayd Robyn,;
    'Or elles I were a fole;
Another day ye wyll me clothe,
    I trowe, ayenst the Yole.'[3]

421
The kynge kest of his cole[4] then,
    A grene garment he dyde on,
And every knyght had so i wys.
    Another had full sone.

422
Whan they were clothed in Lyncolne
        grene,
    They keste away theyr graye,
'Now we shall to Notyngham,'
    All thus our kynge gan say.

423
Their bowes bente and forth they went,
    Shotynge all in fere,
Towarde the towne of Notyngham,
    Outlawes as they were.

[1] donne: *brown*   [2] meyne: *retinue*
[3] i.e. 'provide me with a livery at Christmas'
[4] kest of his cole: *cast off his cowl*

424

Our kynge and Robyn rode togyder
 For soth as I you say,
And they shote plucke buffet,[1]
 As they went by the way.

425

And many a buffet our kynge wan,[2]
 Of Robyn Hode that day :
And nothynge spared good Robyn
 Our kynge in his pay.

426

'So God me helpe,' sayd our kynge,
 'Thy game is nought to lere,[3]
I sholde not get a shote of the,
 Though I shote all this yere.'

427

All the people of Notyngham
 They stode and behelde,
They sawe nothynge but mantels of grene
 That covered all the felde.

428

Than every man to other gan say,
 'I drede our kynge be slone ;[4]
Come Robyn Hode to the towne, i wys,
 On lyve he lefte never one.'

429

Full hastly they began to fle,
 Both yemen and knaves,
And olde wyves that myght evyll goo,
 They hypped on theyr staves.[5]

430

The kynge loughe full fast,
 And commaunded theym agayne ;
When they se our comly kynge,
 I wys they were full fayne.[6]

431

They ete and dranke, and made them glad,
 And sange with notes hye,
Than bespake our comly kynge
 To Syr Rycharde at the Lee.

432

He gave hym there his londe agayne,
 A good man he bad hym be.
Robyn thanked our comly kynge,
 And set hym on his kne.

433

Had Robyn dwelled in the kynges courte
 But twelve monethes and thre,
That he had spent an hondred pounde,
 And all his mennes fe.

434

In every place where Robyn came
 Ever more he layde downe,
Both for knyghtes and for squyres,
 To gete hym grete renowne.

435

By than the yere was all agone
 He had no man but twayne,
Lytell Johan and good Scathelocke
 With hym all for to gone.

436

Robyn sawe yonge men shote
 Full fayre upon a day ;
'Alas !' than sayd good Robyn,
 'My welthe is went away.[7]

437

'Somtyme I was an archere good,
 A styffe[8] and eke a stronge ;
I was compted the best archere
 That was in mery Englonde.

---

[1] An archery competition with the forfeit of receiving a 'pluck' or knock for missing the
 target (as in stanzas 400–9 above)
[2] wan: *received* [3] to lere: *to be learnt* [4] slone: *slain*
[5] hypped on theyr staves: *hopped on their crutches* [6] fayne: *pleased*
[7] welthe is went: *wealth is gone* [8] Supplied from P.

438

'Alas!' then sayd good Robyn,
  'Alas and well a woo.'[1]
Yf I dwele lenger with the kynge,
  Sorowe wyll me sloo.'

439

Forth than went Robyn Hode
  Tyll he came to our kynge :
'My lorde the kynge of Englonde,
  Graunte me myn askynge.

440

'I made a chapell in Bernysdale,[2]
  That semely is to se,
It is of Mary Magdaleyne,
  And thereto wolde I be.

441

'I myght never in this seven nyght
  No tyme to slepe ne wynke,
Nother[3] all these seven dayes
  Nother ete ne drynke.

442

'Me longeth sore to Bernysdale,
  I may not be therfro ;
Barefote and wolwarde[4] I have hyght
  Thyder for to go.'

443

'Yf it be so,' than sayd our kynge,
  'It may no better be,
Seven nyght I gyve the leve,[5]
  No lengre, to dwell fro me.'

444

'Grammercy, lorde,' then sayd Robyn,
  And set hym on his kne :
He toke his leve full courteysly,
  To grene wode then went he.

445

Whan he came to grene wode,
  In a mery mornynge,
There he herde the notes small
  Of byrdes mery syngynge.

446

'It is ferre gone,' sayd Robyn,
  'That I was last here ;
Me lyste[6] a lytell for to shote
  At the donne dere.'

447

Robyn slewe a full grete harte ;
  His horne than gan he blow,
That all the outlawes of[7] that forest
  That horne coud they knowe,

448

And gadred them togyder,
  In a lytell throwe.[8]
Seven score of wyght yonge men
  Came redy on[9] a rowe,

449

And fayre dyde of theyr hodes,
  And set them on theyr kne :
'Welcome,' they sayd, 'our[10] mayster,
  Under this grene wode tre.'

450

Robyn dwelled in grene wode
  Twenty yere and two ;
For all drede of Edwarde our kynge,
  Agayne wolde he not goo.

451

Yet he was begyled, i wys,
  Through a wycked woman,
The pryoresse of Kyrkesly, [11]
  That nye was of hys kynne,

---

[1] Supplied from P.   [2] Supplied from D.   [3] P reads 'Nor'
[4] wolwarde: *clothed in wool, next to the skin* (i.e. as a penance)
[5] From this point, only the concluding portion of each line survives in P.
[6] me lyste: *it pleases me*   [7] P. reads 'in'   [8] throwe: *period of time*   [9] P. reads 'in'
[10] P. reads 'dere'   [11] Kyrkesly: presumably *Kirklees Priory near Huddersfield*

452

For the love of a knyght,
  Syr Roger of Donkesly,[1]
That was her owne speciall :
  Full evyll mote they the !

453

They toke togyder theyr counsell
  Robyn Hode for to sle,
And how they myght best do that dede,
  His banis[2] for to be.

454

Than bespake good Robyn,
  In place where as he stode,
'To-morow I muste to Kyrkesly,
  Craftely[3] to be leten blode'.

455

Syr Roger of Donkestere,
  By the pryoresse he lay,
And there they betrayed good Robyn Hode,
  Through theyr false playe.

456

Cryst have mercy on his soule,
  That dyed on the rode !
For he was a good outlawe,
  And dyde pore men moch god.

---

[1] Sir Roger of 'Donkester' in other versions. Cf. the ballad of *Robin Hood's Death* (below pp. 134–6)
[2] banis: *murderers*   [3] craftely: *skilfully*

'Here begynneth a lytell geste': the frontispiece of Wynkyn de Worde's edition of the *Gest of Robin Hood* (Cambridge University Library, Sel. 5. 18).

2

ROBIN HOOD AND THE MONK (Child 119)

Source:
Cambridge University Library, MS. Ff. 5. 48, fos. 128v–135v.

Other Editions:
R. Jamieson, *Popular Ballads and Songs* (Edinburgh, 1806), II, 54–72;
C. H. Hartshorne, *Ancient Metrical Tales* (London, 1829), pp. 179–97;
Ritson, 1832, II, 221–36, Gutch, 1847, II, 7–20; Child, 1888, III,
97–101; Quiller-Couch, 1910, pp. 585–600; Leach, 1955, pp. 340–9;
Faber Book of Ballads (1965), pp. 81–93; *Oxford Book of Ballads* (1969),
pp. 405–19.

'Too much could not be said in praise of this ballad, but nothing need be
said.' (Child, III, 95). Ever since its first publication in the early nineteenth
century, *Robin Hood and the Monk* has held justified pride of place as the
most distinguished and artistically accomplished of all the Robin Hood
ballads. As its central importance to any enquiry into the origins of the Robin
Hood legend has already been discussed at some length,[1] it is perhaps only
necessary to mention here that *Robin Hood and the Monk* has a significance in
English literary history which quite transcends its subject matter. Famous as
the earliest surviving as well as longest (*c.* 2,700 words) Robin Hood ballad,
it has sometimes been argued that it may be the first really 'popular' ballad
of any type in Child's great collection.[2] On the other hand, there are some
grounds for refusing to believe that this poem is a 'ballad' at all. It is highly
unlikely that the 'talkyng of the munke and Robyn Hode' was ever meant to
be sung: it is indeed the supreme example in medieval English literature of
the genre of 'yeoman minstrelsy'. Although *Robin Hood and the Monk* shows
interesting anticipations of later ballad formulae, particularly in its use of
incantatory repetition and a 'leaping and lingering' technique,[3] its literary
style as well as its general approach to its subject are highly derivative from
the traditions of medieval metrical romance. Here we can see, as nowhere

[1] See above, pp. 9–10.
[2] E.g., by Chambers, *English Literature at the Close of the Middle Ages*, p. 153.
[3] See especially stanzas 21–22, 47–48, 54–55 below, and the comments by Fowler,
Literary History of the Popular Ballad, pp. 81–3.

else, the 'traditional English ballad' at the very point of birth.

It is therefore highly appropriate that the unique copy of *Robin Hood and the Monk* (a title first given to the piece in the 1832 edition of Ritson's *Robin Hood*) should be found in a Cambridge University manuscript which contains, among its very miscellaneous contents, several examples of metrical narrative. The manuscript includes the well-known *King Edward and the Shepherd*, a chivalric burlesque entitled *The Turnament of Tottenham*, a courtly debate on the worth of women by *The Clerk and the Nightingale*, as well as many explicitly devotional and didactic pieces—including even a Latin prayer '*contra fures et latrones*'. Of the two somewhat different explanations of the collection put forward by Professor Fowler—that the manuscript 'served primarily as a priest's source book' and that 'the man behind the collection may well have been one of that class of minstrel that the author of *Piers the Plowman* praises for having *holy writ ay in his mouth*'[1]—the latter seems the more probable. Although the last twenty folios of the manuscript, which include this tale of Robin Hood, are badly stained with damp, most of the text is still quite easily recovered. Occasional illegibility is in fact a less serious obstacle to the interpretation of the ballad than two hiatuses (at stanzas 30 and 36) apparently caused by the carelessness of the scribe when copying the text into his manuscript. The hand itself is a very clear cursive one and would appear to date from the period after rather than before *c.* 1450, the date customarily assigned to it. Similarly the vocabulary of the poem, although still not subjected to a thoroughgoing linguistic analysis, seems to suggest a date of composition or re-writing in the late rather than early fifteenth century. Quite why the anonymous and possibly clerical compiler of a heterogeneous collection of generally highly didactic verse and prose should have seen fit to preserve a copy of a tale of Robin Hood must remain something of a mystery. But students of Robin Hood must always be grateful for his catholicity of taste.

A probable, although of course unprovable, implication of this unique survival is that many other manuscript copies of this and other Robin Hood 'talkyngs' may have been circulating in England during the late fifteenth century. This supposition does indeed receive some slight support from the survival on a stray fifteenth-century manuscript leaf, now among the Bagford Ballads in the British Library, of stanzas 69[3]–72 and 77[2]–80[2] of the following 'ballad'.[2] But it is of course entirely impossible to know exactly how popular *Robin Hood and the Monk* really was in the later middle ages. It certainly failed to take a place in the standard, and much less enterprising, repertoire of sung Robin Hood ballads of the sixteenth and seventeenth centuries.

---

[1] Fowler, pp. 80–1.

[2] Printed in *Roxburghe Ballads*, VIII, part 2, 538, and collated with the Cambridge University Library MS. Ff. 5. 48. text by Child (III, 101). As the textual variations are of only minor significance, they have been ignored in this edition.

Although occasionally noticed by early antiquaries, its real importance was not appreciated until Hartshorne somewhat diffidently transcribed it for inclusion in his collection of metrical verse in 1829.[1] Only then was it possible to see how many of the most famous themes within the Robin Hood legend—the outlaw's devotion to the Virgin Mary, his strangely turbulent relationship with Little John, and many others—must have owed their early popularity to a medieval literary genre more simple but rather more effective than the lengthy *Gest*. Here is a tale of Robin Hood which audiences of the late fifteenth century must have actually heard, an invaluable survival of the period before the transition from script to print.

1

In somer, when the shawes be sheyne,[2]
  And leves be large and long,
Hit is full mery in feyre foreste
  To here the foulys song.

2

To se the dere draw to the dale,
  And leve the hilles hee,[3]
And shadow hem in the leves grene,
  Under the grene wode tre.

3

Hit befel on Whitson(tide),[4]
  Erly in a May mornyng,
The sun up feyre can shyne,
  And the briddis mery can syng.

4

'This is a mery mornyng,' seid Litull
    John,
  'Be hym that dyed on tre;[5]
A more mery man then I am one
  Lyves not in Cristiante.

5

'Pluk up thi hert, my dere mayster,'
  Litull John can sey,
'And thynk hit is a full fayre tyme
  In a mornyng of May.'

6

Ye[a], on thyng greves me,' seid Robyn,
  'And does my hert mych woo;
That I may not no solem day
  To mas nor matyns goo.

7

'Hit is a fourtnet and more,' seid h[e],
  'Syn I my savyour see;
To day wil I to Notyngham,' seid
    Robyn,
  'With the myght of mylde Marye.'

8

Then spake Moche, the mylner sun,
  Ever more wel hym betyde!
'Take twelve of thi wyght yemen,[6]
  Well weppynd, be thi side.
Such on wolde thi selfe slon,
  That twelve dar not abyde.'[7]

---

[1] Gutch, II, 2–3; Hartshorne, *Ancient Metrical Tales*, p. xvii.
[2] shawes be sheyne: *woods are bright* Cf. the opening lines of *Robin Hood and Guy of Gisborne, Robin Hood and the Potter, Robin Hood and the Curtal Friar* and *The Noble Fisherman* for varied treatments of the conventional seasonal *incipit*, praising greenwood leaves in spring or summer and widely used in other types of medieval poetry.
[3] hee: *high*   [4] -tide: no longer legible   [5] hym. . .tre: *Christ*
[6] wyght yemen: *sturdy yeomen*
[7] Such. . . abyde: *he who would kill yourself will not dare face those twelve*

9

'Off all my mery men,' seid Robyn,
 'Be my feith I wil none have,
But Litull John shall beyre my bow,
 Til that me list[1] to drawe.'

10

'Thou shall beyre thin own,' seid Litull
 Jon,
 'Maister, and I wyl beyre myne,
And we well shete a peny,'[2] seid Litull
 Jon,
 'Under the grene wode lyne.'[3]

11

'I wil not shete a peny,' seyd Robyn
 Hode,
 'In feith, Litull John, with the,
But ever for one as thou shetis,' seide
 Robyn,
 'In feith I holde[4] the thre.'

12

Thus shet thei forth, these yemen too,
 Bothe at buske and brome,[5]
Til Litull John wan of his maister
 Five shillings to hose and shone.[6]

13

A ferly[7] strife fel them betwene,
 As they went bi the wey;
Litull John seid he had won five
 shillings,
 And Robyn Hode seid schortly nay.

14

With that Robyn Hode lyed Litul Jon,[8]
 And smote hym with his hande;
Litul Jon waxed wroth therwith,
 And pulled out his bright bronde.[9]

15

'Were thou not my maister,' seid Litul
 John,
 'Thou shuldis by hit ful sore;
Get the a man wher thou wil[t],
 For thou getis me no more.'

16

Then Robyn goes to Notyngham,
 Hym selfe mornyng[10] allone,
And Litull John to mery Scherwode,
 The pathes he knew ilkone.[11]

17

Whan Robyn came to Notyngham,
 Sertenly withouten layn,[12]
He prayed to God and myld Mary
 To bryng hym out save agayn.

18

He gos in to Seynt Mary chirch,
 And kneled down before the rode;
Alle that ever were the church within
 Beheld wel Robyn Hode.

19

Beside hym stode a gret-hedid munke,
 I pray to God woo he be!
Fful sone he knew gode Robyn,
 As sone as he hym se.

---

[1] that me list: *it pleases me*
[2] shete a peny: *shoot for a penny-stake*
[3] lyne: *linden* [4] holde: *wager*
[5] buske and brome: *brush and broom* (the targets)
[6] to hose and shone: *for stockings and shoes*
[7] ferly: *wondrous* The 'ferly' theme of Robin's bitter quarrel with Little John recurs in *Robin Hood and Guy of Gisborne* (below, p. 142); and in *Robin Hood's Death* (below, p. 135) the outlaw leader's wrath is directed against Will Scarlett.
[8] lyed Litul Jon: *called Little John a liar* (lyed is crossed out in the MS)
[9] bronde: *sword* [10] mornyng: *sorrowing* [11] ilkone: *every one* [12] layn: *disguise*

20

Out at the durre he ran,
  Fful sone and anon;
Alle the gatis of Notyngham
  He made to be sparred[1] everychon.

21

'Rise up,' he seid, 'thou prowde schereff,
  Buske the and make the bowne;[2]
I have spyed the kynggis felon,
  Ffor sothe he is in this town.

22

'I have spyed the false felon,
  As he stondis at his masse,
Hit is long of the,' seid the munke,
  'And ever he fro us passe.[3]

23

'This traytur name is Robyn Hode,
  Under the grene wode lynde;
He robbyt me onys of a hundred pound,
  Hit shalle never out of my mynde.'[4]

24

Up then rose this prowd schereff,
  And radly made hym yare;[5]
Many was the moder son
  To the kyrk with hym can fare.

25

In at the durres thei throly thrast,[6]
  With staves ful gode wone;[7]

'Alas, alas!' seid Robyn Hode,
  'Now mysse I Litull John.'

26

But Robyn toke out a too-hond sworde,[8]
  That hangit down be his kne;
Ther as the schereff and his men stode thyckust,
  Thedurwarde wolde he.

27

Thryes thorow at them he ran,
  [As][9] for sothe as I yow sey,
And woundyt mony a moder son,
  And twelve he slew that day.

28

His sworde upon the schireff hed
  Sertanly he brake in too;
'The smyth that the made,' seid Robyn,
  'I pray to God wyrke hym woo!

29

'Ffor now am I weppynlesse,' seid Robyn,
  'Alasse! agayn' my wyll;
But if[10] I may fle these traytors fro,
  I wot thei wil me kyll.'

30

Robyn . . . .(?) churche . . . . ran,[11]
  Thro out hem everilkon.
. . . .

---

[1] sparred: *barred*
[2] Buske . . . bowne: *prepare yourself and get ready* (cf. *Robin Hood and Guy of Gisborne*, stanza 5).
[3] Hit . . . passe: *It is your fault if he ever escapes from us*
[4] Robin's monastic victim in the *Gest* (stanzas 205–260)—to whose tale there may be an allusion here—was deprived of more than £800.
[5] radly . . . yare: *quickly prepared himself*
[6] throly thrast: *pushed eagerly through*   [7] gode wone: *plenty*
[8] too-hond sword: *a large sword that needed both hands to wield*
[9] a short illegible word in the MS   [10] But if: *unless*
[11] Except for the first and last words, this line is rendered almost completely illegible by damp. Professor Skeat's reading of 'Robyn into the churche ran' (accepted by Child, III, 98, 101) is certainly not completely correct and contradicts the logic of the situation which demands that Robin should run *out* of the church.

31

Sum fel in swonyng as thei were dede,[1]
  And lay stil as any stone;
Non of theym wer in her mynde
  But only Litull Jon.

32

'Let be your rule,'[2] seid Litull Jon,
  'Ffor his luf that dyed on tre;
Ye that shulde be dughty[3] men
  Het is gret shame to se.

33

'Oure maister has bene hard bystode[4]
  And yet scapyd away;
Pluk up your hertis, and leve this mone,
  And harkyn what I shal say.

34

'He has servyd Oure Lady many a day,
  And yet wil, securly;
Therfor I trust in Hir specialy;
  No wyckud deth shal he dye.

35

'Therfor be glad,' seid Litul John,
  'And let this mournyng be;
And I shal be the munkis gyde,[5]
  With the myght of mylde Mary.'

36

[Then spake Moche, the mylner son,
  'We will go, but we too,'
'And I mete hym,' seid Litul John,
  I trust to wyrke hym woo.][6]

37

'Loke that ye kepe wel oure tristil tre,[7]
  Under the leves smale,
And spare non of this venyson,
  That gose in thys vale.'

38

Fforthe then went these yemen too,
  Litul John and Moche on fere,[8]
And lokid on Moch emys hows[9]
  The hye way lay full nere.

39

Litul John stode at a wyndow in the
    mornyng,
  And lokid forth at a stage;[10]
He was war wher the munke came
    ridyng,
  And with hym a litul page.

40

'Be my feith,' seid Litul John to Moch,
  'I can the tel tithyngus[11] gode;
I se wher the munke cumys rydyng,
  I know hym be his wyde hode.'

41

They went in to the way, these yemen
    bothe,
  As curtes men and hende;[12]
Thei spyrred[13] tithyngus at the munke,
  As they hade bene his frende.

---

[1] This sudden transition to Sherwood Forest where Robin's men are lamenting the news of his capture is only explicable in terms of the omission of a quite lengthy passage between stanzas 30 and 31 (at the foot of fo. 130v. and the head of fo. 131r. respectively).
[2] rule: *noisy wailing*   [3] dughty: *doughty, valiant*   [4] bystode: *beset*
[5] be . . . gyde: *take care of* (the outlaws already know that the monk had been dispatched to the king with news of Robin's capture—see stanza 51)
[6] The most plausible reconstruction of an apparently muddled and certainly incomplete stanza: the MS. reads

  And I mete hym, seid Litul John,
    We will go but we too.

[7] tristil tre: *trysting tree* (cf. below, pp. 130, 267)   [8] on fere: *together*
[9] emys hows: *uncle's house*   [10] at a stage: *from an upper room*
[11] tithyngus: *tidings*   [12] hende: *gracious*   [13] spyrred: *asked*

42

'Ffro whens come ye?' seid Litull Jon,
　'Tel us tithyngus, I yow pray,
Off a false owtlay [callid Robyn Hode],[1]
　Was takyn yisterday.

43

'He robbyt me and my felowes bothe
　Of twenti marke in serten;
If that false owtlay be takyn,
　Ffor sothe we wolde be fayn.[2]

44

'So did he me,' seid the munke,
　'Of a hundred pound and more;
I layde furst hande hym apon,
　Ye may thonke me therfore.'

45

'I pray God thanke you,' seid Litull
　John,
　'And we wil when we may;
We wil go with you, with your leve,
　And bryng yow on your way.

46

'Ffor Robyn Hode hase many a wilde
　felow,
　I tell you in certen;
If thei wist ye rode this way,
　In feith ye shulde be slayn.'

47

As thei went talking be the way,
　The munke and Litull John,
John toke the munkis horse be the hede,
　Fful sone and anon.

48

Johne toke the munkis horse be the hed,
　Ffor sothe as I yow say;
So did Much the litull page,
　Ffor he shulde not scape away.

49

Be the golett[3] of the hode
　John pulled the munke down;
John was nothyng of hym agast,[4]
　He lete hym falle on his crown.

50

Litull John was so[5] agrevyd,
　And drew owt his swerde in hye;[6]
This munke saw he shulde be ded,
　Lowd mercy can[7] he crye.

51

'He was my maister,' seid Litull John,
　'That thou hase browght in bale;[8]
Shalle you never cum at our kyng,
　Ffor to telle hym tale.'

52

John smote of the munkis hed,
　No longer wolde he dwell;[9]
So did Moch the litull page,
　Ffor ferd lest he wold tell.

53

Ther their beryed hem bothe,
　In nouther mosse nor lyng,[10]
And Litull John and Much in fere[11]
　Bare the letturs to oure kyng.

54

. . . .
　He knelid down upon his kne:
'God yow save, my lege lorde,
　Ihesus yow save and se!'

55

'God yow save, my lege king!'
　To speke John was full bolde;
He gaf hym the letturs in his hond,
　The kyng did hit unfold.

---

[1] callid Robyn Hode, *not in the MS., probably ought to be inserted here*　　[2] fayn: *glad*
[3] golett: *throat*　　[4] of hym agast: *concerned about him*　　[5] so: *probably should read 'sore'*
[6] hye: *haste*　　[7] can: *gan, began*　　[8] bale: *harm*　　[9] dwell: *wait*
[10] nouther mosse nor lyng: *neither bog nor heath*　　[11] in fere: *together*

56

The kyng red the letturs anon,
And seid, 'So mot I the,[1]
Ther was never yoman in mery Ingland
I longut so sore to se.

57

'Where is the munke that these shuld
have brought?'
Oure kyng can say;
'Be my trouth,' seid Litull John,
'He dyed after[2] the way.'

58

The kyng gaf Moch and Litul Jon
Twenti pound in sertan,
And made theim yemen of the crown,
And bade theim go agayn.

59

He gaf John the seel in hand,
The schereff for to bere,
To bryng Robyn hym to,
And no man do hym dere.[3]

60

John toke his leve at oure kyng,
The sothe as I yow say;
The next[4] way to Notyngham
To take, he yede[5] the way.

61

Whan John came to Notyngham
The gatis were sparred[6] ychon;
John callid up the porter,
He answerid sone anon.

62

'What is the cause,' seid Litul Jon,
'Thou sparris the gates so fast?'
'Because of Robyn Hode,' seid (the)
porter,
'In depe prison is cast.

63

'John and Moch and Wyll Scathlock,
Ffor sothe as I yow say,
Thei slew oure men upon our wallis,
And sawten[7] us every day.'

64

Litull John spyrred after the schereff,
And sone he hym fonde;
He oppyned the kingus prive seell,
And gaf hym in his honde.

65

Whan the scheref saw the kyngus seell
He did of his hode anon;
'Where is the munke that bare the
letturs?'
He seid to Litull John.

66

'He is so fayn of[8] hym,' seid Litul John,
'Ffor sothe as I yow say,
He has made hym abot of Westmynster,
A lorde of that abbay.'

67

The scheref made John gode chere,
And gaf hym wyne of the best;
At nyght thei went to her bedde,
And every man to his rest.

68

When the scheref was on slepe,
Dronken of wyne and ale,
Litul John and Moch for sothe
Toke the way unto the jale.

69

Litul John callid up the jayler,
And bade hym rise anon;
He seyd Robyn Hode had brokyn prison,
And out of hit was gon.

---

[1] mot I the: *may I thrive*   [2] after: *back on*   [3] dere: *injury*   [4] next: *nearest*
[5] yede: *went*   [6] sparred: *barred*   [7] sawten: *assaulted*   [8] fayn of: *fond of, pleased with*

70

The porter rose anon sertan,
  As sone as he herd John calle;
Litul John was redy with a swerd,
  And bare hym to the walle.

71

'Now wil I be porter,' seid Litul John,
  'And take the keyes in honde.'
He toke the way to Robyn Hode,
  And sone he hym unbonde.

72

He gaf hym a gode swerd in his hond,
  His hed (ther) with for to kepe,
And ther as the walle was lowyst
  Anon down can thei lepe.

73

Be that the cok began to crow,
  The day began to spryng;
The scheref fond the jaylier ded,
  The comyn bell[1] made he ryng.

74

He made a crye[2] thoroowt al the tow[n],
  Wheder he be yoman or knave,
That cowthe[3] bryng hym Robyn Hode,
  His warison[4] he shuld have.

75

'Ffor I dar never,' said the scheref,
  'Cum before oure kyng;
Ffor if I do, I wot serten
  Ffor sothe he wil me heng.'

76

The scheref made to seke Notyngham,
  Both be strete and stye,[5]
And Robyn was in mery Scherwode,
  As light[6] as lef on lynde.[7]

77

Then bespake gode Litull John,
  To Robyn Hode can he say,
'I have done the a gode turne for an
    evyll,
  Quyte[8] the whan thou may.

78

'I have done the a gode turne,' seid
    Litull John,
  'Ffor sothe as I yow say;
I have brought the under grene-wode
    lyne;[7]
  Ffare wel, and have gode day.'

79

'Nay, be my trouth,' seid Robyn Hode,
  'So shall hit never be;
I make the maister,' seid Robyn Hode,
  'Off alle my men and me.'

80

'Nay, be my trouth,' seid Litull John,
  'So shalle hit never be;
But lat me be a felow,' seid Litull John,
  'No noder kepe I be.'[9]

81

Thus John gate Robyn Hod out of
    prison,
  Sertan withoutyn layn,[10]
Whan his men saw hym hol and sounde,
  Ffor sothe they were full fayne.

82

They filled in wyne, and made hem glad,
  Under the levys smale,
And yete[11] pastes of venyson,
  That gode was with ale.

83

Than worde came to oure kyng
  How Robyn Hode was gon,
And how the scheref of Notyngham
  Durst never loke hym upon.

---

[1] comyn bell: *town bell*   [2] crye: *proclamation*   [3] cowthe: *could*   [4] warison: *reward*
[5] stye: *alley*   [6] light: *carefree*   [7] lynde, lyne: *linden*   [8] Quyte: *requite, repay*
[9] No . . . be: *nothing else do I care to be*   [10] layn: *disguise*   [11] yete: *ate*

84

Then bespake oure cumly kyng,
 In an angur hye:
'Little John hase begyled the schereff,
 In faith so hase he me.

85

'Litul John has begyled us bothe,
 And that full wel I se;
Or ellis the schereff of Notyngham
 Hye hongut shulde he be.

86

'I made hem yemen of the crowne,
 And gaf hem fee with my hond;
I gaf hem grith[1],' seid oure kyng,
 Thorowout all mery Inglond.

87

'I gaf theym grith,' then seid oure kyng;
 'I say, so mot I the,[2]
Ffor sothe soch a yeman as he is on
 In all Inglond ar not thre.

88

'He is trew to his maister,' seid our
 kyng,
 'I sey, be swete Seynt John,
He lovys better Robyn Hode
 Then he dose us ychon.

89

'Robyn Hode is ever bond to hym,
 Bothe in strete and stalle;[3]
Speke no more of this mater,' seid oure
 kyng,
 'But John has begyled us alle.'

90

Thus endys the talkyng of the munke
 And Robyn Hode I wysse;[4]
God, that is ever a crowned kyng,
 Bryng us all to his blisse!

[1] grith: *pardon*
[2] mot I the: *may I prosper*
[3] I.e. whether travelling (in street) or stationary
[4] I wysse: *i-wysse, indeed*

3

ROBIN HOOD AND THE POTTER (Child 121)

Source:
Cambridge University Library, MS. Ee. 4. 35, fos. 14v–19r.

Other Editions:
Ritson, 1795, I, 81–96; Gutch, 1847, II, 22–35; Child, 1888, III, 109–13; Leach, 1955, pp. 352–60.

'There can be little doubt, but that this ballad may be reckoned the second in point of antiquity of the Robin Hood series' (Gutch, II, 21). Like *Robin Hood and the Monk*, the 'ballad' of *Robin Hood and the Potter* (a title first given to the piece by Ritson) survives in a unique manuscript copy within a volume now in the Cambridge University Library. A comparatively small paper manuscript, of 24 leaves with approximately 30 lines to each page, it appears to have been written throughout in the same clear bastard hand of either the very late fifteenth or, more probably, early sixteenth century. Like the Cambridge University Library manuscript which contains the text of *Robin Hood and the Monk*, it is an anthology compiled on no obvious principle—to serve, one might surmise, the didactic and other purposes of a late medieval clerk. Among the miscellaneous collection of romantic tales and homiletic pieces included in the volume are *The Child and the Shepherd* (fos. 6v–13v) and *The King and the Barker* (fos. 19v–21r). More revealing still is a record, to be found immediately before the text of *Robin Hood and the Potter*, of the 'exspences of fflesche at the mariage of my ladey Margaret, that sche had owt off Eynglonde'. This reference is almost certainly to Margaret Tudor's famous and well-publicized marriage to James IV of Scotland on 8 August 1503 and therefore supports the assertion made by Ritson, when he first published the ballad in 1795, that the manuscript was copied in 'the age of Henry the seventh, that is about the year 1500'.[1] The unusually corrupt

---

[1] Thomas Wright's completely unfounded belief that the MSS. of *Robin Hood and the Monk* and *Robin Hood and the Potter* could be dated to the reigns of Edward II and Henry VI respectively almost deserves to be treated with the same contempt ('the barren production of a poor mind') that he applied to Ritson: T. Wright, *Essays on subjects connected with the literature, popular superstitions and history of England in the Middle Ages* (London, 1846), I, 174, 184, 201.

orthography of the manuscript as well as the many inadvertent repetitions (e.g. in stanzas 74–5 and 80 below) suggest either that the scribe transcribed from his copy-text extremely carelessly or that the latter was an orally transmitted version written down by a semi-literate 'minstrel'. As a result, the following text offers more difficulties to the modern reader than any other item in Robin Hood literature. Some of these difficulties, and in particular the vagaries of spelling, reflect the strong influence of Midland dialectical linguistic forms, but this of course provides no real indication of exactly where and when the story of Robin Hood and the potter may have originated. The reference to 'Went breg' or Wentbridge in stanza 6 is, however, of prime importance in showing that parts of this adventure of Robin Hood had once been deliberately sited in the Barnsdale area as well as at Nottingham itself.[1]

Like *Robin Hood and the Monk*, *Robin Hood and the Potter* will always be one of the few fundamental sources for any attempt to describe both the evolution of the Robin Hood legend and the development of the English popular ballad. There would now seem to be no doubt whatsoever that it was designed to be recited aloud, rather than sung, by a minstrel to an audience of yeomen or would-be yeomen. The direct form of address in the second stanza ('Herkens, god yemen, Comley, corteys, and god') and the final appeal to God to 'saffe all god yemanrey!' deserve, in other words, to be taken at their face value.[2] In several ways indeed, and particularly in its use of an ABAB rhyming pattern within several stanzas,[3] *Robin Hood and the Potter* is closer to the traditions of minstrel style—and further removed from either the common measures or the incremental repetition of the later popular ballad—than is *Robin Hood and the Monk*. Although a much less skilful work of literary composition than the latter, *Robin Hood and the Potter* may however be much more representative of the type of fifteenth-century poem from which the main outlines of the later outlaw legend derived. Robin Hood himself is 'corteys', 'ffre' and devoted to Our Lady in both of these early 'ballads', but his exploits in *Robin Hood and the Potter* are approached in a much more deliberately light-hearted manner than in *Robin Hood and the Monk*. Although the fight between Robin and the potter is presented as a strenuous enough contest, no one is actually killed in the following poem, which is quite devoid of the savage elements in *Robin Hood and the Monk* or *Robin Hood and Guy of Gisborne*. The primary aim of the minstrel who recited the adventure of Robin Hood and the potter was, in other words, apparently to provoke

---

[1] See Introduction, above p. 19.

[2] Note too the minstrel's readiness to break the continuity of his narrative by a direct remark to his audience in the closing couplets of stanzas 30 and 80, as well as the use of the conventional 'literary' seasonal incipit, comparable to that of *Robin Hood and the Monk*.

[3] Stanzas 1, 9–10, 35, 37, 45, 51, 53, 60, 62: see Fowler, *Literary History of the Popular Ballad*, pp. 83–4.

2. 'In schomer when the leves spryng': the opening lines of the only extant copy of *Robi nHood and the Potter*, c. 1500 (reproduced by courtesy of Cambridge University Library. MS. Ee. 4. 35, fo. 14v.)

from his audience a 'lowde lawhyng' similar to that of the sheriff's wife herself in stanza 79.

More specifically, *Robin Hood and the Potter* already combines within its relatively short compass many of the most popular ingredients in the later Tudor and Stuart legend: single and by no means inevitably successful combat with one adversary; dramatic victory in an archery competition; and the inveiglement of a remarkably naive sheriff into the 'ffeyre fforeyst' where he was completely at Robin's mercy. An even more significant feature of *Robin Hood and the Potter* is that it provides the first clear expression of the motif of the greenwood hero in disguise, 'the wonted and simplest expedient of an outlaw mixing among his foes' (Child, III, 109). This theme itself was certainly not a novel one, Robin's disguise as a potter having been anticipated by such earlier heroes of medieval British legend as Hereward the Wake, Eustace the Monk and William Wallace.[1] More interesting is the way in which so many Robin Hood ballads, beginning with *Robin Hood and the Potter*, deliberately refrain from exalting either the valour or the social status of the outlaw leader above those he fights and subsequently impersonates, whether potters, tanners, tinkers, butchers, shepherds or even beggars. Both Robin *and* the potter are categorized as 'yemen' (stanza 16) in the following poem; and it is hard to resist the view that *Robin Hood and the Potter* marks the first surviving stage of a process whereby the outlaw legend was deliberately distorted to flatter the aspirations of the lesser craftsmen of sixteenth and seventeenth-century England. Of the long-term influence of some fifteenth-century version of *Robin Hood and the Potter* there can, in any case, be no doubt: the story told below forms a probable source not only of the play of 'Robin Hood and the Potter' (No. 21 below) but also of the earliest text of the ballad of *Robin Hood and the Butcher* (No. 7).

1

In schomer, when the leves spryng,
  The bloschems on every bowe,
So merey doyt the berdys syng
  Yn wodys merey now.

2

Herkens, god yemen,
  Comley, cortessey,[2] and god,
On of the best that yever bare bou',
  Hes name was Roben Hode.

3

Roben Hood was the yeman's name,
  That was boyt corteys and ffre;
Ffor the loffe of owre ladey,
  All wemen werschep[yd] ye [he].

4

Bot as the god yeman stod on a day,
  Among hes mery maney,[3]
He was ware of a prowd potter,
  Cam dryfyng owyr the lefe [ley].

---

[1] Keen, *Outlaws*, pp. 18–19, 23–4, 56, 73; Child, III, 109.

[2] cortessey: a corruption of *corteys, courteous*

[3] maney: *meny, followers*

5

'Yonder comet a prod potter,' s[e]yde
  Roben,
  'That long hayt hantyd this wey;
He was never so corteys a man
  On peney of pawage[1] to pay.'

6

'Y met hem bot at Went breg,' s[e]yde
  Lytyll John,
  'And therefore yeffell mot he the![2]
Seche thre strokes he me gafe,
  Yet yey cleffe by my seydys.[3]

7

'Y ley forty shillings,' seyde Lytyll
  John,
  'To pay het thes same day,
Ther ys nat a man among hys [us] all
  A wed schall make hem leffe.'[4]

8

'Here ys forty shillings,' seyde Roben,
  'More, and thow dar say,
That y schall make that prowde potter,
  A wed to me schall he ley.'

9

There thes money they leyde,
  They toke het a yeman to kepe;
Roben beffore the potter he breyde,[5]
  A[nd] bad hem stond stell.

10

Handys apon hes hors he leyde,
  And bad the potter stonde foll stell;
The potter schorteley to hem seyde,
  'Ffelow, what ys they well?'

11

'All thes thre yer, and more, potter,' he
  seyde,
  'Thow hast hantyd thes wey,
Yet were tow never so cortys a man
  On peney[6] of pavage to pay.'

12

'What ys they name,' seyde the potter,
  'Ffor pavage thow aske of me?'
'Roben Hod ys mey name,
  A wed schall thow leffe me.'

13

'Wed well y non leffe,' seyde the potter,
  'Nor pavag well y non pay;
Awey they honde ffro mey hors!
  Y well the tene eyls, be mey ffay.'[7]

14

The potter to hes cart he went,
  He was not to seke;[8]
A god to-hande staffe therowt he hent,[9]
  Beffore Roben he leppyd.

15

Roben howt with a swerd bent,
  A bokeler en hes honde;
The potter to Roben he went,
  And seyde, 'Ffelow, let mey hors go.'

16

Togeder then went thes to yemen,
  Het was a god seyt to se;
Thereof low Robyn hes men,[10]
  There they stod onder a tre.

---

[1] pawage: *pavage*, a toll levied on road traffic
[2] yeffell . . . the: *evilly must he prosper*
[3] The text seems corrupt here: 'that my sides are still sore' seems a possible meaning
[4] A . . . leffe: *can force him to pay a fine*   [5] breyde: *rushed*
[6] 1 peney. Numbers are usually given as figures and not as words in the original manuscript
[7] Y . . . ffay: *otherwise I'll do you harm, by my faith*
[8] He . . . seke: *he did not have to search.* 'And teke' *crossed out at the beginning of this line*
[9] hent: *took*   [10] low . . . men: *laughed Robin's men*

17

Leytell John to hes ffelow[s] he seyde,
  'Yend potter well steffeley[1] stonde.'
The potter, with a caward[2] stroke,
  Smot the bokeler owt of hes honde.

18

A[nd] ar Roben meyt get het agen,
  Hes bokeler at hes ffette,
The potter yn the neke hem toke,
  To the gronde sone he yede.[3]

19

That saw Roben hes men,
  As thay stod onder a bow;
'Let us helpe owre master,' seyde Lytell
    John,
  'Yonder potter,' seyde he, '[e]ls well
    hem sclo.'[4]

20

Thes went yemen [yemen went] with
    a breyde,
  To thes [ther] master they cam.
Leytell John to hes mast[er] seyde,
  'Ho haet the wager won?

21

'Schall y haffe yowre forty shillings,'
    seyde Lytl' John,
  'Or ye, master, schall haffe myne?'
'Yeff they were a hundred,' seyde Roben,
  'Y ffeythe, they ben all theyne.'

22

'Het ys ffol leytell cortesey,' seyde the
    potter,
  'As y haffe harde weyse men saye,
Yeffe a pore yeman com drywyng on
    the wey,
  To let hem of hes gorney.'[5]

23

'Be mey trowet, thow seys soyt,'[6]
    seyde Roben,
  'Thow seys god yeme[n]rey;
And thow dreyffe fforthe yevery day,
  Thow schalt never be let ffor me.

24

'Y well prey the, god potter,
  A ffelischepe well thow haffe?
Geffe me they clothyng, and thow
    schalt hafe myne;
  Y well go to Notynggam.'[7]

25

'Y gra[n]t thereto,' seyde the potter,
  'Thow schalt ffeynde me a ffelow
    gode;
Bot thow can sell mey pott[ys] well,
  Come ayen as thow yede.'

26

'Nay, be mey trowt,' seyde Roben,
  'And then y bescro[8] mey hede,
Yeffe y bryng eney pottys ayen,
  And eney weyffe well hem chepe.'[9]

27

Than spake Leytell John,
  And all hes ffelowhes heynd,[10]
'Master, be well ware of the screffe of
    Notynggam,
  Ffor he ys leytell howr ffrende.'

28

'Thorow the helpe of Howr Ladey,
  Ffelowhes, let me a lone;
Heyt war howte,'[11] seyde Roben,
  'To Notynggam well y gon.'[12]

---

[1] steffeley: *staunchly*   [2] caward: a mistake for *acward, back-handed* (cf. below, p. 144)
[3] yede: *went*   [4] sclo: *slo, slay*   [5] let . . . gorney: *hinder him in his journey*
[6] Be . . . soyt: *by my troth, you speak truth*
[7] In the MS., stanza 29 below is inserted here—out of narrative sequence
[8] bescro: *beshrew, curse*   [9] chepe: *buy*   [10] heynd: *friendly*
[11] Heyt war howte: ? *Let my horse go on* (both 'Heyt' and 'war-oute' were terms used in
    riding)
[12] For an alternative arrangement of these four lines (hardly necessary), see Child III, 111

29

Robyn went to Notynggam,
  Thes pottys ffor to sell;
The potter abode with Robens men,
  Ther he ffered not eylle.

30

Tho Roben droffe on hes wey,
  So merey ower the londe:
Her es more, and affter ys to saye,
  The best ys be heynde.[1]

31

When Roben cam to Notynggam,
  The soyt yef y scholde saye,[2]
He set op hes hors anon,
  And gaffe hem hotys[3] and haye.

32

Yn the medys[4] of the towne,
  There he schowed hes ware;
'Pottys! pottys!' he gan crey foll sone,
  'Haffe hansell ffor the mare!'[5]

33

Ffoll effen agenest the screffeys gate
  Schowed he hes chaffare;[6]
Weyffes and wedowes abowt hem drow,
  And chepyd ffast of hes ware.

34

Yet, 'Pottys, gret chepe!' creyed Robyn,
  'Y loffe yeffell thes to stonde;'[7]
And all that say[8] hem sell
  Seyde he had be no potter long.

35

The pottys that were werthe pens ffeyffe,
  He solde tham ffor pens thre;
Preveley[9] seyde man and weyffe,
  'Ywnder potter schall never the.'[10]

36

Thos Roben solde ffoll ffast,
  Tell he had pottys bot ffeyffe;
Op he hem toke of hes car'[11]
  And sende hem to the screffeys weyffe.

37

Thereof sche was ffoll ffayne,[12]
  'Gere amarsey'[13] seyde sche' than;
'When ye com to thes contre ayen,
  Y schall bey of the[y] pottys, so mo
   y the.'[14]

38

'Ye schall haffe of the best.' seyde
   Roben,
  And sware be the Treneyte;
Ffoll corteysley he gan hem call,
  'Come deyne with the screfe and me.'

---

[1] be heynd: *still to come* (Ritson assumed that this phrase marked the end of the first of the tale's two fyttes; and it is certainly probable that *Robin Hood and the Potter* was recited in two parts).

[2] The . . . saye: *if I were to tell the truth*

[3] hotys: *oats*

[4] medys: *middle*

[5] Haffe . . . mare: ? *you will have a present the more you buy*

[6] chaffare: *merchandise*

[7] Y . . . stonde: *I hate standing thus* or ? *I would hate not to sell these*

[8] say: *saw*

[9] Preveley: *privately*

[10] the: *thrive*

[11] car': *cart* (a preferable reading to Skeat's and Child's 'care')

[12] ffayne: *pleased*

[13] Gere amarsey: *gramercy, thank you* (Child re-phrased this line as follows: 'Gereamarsey, ser, than seyde sche')

[14] so . . . the: *so may I prosper* ('of the' is crossed out immediately before these words)

39

'God amarsey,' seyde Roben,
  'A Yowre bedyng schall be doyn;[1]
    mayden yn the pottys gan bere,
    Roben and the screffe weyffe fholowed
      anon.

40

Whan Roben yn to the hall cam,
    The screffe sone he met;
The potter cowed of corteysey,[2]
    And sone the screffe he gret.[3]

41

'Lo, ser, what thes potter hayt geffe yow
      and me;
  Ffeyffe pottys smalle and grete!'
'He ys ffoll wellcom,' seyd the screffe;
  'Let os was,[4] and to [go] to mete.'

42

As they sat at her methe,[5]
    With a nobell chere,
To of the screffes men gan speke
    Off a gret wager;

43

Off a schotyng, was god and ffeyne,
    Was made the thother daye,
Off forty shillings, the soyt[6] to saye,
    Who scholde thes wager wen.

44

Styll than sat thes prowde potter,
    Thos than[7] thowt he;
As y am a trow cerstyn[8] man,
    Thes schotyng well y se.

45

Whan they had ffared of the best,
    With bred and ale and weyne,
To the p[b]ottys the made them prest,[9]
    With bowes and boltyt[s] ffoll ffeyne.

46

The screffes men schot ffoll ffast,
    As archares that weren godde,
There cam non ner ney the marke
    Bey halffe a god archares bowe.

47

Stell then stod the prowde potter,
    Thos than seyde he;
'And y had a bow, be the rode,[10]
    On schot scholde yow se.'

48

'Thow schall haffe a bow,' seyde the
      screffe,
  'The best that thow well cheys[11] of
      thre;
Thou sen[m]yst a stalward and a
      stronge,
    Asay[12] schalt thow be.'

49

The screffe commandyd a yeman that
      stod hem bey
    Affter bowhes to weynde;[13]
The best bow that the yeman browthe
    Roben set on a stryng.

50

'Now schall y wet and thow be god[14]
    And polle het op to they nere;'[15]
'So God me helpe,' seyde the prowde
      potter,
    'Thys ys bot ryght weke gere.'[16]

---

[1] bedyng . . . doyn: *bidding shall be done*
[2] cowed . . . corteysey: *understood courteous manners*   [3] gret: *greeted, saluted*
[4] os was: *us wash*   [5] methe: *meat*   [6] soyt: *sooth, truth*   [7] Thos than: *thus then*
[8] cerstyn: *Christian*   [9] bottys . . . prest: *they made themselves ready for the (archery) butts*
[10] be the rode: *by the Cross*   [11] cheys: *choose*   [12] Asay: *assayed, tried*
[13] Affter . . . weynde: *to go (and search) for bows*
[14] y . . . god: *I know whether you are good*
[15] nere: *ear*   [16] gere: *gear, stuff*

51

To a quequer[1] Roben went,
   A god bolt owthe he toke;
So ney on to the marke he went,
   He ffayled not a fothe.[2]

52

All they schot abowthe agen,
   The screffes men and he;
Off the marke he welde not ffayle,
   He cleffed the preke on thre.[3]

53

The screffes men thowt gret schame
   The potter the mastry wan;
The screffe lowe[4] and made god game,
   And seyde, 'Potter, thow art a man;

54

. . . .
. . . .
Thow art worthey to bere a bowe
   Yn what plas that thow goe.'[5]

55

'Yn mey cart y haffe a bowe,
   'Ffor soyt,' he seyde, 'and that a
     godde;
Yn mey cart ys the bow
   That gaffe me Robyn Hode.'[6]

56

'Knowest thow Robyn Hode?' seyde
   the screffe,
   'Potter, y prey the tell thow me;'
'A hundred torne[7] y haffe schot with
   hem,
   Under hes tortyll-tre.'[8]

57

'Y had lever nar[9] a hundred ponde,'
   seyde the screffe,
   'And sware be the Trenite,
. . . .[10]
That the ffals owtelawe stod be me.'

58

'And ye well do afftyr mey red,'[11] seyde
   the potter,
   'And boldeley go with me,
And to morow, or we het bred,
   Roben Hode well we se.'

59

'Y wel queyt the,' kod the screffe,[12]
   'And swere be God of meythey;'[13]
Schetyng thay left, and hom they went,
   Her scoper was redey deythe.[14]

60

Upon the morow, when het was day,
   He boskyd hem fforthe to reyde;[15]
The potter hes cart fforthe gan ray,[16]
   And wolde not leffe beheynde.

61

He toke leffe of the screffys wyffe,
   And thankyd her of all thyng;
'Dam, ffor mey loffe and ye well thys
   were,[17]
   Y geffe yow here a golde ryng.'

62

'Gramarsey,' seyde the weyffe,
   'Ser, God eylde het the.'[18]
The screffes hart was never so leythe,
   The ffeyre fforeyst to se.

---

[1] quequer: *quiver*   [2] fothe: *foot*

[3] I.e. Robin broke the prick (the wooden marker in the centre of the target) into three pieces. The description of the archery contest here, more detailed than its counterparts in the *Gest*, stanzas 289–95, 397–403, is the most valuable in early Robin Hood literature.

[4] lowe: *laughed*

[5] Child's stanza divisions have been retained here, although there is no break in the MS. or indeed the sense.

[6] MS. reads 'that Robyn gaffe me'   [7] torne: *turns, bouts*

[8] tortyll-tre: a corruption of *trystill* or *trysting tree* (see above, p. 99)

[9] lever nar: *rather than*   [10] No hiatus in the MS   [11] red: *counsel, advice*

[12] Y . . . screffe: '*I will recompense you,*' *quoth the sheriff*

[13] meythey: *for meythe, might*   [14] Her . . . deythe: *Her supper was ready prepared*

[15] He . . . reyde: *He got them ready to ride forth*   [16] gan ray: *began to make ready*

[17] and . . . were: *and if you will wear this*   [18] eylde het the: *requite thee for it*

63

And when he cam yn to the fforeyst,
  Yonder the leffes grene,
Berdys there sange on bowhes prest,[1]
  Het was gret goy[2] to se.

64

'Here het ys merey to be,' seyde Roben,
  'Ffor a man that had hawt[3] to spende;
Be mey horne he [I] schall awet[4]
  Yeff Roben Hode be here.'

65

Roben set hes horne to hes mowthe,
  And blow a blast that was ffoll god;
That herde hes men that there stode,
  Ffer downe yn the wodde.

66

'I her mey master blow,' seyde Leytyll
  John,
. . . .
. . . .
  They ran as they were wode.[5]

67

Whan thay to that master cam,
  Leytell John wold not spare;[6]
'Master, how haffe yow ffare yn
  Notynggam?
How haffe yow solde yowre ware?'

68

'Ye, be mey trowthe, I leyty (*sic : for*
  Little) John,
  Loke thow take no care;

Y haffe browt the screffe of Notynggam,
  Ffor all howre chaffare.'[7]

69

'He ys ffoll wellcom,' seyde Lytyll John,
  'Thes tydyng ys ffoll godde.'
The screffe had lever nar a hundred
    ponde
  He had [never sene Roben Hode].[8]

70

'[Had I] west that befforen,[9]
  At Notynggam when we were,
Thow scholde not com yn ffeyre fforest
  Of all thes thowsande eyre.'[10]

71

'That wot y well,' seyde Roben,
  'Y thanke God that ye be here;
Thereffore schall ye leffe yowre hors
    with hos,[11]
  And all yowre hother gere.'

72

'That ffend I Godys fforbod,'[12]
  kod the screffe,
  'So to lese mey godde;[13]
. . . .
. . . .[14]

73

'Hether ye cam on hors ffoll hey,[15]
  And hom schall ye go on ffote;
And gret well they weyffe at home,
  The woman ys ffoll godde.

---

[1] prest: *freely, with expression*
[2] goy: *joy*   [3] hawt: *aught, anything*   [4] awet: *discover*
[5] wode: *mad* (Child's arrangement of this stanza has been followed: there is no break in the MS)
[6] spare: *pause*   [7] Ffor . . . chaffare: *as merchandise for us all*
[8] These 4 words, and the first 2 of the next stanza, do not occur in the MS, which reads 'He had west that befforen'
[9] west . . . befforen: *known that before*   [10] eyre: *years*
[11] hos: *us*   [12] That . . . fforbod: *? I protest (and) God forbid*
[13] godde: *goods*   [14] Child's stanza arrangement (no break in the MS)
[15] ffoll hey: *at rapid speed*

74

'Y schall her sende a wheyt palffrey,
    Het ambellet be mey ffey,[1]

. . . .
    . . . .[2]

75

'Y schall her sende a wheyt palffrey,
    Het hambellet as the weynde;
Nere[3] ffor the loffe of yowre weyffe,
    Off more sorow scholde yow seyng.'

76

Thes parted Robyn Hode and the
    screffe;
    To Notynggam he toke the waye;
Hes weyffe ffeyre welcomed hem hom,
    And to hem gan sche saye:

77

'Seyr, how haffe yow ffared yn grene
    fforeyst?
    Haffe ye browt Roben hom?'
'Dam, the deyell spede hem, bothe
    bodey and bon;[4]
    Y haffe hade a ffoll gret skorne.'

78

'Of all the god that y haffe lade[5] to grene
    wod,
    He hayt take het ffro me;
All bot thes ffeyre palffrey,
    That he hayt sende to the.'

79

With that sche toke op a lowde
    lawhyng,[6]
    And swhare be hem that deyed on tre,

'Now haffe yow payed ffor all the pottys
    That Roben gaffe to me.

80

'Now ye be com hom to Notynggam,
    Ye schall haffe god ynowe.'[7]
Now speke we of Roben Hode,
    And of the pottyr ondyr the grene
        bowhes.

81

'Potter, what was they pottys worthe
    To Notynggam that y ledde with me?'
'They wer worthe to nobellys,'[8] seyde
    he,
    'So mot y treffe or the;[9]
So cowde y (haffe) had ffor tham,
    And y had be there (there be).'

82

'Thow schalt hafe ten ponde,' seyde
    Roben,
    'Of money ffeyre and ffre;
And yever whan thow comest to grene
    wod,
    Wellcom, potter, to me.'

83

Thes partyd Robyn, the screffe, and the
    potter,
    Ondernethe the grene-wod tre;
God haffe mersey on Roben Hodys
    solle,
    And saffe all god yemanrey!

Expleycyt Robyn Hode

---

[1] Het . . . ffey: *that can amble* (i.e. move at a smooth and easy pace) *by my faith*
[2] Child's stanza arrangement; but, as he points out (III, 114), these two lines probably ought to be deleted, for the scribe repeats them in a corrected form at the beginning of the next stanza.
[3] Nere: *were it not*   [4] bon: *bone*
[5] lade: *led, taken*   [6] lawhyng: *laughing*
[7] This line is inadvertently repeated after 'Now speke we of Roben Hode'
[8] nobellys: *nobles* (gold coins first coined by Edward III and usually current at 6s. 8d. or half a mark)
[9] So . . . the: *so may you or I thrive*

4

ROBIN HOOD'S DEATH (Child 120)

Sources:
A. Percy Folio version: British Library, Additional MS. 27, 879, fos. 9–10; printed in *Bishop Percy's Folio Manuscript*, ed. Hales and Furnivall, I, 53–8, and Child, III, 104–5.
B. Garland version: *The English Archer; or, Robert, Earl of Huntington, Vulgarly call'd Robin Hood. York. Printed by N. Nickson, in Feasegate. Price Fourpence* (c. 1767[1]). (Bodleian Library, Douce F.F. 71, no. 4).

Other Editions of B:
Ritson, 1795, II, 183–7; Evans, 1810, II, 262–5; Gutch, 1847, II, 312–16; Child, 1888, III, 106–7; Quiller-Couch, 1910, pp. 635–9; *Faber Book of Ballads* (1965), pp. 94–6.

First printed by Hales and Furnivall in 1867, the unique A version of the ballad of *Robin Hood's Death* is unquestionably the more valuable to survive. It is therefore particularly regrettable that it should do so in such a deplorably fragmentary state. As approximately a half of each page in this section of the Percy Folio has been torn away, only twenty-seven stanzas of a probable total of more than fifty remained when the manuscript was rescued from complete destruction by Bishop Percy in the early eighteenth century. At three separate sections of the ballad (between stanzas 8 and 9, between stanzas 18 and 19, and at the very end) there are accordingly omissions of such length that it has proved impossible to speculate at all convincingly upon their content. Mutilated though it is, 'Robin Hoode his Death' (the title inserted into the Percy Folio by its seventeenth-century scribe) is more or less completely in agreement with the summary outline of the close of Robin Hood's career provided by the six last stanzas of the *Gest* (see above pp. 111–12). In particular, Robin's two arch-enemies in that poem, 'the pryoresse of Kyrkesly' and 'Syr Roger of Donkesly', reappear in *Robin Hood's Death* as the prioress of Churchlees and the mysterious Red Roger. It is hard to resist the conclusion that the author of the *Gest* was familiar with a late medieval story of Robin Hood's death by treachery substantially similar to that preserved in partial and no doubt modified form by the compiler of the Percy

[1] R. Davies, *Memoir of the York Press* (Westminster, 1868), p. 328.

Folio. Such a suggestion, of course, makes it all the more frustrating that we will never know why the 'old woman' of stanza 8 cursed Robin Hood or what the outlaw hero's last words really were.

Although deservedly famous in its own right,[1] the garland version (B) of *Robin Hood's Death* is inevitably of much less interest to the development of the outlaw legend. Indeed it is questionable whether it had attained its present form much before the middle of the eighteenth century, when it first begins to appear as the final item in collections of Robin Hood songs. Despite its obvious dramatic merits, *Robin Hood's Death* was included in only a small minority of garlands and seems to have been much more popular in the north than the south of England. Most of the surviving copies were printed at York, the version printed below from Nicholas Nickson's edition being one of the earliest and least corrupt. Comparison between this text and that provided by the Percy Folio offers an exceptionally instructive object-lesson in the literary evolution of the English popular ballad. In the late eighteenth-century garlands, *Robin Hood's Death* is not only a shorter but also a much more simplified poem than was the work known to the copyist of the Percy Folio: Will Scarlet, the old woman 'banning Robin Hoode' and Red Roger have all disappeared, together with the doom-laden atmosphere that pervades the whole of the earlier ballad. On the other hand, the author of the chapbook version has introduced into the story of Robin Hood's death two apparently new incidents. It is by the traditional three blasts of his horn that Robin brings Little John to his rescue, a theme common to a great number of popular ballads, including *Robin Hood and the Curtal Friar* (No. 8 below) and *Robin Hood and the Shepherd* (Child 135). Much more striking—and one of the most celebrated episodes in the entire Robin Hood saga—is the dying outlaw's determination to shoot one last arrow to mark the site of his grave; but exactly when this legend began, and whether it preceded or was invented to justify the discovery of a grave of Robin Hood within the Kirklees Estate, remain among the more insoluble of the Robin Hood mysteries.[2]

A. 'Robin Hoode his Death'

1

'I will never eate nor drinke,' Robin
   Hood said,
  'Nor meate will doo me noe good,
Till I have beene att merry Church
   Lees,
  My vaines for to let blood.'

2

'That I reade[3] not,' said Will Scarllett,
  'Master, by the assente of me,
Without halfe a hundred of your best
   bowmen
  You take to goe with yee.

---

[1] For a variant Virginian version, possibly introduced to America by a Pennsylvania settlement of Scotch–Irish, see Bronson, *Traditional Tunes*, III, 18–19.
[2] See below, p. 309; Keen, *Outlaws*, pp. 179–82   [3] reade: *rede, advise*

3

'For there is a good yeoman[1] doth abide
   Will be sure to quarrell with thee,
And if thou have need of us, master,
   In faith we will not flee.'

4

'And thou be feard, thou William
      Scarlett,
   Att home I read thee bee:'
'And you be wrothe, my deare master,
   You shall never heare more of mee.'

5

'For there shall noe man with me goe,
   Nor man with mee ryde,
And Litle John shall be my man,
   And beare my benbow by my side.'

6

'You'st[2] beare your bowe, master, your
      selfe,
   And shoote for a peny with mee:'
'To that I doe assent,' Robin Hood
      sayd,
   'And soe, John, lett it bee.'

7

They two bolde children shotten[3]
      together
   All day theire selfe in ranke,
Untill they came to blacke water,
   And over it laid a planke.

8

Upon it there kneeled an old woman,
   Was banning[4] Robin Hoode;
'Why dost thou bann Robin Hoode?'
      said Robin,
         (*half a page missing*)

9

. . . .
   'To give to Robin Hoode;
Wee weepen for his deare body,
   That this day must be lett bloode.'

10

'The dame prior is my aunts daughter,
   And nie unto my kinne;
I know shee wold me noe harme this
      day,
   For all the world to winne.'

11

Forth then shotten these children two,
   And they did never lin,[5]
Untill they came to merry Churchlees,
   To merry Churchlee with-in.

12

And when they came to merry Church
      Lees,
   They knoced upon a pin;
Upp then rose dame prioresse,
   And lett good Robin in.

13

Then Robin gave to dame prioresse
   Twenty pound in gold,
And bad her spend while that wold last,
   And shee shold have more when shee
      wold.

14

And downe then came dame prioresse,
   Downe she came in that ilke,[6]
With a pair off blood irons[7] in her hands
   Were wrapped all in silke.

---

[1] The 'good yeoman' is presumably Red Roger. However, this reference and the sub-sequent and partly inexplicable quarrel between Robin and Scarlet may (as Child suggested, *Ballads* III, 102) betray the influence on this section of the ballad of some version of *Robin Hood and Guy of Gisborne* (see below, p. 144) and/or *Robin Hood and the Monk* (above, p. 116).

[2] You'st: *you must*   [3] shotten: *went quickly*   [4] banning: *cursing*   [5] lin: *stop*

[6] in that ilke: *at that very time*   [7] blood irons: *lancing knives*

15

'Sett a chaffing-dish to the fyer,' said
 dame prioresse,
 'And stripp thou up thy sleeve:'
I hold him but an unwise man
 That will noe warning leeve.[1]

16

Shee laid the blood irons to Robin
 Hoods vaine,
 Alacke, the more pitye!
And pearct the vaine, and let out the
 bloode,
 That full red was to see.

17

And first it bled, the thicke, thicke
 bloode,
 And afterwards the thinne,
And well then wist good Robin Hoode
 Treason there was within.

18

'What cheere my master?' said Litle
 John;
 'In faith, John, litle goode;'
  (*half a page missing*)

19

'I have upon a gowne of greene,[2]
 Is cut short by my knee,
And in my hand a bright browne brand
 That will well bite of thee.'

20

But forth then of a shot[3] windowe
 Good Robin Hood he could glide;

Red Roger, with a grounding glave,[4]
 Thrust him through the milke white
 side.

21

But Robin was light and nimble of
 foote,
 And thought to abate his pride,
Ffor betwixt his head and his shoulders
 He made a wound full wide.

22

Says, 'Ly there, ly there, Red Roger,
 The doggs they must thee eate;
'For I may have my houzle',[5] he said,
 'For I may both goe and speake.'

23

'Now give me mood,'[6] Robin said to
 Litle John,
 'Give me mood with thy hand;
I trust to God in heaven soe hye,
 My houzle will me bestand.'[7]

24

'Now give me leave, give me leave,
 master,' he said,
 'For Christs love give leave to me,
To set a fier with in this hall,
 And to burne up all Churchlee.'

25

'That I reade not,' said Robin Hoode
 then,
 'Litle John, for it may not be;
If I shold doe any widow hurt, at my
 latter end,
 God,' he said, 'wold blame me;

---

[1] leeve: *believe*

[2] This line is copied into the MS. by Percy: the speaker is presumably Robin Hood, talking to Red Roger outside the room?

[3] shot: *hinged* (cf. p. 262 below)

[4] grounding glave: *sword*

[5] houzle: *housel*; Robin must receive the last sacraments

[6] mood: ? *help*, ? *God, i.e. the sacraments*

[7] me bestand: *serve me well*

26

'But take me upon thy backe, Litle
    John,
  And beare me to yonder streete,
And there make me a full fayre grave,
  Of gravell and of greete.[1]

27

'And sett my bright sword at my head,
  Mine arrowes at my feete,
And lay my vew-bow[2] by my side,
  My met-yard[3] wi . . . . .
    (*half a page missing*)

B. *Robin Hood's death and burial: shewing how*
he was taken ill, and how he went to his
cousin at Kirkley Hall, who let him blood,
which was the cause of his death.

I

When Robin Hood and Little John
  Went over yon bank of broom,
Said Robin Hood to Little John,
  'We have shot for many a pound.

2

'But I am not able to shoot one shot
    more,
  My arrows will not flee;
But I have a cousin lives down below,
  Please God, she will bleed me.'

3

Now Robin is to fair Kirkley gone,
  As fast as he cou'd wen;[4]
But before he came there, as we do hear,
  He was taken very ill.

4

And when that he came to fair Kirkley
    hall,
  He knocked at the ring,
But none was so ready as his cousin
    herself
  For to let bold Robin in.

5

'Will you please to sit down, cousin
    Robin,' she said,
  'And drink some beer with me?'

'No, I will neither eat nor drink,
  Till I blood letted be.'

6

'Well, I have a room, cousin Robin,'
    she said,
  'Which you did never see,
And if you please to walk therein,
  You blood shall letted be.'

7

She took him by the lilly white hand,
  And let him into a private room,
And there she blooded bold Robin
    Hood,
  Whilst one drop of blood would run.

8

She blooded him in the vein of the arm,
  And lock'd him up in a room;
There did he bleed all the live-long day,
  Untill the next day at noon.

9

He then bethought him of a casement
    door,
  Thinking for to be gone;
He was so weak he could not leap,
  Nor he could not get down.

---

[1] greete: *grit*   [2] vew-bow: ? *yew-bow*, altered by Percy to *ben-bow*
[3] met-yard: *measuring yard or rod*, no doubt used by archers to measure the distance to
  their targets (as below, p. 143)
[4] wen: *go*

10

He then bethought him of his bugle
    horn,
  Which hung low down to his knee;
He set his horn unto his mouth,
  And blew out strong[1] blasts three.

11

Then Little John, when hearing him,
  As he sat under the tree,
'I fear my master is near dead,
  He blows so wearily.'

12

Then Little John to fair Kirkley is gone,
  As fast as he could dree;[2]
But when he came to Kirkley-hall,
  He broke locks two or three;

13

Untill he came bold Robin to,
  Then he fell on his knee;
'A boon, a boon;' cries Little John,
  'Master, I beg of thee.'

14

'What is that boon,' quoth Robin Hood,
  'Little John, thou begs of me?'
'It is to burn fair Kirkley-hall,
  And all their nunnery.'

15

'I ne'er hurt fair maid in all my time,
  Nor at my end shall it be;
But give me my bent bow in my hand,
  And my broad arrows I'll let flee.

16

'And where this arrow is taken up,
  There shall my grave digged be.
With verdant sods most neatly put,
  Sweet as the green wood tree.[3]

17

'And lay my bent bow by my side,
  Which was my music sweet,
And make my grave of gravel and green,
  Which is most right and meet.

18

'Let me have length and breadth
    enough,
  With a green sod under my head;
That they may say, when I am dead,
  HERE LIES BOLD ROBIN
    HOOD.'

19

These words they readily granted him,
  Which did bold Robin please;
And there they buried bold Robin Hood,
  Near to the fair Kirkleys.[4]

20

Kirkleys was beautiful of old,
  Like Winifrid's of Wales,
By whose fair well strange cures are
    told
  In legendary tales.[5]

21

Upon his grave was laid a stone,
  Declaring that he dy'd,
And tho' so many years ago,
  Time can't his actions hide.

---

[1] Other garlands read the preferable 'weak' here: see stanza 11[4]

[2] could dree: *was able*

[3] These two lines are inferior to a variant reading found in other garlands: 'Lay me a green sod under my head, And another at my feet'.

[4] The original version of *Robin Hood's Death* B no doubt ended here; the following four stanzas, which include some borrowings from *Robin Hood and the Valiant Knight* (below, p. 186), were obviously added later to establish a link with the epitaph, the last item in a Robin Hood Garland.

[5] Dr Johnson saw people bathing at St Winifred's Well (Holywell in Flintshire) as late as 1774.

22

Thus he that fear'd neither bow nor
   spear
  Was murder'd by letting blood;
And so, loving friends, the story ends,
  Of valiant bold Robin Hood.

23

There is nothing remains but his
   epitaph now,
  Which, reader, here you have,
To this very day, which read you may,
  As it was upon the grave.

Hey down a derry derry down.

*Robin Hood's Epitaph, set on his tomb by
the Prioress of Kirkley Monastry, in Yorkshire.*

Robert Earl of Huntington
Lies under this little stone.
No archer was like him so good:
His wildness nam'd him Robin Hood.
Full thirteen years, and something more,
These no(r)thern parts he vexed sore.
Such out-laws as he and his men
May England never know again!

Robin Hood and the Ballad Monger: a
broadside copy of *Robin Hood and the
Shepherd*, printed at London for John
Andrews, *c.* 1660 (Bodleian Library,
Oxford, Wood MS. 401, leaf 13v.).

ROBIN HOOD AND GUY OF GISBORNE
(Child 118)

Source:
British Library, Additional MS. 27, 879, fos. 129r–130v; printed in
Bishop Percy's Folio Manuscript, ed. Hales and Furnivall, II, 227–37.

Other Editions:
Percy's *Reliques*, 1765, I, 74; Ritson, 1795, I, 114–15; Gutch, 1847, II,
74–83; Child, 1888, III, 91–4; Quiller-Couch, 1910, pp. 575–84;
Leach, 1955, pp. 334–40.

As Bishop Percy noticed when he included *Robin Hood and Guy of Gisborne*
in the first edition (1765) of the *Reliques of Ancient English Poetry*, 'We have
here a ballad of Robin Hood (from the Editor's folio manuscript) which was
never before printed, and carries marks of much greater antiquity than any
of the common popular songs on this subject.' So much may be generally
agreed, despite the impossibility of dating this poem, like the other Robin
Hood ballads in the Percy Folio, at all precisely. The archaic features of much
of the language of *Robin Hood and Guy of Gisborne* together with the remarkable similarity of its first verse to that of *Robin Hood and the Monk* (see page
115 above) make it at least probable that the Percy Folio preserves the substance of a late medieval ballad. Above all, and as Child was the first to
emphasize, the survival of a late fifteenth-century dramatic fragment which
centres on Robin's fight with a knight whom he subsequently beheads and
then impersonates (No. 19 below) leaves no doubt that at least the main
elements of the story of Guy of Gisborne were present before the end of the
middle ages.

This unique copy of the ballad of *Robin Hood and Guy of Gisborne* presents
other difficulties besides that of its original date. As will be seen, the scribe of
the Percy Folio seems to have accidentally omitted several lines between the
second and third lines of the second stanza. We are consequently deprived of
a full knowledge of Robin's dream which foreshadows the later action of the
ballad. Nor does the text in its present state explain how Robin, after the
successful completion of his fight with Guy of Gisborne, could have known
of Little John's capture and the need to rescue him. It is hard not to agree

with Child that the story as it survives in the Percy Folio must have undergone 'considerable derangement' (Child, III, 90.) Nevertheless *Robin Hood
and Guy of Gisborne* remains one of the most important as well as most
intriguing ballads in the Robin Hood canon, not least because of its exceptionally violent tone and concisely dramatic qualities.[1]

1
When shales beene sheene, and shradds
    full fayre,[2]
  And leeves both large and longe,
Itt is merrry, walking in the fayre
    fforrest,
  To heare the small birds singe.

2
The woodweete[3] sang and wold not
    cease,
  Amongst the leaves a lyne;[4]
. . . .[5]
'And it is by two wight[6] yeomen,
  By deare God that I meane.

3
Me thought they did mee beate and
    binde,
  And tooke my bow mee froe;
If I bee Robin a-live in this lande.
  I'le be wrocken[7] on both them towe.'

4
'Sweavens[8] are swift, master,' quoth
    John,
  'As the wind that blowes ore a hill;
Ffor if itt be never soe lowde this night,
  To-morrow it may be still.'

5
'Buske yee, bowne yee,[9] my merry men
    all,
  Ffor John shall goe with mee;
For I'le goe seeke yond wight yeomen,
  In greenwood where the bee.'

6
The cast on their gowne of greene,
  A shooting gone are they,
Untill they came to the merry
    greenwood,
  Where they had gladdest bee;
There were the ware of [a] wight
    yeoman,
  His body leaned to a tree.

7
A sword and a dagger he wore by his
    side,
  Had beene many a mans bane,
And he was cladd in his capull hyde,[10]
  Topp, and tayle, and mayne.

8
'Stand you still, master,' quoth Litle
    John,
  'Under this trusty tree,[11]
And I will goe to yond wight yeoman,
  To know his meaning trulye.'

---

[1] The ballad is well discussed in Keen, *Outlaws*, pp. 118–21.
[2] For shales probably read *shawes*, in which case the line means 'When woods are bright, and twigs full fair'
[3] woodweete: *woodwall*, usually identified with the golden oriole, noted for its singing voice
[4] a lyne: *of lime*
[5] 'there are certainly some lines wanting and we can no where better fix the *hiatus*' (*Bishop Percy's Folio Manuscript*, ed. Hales and Furnivall, II, 228)
[6] wight: *strong*   [7] wrocken: *revenged*   [8] Sweavens: *dreams*
[9] Buske yee, bowne yee: *prepare yourselves and get ready*
[10] Capull hyde: *horse-hide*   [11] trusty tree: *trysting tree* (see above, p. 99)

9

'A, John, by me thou setts noe store,
    And that's a ffarley[1] thinge;
How offt send I my men beffore,
    And tarry my-selfe behinde?

10

'It is noe cunning a knave to ken,
    And a man but heare him speake;
And itt were not for bursting of my
      bowe,
    John, I wold thy head breake.'

11

But often words they breeden ball;[2]
    That parted Robin and John;
John is gone to Barn[e]sdale,
    The gates[3] he knowes eche one.

12

And when hee came to Barnesdale,
    Great heavinesse there hee hadd;
He ffound two of his own fellowes
    Were slaine both in a slade,[4]

13

And Scarlett a ffote flyinge was,
    Over stockes and stone,
For the sheriffe with seven score men
    Fast after him is gone.

14

'Yett one shoote I'le shoote,' sayes
    Litle John,
    'With Crist his might and mayne;
I'le make yond fellow that flyes soe fast
    To be both glad and ffaine.'[5]

15

John bent up a good veiwe bow,[6]
    And ffetteled[7] him to shoote;

The bow was made of a tender boughe,
    And fell downe to his foote.

16

'Woe worth thee, wicked wood!' sayd
    Litle John,
    'That ere thou grew on a tree!
Ffor this day thou art my bale,
    My boote[8] when thou shold bee!'

17

This shoote it was but looselye shott,
    The arrowe flew in vaine,
And it mett one of the sheriffes men;
    Good William a Trent was slaine.[9]

18

It had beene better for William a Trent
    To hange upon a gallowe
Then for to lye in the greenwoode,
    There slaine with an arrowe.

19

And it is sayd, when men be mett,
    Six can doe more then three:
And they have tane Litle John,
    And bound him ffast to a tree.

20

'Thou shalt be drawen by dale and
      downe,' quoth the sheriffe,[10]
    'And hanged hye on a hill:'
'But thou may ffayle,' quoth Litle John,
    'If itt be Christs owne will.'

21

Let us leave talking of Litle John,
    For hee is bound fast to a tree,
And talke of Guy and Robin Hood,
    In the green woode where they bee.

---

[1] ffarley: *marvellous*   [2] ball: *bale, misery*   [3] gates: *ways, routes*   [4] slade: *forest glade*
[5] ffaine: *joyful*   [6] veiwe bow; ? *yew bow* (the first word is partly obliterated in the MS)
[7] ffetteled: *prepared*   [8] boote: *help*
[9] The confusion of sense in this stanza makes it probable that the text hereabouts is corrupt
[10] The last three words appear to have been added to the original in an attempt—no doubt correct—to identify the speaker

22

How these two yeomen together they
	mett,
	Under the leaves of lyne,
To see what marchandise they made
	Even at that same time.

23

'Good morrow, good fellow,' quoth Sir
	Guy;
	'Good morrow, good ffellow,' quoth
	hee;
'Methinkes by this bow thou beares in
	thy hand,
	A good archer thou seems to bee.'

24

'I am wilfull[1] of my way,' quoth Sir
	Guye,
	'And of my morning tyde.'
'I'le lead thee through the wood,' quoth
	Robin,
	'Good ffellow, I'le be thy guide.'

25

'I seeke an outlaw,' quoth Sir Guye,
	'Men call him Robin Hood:
I had rather meet with him upon a day
	Then forty pound of golde.'

26

'If you two mett, itt wold be seene
	whether were better
	Afore yee did part away;
Let us some other pastime find,
	Good ffellow, I thee pray.

27

'Let us some other masteryes[2] make,
	And wee will walke in the woods even;
Wee may chance mee[t] with Robin
	Hoode
	Att some unsett steven.'[3]

28

They cutt them downe the summer
	shroggs[4]
	Which grew both under a bryar,
And sett them three score rood in twinn,
	To shoote the prickes full neare.[5]

29

'Leade on, good ffellow,' sayd Sir Guye,
	'Lead on, I doe bidd thee:'
'Nay, by my faith,' quoth Robin Hood,
	'The leader thou shalt bee.'

30

The first good shoot that Robin ledd,
	Did not shoote an inche the pricke
	ffroe;
Guy was an archer good enoughe,
	But he cold neere shoote soe.

31

The second shoote Sir Guy shott,
	He shott within the garlande;[6]
But Robin Hoode shott it better than
	hee,
	For he clove the good pricke-wande.

32

'God's blessing on thy heart!' sayes
	Guye,
	'Goode ffellow, thy shooting is goode;
For an thy hart be as good as thy hands,
	Thou were better then Robin Hood.

33

'Tell me thy name, good ffellow,' quoth
	Guy,
	'Under the leaves of lyne.'
'Nay, by my faith,' quoth good Robin,
	'Till thou have told me thine.'

---

[1] wilfull: *doubtful*	[2] masteryes: *trials of skill*
[3] unsett steven: *unexpected moment*	[4] shroggs: *shrubs*
[5] The prickes (long thin branches stuck in the ground to shoot at) were thus set at the
	remarkably long range of 60 roods or 330 yards
[6] garlande: *ring on the target within which the mark is set* (see above, p. 108).

34

'I dwell by dale and downe,' quoth
    Guye,
  'And I have done many a curst turne;
And he that calles me by my right name
    Calles me Guye of good Gysborne.'

35

'My dwelling is in the wood,' sayes
    Robin;
  'By thee I set right nought;
My name is Robin Hood of Barnesdale,
    A ffellow thou has long sought.'

36

He that had neither beene a kithe nor
    kin
  Might have seene a full fayre sight,
To see how together these yeomen went,
    With blades both browne[1] and bright.

37

To have seene how these yeomen
    together foug[ht],
  Two howers of a summers day;
Itt was neither Guy nor Robin Hood
    That ffettled them to flye away.

38

Robin was reacheles[2] on a roote,
    And stumbled at that tyde,
And Guy was quicke and nimble
    with-all,
    And hitt him ore the left side.

39

'Ah, deere Lady!' sayd Robin Hoode,
  'Thou art both mother and may!
I thinke it was never mans destinye
    To dye before his day.'

40

Robin thought on Our Lady deere,
    And soone leapt up againe,

And thus he came with an awkwarde
    stroke;
  Good Sir Guy hee has slayne.

41

He tooke Sir Guys head by the hayre,
  And sticked itt on his bowes end:
'Thou hast beene traytor all thy liffe,
    Which thing must have an ende.'

42

Robin pulled forth an Irish kniffe,
  And nicked Sir Guy in the fface,
That hee was never on a woman borne
    Cold tell who Sir Guye was.

43

Saies, 'Lye there, lye there, good Sir
    Guye,
  And with me be not wrothe;
If thou have had the worse stroakes at
    my hand,
    Thou shalt have the better cloathe.'

44

Robin did off his gowne of greene,
  Sir Guy hee did it throwe;[3]
And hee put on that capull-hyde,
    That cladd him topp to toe.

45

'The[4] bowe, the[4] arrowes, and litle
    horne,
  And with me now I'le beare;
Ffor now I will goe to Barnsdale,
    To see how my men doe ffare.'

46

Robin sett Guyes horne to his mouth;
  A lowd blast in it he did blow;
That beheard the sheriffe of
    Nottingham,
    As he leaned under a lowe.[5]

---

[1] browne: *gleaming*   [2] reacheles: *reckless, careless*
[3] i.e. Robin threw his gown over Sir Guy's corpse   [4] The: *thy*   [5] lowe: *hill*

47

'Hearken! hearken!' sayd the sheriffe,
  'I heard noe tydings but good;
For yonder I heare Sir Guyes horne
    blowe,
  For he hath slaine Robin Hoode.

48

'For yonder I heare Sir Guyes horne
    blow,
  Itt blowes soe well in tyde,
For yonder comes that wighty yeoman,
  Cladd in his capull-hyde.

49

'Come hither, thou good Sir Guy,
  Aske of mee what thou wilt have!'
'I'le none of thy gold,' sayes Robin
    Hood,
  'Nor I'le none of itt have.

50

'But now I have slaine the master,' he
    sayd,
  'Let me goe strike the knave;
This is all the reward I aske,
  Nor noe other will I have.'

51

'Thou art a madman,' said the shiriffe,
  'Thou sholdest have had a knights
    ffee;
Seeing thy asking (hath) beene soe badd,
  Well granted it shall be.'

52

But Litle John heard his master speake,
  Well he knew that was his steven;[1]
'Now shall I be loset,'[2] quoth Litle
    John,
  'With Christs might in heaven.'

53

But Robin hee hyed him towards Litle
    John,
  Hee thought hee wold loose him
    belive;[3]
The sheriffe and all his companye
  Fast after him did drive.

54

'Stand abacke! stand abacke!' sayd
    Robin;
  'Why draw you mee soe neere?
Itt was never the use in our countrye
  One's shrift[4] another shold heere.'

55

But Robin pulled forth an Irysh kniffe,
  And losed John hand and ffoote,
And gave him Sir Guyes bow in his
    hand,
  And bade it be his boote.

56

But John tooke Guyes bow in his hand,
  His arrowes were rawstye by the
    roote;[5]
The sherriffe saw Litle John draw a bow
  And ffettle him to shoote.

57

Towards his house in Nottingam
  He ffled full fast away,
And soe did all his companye,
  Not one behind did stay.

58

But he cold neither soe fast goe,
  Nor away soe fast runn,
But Litle John, with an arrow broade,
  Did cleave his heart in twinn.

---

[1] steven: *voice*   [2] loset: *set loose*   [3] belive: *at once*   [4] shrift: *confession*
[5] ? rusty (with blood) to their ends

THE JOLLY PINDER OF WAKEFIELD (Child 124)

Sources :

A. Broadside version: Bodleian Library, Oxford, Wood MS. 402, leaf
42 (a broadside printed for F. Coles, T. Vere and W. Gilbertson, *c.*
1650–60).
B. Percy Folio version: British Library, Additional MS. 27,879, fo. 6r;
printed in *Bishop Percy's Folio Manuscript*, ed. Hales and Furnivall, I,
34–6, and Child, III, 131–2.

Other Editions of A :

Evans, 1777, I, 99; Ritson, 1795, II, 16–18; Gutch, 1847, II, 144–6;
Child, 1888, III, 131; Leach, 1955, pp. 365–6.

Like all legendary heroes, Robin Hood has owed much of his fame to his
constant readiness to engage in personal combat with a wide variety of very
different but always redoubtable opponents. But the really distinctive
feature of the majority of post-medieval Robin Hood ballads is the number of
occasions on which the outlaw leader met his match and only escaped from
the ignominy of defeat by persuading his adversary to join his company. Of
the many and often monotonous variations on this theme, the ballad of *The
Jolly Pinder of Wakefield* was certainly one of the earliest and always remained
one of the most popular. Although the first surviving copies of this ballad
date from the middle of the seventeenth century, there are good grounds for
believing that the main outlines of its story were already well known at least
a hundred years earlier. 'A ballett of *Wakefylde and a grene*' was entered to
Master John Wallye and Mistress Toye in the Stationers' Registers as early as
1557–58.[1]
    Indeed, to judge from the various references and allusions to the ballad
of *The Jolly Pinder of Wakefield* in Elizabethan literature, it was extremely
well known at all levels of society. By 1599 George a Green, the Pinner of
Wakefield, had become an important figure in his own right, the subject not
only of a play but a character whose personal strength entered proverbial
expression ('As good as George-a-Green').[2] In Michael Drayton's words, the

[1] Arber, I, 76.
[2] *The Comedy of George a Green, 1599* (Malone Society Reprints, 1911).

valiant fight between Robin and George a Green had become so famous 'that every freeman's song / Can tell you of the same.'[1] Unfortunately, the historical origins (if any) of the Pinner of Wakefield are even more mysterious than those of Robin Hood himself. However it seems probable that, like Maid Marian, he entered the world of the outlaw hero through the agency of the May Games, perhaps those at Wakefield itself.[2] As the ballad seems to have been (in Child's words) 'pretty well sung to pieces before it was printed', the first surviving broadside copies provide disappointingly little in the way of circumstantial detail. Nor does the fragmentary concluding section of the ballad preserved in the Percy Folio—although printed below because it seems to be copied from an earlier text than any now extant—add much of substance to what was always one of the shortest but most spirited ballads in the Robin Hood Garlands of later years.

A. *The Jolly Pinder of Wakefield*

1

In Wakefield there lives a jolly pinder,[3]
  In Wakefield, all on a green,
  In Wakefield, all on a green;
'There is neither knight nor squire' said
    the pinder,
  'Nor baron that is so bold,
  Nor baron that is so bold,
Dare make a trespasse to the town of
    Wakefield,
  But his pledge goes to the pinfold,
  But his pledge goes to the pinfold.'

2

All this beheard three witty[4] young men,
  'Twas Robin Hood, Scarlet and
    John;[5]
With that they spyed the jolly pinder,
  As he sate under a thorn.

3

'Now turn again, turn again,' said the
    pinder,
  'For a wrong way have you gone;
For you have forsaken the king his
    highway,
  And made a path over the corn.'

4

'O that were great shame,' said jolly
    Robin,
  'We being three, and thou but one.'
The pinder leapt back then thirty good
    foot,
  'T was thirty good foot and one.

5

He leaned his back fast unto a thorn,
  And his foot unto a stone,

---

[1] *The Works of Michael Drayton*, ed. J. W. Hebel (Oxford, 1933), IV, 528–30. See the early lute music printed in Bronson, *Traditional Tunes*, III, pp. 24–5.
[2] Ritson, 1795, I, xxvii–xxix.
[3] pinder: *pound-keeper*, whose duty it was to impound all stray cattle, etc.
[4] witty: clearly a corruption of *wight*, strong
[5] This, like the second and also the fourth lines of each stanza, would be repeated during the singing of the ballad. Justice Silence sings this particular line in Shakespeare's *King Henry IV, Part II*, Act V, Sc. 3, l. 100.

And there he fought a long summer's
    day,
    A summer's day so long,
Till that their swords, on their broad
    bucklers,
    Were broken fast unto their hands.[1]

6

'Hold thy hand, hold thy hand,' said
    Robin Hood,
    'And my merry men every one;
For this is one of the best pinders
    That ever I try'd with sword.

7

'And wilt thou forsake thy pinder his
    craft,
    And live in the green wood with me?'
'At Michaelmas next my covnant comes
    out,
    When every man gathers his fee;

8

'I'le take my blew blade all in my hand,
    And plod to the green wood with
    thee.'

'Hast thou either meat or drink,' said
    Robin Hood,
    For my merry men and me?'

9

'I have both bread and beef,' said the
    pinder,
    'And good ale of the best;'
'And that is meat good enough,' said
    Robin Hood,
    'For such unbidden guest.

10

'O wilt thou forsake the pinder his
    craft,
    And go to the green wood with me?
Thou shalt have a livery twice in the
    year,
    The one green, the other brown.'[2]

11

'If Michaelmas day were once come and
    gone
    And my master had paid me my fee,
Then would I set as little by him
    As my master doth set by me.'

B. *Percy Folio Version* (concluding stanzas only)

1

. . . .
. . . .
'But hold y . . . , hold y . . .' says
    Robin,[3]
    My merrymen, I bid yee.

2

'For this [is] one of the best pindars
    That ever I saw with mine eye.
But hast thou any meat, thou jolly
    pindar,
    For my merry men and me?'

[1] The ballad shows signs of undue compression and no doubt corruption here: it is clear from the play of *George a Green* and other sources that in the original story the Pinner of Wakefield fought Robin Hood, Will Scarlet and Little John in turn rather than simultaneously.
[2] ? *add* 'shall be'
[3] This line in the MS. now shares the fate of all its predecessors and has completely disappeared.

3
'But I have bread and cheese,' sayde
   the pindar,
  'And ale all on the best.'
'That's cheere good enoughe,' said
   Robin,
  'For any such unbidden guests.

4
'But wilt be my man?' said good Robin,
  'And come and dwell with me?
And twise in a yeere thy clothing be
   changed
  If my man thou wilt bee.

5
'The tone shall be of light Lincolne
   greene,
  The tother of Picklory.'
'Att Michallmass comes a well good
   time,
  When men have gotten in their ffee.[1]

6
I'le sett as litle by my master
  As he now setts by me,
I'le take my benbowe in my hande,
  And come into the grenwoode to
   thee.'

[1] The last two lines of this stanza were presumably meant to be spoken by the Pinder rather than by Robin Hood. Like all the later printed copies of *The Jolly Pinder*, the Percy Folio fragment owes a good deal of its ambiguities to the forgetting of some of the original lines: for a conjectural reconstruction of the whole piece in alternative and sometimes six-line stanza form, see Child, III, 131–2.

'Robin Hood, William Scadlock and Little John': a broadside copy of *Robin Hood and the Prince of Aragon*, printed at London for W. Onley, *c.* 1660 (British Library, Roxburghe I, 358).

7

ROBIN HOOD AND THE BUTCHER (Child 122)

Sources :
A. Percy Folio version: British Library, Additional MS. 27, 879, fos. 3r–4v; printed in *Bishop Percy's Folio Manuscript*, ed. Hales and Furnivall, I, 19–25, and Child, III, 116–18.
B. Broadside version: Bodleian Library, Oxford, Wood MS. 401, leaves 19v, 20r (a broadside printed for F. Grove on Snow Hill, *c.* 1640).

Other Editions of B :
Evans, 1777, I, 106; Ritson, 1795, II, 24–9; Gutch, 1847, II, 152–7; Child, 1888, III, 118–19; Quiller-Couch, 1910, pp. 607–12.

With its ingeniously concise story of the outlaw hero's entry into the town of Nottingham and his subsequent inveiglement of the sheriff into Sherwood Forest, the broadside version of this ballad deservedly held an important place in the Robin Hood canon from at least the mid-seventeenth to the mid-nineteenth centuries. To the modern student of the greenwood legend, *Robin Hood and the Butcher* is more significant still: no other ballad illustrates in such detail the process whereby a late medieval story of Robin Hood was gradually transformed into a regular 'sung ballad' of the early modern period. A reading of the later version of the ballad (B) itself reveals a close similarity with parts of the story of *Robin Hood and the Potter*, as preserved in a unique manuscript of *c.* 1500 (No. 3 above). But it was the publication by Hales and Furnivall in 1867 of the Percy Folio fragment of *Robin Hood and the Butcher* (A) which first revealed the existence of an all-important missing link in the sequence and showed how the comparatively casual simplicity of a late medieval ballad was re-worked into more regular but more monotonous broadside ballad form.

The close relationship between the Percy manuscript version of *Robin Hood and the Butcher* and the earlier *Robin Hood and the Potter* needs no particular urging. Apart from the fundamental resemblances between both narratives, the former often echoes the very words of the latter.[1] On the other

[1] Compare, e.g., *Robin Hood and the Potter*, stanza 4, line 3, with *Robin Hood and the Butcher* A, stanza 4, line 3; and also stanza 67, lines 3–4, of the former with stanza 25, lines 3–4 of the latter.

hand, the two tales are by no means identical: the Percy Folio fragment (unfortunately incomplete and impossible to date) employs a considerably more modern vocabulary and appears to have been simplified and condensed in various ways, most notably by the omission of any reference to an archery contest in Nottingham itself (compare p. 129 above). It will be noticed that this process of simplification was carried much further by the composer—possibly the T. R. (Thomas Robins) whose initials appear at the end of the broadside—of version B below. Various details in common (the use of the phrase 'horn' or 'horned beasts', the fact that the sheriff is prepared to pay £300 in both versions) make it highly probable that this author had a text not very unlike the Percy Folio fragment before him when he began to revise the ballad. But the result of his labours was an almost completely re-written song, in which the preliminary fight between Robin and the potter had been discarded together with all but one, rather cryptic, reference to the sheriff's wife (B, stanza 30, line 3). Such extensive re-writing was no doubt forced upon the composer of the broadside version of *Robin Hood and the Butcher* by the need to insert middle rhyme in the third line of each stanza and to convert the ballad into one which could be sung to the familiar tune of 'Robin Hood and the Beggar', alias 'Robin Hood and the Stranger'.[1] The end result was a ballad which had certainly been printed in black-letter for a commercial audience before 1655 (the terminal date of the earliest known version of B, that copied below) and which should probably be identified with the two versions of *Robin Hood and the Butcher* entered in the Stationers' Registers during July 1657.[2] From approximately this date onwards, *Robin Hood and the Butcher*, like the great majority of the so-called 'traditional' Robin Hood ballads, was fixed in a more or less permanent form, quite rigidly preserved within a series of innumerable garlands, all dependent upon one another and ultimately derived from mid-seventeenth-century broadsides.

---

[1] Bronson, *Traditional Tunes*, III, 20; and see below, p. 166 n.1.
[2] H. E. Rollins, *An Analytical Index to the Ballad Entries (1557–1709) in the Registers of the Company of Stationers of London* (North Carolina University, *Studies in Philology*, XXI, 1924), Nos. 2312, 2313 (p. 200).

A. '*Fragment of Robin Hood and the Butcher*'[1]

1

But Robin he walkes in the g[reene]
    fforest,[2]
  As merry as bird on bughe,
But he that feitches good Robins head,
  Hee'le find him game enoughe.

2

But Robin he walkes in the greene
    fforest,
  Under his trusty tree,[3]
Sayes, 'Hearken, hearken, my merrymen
  all,
  What tydings is come to me.

3

'The sheriffe he hath made a cry,[4]
  Hee'le have my head I wis;
But ere a twelvemonth come to an end
  I may chance to light on his.'

4

Robin he marcht in the grene fforest,
  Under the greenwood scray,[5]
And there he was ware of a proud
  bucher
Came driving flesh by the way.

5

The bucher he had a cut taild dogg,[6]
  And at Robins face he flew;

But Robin he was a good sword,
  The buchers dogg he slew.

6

'Why slayes thou my dogg?' sayes the
  bucher,
  'For he did none ill to thee;
By all the saints that are in heaven,
  Thou shalt have buffetts three.'

7

He tooke his staffe then in his hand,
  And he turnd him round about,
'Thou hast a little wild blood in thy
  head,
  Good fellow, thoust[7] have it letten
  out.'

8

'He that does that deed,' sayes Robin,
  'I'le count him for a man,
But that while will I draw my sword,
  And fend it[8] if I can.'

9

But Robin he stroke att the bloudy
  bucher,
  In place where he did stand,
(*half a page missing: i.e. c. 9 stanzas*)

---

[1] A title inserted in the manuscript by Bishop Percy

[2] The whole of this line is now missing in the original MS. The fact that it is almost exactly repeated at the beginning of the fourth stanza suggests that the first three stanzas of this version of *Robin Hood and the Butcher* may have strayed from a now lost ballad of 'Robin's revenge on the sheriff'. The latter had earlier been absorbed into the sixth fitte of the *Geste*, whose 329th stanza also begins with the words 'Robyn Hode walked in the forest'. See Clawson, *Gest of Robin Hood*, p. 127.

[3] trusty tree: an obvious corruption of *trysting tree*, chosen as a rendezvous

[4] cry: *proclamation*   [5] scray: *? spray, branches*

[6] A dog with its tail docked as a sign that it was a common dog, not meant for sport: for the Curtal Friar's 'curtall dogs', see below, p. 163.

[7] thoust: *thou is to* (clear evidence of the northern provenance of this text of the ballad)

[8] fend it: *ward off the 'deed' or blow*

10

'I (am) a younge bucher,' sayes Robin,[1]
   'You fine dames am I come amonge;
But ever I beseech you, good Mrs
    Sheriffe,
   You must see me take noe wronge.'

11

'Thou art verry welcome,' said Master
    Sherriff's wife;
   Thy inne heere up take:
If any good ffellow come in thy
    companie,
   Heest be welcome for thy sake.'

12

Robin called ffor ale, soe did he for wine,
   And for it he did pay:
'I must to my markett goe,' says Robin,
   'For I hold time itt of the day.'

13

But Robin is to the markett gone,
   Soe quickly and belive,[2]
He sold more flesh for one peny
   Then othe(r) buchers did for five.

14

The drew about the younge bucher
   Like sheepe into a fold,
Yea never a bucher had sold a bitt
   Till Robin he had all sold.

15

When Robin Hood had his markett
    made,
   His flesh was sold and gone;
Yea he had received but a litle mony,
   But thirty pence and one.

16

Seaven buchers, the garded[3] Robin
    Hood,
   Ffull many time and oft;
Sayes, 'We must drinke with you,
    brother bucher,
   It's custom of our crafte.'

17

'If that be the custome of your crafte,
   As heere you tell to me,
Att four of the clocke in the afternoone
   At the sheriffs hall I wilbe.'

(half a page missing: i.e. c. 9 stanzas)

18

. . . .
   'if thou doe like it well,'[4]
'Yea heere is more by three hundred
    pound
   Then thou hast beasts to sell.'

19

Robin sayd naught, the more he
    thought:
   'Mony neere comes out of time;
If once I cacth[5] (thee) in thy greene
    fforest,
   That mony it shall be mine.'

20

But on the next day seven butchers
   Came to guard the sheriffe that day,
But Robin he was the whighest[6] man,
   He led them all the way.

---

[1] Robin has now entered Nottingham (see stanza 25) disguised in the clothes of his former
adversary, exactly as in *Robin Hood and the Potter*. But in the latter ballad he is asked to
dinner by the sheriff's wife and not (as here) asked to lodge with her.

[2] belive: *immediately*

[3] garded: *regarded, looked at*

[4] At the conclusion of the feast, Robin offers to sell some deer to the sheriff (who speaks
the next two lines).

[5] cacth: *catch* (possibly a northern dialect peculiarity rather than the result of a scribal
error)

[6] whighest: *wightest, most nimble*

21

He led them into the greene fforest,
  Under the trusty tree;
Yea, there were harts, and ther were
    hynds,
  And staggs with heads full high.[1]

22

Yea, there were harts and there were
    hynds,
  And many a goodly ffawne:
'Now praised be God,' says bold Robin,
  'All these they be my owne.

23

'These are my horned beasts,' says
    Robin,
  'Master sherriffe, which must make
    the stake.'
'But ever alacke now,' said the sheriffe,
  'That tydings comes to late!'

24

Robin sett a shrill horne to his mouth,
  And a loud blast he did blow,
And then halfe a hundred bold archers
  Came rakeing on a row.[2]

25

But when the came befor bold Robin,
  Even there the stood all bare,
'You are welcome, Master, from
    Nottingham:
  How have you sold your ware?'

(*half a page missing; i.e. c. 9 stanzas*)

26

. . . .
  'It proves bold Robin Hood.'[3]

27

'Yea, he hath robbd me of all my gold
  And silver that ever I had;
But that I had a verry good wife at home,
  I shold have lost my head.

28

'But I had a verry good wife at home,
  Which made him gentle cheere,
And therfor, pro[4] my wifes sake,
  I shold have better favor heere.

29

'But such favor as he shewed me
  I might have of the devills dam,
That will rob a man of all he hath,
  And send him naked home'.

30

'That is very well done,' then says his
    wiffe,
  'Itt is well done, I say,
You might have tarryed att Nottingham,
  Soe fayre as I did you pray'.

31

'I have learned wisdome,' sayes the
    sherriffe,
  'And, wife, I have learned of thee,
But if Robin walke east, or he walke
    west,
  He shall never be sought for me.'

---

[1] This part of the story seems to bear a closer similarity to stanzas 181–204 of the *Gest* (based on a tale of Little John enticing the sheriff into Robin's power) than to the equivalent section of *Robin Hood and the Potter* (above, pp. 130–2).

[2] Rakeing on a row: *advancing in a line*: cf. the very similar couplet in *Robin Hood and the Curtal Friar*, stanza 16 (below, p. 161).

[3] The sheriff has now been deprived of his money by Robin Hood and sent home to Nottingham, where he is in the middle of a conversation with his wife (longer and more subdued than its counterpart in *Robin Hood and the Potter*, stanzas 77–80).

[4] pro: *for*

B. *Robin Hood and the Butcher. To the Tune of Robin Hood and the Beggar.*
At the end: *London. Printed for F. Grove on Snow Hill. Entered according to
Order. Finis. T.R.* (1620–55).

1

Come, all you brave gallants, and listen
    a while,
    With hey down, down, down an a
    down,
    That are in the bowers within;
For of Robin Hood, that archer good,
    A song I intend for to sing.

2

Upon a time it chanced so
    Bold Robin in fforest did spy
A jolly butcher, with a bonny fine mare,
    With his flesh to the market did hye.

3

'Good morrow, good fellow,' said jolly
    Robin,
    'What food hast? tell unto me;
And thy trade to me tell, and where
    thou dost dwell,
    For I like well thy company.'

4

The butcher he answered jolly Robin:
    'No matter where I dwell;
For a butcher I am, and to Notingham
    I am going, my flesh to sell.'

5

'What is price of thy flesh?' said jolly
    Robin,
    'Come, tell it soon unto me;
And the price of thy mare, be she never
    so dear,
    For a butcher fain would I be.'

6

'The price of my flesh,' the butcher
    repli'd,
    'I soon will tell unto thee;
With my bonny mare, and they are not
    dear,
    Four mark thou must give unto me.'

7

'Four mark I will give thee,' saith jolly
    Robin,
    'Four mark it shall be thy fee;
Thy mony come count, and let me
    mount,
    For a butcher I fain would be.'

8

Now Robin he is to Notingham gone,
    His butcher's trade for to begin;
With good intent, to the sheriff he went,
    And there he took up his inn.

9

When other butchers they opened their
    meat,
    Bold Robin he then begun;
But how for to sell he knew not well,
    For a butcher he was but young.

10

When other butchers no meat could sell,
    Robin got both gold and fee;
For he sold more meat for one peny
    Than others could do for three.

11

But when he sold his meat so fast,
    No butcher by him could thrive;
For he sold more meat for one peny
    Than others could do for five.

12

Which made the butchers of Notingham
    To study as they did stand,
Saying, surely he was some prodigal,
    That hath sold his father's land.

13

The butchers they stepped to jolly
    Robin,
    Acquainted with him for to be;
'Come brother,' one said, 'we be all of
    one trade,
    Come, will you go dine with me?'

14

'Accurst of his heart,' said jolly Robin,
  'That a butcher doth deny;
I will go with you, my brethren true,
  And as fast as I can hie.'

15

But when to the sheriff's house they
    came,
  To dinner they hied apace,
And Robin he the man must be
  Before them all to say grace.

16

'Pray God bless us all,' said jolly Robin,
  'And our meat within this place;
A cup of sack so good will nourish our
    blood,
  And so I do end my grace.

17

'Come fill us more wine,' said jolly
    Robin,
  'Let us merry be while we do stay;
For wine and good cheer, be it never so
    dear,
  I vow I the reckning will pay.

18

'Come, brother(s), be merry,' said jolly
    Robin,
  'Let us drink, and never give ore,
For the shot[1] I will pay, ere I go my
    way,
  If it cost me five pounds and more.'

19

'This is a mad blade,' the butchers then
    said;
  Saies the sheriff, 'He is some prodigal,
That some land has sold, for silver and
    gold,
  And now he doth mean to spend all.

---

[1] shot: *account* (especially at a tavern)

20

'Hast thou any horn beasts,' the sheriff
    repli'd,
  'Good fellow, to sell unto me?'
'Yes, that I have, good Master Sheriff,
  I have hundreds two or three.

21

'And a hundred aker of good free land,
  If you please it to see;
And I'le make you as good assurance of
    it
  As ever my father made me.'

22

The sheriff he saddled a good palfrey,
  With three hundred pound in gold,
And away he went with bold Robin
    Hood,
  His horned beasts to behold.

23

Away then the sheriff and Robin did
    ride,
  To the forrest of merry Sherwood;
Then the sheriff did say, 'God bless us
    this day
  From a man they call Robin Hood.'

24

But when that a little further they came,
  Bold Robin he chanced to spy
A hundred head of good red deer,
  Come tripping the sheriff full nigh.

25

'How like you my horn'd beasts, good
    Master Sheriff?
  They be fat and fair for to see;'
'I tell thee, good fellow, I would I were
    gone,
  For I like not thy company.'

26

Then Robin he set his horn to his
  mouth,
  And blew but blasts three;
Then quickly anon there came Little
  John,
  And all his company.

27

'What is your will?' then said Little
  John,
  'Good master come tell it to me.'
'I have brought hither the sheriff of
  Notingham,
  This day to dine with thee.'

28

'He is welcome to me,' then said Little
  John,
  'I hope he will honestly pay;

I know he has gold, if it be but well told,
  Will serve us to drink a whole day.'

29

Then Robin took his mantle from his
  back,
  And laid it upon the ground,
And out of the sheriff's portmantle[1]
  He told three hundred pound.

30

Then Robin he brought him thorow the
  wood,
  And set him on his dapple gray:
'O have me commended to your wife at
  home!'
  So Robin went laughing away.

[1] Portmantle: i.e. portmanteau or travelling case, a word first recorded in English in 1584
according to O.E.D.

Robin Hood and the Bishop: a broadside
printed at London for W. Onley, *c.* 1660
(British Library, Roxburghe I, 362).

8

ROBIN HOOD AND THE CURTAL FRIAR
(Child 123)

Sources:
A. Percy Folio version: British Library, Additional MS. 27, 879, fos. 4v–6r; printed in *Bishop Percy's Folio Manuscript*, ed. Hales and Furnivall, I, 26–31, and Child, III, 123–4.
B. Broadside version: Bodleian Library, Oxford, Wood MS. 401, leaves 15v, 16r (a broadside printed for F. Coles, T. Vere and W. Gilbertson, *c*. 1660).

Other Editions of B:
Evans, 1771, I, 136; Ritson, 1795, II, 58–65; Gutch, 1847, II, 190–6; Child, 1888, III, 124–6; Quiller-Couch, 1910, pp. 600–7; Leach, 1955, pp. 361–5.

Of all Robin Hood's many adventures, his 'Famous Battel' with the curtal friar has long and deservedly been among the most popular. Ballads devoted to this celebrated contest were already circulating quite widely by the middle of the seventeenth century;[1] and *Robin Hood and the Curtal Friar* takes a prominent place in all the Robin Hood Garlands from the 1660s onwards. Moreover a comparison of the two seventeenth-century versions printed below can leave little doubt that they were both dependent on an even earlier ballad now lost to us. Indeed the main elements in the story—the fight in the river, the blasts on the horn and Robin's final request that the friar should become 'my man'—must have been well known by the beginning of Elizabeth's reign when they formed the basis of one of the plays appended by William Copland to his edition of the *Gest* (see below, No. 20). It is hard to resist the conclusion that the story of the curtal friar originated in the later middle ages and was the product of that ever-popular literary genre of the period—affectionate (as opposed to savage) satire at the expense of the mendicant orders. But the friar's association with Fountains Abbey (mentioned in both ballads printed below) can only be a post-Reformation fabrication.

[1] Including one broadside (Pepys I, 78, No. 37), certainly printed at London before 1641 (Child, III, 126).

Despite the title attached to the ballad by the copyist of the Percy Folio, Child was at great pains to point out that the curtal friar of this ballad should not be too readily identified with Friar Tuck. It is certainly true that like Maid Marian, Allen a Dale, the Pinder of Wakefield and others, the curtal friar plays little or no part in the traditional Robin Hood saga outside his own ballad. In all these cases—and that of Friar Tuck—it seems likely that the protagonist was a legendary figure in his or her own right before being absorbed into the world of Robin Hood. But whether, as Child believed, Friar Tuck owed his association with Robin Hood to the mediation of the May Games 'and not in the least to popular ballads' is more questionable.[1] The name of Friar or 'Frere' Tuck had already become synonymous with that of a notorious robber by the early fifteenth century;[2] and 'Ffrere Tuke' appears as an active member of Robin's company in a dramatic fragment (No. 19 below) of *c.* 1475, earlier than one would expect if Child is correct in suggesting that he owes his fame exclusively to his prominent role in the May Games and morris dances. In any case the fact that Friar Tuck and Robin Hood undoubtedly were associated together in the late fifteenth century must add some weight to the view that this seventeenth-century ballad preserves a story already current in the later middle ages, long before Shakespeare's famous allusion to 'the bare scalp of Robin Hood's fat friar' in *Two Gentlemen of Verona*, IV, 1.

A. '*Robine Hood and Ffryer Tucke*'[3]

1

But how many merry monthes be in the
   yeere?
There are thirteen in May.[4]
The midsummer moone is the merryest
   of all,
Next to the merry month of May.

2

In May, when mayds beene fast
   weepand,

Young men their hands done wringe,
   (*half a page missing*)[5]

3

'I'le.... pe....................,
Over may noe man for villanie.'
'I'le never eate nor drinke,' Robin Hood
   said,
'Till I that cutted[6] friar see'.

---

[1] Child, III, 122. See Introduction, above p. 41.

[2] *C.P.R.*, *1416–22*, pp. 84, 141; *1429–36*, p. 10; cf. C. L. Kingsford, *English Historical Literature in the Fifteenth Century* (Oxford, 1913), p. 267.

[3] The title added by the scribe of the Percy Folio

[4] in May: ? a mistake for 'I say'

[5] This large gap prevents us from knowing why men and maids should be so surprisingly mournful in May.

[6] cutted: *short-frocked*, with the possible but by no means certain implication that the friar was a member of the Franciscan Order, often enjoined to wear short habits in conformity with the instructions of St Francis himself.

4

He builded[1] his men in a brake of fearne,
  A litle from that nunery;[2]
Sayes, 'If you heare my litle horne
    blow,
  Then looke you come to me.'

5

When Robin came to Fontaines Abey,
  Wheras that fryer lay,
He was ware of the fryer where he stood,
  And to him thus can he say :—

6

A payre of blacke breeches the yeoman
    had on,
  His coppe[3] all shone of steele,
A fayre sword and a broad buckeler
  Beseemed him very weell:—

7

'I am a wet weary man,' said Robin
    Hood,
  'Good fellow, as thou may see;
Wilt beare (me) over this wild water,
  Ffor sweete Saint Charity ?'

8

The fryer bethought him of a good deed;
  He had done none of long before;
He hent up Robin Hood on his backe,
  And over he did him beare.

9

But when he came over that wild water,
  A longe sword there he drew:
'Beare me backe againe, bold outlawe,
  Or of this thou shalt have enoughe.'

10

Then Robin Hood hent the fryar on his
    back,
  And neither sayd good nor ill;
Till he came ore that wild water,
  They yeoman he walked still.

11

Then Robin Hood wett his fayre greene
    hoze,
  A span above his knee;
Says, 'Beare me ore againe, thou cutted
    f(ryer)
      (*half a page missing*)

12

· ·
· ·
· · · · · · · · · · · · · · · · · · · [good bowmen
  Came raking] all on a rowe.[4]

13

'I beshrew thy head,' said the cutted
    ffriar,
  'Thou thinkes I shall be shente;[5]
I thought thou had but a man or two,
  And thou hast (a) whole convent.

14

'I lett thee have a blast on thy horne,
  Now give me leave to whistle another;
I cold not bidd thee nóe better play
  And thou wert my owne borne
    brother.'

15

'Now fate on, fute on,[6] thou cutted
    fryar,
  I pray God thou neere be still;
It is not the futing in a fryers fist
  That can doe me any ill'.

---

[1] builded: *concealed*
[2] nunery: Fountains Abbey, near Ripon, was of course a Cistercian monastery, not a
nunnery
[3] coppe: *head*
[4] Only the last four words of this stanza now survive in the MS
[5] shente: *hurt*
[6] fate, fute: *whistle*

THE MERRY FRIAR CARRIETH ROBIN ACROSS THE WATER

3. Robin Hood meets Friar Tuck: Howard Pyle's illustration from his *The Merry Adventures of Robin Hood* (New York, 1883)

16

The fryar sett his neave[1] to his mouth,
  A loud blast he did blow;
Then halfe a hundred good bandoggs[2]
  Came raking all on a rowe.

17

'Every dogg to a man,' said the cutted
    fryar,
  'And I my selfe to Robin Hood.'
'Every dogg to a man,' said the cutted
    fryar,
  'And I my selfe to Robin Hood.'

18

'Ever God's forbott,'[3] said Robin Hood,
  'That ever that soe shold bee;
I had rather be matched with three of
    the tikes[4]
  Ere I wold be matched on thee.

19

'But stay thy tikes, thou fryar,' he said,
  'And freindshipp I'l have with thee;
But stay thy tikes, thou fryar,' he said,
  'And save good yeomanry.'

20

The fryar he sett his neave to his
    mouth,
  A lowd blast he did blow;
They dogges the couch downe every
    one,
  They couched downe on a rowe.

21

'What is thy will, thou yeoman?' he
    said,
  'Have done and tell it me.'
If that thou will goe to merry green-
    wood,
      (*half a page missing*)

B. *The famous Battle between Robin Hood and the Curtall Fryer.*
  To a new Northern Tune.

1

In summer time, when leaves grow
    green,
  And flowers are fresh and gay,
Robin Hood and his merry men
  Were disposed to play.

2

Then some would leap and some would
    run,
  And some would use artilary.
'Which of you can a good bow draw,
  A good archer to be?'

3

'Which of you can kill a buck?
  Or who can kill a doe?

Or who can kill a hart of Greece,[5]
  Five hundred foot him fro?'

4

Will Scadlock he kill'd a buck,
  And Midge he kill'd a doe.
And Little John kill'd an hart of greece,
  Five hundred foot him fro.

5

'God's blessing on thy heart,' said
    Robin Hood,
  That hath such a shot for me;
I would ride my horse a hundred miles,
  To finde one could match thee.'

---

[1] neave: *fist*
[2] bandoggs: dogs so savage that they are usually kept chained
[3] Ever God's forbott: *God forfend!*
[4] tikes: a northern English word for *dogs* or *curs*
[5] hart of greece: *fat hart*

6

That caused Will Scadlock to laugh,
  He laught full heartily:
'There lives a curtal[1] friar in Fountains
    Abby
Will beat both him and thee.

7

'That curtall frier in Fountains Abby
  Well can a strong bow draw;
He will beat you and your yeomen,
  Set them all on a row.'

8

Robin Hood took a solemn oath,
  It was by Mary free,
That he would neither eat nor drink
  Till the fryer he did see.

9

Robin Hood put on his harness good,
  And on his head a cap of steel,
Broad sword and buckler by his side,
  And they became him weel.

10

He took his bow into his hand,
  It was made of a trustie tree,
With a sheafe of arrows at his belt,
  To the Fountains Dale went he.

11

And coming unto Fountains Dale,
  No farther would he ride;
There he was aware of a curtal frier,
  Walking by the water-side.

12

The fryer had on a harnesse good,
  And on his head a cap of steel,
Broad sword and buckler by his side,
  And they became him weel.

13

Robin Hood lighted off his horse,
  And tyed him to a thorn:
'Carry me over the water, thou curtal-
    tyed fryer,
  Or else thy life's forlorn.'

14

The frier took Robin Hood on his back,
  Deep water he did bestride,
And spake neither good word nor bad,
  Till he came at the other side.

15

Lightly stept Robin Hood off the friers
    back;
  The frier said to him again,
'Carry me over this water fine fellow,
  Or it shall breed thy pain.'

16

Robin Hood took the frier on his back,
  Deep water he did bestride,
And spake neither good word nor bad,
  Till he came at the other side.

17

Lightly leapt the fryer off Robin Hood's
    back;
  Robin Hood said to him again,
'Carry me over this water, thou curtall
    frier,
  Or it shall breed thy pain.'

18

The frier took Robin Hood on 's back
    again,
  And stept up to the knee;
Till he came at the middle stream,
  Neither good nor bad spake he.

[1] curtal: probably a more ancient epithet for the friar than the 'cutted' of the Percy Folio version of this ballad. If derived from the Latin *curtilarius*, as Child supposed, its implication would be that the friar kept the *curtile*, or vegetable garden, of his monastery; but, like 'cutted', it is more probably an allusion to the shortness of the friar's habit.

The Second Part, to the same Tune

19

And coming to the middle stream,
   There he threw Robin in:
'And chuse thee, chuse thee, fine fellow,
   Whether thou wilt sink or swim.'

20

Robin Hood swam to a bush of broom,
   The frier to a wicker wand;
Bold Robin Hood is gone to shore,
   And took his bow in hand.

21

One of his best arrows under his belt
   To the frier he let flie;
The curtall frier, with his steel buckler,
   He put that arrow by.

22

'Shoot on, shoot on, thou fine fellow,
   Shoot on as thou hast begun;
If thou shoot here a summers day,
   Thy mark I will not shun.'

23

Robin Hood shot so passing well,
   Till his arrows all were gone;
They took their swords and steel
     bucklers,
   They fought with might and maine;

24

From ten o' th' clock that day,
   Till four i' th' afternoon;
Then Robin Hood came to his knees,
   Of the frier to beg a boon.

25

'A boon, a boon, thou curtall frier,
   I beg it on my knee;
Give me leave to set my horn to my
     mouth,
   And to blow blasts three.'

26

'That will I do,' said the curtall frier,
   'Of thy blasts I have no doubt;
I hope thou'lt blow so passing well
   Till both thy eyes fall out.'

27

Robin Hood set his horn to his mouth,
   He blew but blasts three;
Half a hundred yeomen, with bows bent,
   Came ranging over the lee.

28

'Whose men are these,' said the frier,
   'That come so hastily?'
'These men are mine,' said Robin Hood;
   'Frier, what is that to thee?'

29

'A boon, a boon,' said the curtall frier,
   'The like I gave to thee;
Give me leave to set my fist to my
     mouth,
   And to whute[1] whutes three.'

30

'That will I do,' said Robin Hood,
   'Or else I were to blame;
Three whutes in a friers fist
   Would make me glad and fain.'

31

The frier set his fist to his mouth,
   And whuted whutes three;
Half a hundred good ban-dogs
   Came running the frier unto.

32

'Here's for every man a dog,
   And I my self for thee:'
'Nay, by my faith,' quoth Robin Hood,
   'Friar, that may not be.'

33

Two dogs at once to Robin Hood did go,
   The one behind, the other before;
Robin Hoods mantle of Lincoln green
   Off from his back they tore.

34

And whether his men shot east or west,
   Or they shot north or south,
The curtall[2] dogs, so taught they were,
   They kept their arrows in their
     mouth.

[1] whute: *whistle*   [2] curtall: ? a corruption of 'cut-tailed' (see above, p. 152, n. 6)

35

'Take up thy dogs,' said Little John,
  'Frier, at my bidding be;'
'Whose man art thou,' said the curtall
    frier,
  'Comes here to prate with me?'

36

'I am Little John, Robin Hoods man,
  Frier, I will not lye;
If thou take not up thy dogs soon,
  I'le take up them and thee.'

37

Little John had a bow in his hand,
  He shot with might and main;
Soon half a score of the friers dogs
  Lay dead upon the plain.

38

'Hold thy hand, good fellow,' said the
    curtal frier,
  'Thy master and I will agree;

And we will have new orders taken,
  With all the hast that may be.'

39

'If thou wilt forsake fair Fountains Dale,
  And Fountains Abby free,
Every Sunday throughout the year,
  A noble shall be thy fee.

40

'And every holly-day throughout the
    year,
  Changed shall thy garments be,
If thou wilt go to fair Notingham,
  And there remain with me.'

41

This curtal frier had kept Fountains
    Dale
  Seven long years or more;
There was neither knight, lord, nor earl
  Could make him yield before.

9

ROBIN HOOD AND LITTLE JOHN (Child 125)

Sources:
A. Chapbook version: *Robin Hood's Garland, being a complete History of all the Notable and Merry Exploits Perform'd by him and his Men on divers occasions. York, Printed and sold by J. Jackson in Peter-gate.* (York Minster Library, B. 8; *c*. 1750)[1] pp. 12–16.
B. Traditional American version, from Virginia: MacEdward Leach, ed. *The Ballad Book* (New York, 1955), pp. 370–2.

Other Editions of A:
Evans, 1777, I, 204; Ritson, 1795, II, 138–45; Gutch, 1847, II, 295–301; Child, 1888, III, 134–6; Leach, 1955, pp. 367–70.

From his first appearance as a 'gode yeman' in the third stanza of the *Gest*, Little John has always been the most important and inseparable of Robin Hood's companions. It was consequently no doubt inevitable that, sooner or later, a ballad would be composed to explain both his name and the circumstances by which he joined his master in the greenwood. It was almost as inevitable that this story should take the traditional form of a personal combat between Robin and John, at the conclusion of which the former was compelled to acknowledge that 'thou has got the day'. Whether this particular tale has medieval origins is, however, highly doubtful. The surviving ballad of *Robin Hood and Little John* shows every sign of having been produced by a professional ballad-writer for a popular audience. It can probably be identified with the ballad of Robin Hood and Little John entered in the Stationers' Registers on 29 June 1624;[2] and was certainly circulating in both black- and white-letter broadside form during the second half of the seventeenth century. For no very obvious reason it was omitted from all the early garlands and never became a standard component of the repertoire of Robin Hood chap-books. However, by the middle of the eighteenth century *Robin Hood and*

---

[1] R. Davies, *A Memoir of the York Press* (Westminster, 1868), pp. 312–18.
[2] Rollins, *Analytical Index to the Ballad Entries (1557–1709) in the Registers of the Company of the Stationers of London*, No. 2309 (p. 199). For another 'Robin Hood and Little John' (probably a ballad) entered to Master Oulton on 22 April 1640 see Arber IV, 507.

Little John was often included in the larger printed collections of Robin Hood songs in a very stereotyped text, of which the York version printed below is thoroughly representative.

Like many other seventeenth-century ballads, *Robin Hood and Little John* probably owed most of its considerable popularity to its music rather than its very bathetic verses. In the version printed below, as elsewhere, the ballad was directed to be sung to the tune of 'Arthur a Bland', i.e. the Nottingham tanner of *Robin Hood and The Tanner* (Child 126). 'Arthur a Bland', alternatively known as 'Robin Hood', 'Robin Hood Revived' or 'Hey down, down a down', was much the most popular of the Robin Hood tunes; and there are some grounds for believing that *Robin Hood and Little John* may have played an especially influential part in its dissemination.[1] It will also be noticed that this ballad is characterized by internal rhyme in the third line of each stanza, a feature it shares with at least seven other Robin Hood ballads, all of which bear a strong resemblance to each other (see *Robin Hood and the Butcher*, above, pp. 155–7). Most of these musical characteristics of *Robin Hood and Little John* were preserved relatively intact when the ballad was transmitted to the American colonies. The traditional Virginian version of the ballad printed below (B) reveals how persistently, despite considerable condensation and re-phrasing, what Child called the rank style of the English seventeenth century could survive for many generations in a very different country. Yet another version of the same ballad was recovered from a Mrs Schaupp of Kentucky in 1937.[2]

A. *Robin Hood and Little John. Being an Account of their first Meeting, their fierce Encounter and Conquest. To which is added their friendly Agreement, and how he came to be calld Little John. Tune of Arthur a Bland.*

1

When Robin Hood was about twenty
  years old,
    With a hey down down and a down,
  He happen'd to meet Little John,
A jolly brisk blade, right fit for the trade,
  For he was a lusty young man.

2

Tho' he was call'd Little, his limbs they
  were large,
  And his stature was seven foot high;
Where ever he came, they quak'd at his
  name,
  For soon he would make them to fly.

---

[1] See Child, III, 133, for the argument that the frequently mentioned tune of 'Robin Hood and the Stranger' is an allusion to an alternative title of *Robin Hood and Little John* rather than (as Ritson believed) of *Robin Hood Newly Revived* (Child 128). Bronson (*Traditional Tunes*, III, 26) prefers to 'tip the balance' in favour of Ritson's identification.

[2] Bronson, *Traditional Tunes*, III, 26–7.

3

How they came acquainted, I'll tell you
    in brief,
  If you will but listen a while;
For this very jest, amongst all the rest,
    I think may cause you to smile.

4

Bold Robin said to his jolly bowmen,
  'Pray tarry you here in this grove;
And see that you all observe well my call,
    While thro the forest I rove.

5

We have had no sport for these fourteen
    long days,
  Therefore now abroad will I go;
Now should I be beat, and cannot
    retreat,
    My horn I will presently blow.'

6

Then did he shake hands with his merry
    men all,
  And bid them at present good by;
Then as near a brook his journey he
    took,
    A stranger he chanc'd to espy.

7

They happen'd to meet on a long
    narrow bridge,
  And neither of them would give way;
Quoth bold Robin Hood, and sturdily
    stood,
    'I'll show you right Nottingham play!'

8

With that from his quiver an arrow he
    drew,
  A broad arrow with a goose wing;
The stranger reply'd, 'I'll licker[1] your
    hide
    If thou offer to touch the string.'

9

Quoth bold Robin Hood, 'Thou dost
    prate like an ass,
  For where (*sic*) I to bend but my bow,
I could send a dart quite through thy
    proud heart,
    Before thou could'st strike me **one**
    blow.'

10

'Thou talk'st like a coward,' the stranger
    reply'd;
  'Well arm'd with a long bow you
    stand,
To shoot at my breast, while I, I protest,
    Have nought but a staff in my hand.'

11

'The name of a coward,' quoth Robin,
    'I scorn,
  Wherefore my long bow I'll lay by;
And now, for thy sake, a staff will I take,
    The truth of thy manhood to try.'

12

Then Robin Hood stept to a thicket of
    trees,
  And chose him a staff of ground oak;
Now this being done, away he did run
    To the stranger, and merrily spoke:

13

'Lo! see my staff is lusty and tough,
  Now here on this bridge we will play;
Whoever falls in, the other shall win
    The battle, and so we'll away.'

14

'With all my whole heart,' the stranger
    reply'd,
  'I scorn in the least to give out.'
This said, they fell to't without more
    dispute,
    And their staffs they did flourish
    about.

---

[1] licker: *thrash*

15

And first Robin he gave the stranger a
    bang,
  So hard that it made his bones ring;
The stranger he said, 'This must be
    repaid,
    'I'll give you as good as you bring.

16

'So long as I'm able to handle my staff,
  To die in your debt, friend, I scorn.'
Then to it both go, and follow their
    blows,
  As if they had been threshing of corn.

17

The stranger gave Robin a crack on the
    crown,
  Which caused the blood to appear;
Then Robin, enrag'd, more fiercely
    engag'd,
  And follow'd his blows more severe.

18

So thick and so fast did he lay it on him,
  With a passionate fury and ire,
At every stroke, he made him to smoke,
  As if he had been all on fire.

19

O then in a fury the stranger he grew,
  And gave him a damnable look,
And with it a blow which laid him full
    low,
  And tumbl'd him into the brook.

20

'I prithee, good fellow, O where art
    thou know [*sic*]?',
  The stranger, in laughter, he cry'd;
Quoth bold Robin Hood, 'Good faith,
    in the flood,
  And floating along with the tide.

21

'I needs must acknowledge thou art a
    brave soul;
  With thee I'll no longer contend;
For in truth I must say, thou has got the
    day
  Our battle shall be at an end.'

22

Then unto the bank he did presently
    wade,
  And pull'd himself out by a thorn;
Which done, at the last, he blow'd a
    loud blast
  Straightway on his fine bugle horn.

23

The eccho of which thro' the vallies did
    ring,
  At which his stout bowmen appear'd,
All cloathed in green, most gay to be
    seen;
  So up to their master they steer'd.

24

'O what is the matter?' quoth Will.
    Stutely;[1]
  'Good master, you are wet to the
    skin:'
'No matter,' quoth he; 'the lad that you
    see,
  In fighting hath tumbl'd me in.'

25

'He shall not go scot-free,' the others
    reply'd;
  So straight they were seizing him
    there,
To duck him likewise; but Robin Hood
    cries,
  'He is a stout fellow, forbear!

---

[1] The only other appearance of William Stutely in the traditional Robin Hood ballads is
as the subject of the seventeenth-century *Robin Hood Rescuing Will Stutly* (Child 141)

26

'There's no one shall wrong thee, friend,
  be not afraid;
These bowmen upon me do wait;
There's threescore and ten;[1] if thou
  wilt be mine,
Though shalt have my livery straight,

27

'And other accoutrements fit also;
  Speak up, jolly blade, ne'er fear;
I'll teach you also the use of the bow,
  To shoot at the fat fallow deer.'

28

'O here is my hand,' the stranger reply'd,
  'I'll serve you with all my whole heart;
My name is John Little, a man of good
  mettle;
  Ne'er doubt me, for I'll play my part.'

29

'His name shall be altered,' quoth
  William Stuteley,
  'And I will his godfather be;
Prepare then a feast, and none of the
  least,
  For we will be merry,' quoth he.

30

They presently fetch'd in a brace of fat
  does,
  With humming strong liquor likewise;
They lov'd what was good; so, in the
  green wood,
  This pretty sweet babe they baptiz'd.

31

He was, I must tell you, but seven foot
  high,
  And, maybe, an ell in the waste;
He was a sweet lad; much feasting they
  had;
  Bold Robin the christening grac'd,

32

With all his bowmen, which stood in a
  ring,
  And were of the Nottingham breed.
Brave Stuteley came then, with seven
  yeomen,
  And did in this manner proceed.

33

'This infant was call'd John Little,'
  quoth he,
  'Which name shall be chang'd anon;
The words we'll transpose, so where-
  ever he goes,
  His name shall be call'd Little John.'

34

They all with a shout made the elements
  ring,
  So soon as the office was o'er;
To feasting they went, with true merri-
  ment,
  And tippled strong liquor gallore.

35

Then Robin he took the pretty sweet
  babe,
  And cloath'd him from top to toe
In garments of green, most gay to be
  seen,
  And gave him a curious long bow.

36

'Thou shalt be an archer as well as the
  best,
  And range in the greenwood with us;
Where we will not want gold nor silver,
  behold,
  While bishops have ought in their
  purse.

37

'We live here like squires, or lords of
  renown,
  Without e'er a foot of free land;
We feast on good cheer, with wine, ale,
  and beer,
  And every thing at our command.'

---

[1] Other texts have 'and nine': 69 or 70 is, in any case, the lowest of the various fanciful
estimates of the total size of Robin's company made in the ballads (Child, *Popular
Ballads*, III, 67, 75, 78, 180–1, 228; and see above, p. 100).

38

Then musick and dancing did finish
 the day;
 At length, when the sun waxed low,
Then all the whole train the grove did
 refrain,
 And un o their caves they did go.

39

And so ever after, as long as they liv'd,
 Altho he was proper and tall,
Yet nevertheless, the truth to express,
 Still Little John they did him call.

B. *Traditional American Version, from Virginia*

1

Scarce sixteen years old was bold Robin
 Hood,
 When first he met Little John,
A steady young blade well fit for his
 trade,
 And he was a handsome young man.

2

Although he was Little, his limbs they
 were large,
 His height about seven feet high;
And wherever he came he straight cut
 his name,
 And quickly he made them all fly.

3

'I have not been sporting for fourteen
 long days,
 So now abroad I will go,
And if I get beat, and I can't retreat,
 My horn I will suddenly blow.'

4

Thus took he the leave of his merry men
 all,
 And bid them a pleasant good-by,
And down to the brook a journey he
 took,
 And a stranger he chancd for to spy.

5

There these two fellows met on a long
 narrow bridge,
 And neither of them would give way;
The stranger he said, 'I will lather your
 hide;
 I will show you fine Nottingham play.'

6

'You speak as a fool,' bold Robin
 replied:
 'If I should bend my long bow,
I would shoot a dart then quite through
 your heart,
 Before you could give me one blow.'

7

'You speak as a coward,' the stranger
 replied,
 'To bend your long bow as I stand,
To shoot at my breast, as I do protest,
 And I but a staff in my hand.'

8

'The name of a coward I do disdain;
 Therefore my long bow I'll lay by;
And now for your sake a staff I will take,
 And the strength of your manhood
 I'll try.'

9

Robin stepped down in a thicket of wood,
 And chose him a staff of brown oak,
And that being done, he straight back
 did come,
 To the stranger he merrily spoke:

10

'Oh, here is my staff both steady and
 stout;
 Therefore on this bridge let us play.
Whichever falls in, the other shall win,
 And after all that we'll away.'

11

Robin struck the stranger a crack on the
     crown,
  Which caused the red blood to appear.
The stranger enraged, then closely
     engaged,
  And laid on his blows most severe.

12

'As long as I'm able my staff for to
     handle,
  To die in your debt I would scorn.'
And so thick and fast they laid on each
     other,
  As though they were threshing out
     corn.

13

The stranger struck Robin a crack on
     the crown,
  That caused him a terrible flow,
And with the same blow he laid him
     quite low,
  And tumbled him into the brook.

14

'Oh, where are you now, my gay fellow?'
     he said;
  And with a loud laugh he replied,
'It's I, by my faith,' bold Robin Hood
     said,
  'I am floating away with the tide.'

15

Robin floated down all into the deep,
  And drew himself out by a thorn,
And with his last gasp he blew a loud
     blast,
  A blast on his own bugle-horn,

16

Which caused all the hills and the
     valleys to ring,
  And all his gay men to appear.
There were threescore and ten, all
     clothed in green,
  That straightway to the master did
     steer.

17

'Oh, what is the matter?', said William
     Stellee,[1]
  'Methinks you are wet to the skin.'
'No matter,' said he, 'the lad that you
     see
  By fair fighting has tumbled me in.'

18

'He shall not go free,' said William
     Stellee,
  While still stood the poor stranger
     there;
'We will duck him likewise.' Bold Robin
     replies
  'He is a stout fellow, forbear.'

19

'His name is John Little, he is made of
     good metal,
  No doubt he will play his own part.'
'He shall not go free,' said William
     Stellee,
  'Therefore his godfather I'll be.'

20

They called him a babe; he was none
     of the least;
  They had rum and all liquors like-
     wise,
And there in the woods these bold
     fellows stood,
  While this little babe was baptized.

[1] A corruption of Stutely (above, p. 168) and an excellent illustration of the rule that the
   complete alteration of personal names is likely to be the most obvious consequence of
   ballad transmission: see W. M. Hart, 'Professor Child and the Ballad' *Publications of the
   Modern Language Association of America*, XXI (1906), 769–70.

IO

ROBIN HOOD AND ALLEN A DALE (Child 138)

Source:
Robin Hood's Garland, being a complete History of all the Notable and Merry Exploits Perform'd by him and his Men on divers occasions. York, Printed and sold by J. Jackson in Peter-gate (York Minster Library, B. 8; *c.* 1750) pp. 33–6.

Other Editions:
Evans, 1777, I, 126; Ritson, 1795, II, 46–51; Gutch, 1847, II, 259–63; Child, 1888, III, 173–4; Quiller-Couch, 1910, pp. 616–20; Leach, 1955, pp. 397–400.

After the many monotonous broadside variations on the theme of personal combat with a stranger, the ballad of *Robin Hood and Allen a Dale* must have appeared a welcome and unexpected novelty. At first sight the role of matchmaker would seem to involve a surprising transformation of the *persona* of the forest outlaw. Yet it was perhaps a logical development of the popular belief that Robin was 'a good outlawe, / And dyde pore men moch god' to construct a ballad which extended his magnanimous benevolence to the plight of poor lovers. Despite the mechanical obviousness of the language in which it is expressed, the narrative of *Robin Hood and Allen a Dale* is indeed exceptionally and economically dramatic. A popular and perennially appealing story has been re-worked to include the two traditional Robin Hood motifs of his successful 'disguising' (this time as a 'bold harper') and subsequent discomfiting of a bishop. The ballad was included in most of the larger Robin Hood Garlands, a typical example being the York collection from which the following text is derived. Although *Robin Hood and Allen a Dale* first survives in broadside copies of the late seventeenth century,[1] the basic outlines of the story certainly have a much earlier history. The author of the account of Robin Hood's career in Sloane MS. 780, written *c.* 1600, was evidently aware of a very similar ballad in which, however, the unfortunate lover was Scarlock rather than Allen a Dale, and Robin 'came to the church as a beggar' rather than a harper. Thanks to the sound of his horn, 'Bold Robin Hood he did the young man right, And took the damsel from the doteing knight.' Allen a Dale

[1] Three of which are collated in Child, III, 173–5.

as a character does not appear to have entered the legend until the seventeenth century.

Robin Hood and Allen a Dale : or, the Manner of Robin Hood's rescuing a young Lady from an old Knight, to whom she was going to be married, and restoring her to Allen a Dale. Tune of Robin Hood in the Green woode stood.

1
Come listen to me, you gallants so free,
　All you that love mirth for to hear,
And I will tell you of a bold outlaw,
　That lived in Nottinghamshire,
　That lived in Nottinghamshire.

2
As Robin Hood in the green forest stood,
　All under the green wood tree,
There he was aware of a brave young man,
　As fine as fine might be.

3
The youngster was cloathed in scarlet red,
　In scarlet fine and gay,
And he did frisk it over the plain,
　And chanted a round de la.

4
As Robin Hood next morning stood,
　Amongst the leaves so gay,
There did he 'spy the same young man
　Come drooping along the way.

5
The scarlet he wore the day before,
　It was clean cast away;
And every step he fetch'd a sigh,
　'Alack and well a day!'

6
Then stepped forth brave Little John,
　And Midge the miller's son,[1]
Which made the young man bend his bow,
　When as he see them come.

7
'Stand off, stand off,' the young man said,
　'What is your will with me?'
'You must come before our master strait,
　Under yon greenwood tree.'

8
And when he came bold Robin before,
　Robin ask'd him courteously,
'O hast thou any money to spare
　For my merry men and me?'

9
'I have no money,' the young man said,
　'But five shillings and a ring;
And that I have kept this seven long years,
　To have it at my wedding.

10
'Yesterday I should have married a maid,
　But she from me was ta'en,
And chosen to be an old knight's delight,
　Whereby my poor heart is slain.'

[1] A common corruption in Robin Hood ballads of Much, the Miller's Son, one of the original companions of the outlaw (see above, pp. 79, 161). Some early texts of *Robin Hood and Allen a Dale* read, less happily, 'Nick the miller's son' here.

11

'What is thy name?' then said Robin
    Hood,
  'Come tell to me, without any fail.'
'By the faith of my body,' then said the
    young man,
  'My name it is Allen a Dale.'

12

'What wilt thou give me,' said Robin
    Hood,
  'In ready gold or fee,
To help thee to thy true love again,
  And deliver her unto thee?'

13

'I have no money,' then said the young
    man,
  'No ready gold or fee,
But I will swear upon a book
  Thy true servant to be.'

14

'How many miles is it to thy true love?
  Come tell me without any guile.'
'By the faith of my body,' then said the
    young man,
  'It is but five little miles.'

15

Then Robin he hasted over the plain,
  He did neither stint nor lin,[1]
Until he came unto the church
  Where Allen should keep his wedding.

16

'What dost thou hear [*sic*]?' the bishop
    then said,
  'I prithee now tell me.'
'I am a bold harper,' quoth Robin Hood,
  'And the best in the north country.'

17

'O welcome, O welcome,' the bishop
    then said,
  'That musick best pleaseth me.'

'You shall have no musick,' quoth Robin
    Hood,
  'Till the bride and the bridegroom I
    see.'

18

With that came in a wealthy knight,
  Which was both grave and old,
And after him a finikin[2] lass,
  Did shine like the glittering gold.

19

'This is not a fit match,' quoth bold
    Robin Hood,
  'That you do seem to make here;
For since we are come into the church,
  The bride she shall chuse her own
    dear.'

20

Then Robin Hood put his horn to his
    mouth,
  And blew blasts two or three;
Then four and twenty bowmen bold
  Came leaping over the lee.

21

And when they came into the church-
    yard,
  Marching all on a row,
The first man was Allen a Dale,
  To give bold Robin his bow.

22

'This is thy true-love,' Robin he said,
  'Young Allen, as I hear say;
And you shall be married at the same
    time,
  Before we depart away.'

23

'That may not be,' the bishop he said,
  'For thy word shall not stand;
They shall be three times ask'd in the
    church,
  As is the law of our land.'

---

[1] lin: *stop*   [2] finikin: *fine, finely dressed*

24

Robin Hood pull'd of the bishop's coat,
  And put it upon Little John;
'By the faith of my body,' then Robin
    said,
  'This cloth doth make the a man.'

25

When Little John went to the choir,
  The people began to laugh;
He ask'd them seven times in the church,
  Lest three times should not be
    enough.

26

'Who gives this maid,' said Little John;
  Quoth Robin Hood, 'That do I;
And he that doth take her from Allen a
    Dale
  Full dearly he shall her buy.'

27

And thus having ended this merry
    wedding,
  The bride she look'd like a queen,
And so they return'd to the merry
    greenwood,
  Amongst the leaves so green.

'A New Ballad of bold Robin Hood', or
*Robin Hood's Birth, Breeding, Valour and
Marriage*: a broadside printed at London
for W. Onley, *c.* 1660 (British Library,
Roxburghe I, 360).

I I

ROBIN HOOD AND MAID MARIAN (Child 150)

Source:
Bodleian Library, Oxford, Wood MS. 401, leaves 21v, 22r (a broadside with no mention of the printer; the initials S.S. at the end).

Other Editions:
Ritson, 1795, II, 157–61; Evans, 1810, II, 240–4; Gutch, 1847, II, 303–6; Child, 1888, III, 218–19; Leach, 1955, pp. 423–5.

Only one copy of this ballad is known to survive, that preserved among Antony Wood's collection of seventeenth-century black-letter broadsides. It provides no evidence of either the printer or the date but is signed by one S.S., presumably the author of this original if feeble addition to the canon of Robin Hood ballads. Despite its complete lack of any literary merit, *Robin Hood and Maid Marian* deserves inclusion in this selection as the most extreme and implausible attempt ever made to combine the unusual theme of Robin Hood as a lover with the more traditional motif of his single-handed fight against an opponent unaware of his real identity. In this case we are even expected to believe that Robin failed to recognize his own 'bonny fine maid'. More interestingly still, this is the only serious attempt to provide Maid Marian with an independent role in the Robin Hood ballads. Possibly influenced by the appearance of Marian, alias Matilda, as Robin Hood's lover in Munday's plays *The Downfall* and *The Death of Robert, Earl of Huntington*, (see below, No. 22) it seems highly unlikely that the author of this ballad was relying on any popular tradition. Despite the occasional appearance of her name in other seventeenth-century Robin Hood ballads, Marian was to play a relatively insignificant part in the outlaw legend for many years to come. No doubt for this reason, *Robin Hood and Maid Marian* failed to find its way into the innumerable Robin Hood Garlands of the period from the Restoration to the early nineteenth century: it was only rediscovered when printed from Wood's copy in the first edition (1795) of Ritson's *Robin Hood*.

A famous Battle between Robin Hood and Maid Marian, declaring their Love, Life, and Liberty. Tune, Robin Hood Reviv'd.

1

A bonny fine maid of a noble degree,
   With a hey down down a down down,
  Maid Marian call'd by name,
Did live in the North, of excellent worth,
  For shee was a gallant dame.

2

For favour and face, and beauty most
   rare,
  Queen Hellen shee did excell;
For Marian then was prais'd of all men
  That did in the country dwell.

3

'Twas neither Rosamond nor Jane
   Shore,[1]
  Whose beauty was clear and bright,
That could surpass this country lass,
  Beloved of lord and knight.

4

The Earl of Huntington, nobly born,
  That came of noble blood,
To Marian went, with a good intent,
  By the name of Robin Hood.

5

With kisses sweet their red lips meet,
  For shee and the earl did agree.
In every place, they kindly imbrace,
  With love and sweet unity.

6

But fortune bearing these lovers a
   spight,
  That soon they were forced to part;

To the merry green wood then went
   Robin Hood,
  With a sad and sorrowfull heart.

7

And Marian, poor soul, was troubled in
   mind,
  For the absence of her friend;
With finger in eye, shee often did cry,
  And his person did much comend.

8

Perplexed and vexed, and troubled in
   mind,
  Shee drest her self like a page,
And ranged the wood to find Robin
   Hood,
  The bravest of men in that age.

9

With quiver and bow, sword, buckler,
   and all,
  Thus armed was Marian most bold,
Still wandering about to find Robin out,
  Whose person was better than gold.

10

But Robin Hood, hee himself had
   disguis'd,
  And Marian was strangly attir'd,
That they prov'd foes, and so fell to
   blowes,
  Whose vallour bold Robin admir'd.

11

They drew out their swords, and to
   cutting they went,
  At least an hour or more,
That the blood ran apace from bold
   Robins face,
  And Marian was wounded sore.

[1] 'Fair' Rosamond and Jane Shore, the mistresses of Henry II and Edward IV respectively, were—as paragons of female beauty—themselves the subject of many popular seventeenth-century ballads.

12

'O hold thy hand, hold thy hand,' said
  Robin Hood,
  'And thou shalt be one of my string,
To range in the wood with bold Robin
  Hood,
  And hear the sweet nightingall sing.'

13

When Marian did hear the voice of her
  love,
  Her self shee did quickly discover,
And with kisses sweet she did him greet,
  Like to a most loyall lover.

14

When bold Robin Hood his Marian did
  see,
  Good lord, what clipping[1] was there!
With kind imbraces, and jobbing[2] of
  faces,
  Providing of gallant cheer.

15

For Little John took his bow in his hand,
  And wandring in the wood,
To kill the deer, and make good chear,
  For Marian and Robin Hood.

The Second Parte

16

A stately banquet they had full soon,
  All in a shaded bower,
Where venison sweet they had to eat,
  And were merry that present hour.

17

Great flaggons of wine were set on the
  board,
  And merrily they drunk round
Their boules of sack, to strengthen the
  back,
  Whilst their knees did touch the
  ground.

18

First Robin Hood began a health
  To Marian his onely dear,
And his yeomen all, both comly and tall,
  Did quickly bring up the rear.

19

For in a brave vente[3] they tost off the
  bouls,

Whilst thus they did remain,
And every cup, as they drunk up,
  They filled with speed again.

20

At last they ended their merryment,
  And went to walk in the wood,
Where Little John and Maid Marian
  Attended on bold Robin Hood.

21

In sollid content together they liv'd,
  With all their yeomen gay;
They liv'd by their hands, without any
  lands,
  And so they did many a day.

22

But now to conclude, an end I will make
  In time, as I think it good,
For the people that dwell in the North
  can tell
  Of Marian and bold Robin Hood.

---

[1] clipping: *embracing*   [2] jobbing: *pecking, i.e. kissing*   [3] brave vente: *merry vein*

12

THE NOBLE FISHERMAN (ROBIN HOOD'S PREFERMENT) (Child 148)

Source:
The English Archer, or Robert Earl of Huntington, vulgarly call'd Robin Hood. A 'Robin Hood's Garland' printed and sold by Thomas Gent of York, *c.* 1750[1] (York Minster Library, B. 9) pp. 53–5.

Other Editions:
Evans, 1777, I, 171; Ritson, 1795, II, 110–15; Gutch, 1847, II, 198–202; Child, 1888, III, 211–13; Quiller-Couch, 1910, pp. 630–4.

Robin Hood has never undergone a more bizarre metamorphosis than his conversion in this ballad from a forest outlaw to a hero of the open sea. Nowadays the story of *The Noble Fisherman* may appear, as it did to Child, more than usually infantile; but there can be no doubt that it enjoyed great popularity for at least two hundred years after its first emergence in the early seventeenth century. A ballad of 'The Noble Fisherman, or, Robin Hoods great Prize' (the latter title was later transferred to another ballad) was entered in the Stationers' Registers as early as 13 June 1631; and the first surviving broadside copy of the work—among Antony Wood's collections in the Bodleian Library, Oxford—seems to date from the same decade.[2] An exceptionally large number of late seventeenth-century broadsides of *The Noble Fisherman* are still extant, so it is no surprise to discover that the song was almost always included in Robin Hood Garlands from the beginning to the end of their long history. The York copy printed below is a completely representative example of the eighteenth-century texts of the song, texts which had changed very little during the previous hundred years except for a certain standardization of spelling and modernization of diction. Throughout the entire history of this ballad Robin's port of embarkation was always Scarborough, and his adversaries were always 'French robbers on the sea'.

The Noble Fisherman was itself responsible for spawning a great number of subsidiary and misleadingly influential Robin Hood legends. Even a historian

---

[1] Davies, *Memoir of the York Press*, p. 223.
[2] Arber, IV, 254; Rollins, *Analytical Index to the Ballad Entries in the Registers of the Company of Stationers*, No. 1955 (pp. 169–70); Child, III, 211–13.

as sober as Lionel Charlton, author of the first *History of Whitby*, was capable of believing that when Robin Hood was in danger of capture by 'parties of soldiers . . . sent down from London to apprehend him', he 'always had in readiness near at hand some small fishing vessels, to which he could have refuge, if he found himself pursued; for in these, putting off to sea, he looked upon himself as quite secure, and held the whole power of the English nation at defiance. The chief place of his resort at these times, where his boats were generally laid up, was about six miles from Whitby, to which he communicated his name'.[1] Charlton's ingenious powers of invention may, of course, embroider what is a real possibility—that the author of *The Noble Fisherman* placed Robin's maritime adventure off the north Yorkshire coast because he was well aware of the existence of a 'Robin Hood's Bay' there. But it is almost inconceivable that the story of this ballad was derived from popular tradition, let alone any genuine historical incident. *The Noble Fisherman* bears all the hallmarks of a song composed by a professional ballad writer who was fully conscious of the commercial attractions of inventing a tale about England's most popular hero which could be set within the almost equally popular genre of a successful sea victory over the national enemy.[2]

The noble Fisherman : Or, Robin Hood's Preferment,
Shewing how he won a Prize on the Sea, and how he
gave one half to his Dame, and the other to the
Building of Alms-Houses. Tune of, In Summer Time, etc.[3]

1

In summer time, when leaves grow
    green,
When they do grow both green and
    long,
Of a bould outlaw, call'd Robin Hood,
    It is of him I sing this song.

2

When the lily-leaf and the couslip
    sweet,
    Do bud and spring with merry chear,
This outlaw was weary of the wood-side,
    And chasing of the fallow deer.

3

'The fishermen brave more mony have
    Than any merchant, two or three;
Therefore I will to Scarborough goe,
    That I a fisherman may be.'

4

This outlaw call'd his merry men all,
    As they sat under the green-wood
        tree:
'If any of you have gold to spend,
    I pray you heartily spend it with me.'

---

[1] L. Charlton, *History of Whitby and Whitby Abbey* (York, 1779), pp. 146–7, an account written with such conviction that it was—and is—often taken seriously!

[2] C. H. Firth, *Naval Songs and Ballads* (London, 1908); Gerould, *Ballad of Tradition*, pp. 56–7.

[3] The same tune, and therefore the same opening line, is to be found in broadside and garland versions of *Robin Hood and the Curtal Friar* (above, p. 161) and *Robin Hood and the Tinker* (Child, 127): for the notation of the tune, see Rimbault in Gutch, II, 436, and the important reservations of Bronson, *Traditional Tunes*, III, 69.

5

'Now,' quoth Robin Hood, 'I'l to
    Scarborough goe,
It seems to be a very fair day,'
Who tooke up his inn in a widow
    woman's house,
    Hard by upon the waters gray.

6

Who askt of him, 'Where wast thou
    born?
Or tell me, where thou dost fare?'
'I am a poor fisherman,' said he then,
    'This day intrapped all in care.'

7

'What is thy name, thou fine fellow?
    I pray thee heartily tell me;'
'In my own country where I was born,
    Men call me Simon Over-the-Lee.'

8

'Simon, Simon,' said the good wife,
    'I wish thou mayst well brook[1] thy
    name.'
The outlaw was aware of her courtsie,
    And rejoyc'd he had got such a dame.

9

'Simon, wilt thou now be my man?
    And good round wages I'll give thee;
I have as good a ship of my own
    As any sails upon the sea.

10

'Anchors and planks thou shalt want
    none,
Masts and ropes there are so long;'
'And if that thou so furnish me,'
    Said Simon, 'nothing shall be wrong.'

11

They pluck'd up anchors, and away did
    sail,
More of a day then two or three;
When others cast in their baited hooks,
    The bate[2] lines in the sea cast he.

12

'It will be long,' said the Master then,
    'E'er this great lubber thrive on the
    sea;
He shall have no part in our fish,
    For in truth he is no part worthy.'

13

'O woe is me,' said Simon then,
    'This day that ever I came here!
I wish I were in Plumpton Park,[3]
    A chasing of the fallow deer.

14

'For every man laughs me to scorn,
    And by me sets nothing at all;
If I had them in Plumpton Park,
    I would set little by them all.'

15

They pluck'd up anchors, and away did
    sail,
More of a day then two or three;
But Simon espy'd a ship of war,
    That sail'd to them vigorously.

16

'O woe is me,' said the Master then,
    'This day that ever I was born!
For all the fish that we have got
    Is every bit lost and forlorn.

---

[1] brook: *deserve* (the dame hopes that Robin will prove as good a fisherman as his name-
sake, Simon Peter)

[2] bate: a mistake for 'bare', the word in all the early broadside copies. It is hard to agree
with Child's supposition (III, 211) that Robin was being deliberately perverse rather
than ignorant.

[3] An unexpected place for which Robin should feel nostalgia; possibly borrowed from the
Gest, stanza 357 (above, p. 105).

17

'For these French robbers on the sea,
    They will not spare, no, not one man,
But carry us to the coast of France,
    And lay us in the prison strong.'

18

But Simon said, 'Do not fear them,
    Nor, Master, take you any care;
Give me my bent bow in my hand,
    And ne'er a French man will I spare.'

19

'Hold thy peace then, thou long lubber,
    For thou art nought but brags and
        boast;
If I should cast thee over-board,
    There is but a simple lubber lost.'

20

Simon grew angry at these words,
    And so sore angry then was he
That he took his bent bow in hand,
    And on the ship hatch goeth he.

21

'Master, tye me fast to the mast,
    That at my mark I may stand fair,
And give me my bent bow in hand,
    And ne'er a French man will I spare.'

22

He drew the arrow to the head,
    And drew it with all might and main,
And straight in the twincle of an eye,
    To th' French man's heart the arrow
        gain.

23

The French man fell on the ship hatch,
    And under the hatches down below;
Another French man that him espy'd
    The dead corps in the sea did throw.

24

'O, loose me from the mast,
    And for them all take you no care,
And give me my bent bow in hand,
    And ne'er a French man will I spare.'

25

Then straight they boarded the French
        ship,
    They lying all dead in their sight:
They found within this ship of war
    Twelve thousand pounds in money
        bright.

26

'One half of the ship,' said Simon then,
    'I'll give to my dame and children
        small;
The other half of the ship I'll give
    To you that are my fellow all.'

27

But now bespake the Master then,
    'For so, Simon, it shall not be;
For you have won it with thy own hands,
    And the owner of it you must be.'

28

'It shall be so, as I have said:
    And, with the gold, for the oppress'd
An habitation I will build,
    Where they shall live in peace and
        rest.'

13

ROBIN HOOD AND THE VALIANT KNIGHT
(Child 153)

Source:
Robin Hood; or, A complete History of all the Notable Exploits per-formed by Him and His Merry Men. A 'Robin Hood's Garland' printed by and for Thomas Wilson and Son, High Ousegate, York, 1811 (price: 1/–) (York City Library, Y. 920) pp. 103–6.

Other Editions:
Evans, 1777, I, 232; Ritson, 1795, II, 178–82; Gutch, 1847, II, 307–10; Child, 1888, III, 225–6.

Despite its somewhat misleading title, *Robin Hood and the Valiant Knight* is in fact a story of the forest outlaw's final battle with the forces of authority and his subsequent death. A piece which 'surpasses in platitude everything that has gone before' (Child, III, 225), this song certainly has strong claims to be regarded as the least distinguished Robin Hood ballad ever composed. Indeed no other work illustrates quite so well (hence its inclusion here) the imaginative poverty as well as stylistic debasement which overtook the legend of the greenwood during the course of the eighteenth century. Among many casual liberties taken with the stock ingredients of the Robin Hood saga are the transference of Robin's own name of 'Locksley' to an otherwise com-pletely obscure character and the allegation that Robin was killed by a monk rather than the prioress of Kirklees. Just because of its careless crudity, *Robin Hood and the Valiant Knight* is an unusually instructive example of the dangers of believing that the 'traditional' Robin Hood ballads preserve genuine popular tradition, let alone historical fact. It is probable that this was indeed the very last of these 'traditional' ballads to be composed, almost certainly in an attempt to bring the random collections of Robin Hood songs which made up the standard garlands and chapbooks to a satisfactory close. No seventeenth-century copies of *Robin Hood and the Valiant Knight* are known to survive, and it was only from *c.* 1750 that it began to appear regularly in the garlands, almost always as their last item and leading—as below—directly to the famous Robin Hood's Epitaph.[1] However, towards

[1] See, e.g., the exceptionally well produced garland printed for James Hodges of London

the end of the eighteenth century a version of *Robin Hood's Death* (above, No. 4b) was commonly, and more happily, chosen to conclude the Robin Hood Garlands: when that happened, *Robin Hood and the Valiant Knight* took the penultimate place in the collection.

Robin Hood and the valiant Knight; together with
an Account of his Death and Burial, etc.
Tune of, Robin Hood and the fifteen Foresters.[1]

1

When Robin Hood and his merry men
all,
  Derry, derry, down,
 Had reigned many years,
The king was then told he had been too
bold
 To his bishops and noble peers.
    Hey, down, derry, derry, down.

2

Therefore they call'd a council of state,
 To know what was best to be done
For to quell their pride, or else, they
reply'd,
 The land would be over-run.

3

Having consulted a whole summer's
day,
 At length it was agreed
That one should be sent to try the
event,
 And fetch him away with speed.

4

Therefore a trusty and worthy knight
 The king was pleas'd to call,
Sir William by name;[2] when to him he
came,
 He told him his pleasure all.

5

'Go you from hence to bold Robin
Hood,
 And bid him, without more ado,
Surrender himself, or else the proud elf
 Shall suffer with all his crew.

6

'Take here an hundred bowmen brave,
 All chosen men of might,
Of excellent art for to take thy part,
 In glittering armour bright.'

7

Then said the knight, 'My sov'reign
liege,
 By me they shall be led;
I'll venture my blood against Robin
Hood,
 And bring him alive or dead.'

---

under the common title of *The English Archer* (British Library, C. 67. a. 24) or the texts collated by Child (III, 225).

[1] An alternative tune-title for *Robin Hood's Progress to Nottingham* (Child 139). It will be noted that *Robin Hood and the Valiant Knight* is one of the large group of Robin Hood ballads with middle rhyme in the third line of each stanza (see above, p. 151; Bronson, *Traditional Tunes*, III, 52, 71).

[2] Perhaps the progenitor of Sir William Dale in Howard Pyle's *The Merry Adventures of Robin Hood* (London, 1971 edn.), pp. 245–6, but otherwise a personage rarely mentioned in later Robin Hood literature.

8

One hundred men were chosen straight,
  As proper as e'er a man saw,
On midsummer day they march'd away,
  To conquer that brave outlaw.

9

With long yew bows and shining spears,
  They march'd in mickle pride,
And never delay'd, or halted, or staid,
  Till they came to the green wood side.

10

Said he to his archers, 'Tarry here;
  Your bows make ready all,
That, need should be, you may follow
    me;
  And see that you observe my call.

11

'I'll go in person first,' he cry'd,
  'With the letters of my good king,
Well sign'd and seal'd, and if he will
    yield,
  We need not draw one string.'

12

He wander'd about, till at length he
    came
  To the tent of Robin Hood;
The letters he shows; bold Robin
    arose,
  And there on his guard he stood.

13

'They'd have me surrender,' quoth
    Robin Hood,
  'And lie at their mercy then;
But tell them from me, that never shall
    be,
  While I have full seven score men.'[1]

14

Sir William the knight, both hardy and
    bold,
  Did offer[2] to seize him there;
Which William Locksley by fortune did
    see,
  And bid him that trick to forbear.

15

Then Robin Hood set his horn to his
    mouth,
  And blew a blast or twain,
And so did the knight, at which there in
    sight
  The archers came there all amain.

16

Sir William with care he drew up his
    men,
  And plac'd them in battle array;
Bold Robin, we find, he was not behind;
  Now this was a bloody fray.

17

The archers on both sides bent their
    bows,
  And clouds of arrows flew;
The very first flight, that honoured
    knight
  Did there bid the world adieu.

18

Yet nevertheless their fight did last
  From morning till almost noon;
Both parties were stout, and loath to
    give out;
  This was on the last (day) of June.

19

At length they went off; one part they
    went
  For London with free good will;
And Robin Hood he to the green wood
    tree,
  And there he was taken ill.

---

[1] The usual size of Robin's company in the ballads (see above, p. 100).
[2] offer: *attempt* This is a somewhat cryptic stanza, probably a corruption of an earlier story.

20

He sent for a monk to let him blood,
  Who took his life away;
Now this being done, his archers they
    run,
  It was no time to stay.

21

Some went on board and cross'd the
    seas,
  To Flanders, France and Spain,
And others to Rome, for fear of their
    doom,
  But soon return'd again.

22

Thus he that ne'er fear'd bow nor spear
  Was murder'd by letting of blood;
And so, loving friends, the story now
    ends
  Of valiant bold Robin Hood.

23

There's nothing remains but his epitaph
    now,
  Which, reader, here you have;
To this very day, read it you may,
  As it is upon his grave.

EPITAPH

Robert, Earl of Huntingdon,[1]
Lies here, his labour being done,
No archer like him was so good;
His wildness nam'd him
    ROBIN HOOD.
For thirteen years, and somewhat more,
These northern parts he vexed sore.
Such outlaws as he and his men
May England never know again.

---

[1] 'Robin, Earl of Huntington' in the earliest versions of this ballad (see Child, III, 226, and below, p. 190).

14

THE OPENING AND CLOSING STANZAS OF MARTIN PARKER'S 'A TRUE TALE OF ROBIN HOOD' (Child 154)

Source:
Probable First Edition of 1632 (B.L. copy, press-mark C.39 a. 52).

Other Editions:
Ritson, 1795, I, 126–48; Gutch, 1847, II, 84–106; Child, 1888, III, 227–33.

It is hardly surprising that the legend of Robin Hood should attract the attention of Martin Parker (*c.* 1600–*c.* 1656), the most distinguished of all London professional ballad-writers. In his *True Tale of Robin Hood* he attempted to provide a popular synthesis of the current tales of Robin Hood in much the same way that he wrote ballads on such other famous English heroes as King Arthur, St George and Sir Guy of Warwick.[1] Parker's insistence that his own version of the Robin Hood story was 'true' because of its reliance on chronicles rather than 'many fained tales' should not of course be taken too seriously: the chief interest of his work is that it was derived from so many different sources. These include not only the chronicle tradition as represented by Grafton but a wide variety of current ballad literature. His references to 'the abbot of Saint Maries' must derive from the *Gest*, and it is equally clear that Parker was familiar with several tales which found their way into the later Robin Hood Garlands as *Robin Hood and the Bishop*, *Robin Hood and Queen Katherine*, and *The Noble Fisherman* (Child, III, 227). Parker's *True Tale* is of especial value in preserving the broad outlines of some Robin Hood stories which failed to survive in an independent form.

The *True Tale* was entered to Francis Grove at Stationers' Hall on 29 February 1632[2] and thus provides us with our best opportunity to appreciate the main outlines of the Robin Hood legend as it existed a decade before the Commonwealth's suppression of the ballads for their 'disgrace of religion' and a generation before the outlaw's resurrection as the hero of innumerable

---

[1] H. E. Rollins, 'Martin Parker, Ballad-Monger', *Modern Philology* XVI (1919), pp. 113–38.
[2] Arber, IV, 273.

garlands. The following extracts show that many characteristic themes of the
modern legend had now crystallized. Maid Marian and Friar Tuck remain
conspicuous by their absence; but Robin himself was now firmly identified
with an Earl of Huntington living at the time of Richard I's expedition to the
Holy Land on the Third Crusade. Parker lays more stress than any of his
predecessors on Robin's gentleness and his generosity towards the poor; at
the same time his hostility towards monks and friars, more extreme than that
encountered at earlier or later stages of the evolution of the Robin Hood
legend, appears to reflect the anti-clericalism of his own period. Equally
noticeable is the fact that Parker's *True Tale* lacks the comic ingredients of
the many other seventeenth-century ballads of Robin Hood. Although reprinted in 1686 for Clark, Thackeray and Passenger and later by various
provincial presses, it figured in none of the popular garland collections and
only took a permanent place in the canon of Robin Hood ballads after its
inclusion in the first edition (1795) of Ritson's *Robin Hood*.

A True Tale of Robbin Hood, or, A briefe touch of the life and
death of that Renowned Outlaw, *Robert* Earle of Huntington
vulgarly called *Robbin Hood*, who lived and died in A.D. 1198,
being the 9. yeare of the reigne of King *Richard* the first,
commonly called Richard *Cuer de Lyon*. Carefully collected out
of the truest Writers of our English Chronicles. And published
for the satisfaction of those who desire to see Truth purged from
falsehood. By Martin Parker. Printed at London for T. Cotes,
and are to be sold by F. Grove dwelling upon Snow-hill, neare
the Saracen's head.

1
Both gentlemen, or yeomen bould,
  Or whatsoever you are,
To have a stately story tould,
  Attention now prepare.

2
It is a tale of Robbin Hood,
  That I to you will tell,
Which being rightly understood,
  I know will please you well.

3
This Robbin (so much talked on)
  Was once a man of fame,
Instiled Earle of Huntington,
  Lord Robert Hood by name.

4
In courtship and magnificence,
  His carriage won him prayse,
And greater favour with his prince
  Than any in his dayes.

5
In bounteous liberality
  He too much did excell,
And loved men of quality
  More than exceeding well.

*   *   *   *   *

104
His followers, when he was dead,
  Were some received to grace;
The rest to forraigne countries fled,
  And left their native place.

105

Although his funerall was but meane,
   This woman had in minde
Least his fame should be buried clear
   From those that came behind.

106

For certainely, before nor since,
   No man ere understood,
Under the reigne of any prince,
   Of one like Robbin Hood.

107

Full thirteene yeares, and something
     more,
   These outlawes lived thus,
Feared of the rich, loved of the poore,
   A thing most marvelous.

108

A thing impossible to us
   This story seemes to be;
None dares be now so venturous;
   But times are chang'd, we see.

109

We that live in these latter dayes
   Of civill government,
If neede be, have a hundred wayes
   Such outlawes to prevent.

110

In those dayes men more barbarous
     were,
   And lived lesse in awe;
Now, God be thanked! people feare
   More to offend the law.

111

No roaring guns were then in use,
   They dreampt of no such thing;
Our English men in fight did chuse
   The gallant gray-goose wing.

112

In which activity these men,
   Through practise, were so good,
That in those dayes non equald them,
   Specially Robbin Hood.

113

So that, it seemes, keeping in caves,
   In woods and forrests thicke,
Thei'd beate a multitude with staves,
   Their arrowes did so pricke.

114

And none durst neare unto them come,
   Unlesse in courtesie;
All such he bravely would send home,
   With mirth and jollity.

115

Which courtesie won him such love,
   As I before have told;
'T was the cheefe cause that he did
     prove
More prosperous than he could.

116

Let us be thankefull for these times
   Of plenty, truth and peace,
And leave out great and horrid crimes,
   Least they cause this to cease.

117

I know there's many fained tales
   Of Robbin Hood and 's crew;
But chronicles, which seldome fayles,
   Reports this to be true.

118

Let none then thinke this a lye,
   For, if 't were put to th' worst,
They may the truth of all discry
   I' th' raigne of Richard the first.

119

If any reader please to try,
　As I direction show,
The truth of this brave history,
　Hee'le finde it true I know.

120

And I shall thinke my labour well
　Bestowed, to purpose good,
When 't shall be sayd that I did tell
　True tales of Robbin Hood.

The Epitaph which the Prioress of the Monastery of Kirkes Lay in Yorkeshire set over Robbin Hood, which, as is before mentioned, was to bee reade within these hundred yeares, though in old broken English, much to the same sence and meaning.

Decembris quarto die, 1198: anno regni Richardii Primi 9.

> Robert Earle of Huntington
> Lies under this little stone.
> No archer was like him so good:
> His wildnesse named him Robbin Hood.
> Full thirteene yeares, and something more,
> These northerne parts he vexed sore.
> Such out-lawes as he and his men
> May England never know agen.

Some other superstitious words were in it, which I thought fit to leave out.[1]

---

[1] For discussion of Robin Hood's various epitaphs see Ritson (1846), pp. 13–14; Keen, *Outlaws*, pp. 179–82; and see above, pp. 139, 186.

ROBIN HOOD AND THE DUKE OF
LANCASTER, *1727*

Source:
Robin Hood and the Duke of Lancaster. A Ballad. To the tune of The Abbot of Canterbury. Printed for J. Roberts in Warwick Lane, And sold by the Booksellers of London and Westminster, 1727. (folio pamphlet in the British Library: 1490 f. 4)

Other Editions:
Gutch, 1847, II, 397–40: Milton Percival, ed., *Political Ballads illustrating the Administration of Sir Robert Walpole* (Oxford Historical and Literary Studies, ed. C. H. Firth and W. Raleigh, Vol. VIII, Oxford, 1916), pp. 4–7.

The adaptation of the broadside ballad to the purposes of political satire and propaganda dates from at least the early seventeenth century: indeed the most influential English ballad ever written, *When the King shall enjoy His Own Again* (described by Joseph Ritson as 'the most famous and popular air ever heard of in this country'[1]) was composed by Martin Parker, the author of the previous item in this collection. But it was during the reigns of Queen Anne and the first two Georges, shortly before their functions were largely replaced by those of the more sophisticated newspapers of the mid-eighteenth century, that the political ballads enjoyed their greatest vogue. Some commented scathingly on contemporary grievances or poured scorn on the policies of a particular party, but the great majority—like the one printed below—ruthlessly attacked the personal weaknesses of various political leaders, not sparing the king himself. Of enough importance to be commissioned by prominent politicians from prominent writers (most notably Swift), such ballads owed most of their appeal to the readiness with which a largely London audience could recognize the now often cryptic allusions to the latest gossip of the court: the following work was first advertised in *The Whitehall Evening Post* for 19–21 January 1727.[2]

During his years of political ascendancy Sir Robert Walpole was the most

[1] J. Ritson, *Ancient Songs and Ballads* (London, 1829), II, 257.
[2] Percival, *Political Ballads*, p. 4.

obvious of all targets for bitter personal abuse, and his Christian name was enough to make him the 'Robin' or 'Robin Hood' of contemporary street literature. The stanzas below relate, perhaps not very accurately, the story of an incident which occurred in early 1727 during one of the many periods when rumour was rife that Sir Robert's power was doomed. It describes how the choleric Lord Lechmere, Chancellor of the Duchy of Lancaster (hence the 'Duke of Lancashire'), burst into George I's presence to voice his indignation at Walpole's corruption and at the completely unfounded rumour that he intended to bring the Tory Lord Bolingbroke ('Harry Gambol') back into office. Highly amused at Lechmere's misunderstanding of the situation, the king brought about his complete and embarrassed discomfiture by pretending to offer him Walpole's Prime Ministership.[1] Lechmere died a few months later but Walpole was to survive for many years before the balladeers saw their favourite prophecy, 'Robin Will Be Out At Last', eventually fulfilled in 1742.

I

Come listen, my Friends, to a Story so
    new,
    In the Days of King John, in twelve
      hundred and two,
How the bold little Duke, of the fair
    Lancashire,
    Came to speak to the King like a
    brave Cavalier.
    DERRY DOWN, DOWN,
      DOWN, DERRY DOWN.

2

In a trice he was got to the good King's
    Abode,
    The Horse in a Froth, on which the
    Duke rode;
Tho' the Steed had gallop'd full three
    Miles from Home,
    Not so much at the Mouth as the
    Rider did foam.

3

The Gate it did shake when he knock'd
    at the Door,

As his Hands they did tremble with
    Anger full sore,
And a Message of Haste his Words did
    bespeak,
    Till the Paint, red before, waxed blue
    on his Cheek.

4

Quoth the Porter, who is it that dares be
    so bold,
    As to stun the fair Gate of our Liege's
    Freehold?
Quoth the Duke, I am come some
    Truth to report.
    O ho! quoth the Porter - - - - You're
    just come to Court.

5

He toss'd up his Chin, and a Roll did
    advance
    Of Parchment, I ween, instead of an
    Lance:
Lo here is the Statute we made such a
    Strife for.
    Said the Porter, Lord Sir, - - - - It
    seemeth all Cypher.

---

[1] According to other sources, Lord Lechmere actually found Bolingbroke closeted with the king when he arrived to ask for George's signature to various official papers, perhaps the 'Roll of Parchment' mentioned below: W. Coxe, *Memoirs . . . of Sir Robert Walpole* (London, 1798), I, 264; Percival, *Political Ballads*, p. 4.

6

Then up the high Steps the short Duke
he did stride;
  His Stride so gigantick, his Stature
bely'd
Quoth he, as a Peer, I will free my good
Liege
  From the Vermin and Earwigs his
Grace that besiege.

7

The Yeoman cry'd Stand - - - - Quoth
the Duke I'm a Peer,
  And I bring a good Statute of
Parliament here;
Be the King where he can, I may visit
him still.
This was pass'd in the last of the Con-
queror Will.

8

He found his good Grace just a
trimming his Beard,
  By the Hands of a Dwarf whom he
lately had rear'd:
The Duke was beginning his Speech in
great Wrath;
  Says the King to the Dwarf, This is
nothing but Froth.

9

My good Liege, quoth the Duke, You
are grossly abused
  By Knaves far and near, by your
Grace kindly used;
There's your Keeper so crafty, call'd
Bold Robin Hood,
  Keeps us all but himself, my good
Liege, in a Wood.

10

He riseth, e'er Day-break, to kill your
fat Deer,
  And never calls me to partake of the
Cheer.

For Shoulders and Umbles, and other
good Fees,
  He says, for your Use, he locks up
with his Keys.

11

As I'm learnt in the Law, This is
Robbing direct,
  As appears by the 1st of King Will.
VII. Sect.
Besides what is yours, Sir, is ours - - - -
and then
  He's a Felon, d'ye see, by the 2d of
Hen.

12

What is worse, he will make Harry
Gambol a Keeper,
  And the Plot ev'ry Day is laid deeper
and deeper,
Shou'd he bring him once in, your
Court wou'd grow thinner,
  For instead of a St. - - - - he wou'd
bring in a Sinner.

13

I intreat you, dear Liege, have a Care
what you do;
  To Man, Woman nor Child he was
never yet true;
Shou'd you trust him, he'd serve you as
ill, on my Life,
  As he did his first Friends, as he did
his first Wife.[1]

14

Quoth our Liege, Wou'd you have
Robin out - - - - Is that all?
  I wou'd have, quoth the Duke, Sir,
No Robbing at all.
Why Man! quoth the King, on my troth
you'll bereave
  All my Court of its People, except
'tis my Sheriff.

---

[1] Presumably an allusion to Walpole's complete estrangement from his first wife by the
1720s: see J. H. Plumb, *Sir Robert Walpole, The King's Minister* (London, 1960), p. 78.

15

Besides, who'll succeed him, because
    without Doubt,
  You'd have some one put in sure, as
    well as put out?
Then a Smile so obliging the Duke did
    display,
  And made a low 'beysance, as if ----
    Who shou'd say.

16

Said our Liege, I respect your great
    Depth, on my Word;
  But to cast up vile Sums is beneath
    such a Lord.

As to that, quoth the Duke, I learnt it at
    School,
  And can tell more than twenty ----
    You know I'm no Fool.

17

Quoth our Liege with a Snear, tho'
    with Face right serene,
  I believe, I by this time guess all that
    you mean.
Wou'd you have me hang Robin, and
    Count my own Pelf?
  Oh no, quoth the Duke, ---- I'd be
    Robbing my self.

Robin Hood and the Beggar: a broadside
printed at London for Coles, Vere and
Wright, *c.* 1670 (British Library, Roxburghe
III, 20). The same woodcut had already
appeared in Robin Hood and the Bishop
(see page 157)

16

THE BIRTH OF ROBIN HOOD (*WILLIE AND EARL RICHARD'S DAUGHTER*) (Child 102A)

Source:
Robert Jamieson, *Popular Ballads and Songs, from tradition, manuscripts, and scarce editions* (Edinburgh, 1806), II, 44–8.

The following ballad provides the most interesting of the several cases in which the reputation of medieval England's outlaw hero has invaded the very different world of the eighteenth-century Scottish ballads. Jamieson copied it down from the recitation of the celebrated Mrs Brown of Falkland in 1800 and published it six years later 'without the alteration of a single word'.[1] It need hardly be said that Mrs Brown's ballad owes nothing but Robin Hood's name to the native English cycle of stories: the early stanzas of the poem with their familiar tale of illicit love and secret birth depend heavily on other Scottish ballads, and especially on *Willie O Douglas Dale* (Child 101). For this reason Child was undoubtedly justified in preferring *Willie and Earl Richard's Daughter* to Jamieson's title, *The Birth of Robin Hood*. Whether the popularity of Robin Hood north of the Border 'was in all probability mediated by the name Brown Robin' (Child, II, 305–6) is less certain: the English outlaw figures as the hero of the Scottish greenwood in various other ballads, including an alternative and more tragic version of *The Birth of Robin Hood* (Child 102 B) as well as some copies of the famous *Rose the Red and White Lily* (Child 103), itself partly inspired by *Robin Hood and Maid Marian* (No. 11 above). Robin Hood's fame, to state the obvious, has never been completely confined within the boundaries of his own country. But it remains suspicious that for the missing story of his birth we have to wait until the recitation of a remarkable Scottish woman delivered five years after the first (1795) edition of Ritson's comprehensive collection of the Robin Hood ballads (see Introduction above, p. 54).

[1] The best discussion of Mrs Brown of Falkland as 'the most important single contributor to the canon of English and Scottish ballads' is by Fowler, *Literary History of the Popular Ballad*, pp. 294–331, whose conclusions on Mrs Brown's 'Robin Hood Ballads' are not, however, altogether accepted here.

1

O Willie's large o'limb and lith[1]
   And come o'high degree,
And he is gane to Earl Richard
   To serve for meat and fee.

2

Earl Richard had but ae[2] daughter
   Fair as a lily flower;
And they made up their love-contract
   Like proper paramour.

3

It fell upon a simmer's nicht
   Whan the leaves were fair and green,
That Willie met his gay ladie
   Intil[3] the wood alane.

4

'O narrow is my gown, Willie,
   That wont to be sae wide;
And gane is a' my fair colour
   That wont to be my pride.

5

'But gin[4] my father should get word
   What's past between us twa,
Before that he should eat or drink
   He'd hang you o'er that wa'.

6

'But ye'll come to my bower, Willie,
   Just as the sun gaes down;
And kep me in your arms twa
   And latna me fa' down.'

7

O whan the sun was now gane down
   He's doen him[5] till her bower;
And there by the lee licht[6] o' the moon
   Her window she lookit o'er.

8

Intill a robe o' red scarlet
   She lap, fearless o' harm;
And Willie was large o' lith and limb
   And keppit her in his arm.

9

And they've gane to the gude green
     wood;
   And ere the night was deen,[7]
She's born to him a bonny young son
   Amang the leaves sae green.

10

Whan night was gane and day was come
   And the sun began to peep,
Up and raise the Earl Richard
   Out o' his drowsy sleep.

11

He's ca'd upon his merry young men
   By ane, by twa, and by three;
'O what's come o' my daughter dear,
   That she's nae come to me?

12

'I dreamt a dreary dream last night:
   God grant it come to gude.
I dreamt I saw my daughter dear
   Drown in the saut sea flood.

13

'But gin my daughter be dead or sick,
   Or yet be stown awa,[8]
I make a vow, and I'll keep it true,
   I'll hang ye ane and a'!'

14

They sought her back, they sought her
     fore,
   They sought her up and down;
They got her in the gude green wood
   Nursing her bonny young son.

---

[1] lith: *joint*   [2] ae: *one*   [3] Intil: *Within*   [4] gin: *if*   [5] doen him: *taken himself*
[6] lee licht: *desolate light*   [7] deen: *done*   [8] stown awa: *stolen away*

15

He took the bonny boy in his arms
  And kist him tenderlie;
Says, 'Though I would your father hang,
  Your mother's dear to me.'

16

He kist him o'er and o'er again:
  'My grandson I thee claim;
And Robin Hood in gude green wood,
  And that shall be your name.'

17

And mony ane sings o' grass, o' grass,
  And mony ane sings o' corn,
And mony ane sings o' Robin Hood
  Kens little whare he was born.

18

It wasna in the ha', the ha',
  Nor in the painted bower,
But it was in the gude green wood
  Amang the lily flower.

'Renowned Robin Hood', or *Robin Hood and Queen Katherine*:
a broadside printed at London for F. Grove, *c.* 1640 (British
Library, Roxburghe I, 356).

JOHN KEATS: 'ROBIN HOOD: TO A FRIEND'

Source:
The Poetical Works of John Keats, ed. H. W. Garrod (Oxford, 2nd. edn., 1958), pp. 270–2. First published in *Lamia, Isabella, The Eve of St Agnes and Other Poems* (1820).

1818 has claims to be considered the *annus mirabilis* of Robin Hood literature—the year in which Sir Walter Scott began dictating *Ivanhoe*, Thomas Love Peacock started writing *Maid Marian*, and John Keats composed his own 'dirge of a national legend'.[1] Keats's 'Robin Hood' was dashed off after the author had received two sonnets devoted to the forest outlaw from his friend, J. H. Reynolds;[2] in reply Keats sent the following poem, together with the more famous *Lines on the Mermaid Tavern*, to Reynolds from Hampstead on 3 February.[3] By no means one of Keats's more distinguished works, it is certainly one of his most characteristic. All in all, it remains the best short memorial we have to the period when the cult of Robin Hood attained the highest popularity within English literary circles it has ever known. More significantly, Keats's few lines are thoroughly representative of the profound transformation which overtook the Robin Hood legend during the early years of the nineteenth century. In the very decade (1810–20) when the long tradition of the broadside and garland songs of Robin Hood was at last under threat of imminent decease, the medieval outlaw saga was rescued from oblivion by the professional man of letters. For the first time in the history of the legend, Robin Hood came to be generally regarded as a possible and even proper subject for serious attention on the part of poet and historical novelist as well as antiquary. However, as Keats's lines reveal only too clearly, it henceforth became increasingly difficult to write 'rymes of Robin Hood' except in a spirit of intense and self-conscious nostalgia. Nostalgia itself had of course been an important constituent of the Robin Hood legend since at

---

[1] H. J. Newbolt, *The Greenwood, A Collection of Literary Readings relating to Robin Hood* (London, 1925), p. 213.
[2] Reynolds's two sonnets appear in the author's *The Garden of Florence* (London, 1821), pp. 124–7, and Gutch, II, 426–7; cf. *The Complete Works of William Hazlitt*, ed. P. P. Howe (London, 1930–4), V, 143.
[3] *The Letters of John Keats, 1814–21*, ed. H. E. Rollins (Cambridge, 1958), I, 223–5; cf. R. Gittings, *John Keats* (Pelican edition, 1971), p. 281.

least the reign of Elizabeth; but in this poem there is sounded a sustained note of calculated escapism and fantasy ('So it is: yet let us sing') which has dominated Robin Hood literature ever since. Keats's pious hope that his verses were 'at least written in the Spirit of Outlawry'[1] was sadly misguided: Robin Hood had been converted from a real outlaw into an Arcadian symbol of pre-industrial 'Merry England'.

No! those days are gone away,
And their hours are old and gray,
And their minutes buried all
Under the down-trodden pall
Of the leaves of many years:
Many times have winter's shears,
Frozen North, and chilling East,
Sounded tempests to the feast
Of the forest's whispering fleeces,
Since men knew nor rent nor leases.

No, the bugle sounds no more,
And the twanging bow no more;
Silent is the ivory shrill
Past the heath and up the hill;
There is no mid-forest laugh,
Where lone Echo gives the half
To some wight, amaz'd to hear
Jesting, deep in forest drear.

On the fairest time of June
You may go, with sun or moon,
Or the seven stars to light you,
Or the polar ray to right you;
But you never may behold
Little John, or Robin bold;
Never one, of all the clan,
Thrumming on an empty can
Some old hunting ditty, while
He doth his green way beguile
To fair hostess Merriment,
Down beside the pasture Trent;
For he left the merry tale
Messenger for spicy ale.

Gone, the merry morris din;
Gone, the song of Gamelyn;
Gone, the tough-belted outlaw
Idling in the "grene shawe";
All are gone away and past!
And if Robin should be cast
Sudden from his turfed grave,
And if Marian should have
Once again her forest days,
She would weep, and he would craze:
He would swear, for all his oaks,
Fall'n beneath the dockyard strokes,
Have rotted on the briny seas;
She would weep that her wild bees
Sang not to her—strange! that honey
Can't be got without hard money!

So it is: yet let us sing,
Honour to the old bow-string!
Honour to the bugle-horn!
Honour to the woods unshorn!
Honour to the Lincoln green!
Honour to the archer keen!
Honour to tight little John,
And the horse he rode upon!
Honour to bold Robin Hood,
Sleeping in the underwood!
Honour to maid Marian,
And to all the Sherwood-clan!
Though their days have hurried by
Let us two a burden try.

[1] *Letters of Keats*, I, 225.

18

ALFRED NOYES : 'SHERWOOD'

Source :
Alfred Noyes, *Poems* (Edinburgh and London, 1904), pp. 7–9, provides the first publication in book form. Reprinted in Alfred Noyes, *Collected Poems* (Edinburgh and London, 1914), I, 78–9.

Far and away the most popular Robin Hood poem written during the last hundred years, Alfred Noyes's 'Sherwood' is the obvious choice with which to bring the first part of this selection of 'rymes of Robyn Hood' to a close. Standing in a straight and obvious line of literary descent from the previous poem, 'Sherwood' is an excellent example of a late Victorian and Edwardian poetic tradition now completely out of fashion precisely because it can so often be justifiably dismissed as 'Keats and water'.[1] It is therefore all the more important to remember that no poet since Rudyard Kipling, not even John Betjeman in the 1960s, has been more popular than was Noyes on the eve of the First World War. 'Sherwood', like 'The Highwayman' and 'Come to Kew in Lilac-Time', still lingers on in the more old-fashioned school anthologies; and no work in this century has done more to shape the popular attitudes to the English greenwood legend. The wheel has, in a sense, turned full circle: a medieval English outlaw first immortalized because of his deeds of violent robbery is commemorated by Noyes for everything but his violence.

Robin Hood's appeal for Noyes and the generation to which he spoke is not in fact difficult to explain. A zealous Roman Catholic convert and a bitter opponent of the 'modern' movement in art and literature, Alfred Noyes (1880–1958) projected on to the medieval outlaw his own extremely sentimental longings for the supposedly traditional English virtues. More specifically, the Robin Hood legend provided an ideal medium for the expression of 'that strange yearning for the Infinite and elusive'[2] which, however unprofound, permeated the work of Noyes, Sir James Barrie and many of their contemporaries. This theme is developed at considerable and interesting

---

[1] Not surprisingly it was Dr Leavis who drove the most piercing nail into the coffin of Noyes's literary reputation. For his dismissal of Noyes's now almost forgotten would-be epic, *The Torchbearers* ('complete insignificance as poetry') see F. R. Leavis, *New Bearings in English Poetry* (London, new edition, 1950), p. 24.

[2] The comment of one of Noyes's early reviewers, cited in Noyes, *Poems*, 1904, p. 237.

length by Noyes in his play, *Robin Hood*, originally written in 1908 but first published in England on the eve of its stage performance in 1926.[1] Despite contemporary enthusiasm ('Where Tennyson utterly failed Alfred Noyes has succeeded'),[2] Noyes's debased Shakespearian verse drama lacks the metrical skill of his short poem and would scarcely justify revival. But it must be admitted that Noyes's play does give the Robin Hood legend a genuinely new dimension. Sexual jealousy, in the person of King John's iniquitous sister, Elinor, is made the fundamental cause of Robin's downfall and death; but Robin and Marian are guaranteed immortality in a mystic 'Forest World' presided over by 'the great King' himself and represented in the play by various Puck-like 'Woodland Sprites'.[3] As in Noyes's poem, so in his play, nothing is more significant than the author's refusal to allow Robin Hood to succumb to the ordinary processes of mortality. Noyes's 'Sherwood' shows how the medieval myths of the sleeping Emperor, 'once and future king', and undying hero have never altogether lost their emotional appeal. To the question 'Is Robin Hood awake?' there can still be only one answer.

Sherwood in the twilight, is Robin Hood awake?
Grey and ghostly shadows are gliding through the brake,
Shadows of the dappled deer, dreaming of the morn,
Dreaming of a shadowy man that winds a shadowy horn.

Robin Hood is here again: all his merry thieves
Hear a ghostly bugle-note shivering through the leaves,
Calling as he used to call, faint and far away,
In Sherwood, in Sherwood, about the break of day.

Merry, merry England has kissed the lips of June:
All the wings of fairyland were here beneath the moon,
Like a flight of rose-leaves fluttering in a mist
Of opal and ruby and pearl and amethyst.

Merry, merry England is waking as of old,
With eyes of blither hazel and hair of brighter gold:
For Robin Hood is here again beneath the bursting spray
In Sherwood, in Sherwood, about the break of day.

Love is in the greenwood building him a house
Of wild rose and hawthorn and honey-suckle boughs:
Love is in the greenwood, dawn is in the skies,
And Marian is waiting with a glory in her eyes.

---

[1] A. Noyes, *Robin Hood, A Play in Five Acts* (Edinburgh and London, 1926). An American edition had been published by Frederic A. Stokes of New York in 1911 (Gable, p. 83, No. 576).

[2] Newbolt, *The Greenwood*, p. 213.

[3] Noyes, *Robin Hood*, pp. 8–10, 33, 77, 108: see pp. 13–14 for the 'Song of the Woodland Sprites'.

Hark! The dazzled laverock climbs the
   golden steep!
Marian is waiting: is Robin Hood
   asleep?
Round the fairy grass-rings frolic elf
   and fay,
In Sherwood, in Sherwood, about the
   break of day.

Oberon, Oberon, rake away the gold,
Rake away the red leaves, roll away the
   mould,
Rake away the gold leaves, roll away
   the red,
And wake Will Scarlett from his leafy
   forest bed.

Friar Tuck and Little John are riding
   down together
With quarter-staff and drinking-can
   and grey goose feather.
The dead are coming back again, the
   years are rolled away
In Sherwood, in Sherwood, about the
   break of day.

Softly over Sherwood the south wind
   blows.
All the heart of England hid in every
   rose
Hears across the greenwood the sunny
   whisper leap,
Sherwood in the red dawn, is Robin
   Hood asleep?

Hark, the voice of England wakes him
   as of old
And, shattering the silence with a cry
   of brighter gold
Bugles in the greenwood echo from the
   steep,
SHERWOOD IN THE RED DAWN,
   IS ROBIN HOOD ASLEEP?

Where the deer are gliding down the
   shadowy glen
All across the glades of fern he calls his
   merry men—
Doublets of the Lincoln green glancing
   through the May
In Sherwood, in Sherwood, about the
   break of day—

Calls them and they answer: from aisles
   of oak and ash
Rings the *FOLLOW! FOLLOW!* and
   the boughs begin to crash,
The ferns begin to flutter and the
   flowers begin to fly,
And through the crimson dawning the
   robber band goes by.

ROBIN! ROBIN! ROBIN! All his
   merry thieves
Answer as the bugle-note shivers
   through the leaves,
Calling as he used to call, faint and far
   away,
In Sherwood, in Sherwood, about the
   break of day.

19

THE PLAY OF 'ROBIN HOOD AND THE SHERIFF', c. 1475

Source:
Trinity College, Cambridge, MS. R. 2. 64 (fragment)

Other Editions:
Child, 1888, III, 90–1; J. M. Manly, *Specimens of the Pre-Shaksperean Drama* (London, 1897), I, 279–81; Facsimile edition under the title 'Robin Hood and the Sheriff of Nottingham, A Dramatic Fragment, *c.* 1475', in Malone Society, *Collections* I, Part 2 (Oxford, 1908), pp. 120–4.

Despite its brevity, this unique fifteenth-century fragment can lay claims to being one of the most historically significant items in the entire corpus of Robin Hood literature. Besides providing us with the solitary surviving text of a genuinely medieval Robin Hood play, it marks the first known entry into the outlaw saga of the famous 'ffrere Tuck'; and is at the same time the only certain evidence we have for the fact that the main outlines of the story of *Robin Hood and Guy of Gisborne* (No. 5 above) were medieval in origin. As Child was the first to notice (*Popular Ballads*, III, 90), this dramatic fragment was clearly founded on a pre-existing 'ballad' of Guy of Gisborne: it therefore illuminates the otherwise almost completely obscure process by which Robin Hood passed from the world of popular song into that of the May games and plays.

The following lines were written in a late fifteenth-century hand on the upper half of a single piece of paper (measuring approximately 8″ by 10″) now preserved in the Library of Trinity College, Cambridge. This leaf of paper may at one time have formed part of a larger volume for the remains of the glue by which it was pasted down still survive on it. On the dorse of the fragment are several account entries of sums received by one John Sterndalle during the fifteenth regnal year of Edward IV (1475–76). As the hands are of much the same period it seems safe to infer that the Robin Hood fragment itself dates from *c.* 1475. According to a transcript made of the play by William Stukeley in the early eighteenth century (and first published in *Notes and Queries*, First Series, XII, 321; 27 October 1855) the manuscript was then in the possession of Peter Le Neve, the famous Norfolk antiquary. It later passed into the hands of the Frere family and was eventually presented to Trinity College, Cambridge by W. Aldis Wright. This eighteenth-century provenance makes it highly probable that the fragment once formed part of the famous collection of Paston papers bought by Peter Le Neve from William Paston, second Earl of Yarmouth, a collection which was later acquired by Sir John Fenn and William Frere, the early editors of the Paston letters.[1] Moreover, in a famous letter of 16 April 1473 Sir John Paston lamented the flight of a man Woode whom he had kept 'thys iii yer to pleye Seynt Jorge and Robyn Hod and the Shryff off Nottyngham'.[2] It is hard not to agree with Child and E. K. Chambers (*Mediaeval Stage*, I, 177) that the following lines should be identified with this very play of 'Robyn Hod and the Shryff off Nottyngham', presumably acted before the Paston household in the 1470s.

The text as preserved and printed below presents various difficult problems. Of these the fact that the drama breaks off abruptly at an exciting stage of the action is perhaps the least serious: it is abundantly clear from a comparison with the ballad of *Robin Hood and Guy of Gisborne* that the complete play must have ended with Robin's rescue of his men and the discomfiture and probable death of the sheriff of Nottingham (see above No. 5). It is much less easy, particularly in the second part of the play, to identify the various speakers. The dialogue is often brief to the point of obscurity and was clearly not felt to have much importance in its own right. As in many other early manifestations of English popular drama, attention was focussed on violent action rather than on words: 'The culminating point of the Drama is of course the Combat'.[3] Any reconstruction of this Robin Hood play into its original dramatic elements is therefore bound to be at least partly conjectural: the one printed below owes a good deal to the two previous attempts at reconstituting the play made by J. M. Manly (*Specimens of the Pre-Shaksperean Drama*, I, 279) and the editor of the Malone Society edition (pp. 122–3). Whether or not it was written to be performed as part of the May Games proper, this dramatic version of 'Robyn Hod and the Shryff' provides us with our single most valuable insight into the way in which the outlaw entered the world of those festivities.[4]

---

[1] Stukeley's transcript of the play still survives on p. v of Folger Shakespeare Library, Washington D.C., PR 2125 R6. Malone Society, *Collections*, I, Part 2 (1908), pp. 118–19, provides the fullest account of the fortunes of the manuscript.

[2] *The Paston Letters*, ed. J. Gairdner (London, 1904), V, 185.

[3] E. K. Chambers, *The English Folk-Play* (Oxford, 1933), p. 23.

[4] See Introduction, p. 38 above.

Manuscript Version

Syr sheryffe for thy sake / Robyn Hode wull y take
I wyll the gyffe golde and fee / This be heste[1] thou holde me
Robyn Hode ffayre and fre / Undre this lynde[2] shote we
With the shote y wyll / Alle thy lustes to full fyll
Have at the pryke / And y cleve the styke
Late us caste the stone / I graunte well be Seynt John
Late us caste the exaltre[3] / Have a foote be fore the
Syr knyght ye have a falle / And I the Robyn qwyte shall
Owte on the I blowe myn horne / Hit ware better be un borne
Lat us fyght at ottraunce / He that fleth god gyfe hym myschaunce
Now I have the maystry here / Off I smite this sory swyre[4]
This knyghtys clothis wolle I were / And in my hode his hede woll bere
Welle mete felowe myn / What herst thou of gode Robyn
Robin Hode and his menye / With the sheryffe takyn be
Sette on foote with gode wyll / And the sheryffe wull we kyll
Be holde wele ffrere Tuke / Howe he dothe his bowe pluke
Yeld yow syrs to the sheryffe / Or elles shall your bowes clyffe[5]
Now we be bownden alle in same / ffrere (T)uke this is no game
Come thou forth thou fals outlawe / Thou shall (be) hangyde and y drawe
Now allas what shall we doo / we (m)oste to the prysone goo
Opyn the yatis faste anon / An(d la)te theis thevys ynne gon

Conjectural Reconstruction

SCENE I

Enter the Sheriff of Nottingham and a knight (? Sir Guy of Gisborne)

Knight. Syr sheryffe, for thy sake,
        Robyn Hode wull y take.
Sheriff. I wyll the gyffe golde and fee;
        This be-heste thou holde me.

The Sheriff leaves and Robin Hood enters to be challenged by the knight

Knight. Robyn Hode, ffayre and fre,
        Undre this lynde shote we.
Robin. With the shot y wyll
        Alle thy lustes to full-fyll.

---

[1] be heste: *promise*   [2] lynde: *linden tree*   [3] exaltre: *axle-tree?*
[4] swyre: *neck*   [5] clyffe: *split*

Robin and the knight fight

Knight. Have at the pryke!
Robin. And y cleve the styke.   *Robin wins*
Knight. Late us caste the stone.
Robin. I graunte well, be Seynt John!   *Robin wins again*
Knight. Late us caste the exaltre.
Robin. Have a foot be-fore the!   *They wrestle : Robin wins again*
Syr Knyght, ye have a falle.
Knight. And I the, Robyn, qwyte shall;
Owte on the! I blowe myn horne.
Robin. Hit ware better be un-borne:
Lat us fyght at ottraunce.
He that fleth, God gyfe hym myschaunce!

They fight again : the knight is killed

Robin. Now I have the maystry here,
Off I smyte this sory swyre.   *Robin cuts off the knight's head*
This knyghtys clothis wolle I were,
And in my hode his hede woll bere.   *Robin disguises himself as the knight*

SCENE II

In a different part of the forest, the Sheriff is attacking Robin's men. As one of the outlaws (?Little John) approaches the scene of the conflict, he meets a companion (?Scarlet) in flight.[1]

Little John. Welle mete, felowe myn,
What herst thou of gode Robyn ?
Scarlet. Robyn Hode and his menye
With the sheryffe takyn be.[2]
Little John. Sette on foote with gode wyll
And the sheryffe wull we kyll.

The two outlaws watch the fight still going on in the distance

Little John. Be-holde wele Frere Tuke
Howe he dothe his bowe pluke!

[1] Neither Little John nor Scarlet are mentioned by name in the play; and the suggestion that they speak the next lines derives from a possible analogy with stanzas 11–13 of *Robin Hood and Guy of Gisborne* (above, p. 142).

[2] If the speaker here is telling the truth and Robin himself had been captured by the sheriff, the second part of this dramatic fragment could be quite independent of the first and be a version of the familiar theme of Robin's own rescue from the sheriff. On balance, and despite Child (III, 44), this seems unlikely.

4. Douglas Fairbanks in the film role of Robin Hood, U.S.A. 1922 (reproduced by courtesy of the National Film Archive)

The Sheriff and his men enter, leading Friar Tuck and other outlaws as prisoners : he addresses Little John and Scarlet

Sheriff.   Yeld yow, syrs, to the sheryffe,
            Or elles shall your bowes clyffe.

Little John and Scarlet surrender to the Sheriff

Little John. Now we be bownden alle in same:
            Frere Tuke, this is no game.
Sheriff.   Come thou forth, thou fals outlawe,
            Thou shall be hangyde and y-drawe.
Friar Tuck. Now, allas, what shall we doo?
            We moste to the prysone goo.
Sheriff.   Opyn the yatis faste anon,
            And late theis thevys ynne gon.

In the sequel the disguised Robin Hood enters and rescues his men—no doubt after yet another fight.

20

THE PLAY OF 'ROBIN HOOD AND THE FRIAR', c. 1560

Source:

Sigs. H 2v–H 4v of William Copland's edition of *A Mery Geste of Robyn Hoode*, printed at Three Cranes Wharf, London, *c.* 1560 (British Library copy, press-mark C. 21. c. 63).

Other Editions:

Appended to Edward White's edition of *A Merry Jest of Robin Hood*, printed at London, *c.* 1590 (Bodleian Library, Oxford, Z. 3. Art. Seld.); Ritson, 1795, II, 192–8; Gutch, 1847, II, 52–7; Child, 1888, III, 127–8; J. M. Manly, *Specimens of the Pre-Shaksperean Drama* (Boston, 1897), I, 281–5; Malone Society, *Collections* I, Part 2 (Oxford, 1908), pp. 127–32; *Old English Drama, Students' Facsimile Edition,* ed. J. S. Farmer (Amersham, 1914); F. J. Tickner, ed., *Earlier English Drama from Robin Hood to Everyman* (London, 1926), pp. 17–20.

The fortunate survival of the play of 'Robin Hood and the Friar' and its companion-piece, 'Robin Hood and the Potter', is entirely due to William Copland's decision to append them to his edition of the *Mery Geste of Robyn Hoode* (see above, p. 71), probably published at some date towards the end of the period 1548–69.[1] On the title-page of this edition, Copland described the two dramatic pieces as 'a newe playe for to be played in Maye games very plesaunte and full of pastyme'. This title conceals the fact that Copland actually published, admittedly without a break in his text, two distinct works: the first, apparently complete, based on a version of the ballad of *Robin Hood and the Curtal Friar*; and the second (printed by us as No. 21 below) which stops short in the middle of the action and was derived from the opening stanzas of the ballad of *Robin Hood and the Potter*. In describing these two pieces as 'a *newe* play', Copland was again being somewhat misleading. He had probably published his 'Play of Robyn Hoode' in a separate edition (of which no copy now survives) at some time prior to his publication of the *Gest*;[2] and, in any case, much of their content was highly

---

[1] For these dates, see Malone Society, *Collections* I, Part 2, p. 125.

[2] The play of Robin Hood entered in the Stationers' Register on 30 October 1560 (Arber, I, 152) was probably identical with Copland's 'newe play' (Chambers, *Elizabethan Stage*, IV, 44).

dependent on earlier ballads. It would, in other words, be dangerous to assign too precise a date to the composition of these two plays. Both are written in a very 'popular' and crude style, particularly noticeable in the way many of the lines are clumsily strained to produce a far too obvious rhyming pattern. All in all, the most likely hypothesis is that two existing early Tudor May Game plays had been roughly re-worked for the press in order to allow Copland to exploit the contemporary appetite for such works. The protagonists of Copland's two plays are certainly much more verbose than their predecessors in the late fifteenth-century fragment of 'Robin Hood and the Sheriff' (No. 19); but we are still being faced with a drama where the appeal of the action must have been considerably greater than that of the accompanying dialogue.

The fact that the following play of 'Robin Hood and the Friar' is anterior in date to any extant text of *Robin Hood and the Curtal Friar* (see No. 8 above) inevitably makes it difficult to demonstrate the exact degree of its dependence on the ballad versions circulating in the early Tudor period. However, the basic outlines of the popular story of Robin's encounter with the 'jolly fryer' are all immediately apparent in this play—the fight in the river, Robin's subsequent blowing of his horn, and his final request that his formidable opponent should become 'my man'. Only in one respect did the demands of a dramatic production impose a major difference between play and ballad. The 'half a hundred good ban-dogs' whom the friar summons to attack the outlaws in both the Percy Folio and the garland versions of the ballad (see above, pp. 161, 163) would have proved unmanageable in the play and were consequently sacrificed. They have left their traces, however, in the *three* dogs attendant on Friar Tuck, in Robin's request to summon his 'hounde' by a blast on his horn, and in the appearance of the mysterious 'Cut' and 'Bause' (two men disguised as dogs?) towards the end of the piece. The play is also much more precise than the ballad versions in its identification of the friar with 'Fryer Tucke', so confirming that this perennially popular character had been firmly absorbed into the Robin Hood legend at a quite early date. Other distinctive features of the play are its unusually specific anti-clericalism ('He never loved fryer, nor none of freiers kyn') and, above all, its tone of comic buffoonery. The play actually closes with ten lines of ribaldry, omitted in Child's edition on his own characteristic but dubious grounds that they 'have no pertinency to the traditional Robin Hood and Friar' (Child, III, 128). But the fact that Robin should present his new recruit with a 'lady free' (the Maid Marian of the morris dances) is only a logical extension of the scurrilous elements always latent within the late medieval greenwood legend; and it was, of course, eminently appropriate that a play 'verye proper to be played in Maye Games' should end with a 'daunce in the myre for veri pure joye'.

Here beginnethe the Playe of Robyn Hoode,
verye proper to be played in Maye Games

Robyn Hode

Now stand ye forth my mery men all,
And harke what I shall say;
Of an adventure I shal you tell,
The which befell this other day.[1]
As I went by the hygh way,
With a stoute frere I met,
And a quarter staffe[2] in his hande.
Lyghtely[3] to me he lept,
And styll he bade me stande.
There were strypes two or three,
But I cannot tell who had the worse;
But well I wote the horeson[4] lepte within me,
And fro me he toke my purse.
Is there any of my mery men all
That to that frere wyll go,
And bryng hym to me forth withall,
Whether he wyll or no?

Lytell John

Yes, mayster, I make God avowe,
To that frere wyll I go,
And bryng him to you,
Whether he wyl or no.

Fryer Tucke[5]

Deus hic! Deus hic! God be here!
Is not this a holy worde for a frere?[6]
God save all this company!
But am not I a jolly fryer?
For I can shote both farre and nere,
And handle the sworde and buckler,
And this quarter staffe also.
If I mete with a gentylman or yeman,

---

[1] Note the almost completely identical opening of the play of 'Robin Hood and the Potter' (No. 21).

[2] O.E.D. provides no date earlier than 1550 for this word: the quarter-staff serves a dramatic purpose here, as it would identify the friar when he appeared before the audience.

[3] Lyghtely: *quickly.*　　　[4] horeson: *whoreson*, a word which could imply affection.

[5] Who enters after the others depart.

[6] The line is partly cut away but still legible.

I am not afrayde to loke hym upon,
Nor boldly with him to carpe;[1]
If he speake any wordes to me,
He shall have strypes two or thre,
That shal make his body smarte.
But, maister[s], to shew you the matter
Wherfore and why I am come hither,
In fayth I wyl not spare.
I am come to seke a good yeman,
In Bernisdale men sai is his habitacion.
His name is Robyn Hode,
And if that he be better man than I,
His servaunt wyll I be, and serve him truely;
But if that I be better man than he,
By my truth my knave shall he be,
And lead these dogges all three.

Robyn Hode[2]
Yelde the, fryer, in thy long cote.[3]

Fryer Tucke
I beshrew thy hart, knave, thou hurtest my throt.

Robyn Hode
I trowe, fryer, thou beginnest to dote:
Who made the so malapert and so bolde
To come into this forest here
Amonge my falowe dere?

Fryer
Go louse the,[4] ragged knave.
If thou make mani wordes, I wil geve the on the eare,
Though I be but a poore fryer.
To seke Robyn Hode I am com here,
And to him my hart to breke.

Robyn Hode
Thou lousy frer, what wouldest thou with hym?
He never loved fryer nor none of freiers kyn.

Fryer
Avaunt, ye ragged knave!
Or ye shall have on the skynne.

---

[1] carpe: *talk.*   [2] Who enters, probably in disguise.
[3] Friar Tuck may owe his name to the practice of 'tucking up' the friar's long habit.
[4] louse the: *de-louse yourself.*

Robyn Hode
Of all the men in the morning thou art the worst,
To mete with the I have no lust;
For he that meteth a frere or a fox[1] in the morning,
To spede ell (ill) that day he standeth in jeoperdy.
Therfore I had lever mete with the devil of hell,
Fryer, I tell the as I thinke,
Then mete with a fryer or a fox
In a mornyng, or I drynke.

Fryer
Avaunt, thou ragged knave, this is but a mock!
If you make mani words, you shal have a knock.

Robyn Hode
Harke, frere, what I say here;
Over this water thou shalt me bere;
The brydge is borne away.

Fryer
To say naye I wyll not;
To let the of thine oth it were great pitie and sin;
But upon a fryers backe and have even in.

Robyn Hode[2]
Nay, have over.

Fryer
Now am I, frere, within, and, thou, Robin, without,
To lay the here I have no great doubt.[3]
Now art thou, Robyn, without, and I, frere, within,[4]
Lye ther, knave; chose whether thou wilte sinke or swym.

Robyn Hode
Why, thou lowsy frere, what hast thou doon?

Fryer
Mary, set a knave over the shone.[5]

Robyn Hode
Therfore thou abye.[6]

[1] Friars were often likened to foxes in late medieval literature: Robin's speech here seems most appropriate to a pre-Reformation audience.
[2] Climbing on the friar's back.   [3] Throwing Robin into the water.
[4] The words 'within' and 'without' should be reversed, for otherwise there is no change in the relative situation of the two men.
[5] the shone: *his shoes*
[6] White's edition reads 'shalt abye': *shall suffer the consequences*

Fryer
Why, wylt thou fyght a plucke ?[1]

Robyn Hode
And God send me good lucke.

Fryer
Than have a stroke for Fryer Tucke.

Robyn Hode
Holde thy hande, frere, and here me speke.[2]

Fryer
Saye on, ragged knave,
Me semeth ye begyn to swete.

Robyn Hode
In this forest I have a hounde,
I wyl not give him for a hundreth pound:
Geve me leve my horne to blowe,
That my hounde may knowe.

Fryer
Blowe on, ragged knave, without any doubte,
Untyll bothe thyne eyes starte out.
Here be a sorte of ragged knaves come in,[3]
Clothed all in Kendale grene,
And to the they take their way nowe.

Robyn Hode
Peradventure they do so.

Fryer
I gave the leve to blowe at thy wyll;
Now give me leve to whistell my fyll.

Robyn Hode
Whystell, frere, evyl mote thou fare!
Untyl bothe thine eyes starte.

Fryer[4]
Now Cut and Bause!
Breng forth the clubbes and staves,
And downe with those ragged knaves.

[1] plucke: *bout.*
[2] Robin is being worsted in the fight.
[3] Robin's men enter in response to his blast on the horn.
[4] Addressing his two men, who have entered in response to his whistle.

Robyn Hode

How sayest thou, frere, wylt thou be my man,
To do me the best servyse thou can?
Thou shalt have both golde and fee.
And also here is a lady free:[1]
I wyll geve her unto the,
And her chapplayn I the make
To serve her for my sake.

Fryer

Here is an huckle duckle,
An inch above the buckle.
She is a trul[2] of trust,
To serve a frier at his lust,
A prycker, a prauncer, a terer of sheses,[3]
A wagger of ballockes[4] when other men slepes.
Go home, ye knaves, and lay crabbes in the fyre,
For my lady and I wil daunce in the myre for veri pure joye.

---

[1] Although not here called by that name, the 'lady free' must be the Maid Marian of the May game morris dances, in which she almost invariably partners Friar Tuck: see, e.g. the description of a London May game on 24 June 1559 in *The Diary of Henry Machyn, 1550–63* (Camden Society, Old Series, 42, 1848), p. 201.

[2] trul: *trollop*.

[3] sheses: White's edition reads 'sheetes'.

[4] ballockes: White's edition reads 'buttockes', a variant which only mildly affects the meaning.

21

THE PLAY OF 'ROBIN HOOD AND THE POTTER', *c. 1560*

Source:
Sigs. H 4v–I 2v of William Copland's edition of *A Mery Geste of Robyn Hoode*, printed at Three Cranes Wharf, London, *c.* 1560 (British Library copy, press mark C. 21. c. 63).

Other Editions:
Appended to Edward White's edition of *A Merry Jest of Robin Hood*, printed at London, *c.* 1590 (Bodleian Library, Oxford, Z. 3. Art. Seld.); Ritson, 1795, II, 199–203; Gutch, 1847, II, 57–60; Child, 1888, III, 114–15; J. M. Manly, *Specimens of the Pre-Shaksperean Drama* (Boston, 1897), I, 285–8: Malone Society, *Collections* I, Part 2 (Oxford, 1908), pp. 132–6; *Old English Drama, Students' Facsimile Edition*, ed. J. S. Farmer (Amersham, 1914); F. J. Tickner, ed., *Earlier English Drama from Robin Hood to Everyman* (London, 1926), pp. 20–3.

This fragmentary play of 'Robin Hood and the Potter' forms, as has been seen (p. 208 above), the second part of the so-called 'playe of Robyn Hoode, verye proper to be played in Maye games'[1] appended by William Copland to his edition of the *Gest, c.* 1560. Admittedly it follows the play of 'Robin Hood and the Friar' (No. 20) without the slightest break in the printed text; and both plays show stylistic evidence of having been composed or re-composed by the same very jejune and unskilled author. But Robin Hood's own introduction ('Lysten to me my mery men all') to the 'adventure' of his encounter with the potter leaves us in no doubt from the outset that we are in the presence of a separate play. In this case, moreover, the survival of an *earlier* ballad version of the same story—in a Cambridge University manuscript of *c.* 1500 (No. 3 above)—makes it possible to study the transformation from recited tale to dramatic version with more precision than in the companion play. The results are of considerable significance: not only are the outlines of the story dramatized in the following lines identical with those at the opening of the ballad, but the dramatic dialogue itself is at times a paraphrase of the words of the

---

[1] The title prefixed to the text of the play by Copland, somewhat shorter than that on the title page of the volume.

latter.[1] Such borrowings by 'newe playe' from older ballad make it all the more regrettable that the former breaks off in the middle of the action and before we learn how potter and Robin Hood are reconciled. The fact that there is nothing in Copland's text to indicate that the play is incomplete suggests that he was printing from a copy of an earlier edition (perhaps his own?: see above, p. 208) which had lost a page or more at the end. It is of course extremely unlikely that, even in its complete form, the play of 'Robin Hood and the Potter' was ever anything like as long and complex as its poetic predecessor. Like 'Robin Hood and the Friar', this was a short and simple play, probably designed to end with a morris dance; there are several indications in the following text—in particular the 'rose garlande' on the potter's head[2]—to remind us that it is indeed a May Game play.

Robyn Hode

Lysten to [me] my mery men all
And harke what I shall say
Of an adventure I shall you tell[3]
That befell this other daye.
With a proude potter I met;
And a rose garlande on his head,
The floures of it shone marvaylous freshe.
This seven yere and more he hath used this waye,
Yet was he never so curteyse a potter
As one penny passage to paye.[4]
Is there any of my mery men all
That dare be so bolde
To make the potter paie passage either silver or golde?

Lytell John

Not I, master, for twenty pound redy tolde.
For there is not among us al one
That dare medle with that potter man for man.
I felt his handes not long agone,
But I had lever[5] have ben here by the.

---

[1] Apart from the parallels between Robin's introductory speech in the play and the fifth stanza of the ballad, compare the line 'And I wyll styfly by you stande' in Little John's speech below with his remark 'Yend potter well steffeley stonde' in the 17th stanza of the ballad (above, p.127).

[2] A peculiarity which caused Ritson (1846 edn., p. 108) unnecessarily serious concern.

[3] This line, supplied from White's edition, is almost completely cut away in that of Copland.

[4] Note the very close similarity here (the closest in the entire play) to the ballad of *Robin Hood and the Potter*, stanza 5 (above, p. 126).

[5] lever: *rather*.

Therfore I knowe what he is;
Mete hem when ye wil or mete him whan ye shal
He is as propre a man as ever you medle[d] withal.

Robyn Hode

I will lai with the, Litel John, twenti pound so read,[1]
If I wyth that potter mete,
I wil make him pay passage, maugre his head.

Lettell John

I consente therto, so eate I bread;
If he pay passage, maugre his head,
Twenti pound shall ye have of me for your mede.[2]

The potters boye Jacke[3]

Out alas that ever I sawe this daye!
For I am clene out of my waye[4]
From Notygham towne.
If I hye me not the faster,
Or I come there the market wel be done.

Robyn Hode

Let me se, are the pottes hole and sounde?

Jacke

Yea, meister, but they will not breake the ground.[5]

Robyn Hode

I wil them breke for the cuckold thi maister's sake;
And if they will breake the grounde,
Thou shalt have thre pence for a pound.

Jacke

Out alas! what have ye done?
If my maister come, he will breke your crown.

The Potter[6]

Why, thou horeson, art thou here yet?
Thou shouldest have bene at market.

---

[1] read: *red*, an allusion to the colour of the gold: note that Robin and Little John's wager was only for 'forty shillings' in the ballad (above, p. 126).
[2] mede: *reward*.
[3] Jack presumably enters the stage after all Robin's men have left their master.
[4] Partly cut away, but still legible.
[5] Robin is starting to throw the pots to the ground.
[6] Who must enter at this point.

Jacke

I met with Robin Hode, a good yeman;
He hath broken my pottes,
And called you kuckolde by your name.

The Potter

Thou mayst be a gentylman, so God me save,
But thou semest a naughty knave.
Thou callest me cuckolde by my name,
And I swere by God and Seynt John,
Wyfe had I never none:
This cannot I denye.
But if thou be a good felowe,
I wil sel mi horse, mi harneis, pottes and paniers to,
Thou shalt have the one halfe, and I wil have the other.
If thou be not so content,
Thou shalt have stripes, if thou were my brother.

Robyn Hode

Harke, potter, what I shall say;
This seven yere and more thou hast used this way,
Yet were thou never so curteous to me
As one peny passage to paye.

The Potter

Why should I paye passage to thee?

Robyn Hode

For I am Robyn Hode, chiefe governoure
Under the grene woode tree.

The Potter

This seven yere have I used this way up and downe,
Yet payed I passage to no man;
Nor now I wyl not beginne, to do the worst thou can.

Robyn Hode

Passage shalt thou pai, here under the grene wode tre,
Or els thou shalt leve a wedded[1] with me

The Potter

If thou be a good felowe, as men do the call,
Laye away thy bowe,
And take thy sword and buckeler in thy hande,
And se what shall befall.

---

[1] wedded: for 'wedde', *forfeit*.

Robin Hode

Lyttle John, where art thou?

Lytell[John]

Here, mayster, I make God avowe.
I told you, mayster, so God me save,
That you should fynde the potter a knave.
Holde your buckeler [fast in your hand],[1]
And I wyll styfly by you stande,
Ready for to fyghte;
Be the knave never so stoute,
I shall rappe him on the snoute,
And put hym to flyghte.

Thus endeth the play of Robyn Hode

---

[1] Partly cut away: the last four words are supplied from White's edition.

Robin Hood and the Butcher: a broadside
printed at London for F. Grove, *c.* 1640
(Bodleian Library, Oxford, Wood MS.
401, leaf 19v).

22

EXTRACTS FROM ANTHONY MUNDAY'S 'THE DOWNFALL' AND 'THE DEATH OF ROBERT, EARL OF HUNTINGTON' (*1597–8*)

Source:
The Downfall of Robert Earl of Huntington by Anthony Munday, 1601
(Malone Society Reprint, 1965, prepared by J. C. Meagher and A.
Brown), A 3r–4r; I 2r–v; L 1r–2r; *The Death of Robert Earl of Hunting-*
ton by Anthony Munday, 1601 (Malone Society Reprint, 1967, pre-
pared by J. C. Meagher and A. Brown), C 4v–D 2r.

Other Editions:
J. P. Collier, ed., *Five Old Plays* (published in 1828 as a supplement to
Dodsley's *Old Plays*); W. C. Hazlitt, ed., *A Select Collection of Old*
English Plays, originally published by Robert Dodsley in the year 1744
(London, 1874–6), VIII, 93–207, 209–327; separate facsimile editions
of both plays in *Old English Drama, Students' Facsimile Edition*, ed.
J. S. Farmer (Amersham, 1914).

The legend of Robin Hood, like so many of the traditional themes of medieval
English literature and history, has never completely recovered from the
exhilaratingly imaginative treatment it received at the hands of Elizabethan
and Jacobean dramatists.[1] However, despite the intensive use of the English
greenwood saga made by Shakespeare's contemporaries, the only plays now
extant 'in which the deeds of Robin Hood are treated *in extenso* as the major
theme of a drama'[2] are *The Downfall* and *The Death of Robert, Earl of*
Huntington. Both plays were entered in the Register of the Stationers'
Company on 1 December 1600 and each was first 'Imprinted at London, for
William Leake' in the following year. Evidence for the authorship and date of
composition of the two plays is provided by the famous 'Diary' of the London

---

[1] See Introduction, above pp. 43–5.
[2] F. E. Schelling, *The English Chronicle Play* (1902, reprinted 1964, New York), p. 159;
see Chambers, *Elizabethan Stage*, III, 446–7, and the reference there to 'The Pastoral
Comedy of Robin Hood and Little John' (now lost) entered in the Stationers' Register
on 14 May 1594. This play can presumably be identified with the anonymous 'Robin
Hood and Little John' still extant in 1624 and 1640 (G. E. Bentley, *The Jacobean and*
Caroline Stage, Oxford 1941–68, VII, 54, 100).

theatre manager and proprietor, Philip Henslowe. On 15 February 1598, Henslowe 'layd owt unto antony monday' the sum of £5 for 'a playe boocke called the firste parte of Robyne Hoode'; and in the following month (on 28 March) he licensed 'the ij partes of Robart Hoode' with the Master of the Revels. Although Henslowe paid ten shillings later in the same year to another Elizabethan playwright, Henry Chettle, 'for mendinge of Roben hood for the corte', there are good grounds for believing that the 1601 editions of both *The Downfall* and *The Death* were printed directly from rough manuscript copies dating from early March 1598.[1] In other words, the surviving texts of the two plays are either primarily or exclusively the work of only one dramatist, Anthony Munday. Munday (*c.* 1560–1633), the son of a London draper, was one of the most prolific and best known of Elizabethan and Jacobean playwrights.[2] Comparatively few of his many plays survive; and he is now best known for his autograph manuscript version of *Sir Thomas More* (*c.* 1593), a play of which he was probably originally sole author but in whose revision other dramatists, and possibly Shakespeare, took a hand. Recent research into Munday's career and writings suggests that he provided scenarios for many other playwrights and was one of the most technically inventive dramatists of his generation—a fact which may help to account for the highly original form into which he cast the traditional greenwood legend in his two Robin Hood plays.

The *Downfall of Robert, Earl of Huntington* is itself 'a play within a play'.[3] In the introduction, and at various occasions throughout the course of the drama, Sir John Eltham (who acts the part of Little John) and John Skelton (who plays the role of Friar Tuck) throw aside their dramatic *personae* and discuss the nature and problems of the dramatic piece, which—it is supposed —they are presenting before Henry VIII and his court. In the first extract printed below (1), Skelton 'as Prologue' introduces the various players to his audience as they enter the stage for the first time. Robin Hood himself is immediately identified as Robert, Earl of Huntington, a contemporary of King Richard I who has himself left England to fight the infidel in the Holy Land just before the action of the play begins. At the centre of a very complex plot is Robin's relationship with Matilda (alias Marian), the daughter of the benevolent but somewhat ineffective Lord Fitzwater. The course of true love between hero and heroine is continually thwarted by the desire of Richard's

---

[1] *Henslowe's Diary*, ed. R. A. Foakes and R. T. Rickert (Cambridge, 1961), pp. 86–8, 102; cf. pp. 317–23. For the most recent and convincing conclusions (accepted here) as to the complex problems of authorship and date of *The Downfall* and *The Death*, see the introductions to the Malone Society Reprint editions of the two plays.

[2] C. Turner, *Anthony Munday, an Elizabethan Man of Letters* (University of California Publications in English, II, 1928). Munday was lampooned as 'Post-haste' in the satirical play *Historiomastix* (1589) and also appears as Antonio Balladino in Ben Jonson's *The Case is Altered*.

[3] Tiddy, *The Mummers' Play*, pp. 133–5.

brother, Prince John, for Matilda and that of his mother, Queen Elinor, for Robin. Robin is served by an evil steward (later sheriff of Nottingham) named Warman, who betrays his master to the latter's uncle, Gilbert de Hood, Prior of York. The success of the two conspirators in securing Robin's outlawry inaugurates an unusually tortuous chain of events, so tortuous indeed that in the fourth act, Munday thought it advisable to insert an explanatory 'worde or two beside the play' by Little John (Eltham) and Friar Tuck (Skelton): see (2). More complications ensue, involving several other members of Robin's company (Scarlet, Scathlock, and Much, the Miller's Son) before a more or less happy ending is achieved on the return of King Richard at the conclusion of the play (3).

The 'second part' of Munday's play, *The Death of Robert, Earl of Hunting-ton*, is in many ways a more satisfactorily integrated work despite the fact that Robin himself dies at the end of the first act. He meets his death as the result of swallowing poison, the surprisingly easy victim of an intrigue between his uncle, the Prior of York, and the mysterious Sir Doncaster. Munday's representation of Robin Hood's lingering death in the odour of sanctity (4) differs radically from all ballad accounts of the outlaw hero's demise and has never found many imitators; with its impressive if highly sentimental rhetoric, it remains one of the most remarkable set-pieces in the entire play. Despite the dying Robin's attempts to reconcile his former friends and enemies, they are rapidly at violent and murderous odds with one another as soon as John succeeds his brother Richard as king. The last four acts of the play are devoted to 'the lamentable Tragedie of chaste Matilda' as she is remorselessly pursued by 'the tempestuous rage of tyrant John'.[1] The attempt of Lord Bruce, identified as Matilda's uncle, to oppose John's intrigues leads to the starvation of Lady Bruce and her younger son in the dungeons of Windsor Castle. Matilda herself takes shelter in Dunmow Abbey where she is poisoned by John's evil henchman, Brand, a denouement which finally brings John—at the very end of the play—to a state of repentance.

As this cursory summary of the outlines of his two Robin Hood plays will have made apparent, Munday handled a wide variety of sources with 'a free-dom which occasionally borders on violence'.[2] Most important of all these sources was undoubtedly Michael Drayton's historical poem, *Matilda, the Faire and Chaste Daughter of Lord. R. Fitzwater* (1594) which provided Munday with the basis of his plot. *The Downfall* and *The Death* are also heavily indebted to other recent plays, notably the anonymous *Troublesome Raigne of King John* and *George A Green, the Pinner of Wakefield*, as well as to the chronicles of Holinshed and Grafton, a variety of metrical romances of

---

[1] For the fascination of John 'in the eyes of the writers of chronicle-history plays for over half a century', see F. S. Boas, *An Introduction to Tudor Drama* (Oxford, 1933), pp. 111–28; F. P. Wilson, *The English Drama, 1485–1585* (Oxford, 1969), pp. 36–8.

[2] *The Downfall* (Malone Society Reprint), p. vii.

King Richard, and several Robin Hood ballads. In particular, the appearance of a Prior (*sic*) of York and of Sir Doncaster among Munday's *dramatis personae* makes it clear that the author had read a copy of the *Gest*. The presence of Sir John Eltham and of the poet John Skelton, together with the dramatic fiction that they are presenting a play before Henry VIII's court, raises more mysterious problems; and it is just possible, although by no means certain, that among Munday's sources was a now lost May Day Robin Hood pageant or interlude written by Skelton himself at the beginning of the sixteenth century.[1] The exact degree of Munday's originality must therefore remain somewhat conjectural; but he is unquestionably responsible for making a permanent impression on the Robin Hood legend by identifying Robin Hood with the Earl of Huntington and Marian with one or more of the semi-legendary Matildas persecuted by King John. It would of course be wrong to exaggerate the immediate impact of Munday's cavalier treatment of the English greenwood legend. He had very little effect indeed on the persistently plebeian Robin Hood of most seventeenth- and eighteenth-century broadside and garland ballads; nor is there any certainty that either *The Downfall* or *The Death* 'has been played on any stage since 1599'.[2] However, Munday's two plays did influence several writers over the years (Robert Davenport's *King John and Matilda* of 1655 borrows heavily from *The Death*) and are of the utmost importance in providing the literary foundations for the modern view of Robin Hood as an unjustly dispossessed nobleman.

THE DOWNFALL OF ROBERT, EARL OF HUNTINGTON

(1) *From Act 1*

(*Enter Robert, earle of Huntington, leading Marian, &c*)

SKELTON This youth that leads yon virgin by the hand
(As doth the sunne, the morning richly clad)
Is our Earle Robert, or your Robin Hoode,
That in those daies, was Earle of Huntington.
The ill-fac't miser, brib'd in either hand,
Is Warman, once the Steward of his house,
Who, Judas like, betraies his liberall lord
Into the hands of that relentlesse Prior,
Calde Gilbert Hoode, uncle to Huntington.

---

[1] This argument was first put forward—with a little more conviction than it warrants—by H. L. D. Ward, *Catalogue of Romances in the Department of Manuscripts in the British Museum* (*1883–93*), I, 506–7; cf. Child, III, 519.

[2] Malone Society Reprints of *The Downfall* (p. vii) and *The Death* (p. x); but it is tempting to suppose that the 'Robin Hood, both parts' in the repertoire of Edward Archer in 1656 were Munday's plays (Bentley, *Jacobean and Caroline Stage*, V, 1402–3). For the probable indebtedness of Shakespeare's *As You Like It* to Munday's Robin Hood plays, see A. H. Thorndike, *Journal of English and German Philology*, IV (1902), 59–69.

Those two that seeke to part these lovely friends,
Are Elenor the Queene, and John the Prince:
She loves Earle Robert, he Maide Marian;
But vainely, for their deare affect is such,
As only death can sunder their true loves.
Long had they lov'd, and now it is agreed,
This day they must be troth-plight, after wed.
At Huntington's faire house a feast is helde;
But envie turnes it to a house of teares;
For those false guestes, conspiring with the Prior,
To whome Earle Robert greatly is in debt,
Meane at the banquet to betray the earle
Unto a heavie writ of outlawry.
The manner and escape you all shall see.
    ELTHAM. Which all, good Skelton?
    SKELTON. Why, all these lookers on;
Whom if wee please, the king will sure be pleas'd.
Looke to your entrance; get you in, Sir John.

                                    [*Exit Sir John Eltham.*]

My shift is long, for I play Frier Tucke:
Wherein, if Skelton have but any lucke,
Heele thanke his hearers oft with many a ducke.
For many talk of Robin Hood, that never shot in his bowe,
But Skelton writes of Robin Hood what he doth truly knowe.
        Therefore I pray yee,
        Contentedly stay yee,
        And take no offending,
        But sit to the ending,
        Likewise I desire
        Yea would not admire
        My rime, so I shift;
        For this is my drift,
        So mought I well thrive
        To make yee all blithe:
        But if ye once frowne,
        Poore Skelton goes downe,
        His labour and cost
        He thinketh all lost
        In tumbling of bookes
        Of Mary goe lookes.
        The Sheriffe with staves,
        With catchpoles and knaves,

Are comming, I see:
High time 'tis for mee,
To leave off my babble
And fond ribble rabble.
Therefore with this curtsie
Awhile I will leave yee.

(2) *From Act IV*

LIT. JOHN. Skelton, a worde or two beside the play.
FRIAR. Now, Sir John Eltam, what is't you would say?
LIT. JOHN. Me thinks I see no jeasts of Robin Hoode,
No merry morices of Frier Tuck,
No pleasant skippings up and downe the wodde,
No hunting songs, no coursing of the bucke.
Pray God this play of ours may have good lucke,
And the king's Majestie mislike it not.
FRIAR. And if he doe, what can we doe to that?
I promis't him a play of Robin Hoode,
His honorable life, in merry Sherewod.
His Majestie himselfe survaid the plot,
And bad me boldly write it; it was good;
For merry jeasts, they have bene showne before,
As how the Frier fell into the well
For love of Jinny, that faire bonny belle;
How Greeneleafe rob'd the Shrieve of Notingham,[1]
And other mirthfull matter, full of game.
Our play expresses noble Robert's wrong;
His milde forgetting trecherous injurie:
The Abbot's malice, rak't in cinders long,
Breakes out at last with Robin's tragedie.
If these, that heare the historie rehears't,
Condemne my play, when it begins to spring,
Ile let it wither, while it is a budde,
And never shewe the flower to the king.
LIT. JOHN. One thing beside: you fall into your vaine
Of ribble rabble rimes Skeltonicall,
So oft, and stand so long, that you offend.
FRIAR. It is a fault I hardly can amend.
O, how I champe my tongue to talke these tearmes!
I doe forget oft times my Frier's part;
But pull mee by the sleeve when I exceede,
And you shall see mee mend that fault indeede.

_____
[1] An allusion to the tale recorded in the third fytte of the *Gest* (see above, p. 90).

Wherefore, still sit you,
Doth Skelton intreat you
While he facete
Will breefely repeate you
The history al
And tale tragical,
By whose treachery
And base injury
Robin the good,
Calde Robin Hood,
Died in Sherewodde.

(3) *From Act V*

(*King Richard and other lords and ladies enter in procession*)
 ALL. God save King Richard! Lord preserve your Grace!
 KING. Thanks all; but chiefely, Huntington, to thee.
Arise, poor earle, stand up, my late lost sonne,
And on thy shoulders let me rest my armes,
That have bene toyled long with heathen warres.
True piller of my state, right lord indeede,
Whose honour shineth in the denne of neede,
I am even full of joy, and full of woe,
To see thee, glad; but sad to see thee so.
 ROBIN. O, that I could powre out my soule in prayers,
And praises for this kingly curtesie.
Doe not, dread lord, grieve at my lowe estate;
Never so rich, never so fortunate,
Was Huntington as now himselfe he findes;
And to approve it, may it please your Grace,
But to accept such presents at the hand
Of your poore servant, as he hath prepar'd.
You shall perceive the Emperour of the East,
Whom you contended with at Babilon,
Had not such presents to present you with.
 KING. Art thou so rich? sweet let me see thy gifts.
 ROBIN. First, take againe this jewell you had lost,
Aged Fitzwater, banished by John.
 KING. A jemme indeede! no prince hath such a one.
Good, good old man, as welcome unto mee,
As coole fresh ayre, in heat's extreamitie.
 FITZ. And I as glad to kisse my soveraignes hand,
As the wrackt swimmer, when he feeles the land.

QUEEN. Welcome, Fitzwater, I am glad to see you.

FITZ. I thanke your Grace; but let me hug these twain,
Lester and Richmond, Christes sworne champions,
That follow'd Richard in his holy warre.

RICH. Noble Fitzwater, thanks, and welcome both.

LESTER. O God, how glad I am to see this lord!
I cannot speake; but welcome at a worde.

ROBIN. Next, take good Ely in your royall hands,
Who fled from death and most uncivill bands.

KING. Robin, thy gifts exceede. Moorton, my Chancellour!
In this man giv'st thou holinesse and honour.

ELY. Indeede he gives me, and he gave me, life,
Preserving me from fierce pursuing foes.
When I, to blame, had wrought him many woes.
With me he likewise did preserve this seale,
Which I surrender to your majestie.

KING. Keepe it, good Ely, keepe it still for me.

ROBIN The next faire jewell that I will presente
Is richer than both these; yet in the foyle,
My gracious lord, it hath a foule default
Which if you pardon, boldly I protest,
It will in value farre exceede the rest.

JOHN. That's me he meanes; y'faith, my turne is next.
He calls me foile: y'faith, I feare a foile.
Well, 'tis a mad lord, this same Huntington.

                                      [*Aside*]

ROBIN. Here is Prince John, your brother, whose revolt
And folly in your absence, let me crave,
With his submission may be buried;
For he is now no more the man he was,
But duetifull in all respects to you.

KING. Pray God it proove so. Wel, good Huntington,
For thy sake pardon'd is our brother John,
And welcome to us in all heartie love.

ROBIN. This last I give, as tenants do their lands,
With a surrender, to receive againe
The same into their owne possession;
No Marian, but Fitzwater's chast Matilda;
The precious jewell, that poore Huntington
Doth in this world hold as his best esteeme.
Although with one hand I surrender her,
I holde the other, as one looking still,
Richard returnes her: so I hope he will.

KING. Els God forbid. Receive thy Marian backe,
And never may your love be separate,
But florish fairely to the utmost date.
　　ROBIN. Now please my king to enter Robin's bower,
And take such homely welcome as he findes,
It shall be reckened as my happinesse.
　　KING. With all my heart. Then, as combined friends,
Goe we togither: here all quarrelles ends.　　　　　*[Exeunt.]*

THE DEATH OF ROBERT, EARL OF HUNTINGTON

(4) *From Act I*

　　KING. Robin, wee see what we are sad to see
Death, like a champion, treading downe thy life:
Yet in thy end, somwhat to comfort thee,
Wee freely give to thy betrothed wife,
Beautious and chast Matilda, all those lands,
Falne by thy folly to the Prior's hands,
And by his fault now forfetted to mee:
Earle Huntington, she shall thy Countesse bee;
And thy wight yeomen, they shall wend with mee
Against the faithlesse enemies of Christ.
　　ROBIN. Bring forth a beere, and cover it with greene;
That on my deathbed I may here sit downe.

　　　　　　　　　　[A bier is brought in. He sits.]

At Robin's buriall let no blacke be seene,
Let no hand give for him a mourning gowne;
For in his death, his king hath given him life
By this large gift, given to his maiden wife.
Chaist maid Matilda, Countesse of account,
Chase with thy bright eyes all these clouds of woe
From these faire cheekes; I pray thee, sweete, do so:
Thinke it is bootelesse folly to complaine
For that which never can be had againe.
Queene Elianor, you once were Matilda's foe;
Prince John, you long sought her unlawfull love;
Let dying Robin Hood intreat you both
To change those passions: Madame, turne your hate
To princely love: Prince John, convert your love
To vertuous passions, chast and moderate.
O, that your gracious right hands would infolde
Matilda's right hand, prisoned in my palme,
And sweare to doe what Robin Hood desires!

QUEEN. I sweare I will; I will a mother be
To faire Matilda's life and chastitie.
JOHN. When John solicites chast Matilda's eares
With lawlesse sutes, as he hath often done,
Or offers to the altars of her eyes
Lascivious poems, stuft with vanities,
He craves to see but short and sower daies,
His death be like to Robin's he desires;
His perjur'd body prove a poysoned prey
For cowled monkes and barefoote begging friers.
 ROBIN. Inough, inough! Fitzwater, take your child.
My dying frost, which no sunnes heat can thawe,
Closes the powers of all my outward parts:
My freezing blood runnes backe unto my heart,
Where it assists death, which it would resist:
Only my love a little hinders death,
For he beholds her eyes, and cannot smite;
Then goe not yet, Matilda, stay a while.
Frier, make speede, and list my latest will.
 MAT. O, let me looke for ever in thy eyes,
And lay my warme breath to thy bloodlesse lips,
If my sight can restraine death's tyrannies,
Or keepe live's breath within thy bosome lockt.
 ROBIN. Away, away!
Forbeare, my love; all this is but delay.
 FITZ. Come, maiden daughter, from my maiden sonne,
And give him leave to doe what must be done.
 ROBIN. First, I bequeath my soule to all soules Saver,
And will my bodie to be buried
At Wakefield, underneath the abbey wall;
And in this order make my funerall.
When I am dead, stretch me upon this beere:
My beades and primer shall my pillowe bee;
On this side lay my bowe, my good shafts here;
Upon my brest the crosse, and underneath
My trustie sworde, thus fastned in the sheath.
Let Warman's bodie at my feete be laid,
Poore Warman, that in my defence did die.
For holy dirges, sing me wodmen's songs,
As ye to Wakefield walke with voices shrill.
This for my selfe. My goods and plate I give
Among my yeomen: them I do bestowe
Upon my soveraigne, Richard. This is all.

My liege, farewell! my love, farewell, farewell!
Farewell, faire Queene, Prince John, and noble lords!
Father Fitzwater, heartily adieu!
Adieu, my yeomen tall. Matilda, close mine eyes.
Frier, farewell! farewell to all!

Robin Hood and Little John: a broadside
printed at London by C. Sheppard, 1791
(Bodleian Library, Oxford, Douce F.F. 71,
no. 14).

Robin Hood and the Ranger: a broadside
printed at London by C. Sheppard, 1791
(Bodleian Library, Oxford, Douce F.F. 71,
no. 12).

23

EXTRACTS FROM 'THE SAD SHEPHERD' (BEN JONSON)

Source:
Ben Jonson, ed. C. H. Herford, Percy and Evelyn Simpson (Oxford, 1925–52), Vol. VII, pp. 8, 15, 21–2, 24–6, 42–3. First printed in the second volume of the Folio edition of Ben Jonson's plays under the title *The Sad Shepherd: or, A Tale of Robin-Hood* and with the date 1641.

The Sad Shepherd, written by Ben Jonson towards the end of his life, is without doubt the single most distinguished literary treatment of the Robin Hood legend. The drama is incomplete, consisting of about two and a half acts out of a projected five. It was probably intended to be produced at Court, and it may be that the poet's work on it was interrupted by a seizure or his death in August 1637.

The Sad Shepherd is Jonson's only essay in the genre of pastoral drama, an attempt to produce an idealized English shepherd world comparable to those of Greece and Sicily. Jonson's combination of rustic characters in the persons of Robin Hood and his men with (a) shepherds and shepherdesses, and (b) supernatural figures such as the witch Maudlin, her son Lorel, and her daughter Douce, is a genuinely original *tour de force*. The setting is the Vale of Belvoir in the forest of Sherwood (No. 1 below). The action begins with Robin Hood asking Maid Marian and Friar Tuck to prepare a feast of venison to which shepherds and shepherdesses have been invited (2). Robin hears that the Sad Shepherd, Aeglamour, has lost his beloved Earine, whom he believes to be drowned in the river Trent. Marian returns and greets Robin (3), but in the account of the hunt which follows, the suspicion is voiced that the witch of Papplewick, Maudlin, had been present in the form of a raven. Scathlock says that he has seen her boiling venison that was thrown to the raven. After they have gone, Maudlin appears in the shape of Marian, sends away the venison that has been prepared, and insults Robin (4). As is disclosed in the second act (5), Maudlin was also responsible for the disappearance of Earine, whom she had imprisoned in a hollow tree to serve the nefarious purposes of her son Lorel. Eventually, as we may surmise from the preliminary argument of the incomplete third act (6), this plot was to be foiled, but not before the witch caused much more confusion.

The Sad Shepherd contains numerous allusions to contemporary incidents and personages. Thus Belvoir Castle, near which the action of the play takes place, was the seat of the Earl and Countess of Rutland who probably served as aristocratic models for the parts of Robin and Marian. At a very different level, Friar Tuck's speech against the 'sourer sort of shepherds' in the first act is an attack by Jonson on the hypocrisy of some Puritan reformers of his day. But the influence of Jonson's play on the development of the Robin Hood legend has always remained, perhaps unfortunately, very limited—even after its revival in the 1780s when it was re-edited, with a continuation and conclusion, by F. G. Waldron of the Drury Lane Theatre.[1] Although one might concede that 'to graft the frail exotic growth of pastoral upon the robust stock of English greenwood poetry was a stroke of genius',[2] Jonson's experiment found no followers. In transforming Robin, Marian and 'Their Family' (Friar Tuck, Little John, Scarlet and Scathlock, George a Greene and Much) into the inhabitants of a literary Arcady and making them all speak sophisticated verse, Ben Jonson threatened to uproot the 'robust stock' itself.

(1) *The Argument of the First Act.*

ROBIN-HOOD, having invited all the Shep'erds and Shep'erdesses of the Vale of BE'VOIR, to a Feast in the Forrest of SHERWOOD, and trusting to his Mistris, Maid MARIAN, with her Wood-men, to kill him Venison against the day: Having left the like charge with Friar TUCK his Chaplaine, and Steward, to command the rest of his merry men, to see the Bowre made ready, and all things in order for the entertainment; meeting with his Guests at their entrance into the Wood, welcomes and conducts them to his Bowre. Where, by the way, hee receives the relation of the sad Shep'ard EGLA-MOUR, who is falne into a deepe Melancholy, for the losse of his beloved EARINE; reported to have beene drowned in passing over the TRENT, some few dayes before. They endeavour in what they can to comfort him: but, his disease having taken so strong root, all is in vaine, and they are forced to leave him. In the meane time MARIAN is come from hunting with the Hunts-men, where the Lovers interchangeably expresse their loves. ROBIN-HOOD enquires if she hunted the Deere at force, and what sport he made, how long hee stood, and what head hee bore: All which is briefly answer'd with a relation of breaking him up, and the Raven, and her Bone. The suspect had of that Raven to be MAUDLIN, the Witch of PAPLE-WICK,[3]

---

[1] Ritson, 1846, p. 21; Gable, No. 412, p. 61.

[2] Herford and Simpson, II, 224; cf. W. W. Grey, *Pastoral Poetry and Pastoral Drama* (New York, 1959), pp. 297–317.

[3] A village near Newstead Priory, on the road from Nottingham to Mansfield.

whom one of the Huntsmen met i' the morning, at the rowsing of the Deere, and is confirm'd by her being then in ROBIN-HOODS Kitchin, i' the Chimney-corner, broyling the same bit, which was throwne to the Raven, at the QUARRY or Fall of the Deere. MARIAN being gone in, to shew the Deere to some of the Shepherdesses, returnes instantly to the SCENE discontented, sends away the Venison she had kill'd to her they call the Witch, quarrels with her Love ROBIN-HOOD, abuseth him, and his Guests the Shep'erds; and so departs, leaving them all in wonder and perplexitie.

(2) *From Act I, Scene IV.*

   ROB. Welcome bright CLARION, and sweet MELLIFLEUR,
The courteous LIONEL, faire AMIE; all
My friends and neighbours, to the Jolly Bower
Of ROBIN-HOOD, and to the greene-wood Walkes:
Now that the shearing of your sheepe is done,
And the wash'd Flocks are lighted of their wooll,
The smoother Ewes are ready to receive
The mounting Rams againe; and both doe feed,
As either promist to increase your breed
At eaning time; and bring you lusty twins.
Why should, or you, or wee so much forget
The season in our selves; as not to make
Vse of our youth, and spirits, to awake
The nimble Horne-pipe, and the Timburine,
And mixe our Songs, and Dances in the Wood,
And each of us cut downe a Triumph-bough?
Such are the Rites, the youthfull IUNE allow.

(3) *From Act I, Scene VI.*

   ROB. My MARIAN, and my Mistris!
   MAR. My lov'd ROBIN!
   MEL. The Moone's at full, the happy paire are met!
   MAR. How hath this morning paid me, for my rising!
First, with my sports; but most with meeting you!
I did not halfe so well reward my hounds,
As she hath me to day: although I gave them
All the sweet morsels, Calle, Tongue, Eares, and Dowcets!
   ROB. What? and the inch-pin?[1]
   MAR. Yes.
   ROB. Your sports then pleas'd you?
   MAR. You are a wanton.

[1] inch-pin: *the sweetbread of a deer.*

ROB. One I doe confesse
I wanted till you came, but now I have you,
Ile growe to your embraces, till two soules
Distilled into kisses, through our lips
Doe make one spirit of love.
    MAR. O ROBIN! ROBIN!
    ROB. Breathe, breathe a while, what sayes my gentle MARIAN?
    MAR. Could you so long be absent?
    ROB. What, a weeke?
Was that so long?
    MAR. How long are Lovers weekes,
Doe you think ROBIN, when they are asunder?
Are they not Pris'ners yeares?
    ROB. To some they seem so;
But being met againe, they are Schoole-boyes houres.

(4) *From Act I, Scene VII.*

    (Enter Maudlin as Marian).
Your Hunt holds in his tale, still; and tells more!
    MAR. My Hunt? what tale?
    ROB. How! cloudie, MARIAN!
What looke is this?
    MAR. A fit one, Sir, for you.
Hand off, rude Ranger! Sirrah, get you in
And beare the Venison hence. It is too good
For these course rustick mouthes that cannot open,
Or spend a thanke for't. A starv'd Muttons carkasse
Would better fit their palates. See it carried
To Mother MAUDLINS, whom you call the Witch, Sir.
Tell her I sent it to make merrie with,
Shee'll 'turne us thanks at least! why stand'st thou, Groome?
    ROB. I wonder he can move! that hee's not fix'd!
If that his feeling be the same with mine!
I dare not trust the faith of mine owne senses.
I feare mine eyes, and eares! this is not MARIAN!
Nor am I ROBIN-HOOD! I pray you aske her!
Aske her good Shep'ards! aske her all for me;
Or rather aske your selves, if shee be shee;
Or I, be I.

(5) *The Argument of the Second Act.*

The Witch MAUDLIN, having taken the shape of MARIAN to abuse
ROBIN-HOOD, and perplexe his guests, commeth forth with her

daughter DOUCE, reporting in what confusion shee hath left them; defrauded them, of their Venison; made them suspitious each of the other; but most of all ROBIN-HOOD so jealous of his MARIAN, as shee hopes no effect of love would ever reconcile them; glorying so farre in the extent of her mischiefe, as shee confesseth to have surpriz'd EARINE, strip'd her of her garments, to make her daughter appeare fine, at this feast, in them; and to have shut the maden up in a tree, as her sonnes prize, if he could winne her; or his prey, if he would force her. Her Sonne, a rude bragging swine'ard, comes to the tree to woo her (his Mother, and Sister stepping aside, to over-heare him) and first boasts his wealth to her, and his possessions; which move not. Then he presents her guifts, such as himselfe is taken with, but shee utterly showes a scorne, and loathing both of him, and them. His mother is angry, rates him, instructs him what to doe the next time, and persuades her daughter, to show her selfe about the bower: tells, how shee shall know her mother, when she is transformed, by her broidered belt. Meane while the yong sheep'ardes AMY being kist by KAROLIN, EARINES brother, before, falls in Love; but knowes not what Love is: but describes her disease so innocently, that MARIAN pitties her. When ROBIN-HOOD, and the rest of his Guests invited, enter to MARIAN, upbraiding her with sending away their Venison to Mother MAUDLIN by SCATHLOCK, which shee denies; SCATHLOCK affirmes it, but seeing his Mistres weep, & to forsweare it, begins to doubt his owne understanding, rather then affront her farder; which makes ROBIN-HOOD, and the rest, to examine themselves better. But MAUDLIN entering like her selfe, the Witch, comes to thanke her for her bountie: at which, MARIAN is more angrie, and more denies the deed. SCATHLOCK enters, tells he has brought it againe, & delivered it to the Cooke. The Witch is inwardly vext, the Venison is so recover'd from her, by the rude Huntsman; and murmurs, and curses, be-witches the Cooke, mocks poore AMIE, and the rest, discovereth her ill nature, and is a meane of reconciling them all. For the sage Shepherd suspecteth her mischeife, if shee be not prevented: and so perswadeth to seize on her. Whereupon ROBIN-HOOD dispatcheth out his woodmen to hunt, and take her. Which ends the Act.

(6) *The Argument of the Third Act.*

PUCK-HAIRY discovers himselfe in the Forrest, and discourseth his offices with their necessities, breifly; After which, DOUCE, entring in the habit of EARINE, is pursued by KAROL; who mistaking her at first to be his Sister, questions her, how shee came by those garments. Shee answers, by her mothers gift. The sad Shepherd comming in the while, shee runs away affrighted, and leaves KAROL, sodainely; AEGLAMOUR thinking it to be EARINES ghost he saw, falls into a melancholique expression of his phantsie to KAROL, & questions him sadly about that point, which moves compassion in KAROL of his mistake still. When CLARION, and LIONELL enter to call KAROL to AMIE; KAROL reports to them AEGLAMOURS passion, with much regrete. CLARION resolves to seeke him. KAROL to returne with LIONELL. By the way DOUCE, and her Mother (in the shape of MARIAN) meet them, and would divert them, affirming AMIE to be recovered, which LIONELL wondred at to be so soone. ROBIN-HOOD enters, they tell him the relation of the Witch, thinking her to be MARIAN; ROBIN suspecting her to be MAUDLIN, lay's hold of her Girdle sodainely, but shee striving to get free, they both run out, and he returnes with the belt broken. Shee following in her owne shape, demaunding it, but at a distance, as fearing to be seiz'd upon againe; and seeing shee cannot recover it, falls into a rage, and cursing, resolving to trust to her old artes, which shee calls her daughter to assist in. The Shepherds content with this discovery, goe home triumphing, make the relation to MARIAN. AMIE is gladded with the sight of KAROL, &c. In the meane time enters LOREL, with purpose to ravish EARINE, and calling her forth to that lewd end, he by the hearing of CLARIONS footing, is staid, and forced to commit her hastily to the tree againe, where CLARION comming by, and hearing a voyce singing, draws neere unto it, but AEGLA-MOUR hearing it also, and knowing it to be EARINE'S, falls into a superstitious commendation of it, as being an Angells, and in the aire, when CLARION espies a hand put forth from the tree, and makes towards it, leaving AEGLAMOUR to his wild phantsie, who quitteth the place, and CLARION beginning to court the hand, and make love to it, there ariseth a mist sodainely, which, darkning all the place, CLARION looseth himselfe, and the tree where EARINE is inclosed, lamenting his misfortune, with the unknowne nimphs miserie. The Aire clearing, enters the Witch, with her Son and Daughter, tells them how shee had caused that late darkenesse, to free LORELL from surprisall, and his prey from being reskued from him: bids him looke to her, and lock her up more carefully, and follow her, to assist a work, shee hath in hand, of recovering her lost Girdle; which shee laments the losse of, with cursings, execrations, wishing confusion to their feast, and meeting: sends her Sonne, and Daughter to gather certaine Simples, for her purpose, and bring them to her Dell. This PUCK hearing prevents, & shewes (her) her error still. The Hunts-men having found her footing, follow the tract, and prick after her. Shee getts to her Dell, and takes her Forme. Enter (the Hunts-men, led by ALKEN), ALKEN has spied her sitting with her Spindle, Threds, and Images. They are eager to seize her presently, but ALKEN perswades them to let her begin her charmes, which they doe. Her Sonne and Daughter come to her, the Hunts-men are afrighted as they see her worke goe forward. And over-hastie to apprehend her, shee escapeth them all, by the helpe and delusions of PUCK.

'ROBIN HOOD AND HIS CREW OF SOULDIERS': NOTTINGHAM, 1661

Source:
Robin Hood and his Crew of Souldiers. A COMEDY. Acted at Nottingham on the day of His sacred Majesties Corronation. Vivat Rex. The Actors names: *Robin Hood*, Commander; *Little John, William Scadlocke*, Souldiers; *Messenger from the Shieriffe*.
London, Printed for James Davis, 1661. (Unpaginated quarto pamphlet in the British Museum, E. 1088, 6.)

No Other Editions

The Restoration of King Charles II in 1660 was accompanied by a series of official and popular celebrations throughout the country, reaching their climax when the new monarch was crowned at Westminster Abbey on 23 April in the following year. It is a tribute to the way in which the Robin Hood legend could be adapted by the middle of the seventeenth century that Nottingham's own contribution to the festivities should take the form not of the usual pageant or sermon but of the following unique interlude. The remarkably abrupt transformation of outlaws 'who have been nurs'd and fed fat with blood and slaughter' into loyal subjects of the crown provided an obvious if very heavy-handed comment on the Restoration. Nottingham, a county now firmly established as the 'chiefest abode' of Robin Hood,[1] had produced a large number of active royalist sympathizers during the late Civil Wars, and the opportunity to convert the greenwood hero into a supporter of the new king was clearly too good to be missed. The burgesses of Nottingham may have been particularly anxious to display their own loyalty to Charles II just because they had recently returned a notorious regicide, Colonel Hutchinson, as one of their two members to the first Restoration parliament.[2] The anonymous author, who for no very obvious reasons begins his play in sub-Shakespearian blank verse but then proceeds to even more bathetic prose,

---

[1] T. Fuller, *The History of the Worthies of England* (1662, re-ed. P. A. Nuttall, London, 1840), II, 575–6.
[2] G. Davies, *The Restoration of Charles II, 1658–60* (San Marino, California, 1955), p. 326; *V.C.H., County of Nottingham*, I, 355–6.

displays no signs of any detailed familiarity with the Robin Hood legend; however the work remains a most interesting demonstration of the way in which the greatest of English outlaws was transformed into a supporter of the *status quo*.[1]

ROBBIN HOOD AND HIS CREW OF SOULDIERS

A shout without the Bower.

  Enter Robin Hood, little John, William, Scadlocke, etc.

Whence springs this general joy?
What means this noise that makes Heavens
Arch'd vault eccho? and the neighb'ring woods
Return a dreadfull answer? With what uneven
Measures the amaz'd Birds cut through the
Trembling ayr? How the whole Forrest shakes,
As if with us 'twas sensible of wonder, and
Astonishment.   *Shout again.*
Still the glad noise encreases
And with it our fear and wonder; Thus when
Unruly tempests force the weak banks,
Rolling the foamy billows o're the yielding
Strand, fear and amazement, confusion and
Distracting cares seize the neighbring villages,
And thus it is with us; the guilty breast
Still pants and throbs, when others are at rest.
Look out and learn the cause, and in the meanwhile
Each man betake himself to's armes.

                                        Exit little John

No danger unexpected to a mind
Prepar'd to meet the worst that it can finde.

                        Enter little John and Shierifs Messenger

Rob. Speak, what's the news?
Little Jo. Gives and Fetters, Hatchets and Halters, stincking prisons, and the death of dogs is all we can expect.
Rob. Why, what's the matter?
Jo. Tis the Kings Coronation; and now the Shieriffe with a band of armed men, are marching to reduce us to loyalty, and the miseries of an honest life;

---

[1] In 'Robin Whood Revived, A Cavalier Song' (printed in Gutch, II, 404–7), the young Charles II is actually identified with Robin.

this Messenger here can tell you a rufull tale of obedience, that is expected.

Rob. Peace, and let him declare his errand.

Messen. From my Master I am come to require and command your armes, and a chearfull and ready submission to his Majesties Laws, with a promise of future obedience; and that forthwith you joyn with us to solemnize his happy Coronation, which is this day to be celebrated; this done, and the rest of your lives running in a smooth stream of loyalty and honest allegiance, I here bring pardon of all past misdemeanors; but otherwise, expect the miseries of a sudden destruction: this told you, I wait your answer.

John. Did not I tell you this? he talks of submission to government, and good Laws, as if we were the sons of peace and idleness, or had bin such Whay-blooded fools to live thus long honestly. And hath thy Master so little braine to think that we who know the sweets of theft and rogery, to whom dangers are as pleasant as dried suckets, who have been nurs'd and fed fat with blood and slaughter, can be content to bear part of your generall joy, for that which takes from us the means of our beloved mirth.

Will. Shall I change Venison for salt Cats, and make a bounteous meal, with the reversion of a puddings skin? Or shall I bid adieu to Pheasant and Partrige, and such pleasing Cates, and perswade my hungry maw to satisfaction with the bruis of an Egge-shell? Or shall it be said that thou O famous little John becomes the Attendant of a Tripe-woman?

John. The very thought of it is dangerous, I have got the gout only with the apprehension, I was born for action, but yet I cannot plow nor thresh, except it be mine enemy; and after all my fam'd exploits to hang for stealing sheep 'twould grieve me. I hope our worthy Master will not credit the gingling words of pardon, and acts of grace, and sully all his former glories with a surviving repentance; for my part I had rather trust my self then any other with my life.

Will. If this geare takes then we may turn our Bows into Fiddle-sticks, or strangle ourselves in the strings, for the daies of warre and wantonness will be done. Now must I whimper like a breecht School-boy, and make a face as soure as an Apes when he eates Crabs; and then learn manners, and to make legs with the patience of a setting-dog; and cry, I forsooth, and no forsooth, like a Country wench at a Churching; Wakes and Bear-baitings, and a little Cudgel-play must be all our comfort, and then in some smoaky corner re-count our past adventures, whilst the good wives blesse themselves at the relation. We must not dream of Venison, but be content like the King's liege-people with crusts and mouldy Cheese.

John. Every brave soule is born a King; rule and command o're the fearfull rabble, is natures stamp; courage and lofty thoughts are not ever confin'd to Thrones, nor still th' appendages of an illustrious birth, but the thatcht Hovell or the simple Wood oft times turns forth a mind as fully fraught with Gallantry and true worth as doth the marble Pallace; bounteous nature ties not her selfe to rules of State, or the hard Laws that cruell men impose; shee's free in all her gifts, as the Suns generall light, which when it first peepes o're the Eastern hills, and glads the widdow'd earth with its fresh beams, is not straight snatcht into a Monarchs Court, and there imprisoned to guild his private luxurie, but spreads his welcome rayes, and cheares the poor Orphan and dejected Widdow, with the same heat it doth the Persian Prince.

Rob. Why then should the severities of obedience, and the strait niceties of Law shackle this Noble soul, whom nature meant not onely free but soveraigne, those ties that now by a boundless spreading force doe equally concern the brave and base; first chiefly toucht the vulgar herd and throng of men, that masse of feare and folly, who therefore closed together, and with an easie fondnesse suffered themselves to be manacled by Lawes, because distrustful of their own free strength, and since being nur'st in idlenesse and soft intemperance, have grown inamoured of their Chaines, and caressed their slavery, and doat upon their hateful Bondage. But the bold daring Spirit hath in all times disown'd this sneaking lownesse, and with a commendable brav'ry challeng'd their darling Liberty; and from th'insulting Lawes rescu'd their enslaved honour: Those famous Heroes in this gallant attempt wee've boldly followed, and should we now sit down, and whine a vain repentance; or tamely and coldly yield our hands and legs to fetters, and necks to the mercy of the haltar, the world might well esteem us rash and heady Men, but never bold or truly Valiant. No we have Swords, and Arms, and Lives equally engaged in our past account, and whilest these Armes can wield our Swords, or our uncurdl'd blood give vigor to those Arms, hopes of submission are as vain as is the strange request.

Mess. Doubtless were the quality of actions the justice or injustice to be measured by the boldnesse or fear of the undertakers, what now is your shame, would be your greatest glory, and your Rebellion would be worthy of an honourable memory to eternal Ages; for none have begun and manag'd such wild designs with more unshaken confidence, but since Laws were not made as you formerly imagine, to enslave the Generous, but Curb the Proud and Violent, th' ambitious and unruly nature, your disobedience betrayes aboundlesse pride, and desires unfix'd as mad-mens thoughts, and restless as the Seas watry motion. That by the Laws which careful Princes make, we are commanded to do well and live vertuously, free both from giving and receiving injuries, is not to be esteemed slav'ry but priviledge. And since we know the power of doing wrong is seldome uncompanyed with a will someway answerable, it's our perfection to have that fairly chekt that so virtue and justice, the top and complement of our natures may have their due regard, which is the end of Lawes. Nor can a good or just Man, one who dares be virteous or honest (which is the truest gallantry) think it a loss of freedom to wait and obey the commands of his Prince, especially, when with his regality and Kingly power, are joyn'd the true embellishments of piety and real goodnesse. A Prince of such an influential sweetnesse, that every account teaches a vertue, and the meanest Subject by his great example grows up into an Heroe, as if his Princely Soul was grown his peoples Genious. A King so dear to Heaven as if he was it's onely care; His birth usher'd in by a bright Star, and each minute of his Life link'd to the former by a miracle, whose preservation was the amazement of his Enemies: and though the prayer, yet scarce the hope of his most hearty Subjects; One who hath suffer'd injuries beyond example, yet of such an unparalleld charity, he pardons them beyond hope. Whose Virtue is as great as his Birth and his Goodnesse unlimitted as his Power, To whom the illustrious persons former Ages brag'd of were no more comparable then the Nights Glimmering to the Noon-dayes Splendor.

    This Great, this Gracious Prince is this day Crown'd, and offers Life, and Peace, and Honour, if you will quit your wilde rebellions, and become what your birth challenges of you, nay what ever your boasted gallantry expects of you that is: loyall subjects.

Rob. Ha! whence is this sudden change? That resolution which but now was remo[r]seless as a Rock of Diamonds, and unyielding as the hardned Steel, is now soft and flexible as a weak womans passions. I am quite another man; thaw'd into conscience of my Crime and Duty; melted into loyalty and respect to vertue. What an harsh savage beast I was before, not differing from the fiery Lyon or the cruell Bear, but in my knowledge to doe greater ill, my strength and eager rashness was all my boast. How all my pride now is undermin'd? How am I dwarfd in mine own sight? remov'd from that advantage ground my fancy set me on, and shrunk to mine own low pitch? How am I torn now from my selfe? sure some power great and uncommon hath quite transform'd me, and consum'd all that was bad and vicious in me. Methinks these men, companions in former ills, look like those Grecians, th' enchanted cup transform'd: they've shapes of beasts, rude, uncomely and very affright-full; yet doe I see remorse bud in their blushing brows, as if with me they felt shame and true penitence for their fore-past Crimes. Let us all then joyne in the present sence of our duty, accept the profer'd pardon, - - - - and with one voice sing,

With hearty Wishes, health unto our King.

3 Voc.   Since Heaven with a liberal hand
                 Doth choicest blessings fling,
           And hath (not only to our Land
                 Restor'd but) Crown'd our K I N G.

           Let us to joy and generall mirth
                 This glad day set aside,

Let the Neighb'ring Woods now Eccho forth
Our shouts and Loyal Pride.

May Halters that Mans fate attend
That envies this dayes Glee
And's name meet a perpetual brand
For his Disloyalty.

Exeunt

Robin Hood and the Bishop of Hereford: a
broadside printed at London by C. Sheppard,
1791 (Bodleian Library, Oxford, Douce F.F.
71, no. 11).

25

EXTRACTS FROM 'THE FORESTERS' (ALFRED TENNYSON)

Source:
Tennyson, *Poems and Plays* (Oxford Standard Authors Edition, London, 1965), pp. 750–1, 754–5, 755–6.

The Foresters, first published in 1892, the year of its author's death, is well below the level of Tennyson's best work. But it is precisely because of its lack of genuinely imaginative creativity that it provides so representative and characteristic a nineteenth-century re-working of the legend. Tennyson's play makes Maid Marian the daughter of a certain Sir Richard Lea, who owes two thousand marks (which has gone to pay the ransom of his son Walter in the Holy Land) to the Abbot of St Mary's, York. He is anxious to marry his daughter to a wealthy suitor who will pay off this debt (No. 1 below). Although Marian loves Robin Hood, the outlawed Earl of Huntingdon, Robin himself is penniless, and the Sheriff of Nottingham and Prince John are presented as rivals for the hand of Marian.

The play is in four acts and written in a mixture of prose and Shakespearian blank verse.[1] In the first act the sheriff promises to pay off Sir Richard's debt if Marian will marry him. After Robin and Marian are compelled to part (2), the former is banished and agrees to become the leader of a group of King Richard's partisans in Sherwood Forest (3). The second act sees the flight of Marian to the woods, and Robin's encounter, disguised as an old woman, with the sheriff and Prince John. In the third act Marian is proclaimed and 'crowned' Queen o' the Woods, and Robin meets and robs some beggars and friars, who have lied to him about the amount of money they carry. Finally, in the fourth and final act, King Richard, after beating Friar Tuck, Much and Robin successively at quarterstaff, resolves the situation; and all ends happily with the reappearance of Sir Richard's son.

It is clear that while Tennyson used certain incidents from the *Gest* as the basis of his play, at the same time he introduced new relationships between characters, notably in the case of Sir Richard and Maid Marian. More sig-

---

[1] Tennyson obviously wrote *The Foresters* with the possibility of its stage performance very much in mind. It was first produced in New York on 17 March 1892 (Gable, p. 136), a few months before his death.

nificantly, he also stressed the theme, popular in the nineteenth century, of Robin Hood as a leader of Saxons against Normans, and an agent—like the Locksley of Sir Walter Scott's *Ivanhoe*—of national unity under Richard I. For Tennyson, Robin Hood was 'all England's darling' who leaves 'but happy memories to the forest' and the familiar final promise that

> 'here perhaps a hundred years away
> Some hunter in day-dreams or half-asleep
> Will hear our arrows whizzing overhead,
> And catch the winding of a phantom horn'.
>
> (Act V)

(1) *From Act I Scene I.*

SIR RICHARD

There never was an Earl so true a friend of the people as Lord Robin of Huntingdon.

MARIAN

A gallant Earl. I love him as I hate John.

SIR RICHARD

I fear me he hath wasted his revenues in the service of our good king Richard against the party of John, as I have done, as I have done: and where is Richard?

MARIAN

Cleave to him, father! he will come home at last.

SIR RICHARD

I trust he will, but if he do not I and thou are but beggars.

MARIAN

We will be beggar'd then and be true to the King.

SIR RICHARD

Thou speakest like a fool or a woman. Canst thou endure to be a beggar whose whole life hath been folded like a blossom in the sheath, like a careless sleeper in the down; who never hast felt a want, to whom all things, up to this present, have come as freely as heaven's air and mother's milk?

MARIAN

Tut, father! I am none of your delicate Norman maidens who can only broider and mayhap ride a-hawking with the help of the men. I can bake and I can brew, and by all the saints I can shoot almost as closely with the bow as the great Earl himself. I have played at the foils too with Kate:[1] but is not to-day his birthday?

---

[1] An attendant on Marian. A sub-plot of the play concerns her love affair with Little John.

SIR RICHARD

Dost thou love him indeed, that thou keepest a record of his birthdays?
Thou knowest that the Sheriff of Nottingham loves thee.

MARIAN

The Sheriff dare to love me? me who worship Robin the great Earl of
Huntingdon? I love him as a damsel of his day might have loved Harold the
Saxon or Hereward the Wake. They both fought against the tyranny of the
kings, the Normans. But then your Sheriff, your little man, if he dare to fight
at all, would fight for his rents, his leases, his houses, his monies, his oxen,
his dinners, himself. Now your great man, your Robin, all England's Robin,
fights not for himself but for the people of England. This John—this Norman
tyranny—the stream is bearing us all down, and our little Sheriff will ever
swim with the stream! but our great man, our Robin, against it. And how
often in old histories have the great men striven against the stream, and how
often in the long sweep of years to come must the great man strive against it
again to save his country, and the liberties of his people! God bless our
well-beloved Robin, Earl of Huntingdon.

SIR RICHARD

Ay, ay. He wore thy colours once at a tourney. I am old and forget. Was
Prince John there?

MARIAN

The Sheriff of Nottingham was there—not John.

SIR RICHARD

Beware of John and the Sheriff of Nottingham. They hunt in couples,
and when they look at a maid they blast her.

MARIAN

Then the maid is not high-hearted enough.

SIR RICHARD

There—there—be not a fool again. Their aim is ever at that which flies
highest—but O girl, girl, I am almost in despair. Those two thousand marks
lent me by the Abbot for the ransom of my son Walter—I believed this
Abbot of the party of King Richard, and he hath sold himself to that beast
John—they must be paid in a year and a month, or I lose the land. There is
one that should be grateful to me overseas, a Count in Brittany—he lives
near Quimper. I saved his life once in battle. He has monies. I will go to
him. I saved him. I will try him. I am all but sure of him. I will go to him.

MARIAN

And I will follow thee, and God help us both.

SIR RICHARD

Child, thou shouldst marry one who will pay the mortgage. This Robin, this Earl of Huntingdon—he is a friend of Richard—I know not, but he may save the land, he may save the land.

(2) *FROM Act I, Scene II.*

SIR RICHARD (*coming forward with MAID MARIAN*)
How close the Sheriff peer'd into thine eyes!
What did he say to thee?

MARIAN
Bade me beware
Of John: what maid but would beware of John?

SIR RICHARD
What else?

MARIAN
I care not what he said.

SIR RICHARD
What else?

MARIAN
That if I cast an eye of favour on him,
Himself would pay this mortgage to his brother,
And save the land.

SIR RICHARD
Did he say so, the Sheriff?

ROBIN
I fear this Abbot is a heart of flint,
Hard as the stones of his abbey.
O good Sir Richard,
I am sorry my exchequer runs so low
I cannot help you in this exigency;
For though my men and I flash out at times
Of festival like burnish'd summer-flies,
We make but one hour's buzz, are only like
The rainbow of a momentary sun.
I am mortgaged as thyself.

SIR RICHARD
Ay! I warrant thee—thou canst not be sorrier than
I am. Come away, daughter.

ROBIN

Farewell, Sir Richard; farewell, sweet Marian.

MARIAN

Till better times.

ROBIN

But if the better times should never come?

MARIAN

Then I shall be no worse.

ROBIN

And if the worst time come?

MARIAN

Why then I will be better than the time.

ROBIN

This ring my mother gave me: it was her own
Betrothal ring. She pray'd me when I loved
A maid with all my heart to pass it down
A finger of that hand which should be mine
Thereafter. Will you have it? Will you wear it?

MARIAN

Ay, noble Earl, and never part with it.

SIR RICHARD LEA (*coming up*)

Not till she clean forget thee, noble Earl.

MARIAN

Forget *him*—never—by this Holy Cross
Which good King Richard gave me when a child—
Never!
Not while the swallow skims along the ground
And while the lark flies up and touches heaven!
Not while the smoke floats from the cottage roof,
And the white cloud is roll'd along the sky!
Not while the rivulet babbles by the door,
And the great breaker beats upon the beach!
Never—
Till Nature, high and low, and great and small
Forgets herself, and all her loves and hates
Sink again into chaos.

(3) *From Act I, Scene III.*

Enter a PURSUIVANT who reads.

O yes, O yes, O yes! In the name of the Regent. Thou Robin Hood Earl of Huntingdon, art attainted and hast lost thine earldom of Huntingdon. Moreover thou art dispossessed of all thy lands, goods, and chattels; and by virtue of this writ, whereas Robin Hood Earl of Huntingdon by force and arms hath trespassed against the king in divers manners, therefore by the judgment of the officers of the said lord king, according to the law and custom of the kingdom of England Robin Hood Earl of Huntingdon is outlawed and banished.

ROBIN

I have shelter'd some that broke the forest laws.
This is irregular and the work of John.

['Irregular, irregular! (*tumult*) Down with
him, tear his coat from his back!']

MESSENGER

Ho there! ho there, the Sheriff's men without!

ROBIN

Nay, let them be, man, let them be. We yield.
How should we cope with John? The London folkmote
Has made him all but king, and he hath seized
On half the royal castles. Let him alone! (*to his men*)
A worthy messenger! how should he help it?
Shall *we* too work injustice? what, thou shakest!
Here, here—a cup of wine—drink and begone!

Exit MESSENGER.

We will away in four-and-twenty hours,
But shall we leave our England?

TUCK
Robin, Earl—

ROBIN

Let be the Earl. Henceforth I am no more
Than plain man to plain man.

TUCK
Well, then, plain man,

There be good fellows there in merry Sherwood
That hold by Richard, tho' they kill his deer.

ROBIN

In Sherwood Forest. I have heard of them.
Have they no leader?

TUCK
Each man for his own.
Be thou their leader and they will all of them
Swarm to thy voice like bees to the brass pan.

ROBIN
They hold by Richard—the wild wood! to cast
All threadbare household habit, mix with all
The lusty life of wood and underwood,
Hawk, buzzard, jay, the mavis and the merle,
The tawny squirrel vaulting thro' the boughs,
The deer, the highback'd polecat, the wild boar,
The burrowing badger—By St. Nicholas
I have a sudden passion for the wild wood—
We should be free as air in the wild wood—
What say you? shall we go? Your hands, your hands!

26

AN OUTLAW'S SONG OF TRAILBASTON, *c. 1305*

Source:
British Library, Harley MS. 2253, fos. 113v–114v.

Other Editions:
T. Wright, ed., *The Political Songs of England* (Camden Society, Old Series, VI, 1839), pp. 231–6; I. S. T. Aspin, *Anglo-Norman Political Songs* (Anglo-Norman Texts XI, Oxford, 1953), pp. 67–78.

The following lines are translated from a French poem preserved in an early fourteenth-century manuscript, otherwise notable for its collection of Middle English lyrics. Untitled in the original text, the poem comprises twenty-five four-line stanzas, all rhyming *AAAA*. Although purporting to have been written on parchment '*al bois, desouz un lorer*' and then dropped on the high-road so that it might fall into the hands of travellers (stanza 25), there can be little doubt that it was a work of calculated and quite sophisticated political propaganda. The author's bitter grievance was the injustice caused by the recent innovation of royal commissions of trailbaston. The latter directed specially appointed groups of justices to prosecute and punish armed criminals ('trailbastons') guilty of acts of robbery, assault and intimidation against the king's subjects. The first commissions of trailbaston dated from 1304–5 and were renewed—despite considerable opposition—at frequent intervals throughout the fourteenth century.[1] The fact that the four men (William Martin, Gilbert de Knovill, Henry Spigurnel and Roger de Bella Fago) to whom allusion is made in stanza 9 were indeed justices of trailbaston assigned to the south-western counties in April 1305 helps to establish the date of the poem and the probability that its author lived in that part of England.[2] His

---

[1] It is worth noting that the most fully recorded opposition to the commissions of trailbaston came from bishops and parliamentary knights of the shire, not the lowest orders of society: see M. McKisack, *The Fourteenth Century* (Oxford 1959) pp. 171, 200, 206. As these commissions, variants of the general royal judicial commissions of oyer and terminer, apparently gave justices the additional power of deciding suits between parties, they could be 'easily used as declarations of war by particular groups in the community against other groups': A. Harding, *The Law Courts of Medieval England* (London, 1973), p. 90.

[2] Aspin, pp. 67–8.

claim that he knew the law as well as his legal persecutors (stanza 23) seems absolutely confirmed by his copious and accurate use of legal vocabulary. All the evidence indeed points to the hypothesis that the supposedly self-confessed outlaw who wrote this poem was a well-informed and remarkably self-confident member of local society, one who had presumably served in Edward I's military campaigns (stanza 7). He was possibly a knight or an esquire but more probably (see stanzas 15–17) a well-connected clerk.

The *Outlaw's Song* is therefore in no sense a popular poem. Written in Anglo-Norman, the language used in early fourteenth-century law courts, it was obviously addressed to a knowledgeable local audience. Despite the author's use of a sort of literary Arcadianism ('There is no deceit there, nor any bad law'), it is clear enough that he has no desire to be a permanent resident of the forest.[1] Yet the *Outlaw's Song* undoubtedly throws exceptionally valuable light on three aspects of late medieval English social thinking which helped to promote the early evolution of the Robin Hood legend. Outlawry itself is assumed to be the outcome of intrigue, false accusations and local oppression rather than of deliberate crime (stanza 24); the lawless '*compagnie*' or band (stanza 22) is already a well-known feature of the English forest; and, on balance, the outlaw himself is presented as a sympathetic and unjustly persecuted individual.[2] On the evidence of this poem alone, considerable numbers of the English gentry and clergy were already predisposed —at the beginning of the fourteenth century—to admire and identify themselves with the exploits of the 'noble outlaw' whom Robin Hood was soon to represent and typify.

Translation

I

I am seized with the desire to rhyme and make a story
About an ordinance which is provided in the land.
It would have been better if this act had still to be done;
If God does not prevent it, I think that war will arise.

2

These are the articles of Trailbaston;
Except for the king himself, may he have God's curse
Who first granted such a commission!
For there is little right in several of its points.

3

Sir, if I wish to chastise my boy
With a slap or two, to correct him,
He will take out a bill against me, and have me attached,
So that I will have to give a big ransom before I get out of prison.

[1] Hilton, 'Origins of Robin Hood', p. 38; cf. Keen, *Outlaws*, pp. 204–5.
[2] Cf. Stones, 'The Folvilles of Ashby-Folville', *T.R.H.S.*, 5th. series, VII (1957), pp. 117–36; Bellamy, *Crime and Public Order*, p. 82.

4

They take forty shillings for my ransom,
And the sheriff comes for his reward
For not placing me in a deep prison.
Now consider, lords, is this right?

5

For this reason, I will keep myself within the woods, in the beautiful shade;
There is no deceit there, nor any bad law,
In the wood of Belregard,[1] where the jay flies
And the nightingale sings every day without ceasing.

6

But people of evil disposition, on whom may God never have pity,
Have indicted me out of their false mouths
For wicked robberies and other misdeeds,
So that I do not dare to be received among my friends.

7

I have served my lord the king in peace and war,
In Flanders, Scotland and Gascony, his own land;
But now I do not know how to make a livelihood.
I have spent all my time in vain to please such a man.

8

If these wicked jurors will not amend themselves
So that I may ride and go to my country,
I will make their heads fly off if I can reach them;
I will not give a penny for all their threats.

9

The Martin and the Knoville are pious men,
And pray for the poor that they may have safety;
Spigurnel and Belflour are cruel men;[2]
If they were in my jurisdiction they would not be returned.

10

I would teach them the game of Trailbaston,
And would break their backs and their rumps,
Their arms and their legs: it would be right;
I would also cut out their tongues and their mouths.

11

He who first began these things
Will never be reformed all the days of his life;
I tell you, in truth, there is too great a sin involved,
Because for fear of prison many a robber will be made.

[1] A fictitious name, chosen to emphasize the delights of living in the forest.
[2] For notes on the four men mentioned in this stanza, see Aspin, p. 77.

12

Some will become thieves who were never such before,
Because, for fear of prison, they dare not come to peace;
To live at all one must have sufficient every day;
Whoever began this thing undertook a heavy task.

13

Merchants and monks should indeed deliver a curse
On all those who have ordained the Trailbaston;
Royal protection will not be worth a leek to them,
Unless they hand over the money without recompense.

14

You who are indicted, I advise you, come to me,
To the green forest of Belregard, where there is no annoyance
But only the wild animal and the beautiful shade;
For the common law is too uncertain.

15

If you know your letters and are tonsured,
You will be summoned before the justices;
You may be returned again to prison,
Under the bishop's care, until you have acquitted yourself.[1]

16

. . . .
. . . .[2]
And suffer privation and very hard penance,
And perhaps you will never have deliverance.

17

Therefore it is better to stay with me in the woods
Than to lie chained in the bishop's prison.
The penance is too great and too hard to bear;
Whoever can choose the best is a fool not to choose.

18

Formerly I knew a little about what was good, now I am less wise;
This is what the evil laws do to me by their very great outrage,
So that I dare not come into peace among my kinsmen.
The rich are put to ransom, the poor dwindle away.

19

It would be serious to pledge what cannot be acquitted,
That is to say a man's life which is so dearly loved;
And I have not the chattels to be redeemed.
But if I were in their power I should be delivered to death.

---

[1] Those in clerical orders (i.e. tonsured) would plead 'benefit of clergy' and eventually
come within episcopal rather than lay jurisdiction.
[2] Two lines seem to have been omitted by the scribe at this point.

20

Yet I shall receive pardon and hear people speak.
Some speak ill of me who dare not approach me,
And they would willingly see my body ill-treated;
But God can save a man in the midst of a thousand devils.

21

He can save me, who is the Son of Mary;
For I was not culpable, but was indicted out of malice.
May God curse whoever caused me to be in this place!
The world is so fickle, he who trusts it is a fool.

22

If I become a 'companion' and know about archery,
My neighbour will go around saying: 'That man is of a company
Which goes to hunt in the woods and to do other follies;
If he wishes to live, he will lead his life like a swine.'

23

If I know more about the law than they do,
They will say, 'That conspirator begins to be untrustworthy'.
And I will not come within ten or two leagues of home.
Let them be disgraced in all neighbourhoods.

24

I beg all good people that they will pray for me,
That I can go and ride to my country.
I was never a homicide, of my own will anyway;
Nor was I a wicked robber to do people harm.

25

This rhyme was made in the wood, beneath a laurel tree;
There sing the blackbird and nightingale, and there hovers the hawk;
It was written on parchment to be better remembered,
And thrown on the highroad so that people should find it.

27

ROBYN AND GANDELEYN (Child 115)

Source:
British Library, Sloane MS. 2593, fos. 14v–15v.

Other Editions:
Ritson, *Ancient Songs* (London, 1790), p. 48; T. Wright, *Songs and Carols printed from a Manuscript in the Sloane Collection in the British Museum* (London, 1836), No. X; Gutch, 1847, II, 36–8; Child, 1888, III, 13–14; Quiller-Couch, 1910, pp. 462–5; Leach, 1955, pp. 332–4; *Oxford Book of Ballads* (1969), pp. 374–7; *Oxford Book of Medieval English Verse* (1970), pp. 437–40.

The unique copy of this famous poem occurs in a volume of miscellaneous verse, almost all written in the same mid-fifteenth-century hand. The manuscript contains 74 different lyrics, of which over 50 are carols and most of the others devoted to religious subjects. This anthology has been attributed—on no very secure grounds—to the abbey of Bury St Edmunds by R. L. Greene in his edition of *A Selection of English Carols* (Oxford, 1962), p. 173. There are several indications, including the accidental repetition of the two last lines of stanza 11 below, that the manuscript was copied hastily and somewhat inaccurately by its scribe. Child's division into stanzas has been followed below, but it should be noted that the manuscript text is written continuously with a somewhat erratic use of punctuation marks to signify the close of the poetic line.

'Robyn and Gandeleyn' has been printed many times since it was first published by Joseph Ritson in 1790 and it finds a place in most modern collections of English ballads. Few medieval lyrics have been subjected to more diverse and often ludicrous interpretations. According to Ritson, the Robin of this poem was a 'Robin Lyth' who gave his name to a cave near Flamborough; while for Robert Graves (*English and Scottish Ballads*, 1957, pp. 149–50), 'Although this seems to be a ballad about Robin Hood the Archer, its real subject is the New Year's hunting of the wren in vengeance of the robin murdered at midsummer'. Thought, as Child pointed out in this connection, is free; but even the more prosaic attempts to suggest that 'Robyn and Gandeleyn' is a poaching ballad fail to provide a satisfactory explanation of this mysterious poem. Only one thing seems certain: by no stretch of the imagination can the 'Robyn' of this lyric be properly identified with the Robin Hood of the other ballads. Nevertheless it demands inclusion in this collection not only because of its intrinsic merits but because of the light it throws on the ambiguity of late medieval attitudes to the 'grene wode'.

1

Robyn lyth in grene wode bowndyn
I herde a carpyng of a clerk,
　Al at yone wodes ende,
Of gode Robyn and Gandeleyn;
　Was ther non other gynge.[1]

2

Stronge thevys wern tho chylderin non,
　But bowmen gode and hende;
He wentyn to wode to getyn hem fleych,
　If God wold it hem sende.

3

Al day wentyn tho chylderin too,
　And fleych fowndyn he non,
Til it were ageyn[2] evyn;
　The chylderin wold gon hom.

4

Half an honderid of fat falyf der[3]
　He comyn ayon,[4]
And alle he wern fayr and fat inow,
　But markyd was ther non;
'Be dere God', seyde gode [Robyn,][5]
　Here of we shul have on.'

5

Robyn bent his joly bowe,
　Ther in he set a flo; [6]
The fattest der of alle
　The herte he clef a to.

6

He hadde not the der iflawe[7],
　Ne half out of the hyde,

Ther cam a schrewde arwe out of the
　　west,
　That felde Robertes pryde.

7

Gandeleyn lokyd hym est and west,
　Be every syde:
'Hoo hat myn mayster slayin?
　Ho hat don this dede?
Shal I never out of grene wode go
　Til I se sydis blede.'

8

Gandeleyn lokyd hym est and lokyd
　　west,
　And sowt under the sunne;
He saw a lytil boy
　He clepyn[8] Wrennok of Donne.

9

A good bowe in his hond,
　A brod arwe therine,
And fawre and twenti goode arwys,
　Trusyd in a thrumme:[9]
'Be war the, war the, Gandeleyn,
　Her-of th(o)u shalt han summe.

10

'Be war the, war the, Gandeleyn,
　Her of th(o)u gyst[10] plente.'
'Ever on for an other,' seyde Gandeleyn;
　'Mysaunter have he shal fle.[11]

11

'Qwer-at shal our marke be?'
　Seyde Gandeleyn:
'Everyche at otheris herte,'
　Seyde Wrennok ageyn.

---

[1] gynge: *company*?　　[2] ageyn: *towards*　　[3] falyf der: *fallow deer*
[4] He comyn ayon: *they came upon*　　[5] Robyn: *omitted in MS*　　[6] flo: *arrow*
[7] iflawe: *flayed*　　[8] He clepyn: *they call*　　[9] thrumme: *bundle*　　[10] gyst: *will get*
[11] Ill fortune may he have who flees

12

'Ho shal yeve[1] the ferste schote?'
   Seyd Gandeleyn:
'And I shul yeve the on be-forn,'[2]
   Seyde Wrennok ageyn.

13

Wrennock schette a ful good schote,
   And he schet not to hye;
Throw the sanchothis of his bryk;[3]
   It towchyd neyther thye.

14

'Now hast thou youvyn me on be-forn,'
   Al thus to Wrennok seyde he,
'And throw the myght of our Lady
   A bettere I shal yeve the.'

15

Gandeleyn bent his goode bowe,
   And set therin a flo;
He schet throw his grene certyl,[4]
   His herte he clef on too.

16

'Now shalt th(o)u never yelpe,[5]
   Wrennok,
   At ale ne at wyn,
That thou hast slawe goode Robyn,
   And his knave[6] Gandeleyn.

17

'Now shalt th(o)u never yelpe, Wrennok,
   At wyn ne at ale,
That th(o)u hast slawe goode Robyn,
   And Gandeleyn his knave.'
Robyn lyeth in grene wode bow(n)dyn

---

[1] yeve: *give*   [2] be-forn: *first*   [3] sanchothis of his bryk: *? fork of his breeches*
[4] certyl: *kirtle*   [5] yelpe: *boast*   [6] knave: *servant*

ADAM BELL, CLIM OF THE CLOUGH, AND WILLIAM OF CLOUDESLY (Child 116)

Source :
'Adambel, Clym of the Cloughe, and Wyllyam of Cloudesle'. 'Imprinted at London in Lothburye by Wyllyam Copland' (1548–68). (British Library copy, press-mark C. 21. c. 64).

Other Editions :
Percy's *Reliques* (included in the 1765 and all later editions); Ritson, *Pieces of Ancient Popular Poetry*, 1791, pp. 5–30; Gutch, 1847, II, 320–43; Child, 1888, III, 22–30; Quiller-Couch, 1910, pp. 468–96; *Oxford Book of Ballads*, 1969, pp. 380–404.

Somewhat ironically the most dramatically exciting of all English outlaw ballads is devoted not to the exploits of Robin Hood and his men but to those of three other famous 'yemen of the north countrey', Adam Bell, Clim of the Clough and William of Cloudesly. Of these three Inglewood outlaws, the hero is undoubtedly William of Cloudesly, captured within Carlisle in the first fytte, rescued by his two blood brothers in the second, and triumphantly successful in shooting an apple off his son's head in the third. Nevertheless the ballad has almost universally gone by the short title of *Adam Bell* since the first record of its entry on the Stationers' Register in 1557–58.[1] The survival of early sixteenth-century printed fragments of the work (B and E below) proves that it was already current in the reign of Henry VIII; but the earliest surviving complete edition of *Adam Bell* is that printed *c.* 1560 by William Copland of London and now preserved in the British Library. This is consequently the text (cited as A) transcribed and reproduced below. As several lines in Copland's edition have been either cut away or omitted, these omissions (together with a few preferable readings cited in the footnotes) have been supplied from some of the following other early editions:

B. Fragments of an edition printed in Fleet Street, London, by John Byddell in 1536 (now preserved in a single copy in Cambridge University Library, Sym. 7. 50. 9). These preserve stanzas 113–28 and 161–70 of the work.

[1] Arber, I, 79. *Adam Bell* was entered in the Stationers' Register twice more (1582, 1594) before the end of the sixteenth century (ibid., II, 405, 651).

C. The edition printed by James Roberts at London in 1605 (now preserved in Bodleian Library, Oxford, S. Selden, d. 45). This also includes 'The Second part of Adam Bell', an 'absurd extravaganza' of the late sixteenth century not printed below but to be found in Child, III, 34–9.

D. The Percy Folio version of Adam Bell, consulted by Bishop Percy for the text he published in the first edition (1765) of the *Reliques*, but first printed in its entirety in *Bishop Percy's Folio Manuscript*, ed. Hales and Furnivall, III, 76–101.

E. Fragment of an edition by an unidentified early sixteenth-century printer, once in the possession of J. Payne Collier who copied the text for Child in 1857. Child's collations (III, 31–4), but not the original, have been consulted here. This fragment preserves stanzas 53–111 of the work.

As the number of these early editions suggests, *Adam Bell* enjoyed a very considerable degree of popularity from the sixteenth century onwards. Allusions to the poem occur in Shakespeare's *Much Ado About Nothing* (Act. I, Scene 1: 'and he that hits me, let him be clapped on the shoulder, and called Adam'), Ben Jonson's *The Alchemist* (Act I: 'No cheating Clim o' the Cloughs'), and Sir William Davenant's *The Long Vacation in London*.[1] Although its reputation never seriously rivalled that of the Robin Hood tales, *Adam Bell* was reprinted at least seven times in the course of the seventeenth century.[2] At an earlier date Robert Laneham's description of the court festivities at Kenilworth in 1575 reveals that the famous collector of 'ballets and songs', Captain Cox of Coventry, was thoroughly familiar with the 'stories' of both Adam Bell and Robin Hood.[3] Not unnaturally, several attempts were made to link the careers of England's two most famous groups of outlaws: much the most ingeniously unlikely of these occurs in the third and fourth stanzas of *Robin Hood's Birth, Breeding, Valor and Marriage* (Child 149) where the Pinder of Wakefield is alleged to have arranged an archery contest between Robin Hood's father and 'Adam Bell, and Clim of the Clugh, and William a Cloudelle'.[4]

It is, however, precisely because *Adam Bell* preserves an outlaw legend originally distinct from the Robin Hood saga that it throws such interesting light on the latter. Despite the lateness of the texts in which it survives, *Adam Bell* is undoubtedly of medieval origin and presumably emerged at about the same period as the earliest extant Robin Hood tales. Like the *Gest*, *Robin Hood and the Monk*, and *Robin Hood and the Potter*, it was probably designed to be read aloud and betrays many characteristic features of the late medieval metrical romance: the seasonal *incipit*, the division of a long work

---

[1] Gutch, II, 318.   [2] Child, III, 14.

[3] Robert Laneham's Letter to Humfrey Martin, ed. F. J. Furnivall, as *Captain Cox, His Ballads and Books* (Ballad Society, 1871), pp. li–liv.

[4] *Robin Hood* (a Garland printed by T. Wilson, York, 1811), p. 5; Child, III, 215.

(*c.* 5,100 words) into fyttes, the minstrel's direct address to his listeners (see especially stanzas 5, 51, 97, 170), the remnants of alliterative poetic diction and the frequent use of an *ABAB* rhyming pattern within the stanzas.[1] As a work of 'yeoman minstrelsy' analogous to the early Robin Hood 'ballads', *Adam Bell* also inevitably introduces several themes of frequent occurrence in the latter. The rescue of William of Cloudesly by Adam Bell and Clim of the Clough is paralleled by Little John's and Much's deliverance of Robin Hood in stanzas 61–82 of *Robin Hood and the Monk*. Like Robin in the *Gest*, Adam Bell and his colleagues eventually receive from their king not only pardon but a place in his household. Such resemblances, and above all the presentation of the three self-confident 'outlawes of the forest' as sympathetic if violent heroes who 'dread for no man', make it clear that the Robin Hood *persona* was not confined to the Sherwood hero alone. Certainly *Adam Bell* has its own distinctive features—most notably its location in Inglewood,[2] and the episode of an archer shooting an apple placed on his son's head;[3] but perhaps its greatest value lies in its confirmation that much of the appeal of the late medieval outlaw lay in his role as an idealized 'noble bandit'.

PART I

1

Mery it was in grene forest
　Amonge the leves grene,
Where that men walke both east and
　　west
　Wyth bowes and arrowes kene;

2

To ryse the dere out of theyr denne;

Suche sightes as hath ofte bene sene;
As by the yemen of the north countrey,
　By them it is as I meane.

3

The one of them hight[4] Adam Bell,
　The other Clym of the Clough,[5]
The thyrd was William of Cloudesly,
　An archer good ynough.

---

[1] Cf. Fowler, *Literary History of Popular Ballad*, p. 71.

[2] Inglewood, a Cumberland forest stretching from Penrith to Carlisle and deservedly famous for its hunting in actuality, was also used as the scene for several of King Arthur's legendary adventures. Perhaps for this reason the Scottish chronicler, Andrew of Wyntoun, made Robin Hood a frequenter of 'Ingilwode' as well as 'Bernysdale' (see above, p. 4). For an extraordinarily unconvincing attempt to identify Adam Bell as 'a genuine personage of history', see Joseph Hunter, *New Illustrations of the Life, Studies, and Writings of Shakespeare* (London, 1845), I, 245–8.

[3] A full discussion of this theme (most famous because of its appearance in the apocryphal history of the Swiss William Tell) in medieval and later literature is provided by Child (III, 16–21). It seems clear enough that the compiler of *Adam Bell* was merely adapting to his own purposes one of the most popular stories of north European literature, a legend already long drained of any genuine mythological content. Child effectively swept away the 'mildew of myth' attached to the story of Adam Bell, as to those of Robin Hood, by nineteenth-century folklorists.

[4] hight: *was called*　　　[5] cloghu in A

5. Robin Hood and Little John: a relief by James Wood (1952) at Castle Green, Nottingham

4

They were outlawed for venyson,
   These thre yemen everechone;
They swore them brethen upon a day,
   To Englysshe-wood[1] for to gone.

5

Now lith and lysten, gentylmen,
   And that of myrthes loveth to here:
Two of them were singele men,
   The third had a wedded fere.[2]

6

Wyllyam was the wedded man,
   Muche more then was hys care:
He sayde to hys brethen upon a day,
   To Carelel[3] he would fare.

7

For to speke with fayre Alse hys wife,
   And with hys chyldren thre:
'By my trouth,' sayde Adam Bel,
   'Not by the counsell of me.

8

'For if ye go to Caerlel, brother,
   And from thys wylde wode wende,
If the justice mai you take,
   Your lyfe were at an ende.'

9

'If that I come not to morowe, brother,
   By pryme[4] to you agayne,
Truste not els but that I am take,
   Or else that I am slayne.'

10

He toke hys leave of hys brethen two,
   And to Carlel he is gone;
There he knocked at hys owne
     wyndowe,
   Shortlye and anone.

11

'Wher be you,[5] fayre Alyce, my wyfe,
   And my chyldren three?
Lyghtly let in thyne husbande,
   Wyllyam of Cloudesle.'

12

'Alas!' then sayde fayre Alyce,
   And syghed wonderous sore,
'Thys place hath ben besette for you
   Thys halfe yere and more.'

13

'Now am I here,' sayde Cloudesle,
   'I woulde that I in were;
Now feche us meate and drynke
     ynoughe,
   And let us make good chere.'

14

She feched him meat and drynke plenty,
   Lyke a true wedded wyfe,
And pleased hym with that she had,
   Whome she loved as her lyfe.

15

There lay an old wyfe in that place,
   A lytle besyde the fyre,
Whych Wyllyam had found,[6] of
     cherytye,
   More than seven yere.

16

Up she rose, and walked full styll,
   Evel mote[7] she spede[8] therefoore!
For she had not set no fote on ground
   In seven yere before.

17

She went ynto the justice hall,
   As fast as she could hye:
'Thys nyght is come unto thys town
   Wyllyam of Cloudesle.'

---

[1] Englysshe wood: *Inglewood Forest*   [2] fere: *companion, wife*
[3] Carelel: *Carlisle*   [4] pryme: *sunrise*   [5] 'your' in A   [6] found: *provided for*
[7] mote: *may*   [8] 'spende' in A

18

Thereof the iustice was full fayne,[1]
  And so was the shirife also:
'Thou shalt not travaile hether, dame,
    for[2] nought,
  Thy meed[3] thou shalt have or thou go.'

19

They gave to her a ryght good goune,
  Of scarlet it was, as I herd saye;
She toke the gyft, and home she wente,
  And couched her doune agayne.

20

They rysed the towne of mery Carlel,
  In all the hast that they can;
And came thronging to Wyllyame's
    house,
  As fast as they might gone.

21

Theyr they besette that good yeman
  Round about on every syde;
Wyllyam hearde great noyse of folkes,
  That heytherward they[4] hyed.

22

Alyce opened a shot-wyndow,[5]
  And loked all about;
She was ware of the justice and the
    shrife bothe,
  Wyth a great full great route.

23

'Alas! treason!' cryed Alyce,
  'Ever wo may thou be!
Go[6] into my chambre, my husband,' she
    sayd,
  'Swete Wyllyam of Cloudesle.'

24

He toke hys sweard and hys bucler,
  Hys bow and hys[7] chyldren thre,

And wente into hys strongest chamber,
  Where he thought surest to be.

25

Fayre Alice folowed him as a lover true,
  With a pollaxe in her hande:
'He shalbe deade that here cometh in
  Thys dore, whyle I may stand.'

26

Cloudesle bent a wel good bowe,
  That was of trusty tre,
He smot the justise on the brest,
  That hys arrowe brest in thre.

27

'God's curse on his hartt,' saide
    William,
  'Thys day thy cote dyd on;[8]
If it had ben no better then myne,
  It had gone nere thy bone.'

28

'Yelde the, Cloudesle,' sayd the justise,
  'And thy bowe and thy arrowes the
    fro:'
'Gods curse on hys hart,' sayde fair
    Alice,[9]
  'That my husband councelleth so.'

29

'Set fyre on the house,' saide the sherife,
  'Syth it wyll no better be,
And brenne we therin William,' he
    saide,
  'Hys wyfe and chyldren thre.'

30

They fyred the house in many a place,
  The fyre flew upon hye;
'Alas!' than cryed fayr Alice,[10]
  'I se we shall here dy.'

---

[1] fayne: *pleased*   [2] 'fore' in A   [3] meed: *reward*   [4] 'they' is missing in A
[5] shot-wyndow: *bay*, or *hinged window* (see above, p. 136): C and D read 'back window'
[6] 'Gy' in A   [7] 's' is missing in A   [8] cote dyd on: *coat put on*   [9] 'Alce' in A
[10] 'Alece' in A

31

William openyd hys backe wyndow,
　That was in hys chambre on hye,
And wyth shetes let hys wyfe downe,
　And hys chyldren thre.

32

'Have here my treasure,' sayde William,
　'My wyfe and my chyldren thre;
For Christes love do them no harme,
　But wreke you all on me.'

33

Wyllyam shot so wonderous well,
　Tyll hys arrowes were all gon,
And the fyre so fast upon hym fell,
　That hys bow[1] stryng brent in two.

34

The spercles brent and fell hym on,
　Good Wyllyam of Cloudesle;
But than was he a wofull man,
　And sayde, 'Thys is a cowardes death
　　to me.'

35

'Lever[2] I had,' sayde Wyllyam,
　'With my sworde in the route to
　　renne,[3]
Then here among myne ennemyes
　　wode[4]
Thus cruelly to bren.'

36

He toke hys sweard and hys buckler,
　And among them all he ran;
Where the people were most in prece,[5]
　He smot downe many a man.

37

There myght no man stand hys stroke,
　So fersly on them he ran;

Then they threw wyndowes and dores
　　on him,
　And so toke that good yeman.

38

There they hym bounde both hand and
　　fote,
　And in depe dongeon hym cast;
'Now, Cloudesle,' sayde the hye justice,
　'Thou shalt be hanged in hast.'

39

'One vow shal I make,' sayde the sherife,
　'A payre of new galowes shall I for
　　the make,
And al the gates of Caerlel shalbe shutte,
　There shall no man come in therat.

40

'Then shall not helpe Clim of the
　　Cloughe,
　Nor yet Adam Bell,
Though they came with a thousand mo,
　Nor all the devels in hell.'

41

Early in the mornyng the justice uprose,
　To the gates fast gan he gon,[6]
And commaunded to be shut full cloce
　Lightile[7] everychone.

42

Then went he to the market place,
　As fast as he coulde hye;
A payre of new gallous there dyd he up
　　set,
　Besyde the pyllory.

43

A lytle boy stod them amonge,
　And asked what meaned that gallow
　　tre;
They sayde, 'To hange a good yeaman,
　Called Wyllyam of Cloudesle.'

---

[1] 'bo' in A   [2] lever: *rather*   [3] renne: *run*   [4] wode: *furious*
[5] in prece: *in a crowd*   [6] gan he gon: *he began to go*   [7] lightile: *quickly*

44

That lytle boye was the towne swyne
    heard,
    And kept there [fayre]¹ Alyce swyne;
Full oft he had sene Cloudesle in the
    wodde,
    And geven² hym there to dyne.

45

He went out of a creves³ in the wall,
    And lightly to the woode dyd gone;
There met he with these wyght⁴ yonge
    men,
    Shortly and anone.

46

'Alas!' then sayde that lytle boye,
    'Ye tary here all to longe;
Cloudesle is taken and dampned to
    death,
    All readye for to honge.'

47

'Alas!' then sayde good Adam Bell,
    'That ever we see thys daye!
He myght her with us have dwelled,
    So ofte as we dyd him praye.

48

'He myght have taryed in grene foreste,
    Under the shadowes sheene,⁵
And have kepte both hym and us in
    reaste,⁶
    Out of trouble and teene.'⁷

49

Adam bent a right good bowe,⁸
    A great hart sone had he slayne;
'Take that, chylde,' he sayde, 'to thy
    dynner,
    And bryng me myne arrowe agayne.'

50

'Now go we hence,' sayed these wight
    yong men,
    'Tary we no lenger here;
We shall hym borowe,⁹ by God's grace,
    Though we bye it full dere.'

51

To Caerlel went these good yemen,
    In a mery mornyng of Maye:
Her is a fyt of Cloudesli,
    And another is for to saye.¹⁰

PART II

52

And when they came to mery Carelell,
    In a fayre mornyng tyde,
They founde the gates shut them untyll
    Round about on every syde.

53

'Alas!' than sayd good Adam Bell,
    'That ever we were made men!
These gates be shut so wonderous wel,
    That we may not come herein.'

54

Then spake Clym of the Clough,
    'Wyth a wyle we wyl us in bryng;
Let us saye we be messengers,
    Streyght come nowe from our king.'

55

Adam said, 'I have a letter written wel,
    Now let us wysely werke,
We wyl saye we have the kinges seales,
    I hold the porter no clerke.'

---

¹ Omitted in A   ² 'geuend' in A   ³ creves: *crevice, gap*   ⁴ wyght: *sturdy*
⁵ sheene: *lovely*   ⁶ reaste: *rest*   ⁷ teene: *vexation*
⁸ This line, missing in A, is supplied from C.D.   ⁹ borowe: *ransom*
¹⁰ At the end of the first fytte, the minstrel addresses his audience directly (cf. above, pp. 89, 102, 124, and below, p. 268).

56

Then Adam Bell bete on the gate
  With strokes great and strong:
The porter herde suche noyse therat,
  And to the gate [faste] he throng.[1]

57

'Who is there now,' sayde the porter,
  'That maketh all thys knocking?'
'We be [two][2] messengers,' sayde Clim
  of the Clough,
'Be come ryght from our kyng.'

58

'We have a letter,' sayd Adam Bel,
  'To the justice we must it bryng;
Let us in our messag[e] to do,
  That we were agayne to our kyng.'

59

'Here commeth none in,' sayd the
  porter,
  'Be hym that dyed upon a tre,
Tyll a false thefe be hanged,
  Called Wyllyam of Cloudesle.

60

Then spake the good yeman, Clym of
  the Cloughe,
  And swore by Mary fre,[3]
'And if that we stande long wythout,
  Lyke a thefe hanged shalt thou be.

61

Lo! here we have the kynges seale:
  What, lordeyn[4] art thou wode?'[5]
The porter had went[6] it had ben so,
  And lyghtly dyd off hys hode.

62

'Welcome be my lordes seale,' he saide;
  'For that ye shall come in.'
He opened the gate full shortlye:
  An evyl openyng for him.

63

'Now are we in,' sayde Adam Bell,
  'Whereof we are full faine;
But Christ know that harowed hell,
  How we shall com out agayne.'

64

'Had we the keys,' said Clim of the
  Clough,
  'Ryght wel then shaulde we spede,
Then might we come out wel ynough
  When we se tyme and nede.'

65

They called the porter to counsell,[7]
  And wronge hys necke in two,
And caste hym in a depe dongeon,
  And toke hys keys hym fro.

66

'Now am I porter,' sayde Adam Bel,
  'Se, brother, the keys have we here,
The worst porter to merry Caerlel,
  That ye had thys hundred yere.

67

Now wyll we our bowes bend,
  Into the towne wyll we go,
For to delyver our dere brother,
  Where he lyeth in care and wo.'

68

They bent theyr bowes,[8]
  And loked theyr stringes were round,[9]
The market place in mery Caerlel
  They beset that stound.[10]

69

And, as they loked them besyde,
  A paire of new galowes ther thei see,
And the justice with a queste[11] of
  squyers,[12]
  That had judged Cloudesle there
    hanged to be.

---

[1] throng: *hastened*   [2] A has 'tow'   [3] fre: *gracious*   [4] lordeyn: *dolt, fool*
[5] wode: *mad*   [6] went: *thought*   [7] The line is partly cut away in A
[8] 'Then they bent theyr good yew bows' in D   [9] round: *in good shape*
[10] stound: *time, moment*   [11] queste: *inquest*   [12] squyers: a corruption of *swerers, jurors*

70

And Cloudesle hymselfe lay redy in a
    carte,
  Fast both fote and hand;
And a stronge rop about hys necke,
  All ready for to hange.

71

The justice called to him a ladde,
  Cloudesle clothes should he have,
To take the measure of that yeman,
  And ther after to make hys grave.

72

'I have sene as great a mearveile,' said
  Cloudesli,
  'As betweyene thys and pryme,
He that maketh thys grave for me,
  Hymselfe may lye therin.'

73

'Thou speakest proudli,' saide the
  justice,
  'I shall the hange with my hande.'
Full wel herd hys brethren two,
  There styll as they dyd stande.

74

Then Claudesle cast his eyen asyde,
  And saw hys to brethen
At a corner of the marked place
With theyr good bows bent in ther hand,
  Redy the justice for to chaunce.

75

'I se comfort,' sayd Cloudesle,
  'Yet hope I well[1] to fare,
If I might have my handes at wyll[2]
  Ryght lytle wolde I care.'

76

Then spake good Adam Bell
  To Clym of the Clough so free,
'Brother se ye marke the justyce wel;
  Lo! yonder you may him see:

77

'And at the shyrfe shote I wyll
  Strongly wyth arrowe kene;'
A better shote in mery Caerlel
  Thys seven yere was not sene.

78

They lowsed thre arrowes both at once,
  Of no man had the dread;
The one hyt the justice, the other the
  sheryfe,
  That both there sedes gan blede.

79

All men voyded[3] that them stode nye,
  When the justece fell downe to the
  grounde,
And the sherife fell nyghe hym by;
  Eyther[4] had his deathes wounde.

80

All the citezens fast gan[5] flye,
  They durst no lenger abyde:
There lyghtly they loused Cloudesle,
  Where he with ropes lay tyde.

81

Wylliam sterte to an officer of the
  towne,
  Hys axe out of hys hande he wronge,
On eche syde he smote them downe,
  Hym thought he taryed all to long.

82

Wyllyam sayde to hys brethren two,
  'Thys daye let us lyve and dye,
If ever you have nede, as I have now,
  The same shall you finde by me.'

83

They shot so well in that tyde,
  For theyr stringes were of silke ful
  sure,
That they kept the stretes on every sede;
  That batayle dyd long endure.

[1] 'will' in A   [2] at wyll: *free*   [3] voyded: *gave room*   [4] eyther: *each*   [5] gan: *did*

84

The fought together as brethren tru,
  Lyke hardy men and bolde,
Many a man to the ground they thrue,
  And made many a herte colde.

85

But when their arrowes were al gon,
  Men preced to them full fast,
They drew theyr swordes then anone,
  And theyr bowes from them cast.

86

They went lyghtlye[1] on theyr way,
  Wyth swordes and buclers round;
By that it was myd of the day,
  They made mani a wound.

87

There was many an out-horne[2] in
    Caerlel blowen,
  And the belles backward[3] dyd ryng,
Many a woman sayde, 'Alas!'
  And many theyr handes dyd wryng.

88

The mayre of Caerlel forth com was,
  And wyth hym a ful great route:[4]
These yemen dred hym full sore,
  For of theyr lyves they stode in great
    doubt.[5]

89

The mayre came armed a full great
    pace,
  With a pollaxe in hys hande;
Many a strong man wyth him was,
  There in that stowre[6] to stande.

90

The mayre smot at Cloudeslee with his
    bil,[7]
  Hys bucler he brust in two,
Full many a yeman with great evyll,
  'Alas! Treason!' they cryed for wo.
'Kepe wel the gates fast,' they bad,
  'That these traytours thereout not go.'

91

But al for nought was that they wrought,
  For so fast they downe were layed,
Tyll they all thre, that so manfulli
    fought,
  Were gotten without at a braide.[8]

92

'Have here your keys,' sayd Adam Bel,
  Yf you do by my councell[9]
'Myne office I here forsake,[9]
  A new porter do we[10] make.'

93

He threw theyr keys at theyr heads,
  And bad them evell to thryve,
And all that letteth[11] any good yeman
  To come and comfort hys wyfe.

94

Thus be these god yeman gon to the
    wod,
  As lyghtly, as lefe on lynde;
The lough[12] and[13] be mery in theyr
    mode,
  Theyr enemyes were fere behynd.

95

When they came to Englyshe wode,[14]
  Under the trusty tre,[15]
They found bowes full good,
  And arrowes full great plentye.

---

[1] lyghtlye: *quickly*   [2] out-horne: *a horn blown to call 'out' the inhabitants of a town*
[3] 'bacward' in A   [4] route: *company*
[5] A part of the line is cut away in A. Supplied from C   [6] stowre: *contest*
[7] bil: *halberd, axe*   [8] braide: *moment*
[9] These lines are correctly transposed in other editions   [10] 'you' in other editions
[11] letteth: *hinder*   [12] the lough: *they laugh*   [13] 'an' in A
[14] Inglyswode in other editions   [15] trusty tre: *trysting tree* (see above, p. 99)

96

'So God me help,' syd Adam Bell,
　And Clym of the Clough so fre,
'I would we were in mery Caerlel,
　Before that fayre meyny.'

97

They set them downe, and made good
　chere,
　And eate and drynke full well.
Here is a fet of these wyght yong men:
　Another I wyll you tell.

PART III

98

As they sat in Englyshe wood,
　Under theyr trusty tre,
They thaught they herd a woman wepe,
　But her they mought not se.

99

Sore syghed the fayre Alyce,
　And sayd, 'Alas that ever I sawe thys
　　day!'
For now is my dere husband slayne:
　Alas! and wel-a-way!

100

'Myght I have spoken wyth hys dere
　　brethren
　Or with eythre of them twayne,
To show to them what him befell,[1]
　My hart were put out of payne.'

101

Cloudesle walked a lytle beside,
　And loked under the grene wood
　　linde,
He was ware of his wife, and chyldren
　　thre,
　Full wo in harte and mynde.

102

'Welcome wyfe,' then sayde Wyllyam,
　'Under this trusti tre:
I had wende[2] yesterday, by swete saynt
　　John,
　Thou shulde me never had se.'

103

'Now well is me,' she sayde, 'that ye be
　　here,
　My hart is out of wo.'
'Dame', he sayde, 'be mery and glad,
　And thanke my brethren two.'

104

'Hereof to speake,' sayd Adam Bel,
　'I wis it is no bote:[3]
The meate, that wee must sup withall,[4]
　It runneth yet fast on fote.

105

Then went they downe into a launde.[5]
　These noble archares all thre;
Eche of them slew a hart of graece,[6]
　The best they could there se.

106

'Have here the best, Alyce[7] my wyfe,'
　Sayde Wyllyam of Cloudesle;
'By cause ye so bouldly stod by me
　When I was slayne full nye.'

107

Then whent they to supper
　And thanked God of ther fortune,[8]
Wyth suche meate as they had;[8]
　They were both mery and glad.

---

[1] The line, omitted in A, is supplied from C　　[2] wende: *thought*
[3] I wis it is no bote: *Truly it is no use*
[4] Most of the line is cut away in A. Supplied from C
[5] launde: *an open space among woods*　　[6] of graece: *fat*　　[7] 'Alce' in A
[8] These lines are correctly transposed in other editions

108

And when they had supped well
 Certayne wythout any lease,[1]
Cloudesle sayd, 'We wyll to our kyng,
 To get us a charter of peace.[2]

109

'Alyce shal be at our sojournyng
 In a nunry here besyde;
My tow sonnes shall wyth her go,
 And there they shall abyde.

110

'Myne eldest son shall go wyth me;
 For hym have I no care:[3]
And he shall you breng worde agayn,
 How that we do fare.'

111

Thus be these good yemen to London
  gone,
 As fast as they myght hye
Tyll they came to the kynges pallace,
 Where they woulde nedes be.

112

And whan they came to the kynges
  courte,
 Unto the pallace gate,
Of no man wold they aske leave,[4]
 But boldly went in therat.

113

They preced prestly[5] into the hall,
 Of no man had they dreade:
The porter came after, and dyd them
  call,
 And with them began to chyde.

114

The usher sayed, 'Yeman, what wold ye
  have?
 I pray you tell me:
You myght thus make offycers shent:[6]
 Good syrs, of whence be ye?'

115

'Syr, we be outlawes of the forest
 Certayne without any lease;
And hether we be come to our kyng,
 To get us a charter of peace.'

116

And whan they came before the kyng,
 As it was the lawe of the lande,
The kneled downe without lettyng,[7]
 And eche held up his hand.

117

The sayed, 'Lord, we besche the here,
 That ye wyll graunt us grace;
For we have slaine your fat falow der
 In many a sondry place.'

118

'What is your nams,' then said our king,
 'Anone that you tell me?'
They sayd, 'Adam Bel, Clim of the
  Clough,
 And Wyllyam of Cloudesle.'

119

'Be ye those theves,' then sayd our king,
 'That men have tolde of to me?
Here to God I make a vowe,
 Ye shal be hanged al thre.

120

'Ye shal be dead withoute mercy,
 As I am kynge of this lande.'
He commaunded his officers everyhone,[8]
 Fast on them to lay hand.

121

There they toke these good yemen,
 And arested them all thre:
'So may I thryve,' sayd Adam Bell,
 'Thys game lyketh not me.

---

[1] lease: *lying*. It is spelt 'leace' in A [2] i.e. *letters of pardon* [3] care: *anxiety*
[4] The line, cut away in A, is supplied from C [5] prestly: *quickly*
[6] shent: *disgraced, ruined* [7] lettyng: *delay* [8] The line, cut away in A, is supplied from C

122

'But, good lorde, we beseche you now,
    That you graunt us grace,
Insomuche as we be to you comen,
    Or els that we may fro you passe,

123

'With sich weapons as we have here,
    Tyll we be out of your place;
And yf we lyve this hundreth yere,
    We wyll aske you no grace.'

124

'Ye speake proudly,' sayd the kynge;
    'Ye shal be hanged all thre.'
'That were great pitye,' then sayd the
        quene,
    'If any grace myght be.

125

'My lorde, whan I came fyrst into this
        lande
    To be your wedded wyfe,
The fyrst bowne[1] that I wold aske,
    Ye would graunt it me belyfe:[2]

126

'And I asked never none tyll now;
    Therefore good lorde, graunt it me.'
'Now aske it, madam,' sayd the kynge,
    'And graunted shall it be.'

127

'Then, good lorde, I you beseche,
    The yemen graunt ye me.'
'Madame, ye myght have asked a bowne,
    That shuld have ben worth them all
        three.

128

'Ye myght have asked towres, and
        towne[s],
    Parkes and forestes plenty'.
'None so pleasant to my pay,'[3] she sayd;[4]
    'Nor none so lefe[5] to me.'

129

'Madame, sith it is your desyre,
    Your askyng graunted shal be;
But I had lever have geven you
    Good market townes thre.'

130

The quene was a glad woman,
    And sayde, 'Lord, gramarcy:
I dare undertake for them,
    That true men shall they be.

131

'But, good lord, speke som mery word,
    That they comfort may se.'
'I graunt you grace,' then said our king;
    'Washe, felos, and to meate go ye.'

132

They had not setten but a whyle
    Certayne without lesynge,
There came messengers out of the north
    With letters to our kyng.

133

And whan the came before the kynge,
    The kneled downe upon theyr kne;
And sayd, 'Lord, your offycers grete
        you wel,
    Of Caerlel in the north cuntre.'

134

'How fare my justice,' sayd the kyng,
    'And my sherife also?'
'Syr, they be slayne without leasynge,[6]
    And many an officer mo.'

135

'Who hath them slayne,' sayd the kyng;
    'Anone thou tell me?'
'Adam Bel, and Clime of the Clough,
    And Wyllyam of Cloudesle.'

136

'Alas for rewth!' then sayd our kynge:
    'My hart is wonderous sore;
I had lever than a thousande pounde,
    I had knowne of thys before;

---

[1] bowne: *boon*   [2] belyfe: *eagerly, immediately*   [3] pay: *liking*
[4] The line, cut away in A, is supplied from C   [5] lefe: *dear*   [6] leasynge: *lying*

137

'For I hav[e] graunted them grace,
　　And that forthynketh me:[1]
But had I knowne all thys before;
　　They had ben hanged all thre.'

138

The kyng opened the letter anone,
　　Himselfe he red it thro,[2]
And founde how these outlawes had slain
　　Thre hundred men and mo:

139

Fyrst the justice, and the sheryfe,
　　And the mayre of Caerlel towne;
Of all the constables and catchipolles[3]
　　Alyve were left not one:

140

The baylyes, and the bedyls both,
　　And the sergeauntes of the law,
And forty fosters of the fe,[4]
　　These outlawes had yslaw:

141

And broken his parks, and slaine his dere;
　　Over all they chose the best;
So perelous outlawes as they were,
　　Walked not by easte nor west.

142

When the kynge this letter had red,
　　In hys harte he syghed sore:
'Take up the tables', anone he bad,
　　'For I may eate no more.'

143

The kyng called hys best archars
　　To the buttes with hym to go:
'I wyll se these felowes shote,' he sayd,
　　'That in the north have wrought this wo.'

144

The kynges bowmen buske them blyve,[5]
　　And the queene's archers also;
So dyd these wight yemen,[6]
　　With them they thought to go.

145

There twyse or thryse they shote about
　　For to assay theyr hande;
There was no shote these thre yemen shot,
　　That any prycke[7] myght them stand.

146

Then spake Wyllyam of Cloudesle;
　　'By God that for me dyed,
I hold hym never no good archar,
　　That shoteth at buttes so wyde.'

147

'Wherat,' then sayd our kyng,
　　'I pray thee tell me?'
'At suche a but, syr,' he sayd,
　　'As men use in my countree.'

148

Wyllyam wente into a fyeld,
　　And his to brothren with him,
There they set up to hasell roddes
　　Twenty score paces betwene.

149

'I hold him an archar,' said Cloudesle,
　　'That yonder wande cleveth in two.'
'Here is none suche,' sayd the kyng,
　　'Nor none that can so do.'

150

'I shall assaye, syr,' sayd Cloudesle,
　　'Or[8] that I farther go.'
Cloudesly with a bearyng arow[9]
　　Clave the wand in to.

---

[1] forthynketh me: *I repent of*　　[2] 'tho' in A　　[3] catchipolles: *sheriff's officers*
[4] fosters of the fe: *foresters of the (feudal) estate*
[5] buske them blyve: *prepared themselves at once*
[6] The line, cut away in A, is supplied from C　　[7] prycke: *target*　　[8] Or: *ere*
[9] A 'bearyng arow' is probably what is now called a flight arrow (specially thin and light to carry long distances like the 400 paces here) as opposed to the 'brode' or broad arrow used in short-range archery (120 paces in stanza 153): see Child, V, 313–14.

151

'Thou art the best archer,' then said
   the king,
  'Forsothe that ever I se.'
'And yet for your love,' sayd Wylliam,
  'I wyll do more maystry.

152

'I have a sonne is seven yere olde,
  He is to me full deare;
I will tie him to a stake;[1]
  All shall se, that be here;

153

'And lay an apple upon hys head,
  And go syxe score paces hym fro,
And I my selfe with a brode arow
  Shall cleve the apple in two.'

154

'Now haste the,' then sayd the kyng,
  'But hym that dyed on a tre,
But yf thou do not, as ye hest sayde,
  Hanged shalt thou be.

155

'And thou touche his head or gowne,
  In syght that men may se,
By all the sayntes that be in heaven,
  I shall hange you all thre.'

156

'That I have promised,' said William,
  'I wyll it never forsake.'
And there even before the kynge
  In the earth he drove a stake:

157

And bound thereto his eldest sonne,
  And bad hym stand styll therat;
And turned the childes face fro him,
  Because he shuld not sterte.

158

An apple upon his head he set,
  And then his bowe he bent:
Syxe score paces they were out met,[2]
  And thether Cloudesle went.

159

There he drew out a fayre brode
   arrowe,
  Hys bowe was great and longe,
He set that arrowe in his bowe,
  That was both styffe and stronge.

160

He prayed the people, that was there,
  That they would styll stande,
For he that shooteth for such a wager,[3]
  Behoveth a stedfast hand.

161

Muche people prayed for Cloudesle,
  That his lyfe saved myght be.
And whan he made hym redy to shote,
  There was many a weping eye.

162

Thus Cloudesle cleft the apple in two,
  That many a man myght se,
'Over Gods forbode,' sayde the kinge,
  'That thou shote at me.

163

'I geve the eightene pence a day,
  And my bowe shalt thou beare,
And over all the north countre
  I make the chyfe rydere.'[4]

164

'And I geve the seventeen pence a day,'
   said the quene,
  'By God, and by my fay;[5]
Come feche thy payment when thou
   wylt,
  No man shall say the nay.

---

[1] The line, partly cut away in A, is supplied from C
[2] out met: *measured out*
[3] The line, missing in A, is supplied from C
[4] rydere: *ranger*
[5] fay: *faith*

165

'Wyllyam, I make the a gentleman
  Of clothyng, and of fe:
And thi two brethen, yemen of my
    chambre,
  For they are so semely to se.

166

'Your sonne, for he is tendre of age,
  Of my wyne seller[1] shal he be;
And when he commeth to mannes
    estate,
  Better avaunced shall he be.

167

'And, Wylliam, bring me your wife,'
    said the quene,
  'Me longeth her sore to se:
She shall be my chefe gentlewoman,
  To governe my nursery.'

168

The yemen thanketh them full
    curteously,
  And sayde, 'To some byshop wyl we
    wend,[2]
Of all the sinnes that wee have done,[3]
  To be assoyld[4] of his hand.'

169

So forth be gone these good yemen,
  As fast as they might hye,
And after came and dwelled with the
    kynge,
  And dyed good men all thre.

170

Thus endeth the lives of these good
    yemen:
  God send them eternall blysse;
And all, that with a hande bowe
    shoteth,
  That of heaven may never mysse.

---

[1] seller: *cellar*
[2] The end of the last *complete* line in B, which (significantly) reads 'Rome' rather than
'some byshop'
[3] The line, missing in A, is supplied from C
[4] assoyld: *absolved*

29

MARSK STIG MADE AN OUTLAW

Source:
A Book of Danish Ballads, selected and with an introduction by Axel
Olrik; translated by E. M. Smith-Dampier (Princeton, 1939), pp.
155-7.

The most universally appealing of all outlaws, Robin Hood is nevertheless
uniquely the product of English social mores and aspirations during the last
six hundred years. Paradoxically, the archetypal 'social bandit' appears under
close scrutiny to be in many ways the least representative of them all.[1] The
search for European analogies to the English greenwood legend seems to
result in a revelation of the differences rather than the similarities between
the Robin Hood saga and any of its apparent counterparts. Although
notorious outlaws have always been—and still are—the subjects of popular
song and story, remarkably few are capable of surviving the fundamental
transition from an oral to a literate culture. As far as late medieval Europe is
concerned, the exceptions to this general rule are almost always figures on the
epic scale who could be transformed into politically conscious national
heroes of a type very unlike Robin Hood.[2]

  The best possible test of these generalizations is afforded by a comparison
between the outlaw hero in Danish and English ballad tradition. The often
close but usually mysterious relationship between the worlds of the English
ballad and the Danish *folkeviser* has lain at the heart of international ballad
scholarship ever since Child modelled his great collection of English balladry
on Svend Grundtvig's *Danmarks gamle Folkeviser*. In particular, much use
has been made in recent years of the argument that the origins and the evolution of the Robin Hood legend may be explicable in terms of an English

---

[1] 'As in so many other respects, Robin Hood, though in most ways the quintessence of
bandit legend, is also rather untypical' (Hobsbawm, *Bandits*, p. 109).

[2] For the most famous case, that of the Serbian national hero, Marko Kraljevic, see D. H.
Low, *The Ballads of Marko Kraljevic* (Cambridge, 1922) and Entwistle, *European
Balladry*, pp. 329-44. Cf. the ballad celebrating Niels Ebbesen, the knight who killed
Count Gert of Holstein at Randers in Jutland on 1 April 1340, the best known Danish
ballad within Denmark because 'symbolical of Danish resistance to German aggression'
(P. N. Mitchell, *A History of Danish Literature*, Copenhagen, 1957, p. 36).

'ballad community' not too far removed in sentiment from that of the late medieval Danish gentry.[1] The inclusion in this anthology of a Danish ballad, even in translation, may therefore help the reader to decide for himself whether the *folkeviser* do indeed 'express much the same code' as the Robin Hood ballads.[2]

Of all the possible medieval parallels to the cult of Robin Hood that of the Danish Marsk Stig would seem the most intriguing. Like the English outlaw, Marsk Stig was the subject of not one but a cycle of ballads, six of which still survive. In particular, his career was treated in considerable detail in *The Long Ballad of Marsk Stig*, a work of 101 stanzas compiled from a series of three short independent ballads and for that reason bearing some superficial resemblance to the *Gest* of Robin Hood.[3] But whether 'the ballad cycle of Robin Hood is exactly paralleled by that of Marsk Stig'[4] is another matter entirely. Far from being an obscure outlaw, Marsk Stig Anderson Hvide was one of the most powerful landowners in east Jutland, and as Marsk or High Constable at the Danish court between 1283 and 1286 played a prominent role in the governmental service of King Eric V Klipping. It was his probable implication in the latter's assassination at Finderup near Viborg on 22 November 1286 which led directly to Stig Anderson's banishment the following May—and to his subsequent exile in Norway and then (from 1290 until his death in 1293) on the island fortress of Hjelm in the Kattegat.[5] The way in which this episode of intrigue and treachery in high places has been simplified and personalized in *Marsk Stig Made An Outlaw* is, of course, typical of the ballad-making process everywhere: to the British reader it is immediately reminiscent of the many famous ballads, notably *Mary Hamilton* (Child 173) and *Earl Bothwell* (Child 174), devoted to political incidents in sixteenth- and seventeenth-century Scottish history. Similarly, the theme of the outlawry and exile of one of the king's most prominent aristocratic subjects is a common ingredient of medieval romance. But the relevance of the 'knight ballads' or *riddarvisor* of Marsk Stig to the Robin Hood legend must seem much more dubious. As the last stanza of *Marsk Stig Made An Outlaw* makes absolutely explicit, this was a hero remembered not for his benevo-

---

[1] W. P. Ker, 'Spanish and English Ballads', *Collected Essays*, ed. C. Whibley (London, 1925), II, 20; 'On the Danish Ballads II', *ibid.* II, 108; Holt, 'Origins and Audience of the Ballads of Robin Hood', pp. 89–90.

[2] Hodgart, *The Ballads*, p. 133.

[3] The *Long Ballad* is printed in translation in *A Book of Danish Ballads*, pp. 159–74, where it is described by Axel Olrik 'as a sort of culminating point in ballad poetry' (*ibid.*, p. 45). Most of the text of *Marsk Stig Made An Outlaw* is absorbed into the *Long Ballad*, unfortunately too long to print here.

[4] Entwistle, *European Balladry*, p. 206.

[5] H. Toldberg, *Marsk Stig-viserne* (Copenhagen, 1963); L. Musset, *Les Peuples Scandinaves au Moyen Age* (Paris, 1951), pp. 192–3; J. H. S. Birch, *Denmark in History* (London, 1938), pp. 85–6.

lence but his ferocity towards the farmer, whether gentleman, yeoman or peasant. Far from being an agent of social justice, Marsk Stig secured immortality as an extreme example of the evils of a situation in which 'So many dwell in Denmark, Would all be masters there!'[1]

1

Now Marstig[2] woke at the mirk
   midnight,
  And to his love he cried:
'Oh, I have dreamt a weary dream,[3]
   God knows what will betide!'
     My noble lord, the young Sir
     Marstig.[4]

2

'Methought to savage swine was
   changed
  Each trusty hunting-hound,
And they wasted all that grew so green
   Within our garden-ground.

3

'And then methought my gallant ship
  Was changed to shallop small,
And anchor she had none, I wis,
  And nought to steer withal.

4

'And then methought across a bridge
  I fared with horse and man,
But my courser threw me from his back
  And went where the wild mares ran.'[5]

5

'Now lay thee down, my noble lord,
  Thy dreams bode good to thee,
The tax shall bring thee gain and gold
  From men of low degree'.

6

Nay, the Court shall be held on the
   morrow
  South by the riverside,[6]
And God alone doth know the hand
   Whereby King Erik died!'

[1] The famous opening lines of the ballad of *The King-Slaying in Finderup* (*A Book of Danish Ballads*, p. 152).

[2] Marsk Stig's two names were commonly amalgamated into this one word, with the accent falling on the first syllable.

[3] An ominous dream is one of the commonest introductions to the action of a ballad and was no doubt a formula derived from the more 'literary' medieval genre of *chansons d'aventure*: perhaps the most famous example is Earl Douglas's 'dreary dream' before the battle of Otterburn (Child, III, 300). For its appearance in the Robin Hood ballads, see above p. 141.

[4] The one-line refrain or burden (probably meant to be sung in chorus) so characteristic of the Scandinavian ballad (J. C. H. R. Steenstrup, *The Medieval Popular Ballad*, translated by E. G. Cox, 1968 edn., Washington D.C., pp. 82–124). For an English example see 'Robyn lyth in grene wode bowndyn' in No. 27 above.

[5] An allusion to the Danish practice of allowing a 'wild stud' of a stallion and a few mares to run wild in the woods until the foals were old enough to be caught and trained.

[6] The *Danehof* at which Marsk Stig Anderson was outlawed and banished actually met in May 1287 at Nyborg in Funen, on the shores of the Great Belt. Like most supposedly 'historical' ballads, *Marsk Stig Made An Outlaw* takes great liberties with the ascertainable historical facts.

7

Now Marstig and his gallant band
  Did on their byrnies brown,
And forth they fared to Skanderborg[1]
  So fast by dale and down.

8

The Queen of Danes in high-loft stood,
  O'er dale and down she spied:
'Lo, hither he comes, Sir Marstig,
  King by the riverside!'

9

'Now cease for shame, my gracious
    dame,
  Thine ill-timed jests to fling!
'Tis Ove, the lordly Seneschal,
  Should bear the name of King.

10

'Now lithe and listen, my gracious dame,
  Nor seek my cause to harm,
'Tis Ove the lordly Seneschal,
  Lay last within thine arm.'[2]

11

Up and spake King Erik's son,
  Clad all in the scarlet red!
'Full ill, I wis, such boot as this
  For my father fallen and dead!'

12

Up and spake King Erik's son
  A word of royal renown:
'Shalt get thee from the land, Marstig,
  An if I wear the crown!'

13

'And must I depart from Denmark
  To hide in wrath and dule,
My food will I fetch in Denmark,
  Both spring and summer and Yule!

14

'And must I depart from Denmark
  To sail the sea so deep,
So many a widow will I make
  That the noblest dames shall weep.'

15

Marstig he builded a castle proud
  That shone o'er wall and tower,
Was never a man in Denmark's realm
  Could win that hold of power.[3]

16

Forth to his field went the farmer,
  All for to sow his corn:
'Now help us, God in heaven above,
  Since Hjelm hath gotten a horn!'

[1] A castle in eastern Jutland to which Queen Agnes fled after the murder of her husband, Eric Klipping, at Finderup 40 miles to the N.W.

[2] In another ballad of the cycle (*Marsk Stig and His Lady*), Marsk's role as a regicide is attributed (equally implausibly) to Eric Klipping's adultery with Stig's own wife rather than that of Queen Agnes with the Seneschal Ove.

[3] Remains of Marsk Stig's thirteenth-century castle are still to be seen on the small island of Hjelm, 12 miles S.E. of Ebeltoft.

THE DEATH OF JESSE JAMES

Source :
C. Sandburg, *The American Songbag* (New York, 1927), pp. 420–1.

The most celebrated outlaw in American popular tradition is unquestionably Jesse Woodson James (1847–82). In 1866, a few months after the end of the American Civil War, in which he and his elder brother Frank (1843–1915) had served as young confederate guerillas, he became the leader of a loosely-knit gang of brigands. For the following fifteen years he led a life of sporadic rather than continuous armed violence, specializing in—often unsuccessful—bank robberies.[1] But it was his famous attack on a Rock Island Railroad train in Iowa (1873) which added a novel crime to the history of American outlawry and so brought him distinctive notoriety.[2] The mysterious circumstances of his death—he was shot in the back of the head on 3 April 1882 by Robert Ford while living in retirement as Thomas Howard—made him much more famous when dead than alive. Between 1901 and 1903 the American publishing house of Street and Smith sold six million copies of 121 hastily produced James novels, 'the all-time record for bandit publicity'.[3] In more recent times the Hollywood feature film has inevitably become the most influential medium in the perpetuation of the Jesse James legend: during the 1950s the release of a full-length film about the career of the outlaw became an almost annual event.

The analogies between the legends of Robin Hood and Jesse James have been often noted and are of course much more a reflection of the popular myth-making process than of any genuine historical parallels. Like Robin Hood, Jesse James was converted, very much against the evidence, into the

---

[1] Compare the 'Full thirteen yeares, and something more' (above, p. 139), during which Robin Hood was traditionally held to have 'vexed' the north of England.

[2] Similarly the now largely forgotten Sam Bass (1851–78) owed his once great fame to the hold-up of a Union Pacific train at Big Springs, Nebraska, in 1877; see the ballad of 'Sam Bass and How his Career was Short' (C. O. Kennedy, ed. *A Treasury of American Ballads*, London, 1957, pp. 272–4; cf. *The Viking Book of Folk Ballads of the English-Speaking World*, ed. A. B. Friedman (New York, 1956), pp. 375–7).

[3] M. Fishwick, *The Hero, American Style* (New York, 1969), p. 150.

stereotyped figure of the 'noble outlaw'—a robber of the rich, a benefactor to the poor and a hero devoted to the correction of social and legal injustice. Similarly Robin Hood's devotion to Our Lady is echoed by Jesse James's activities as a teacher in a Baptist singing-school. And in both cases, 'For the outlaw hero to die by any means other than treachery is unimaginable'.[1] Indeed the great majority of the large number of late nineteenth-century ballads of Jesse James are concerned with this very theme and the final dramatic episode of his life. The following version of *The Death of Jesse James* conforms to the general pattern of such songs and is less banal and more intelligible than most of its counterparts. It seems probable that all of the many Jesse James ballads derived from one basic model with the refrain 'That dirty little coward shot Mister Howard'. The original is alleged to have been the work of a negro convict living in Missouri.[2] Like the best Robin Hood ballads, it is an authentic expression of the hero-making process; unlike them, it is relatively free of the communal discipline of taste which converted the individual components of the English outlaw saga into a uniquely integrated and comprehensive legend.

1

It was on a Wednesday night, the moon
    was shining bright,
    They robbed the Glendale train;
And the people they did say, for many
    miles away,
    'Twas the outlaws Frank and Jesse
    James.

Jesse had a wife to mourn all her life,
    The children they are brave.
'Twas a dirty little coward shot
    Mister Howard,
    And laid Jesse James in his grave.

2

It was Robert Ford, the dirty little
    coward,
    I wonder how he does feel,

For he ate of Jesse's bread and he slept
    in Jesse's bed,
    Then he laid Jesse James in his grave.

3

It was his brother Frank that robbed
    the Gallatin bank,
    And carried the money from the
    town;
It was in this very place that they had a
    little race,
    For they shot Captain Sheets to the
    ground.

4

They went to the crossing not very far
    from there,
    And there they did the same;
And the agent on his knees he delivered
    up the keys
    To the outlaws Frank and Jesse
    James.

[1] K. L. Steckmesser, 'Robin Hood and the American Outlaw', *Journal of American Folklore* 79 (1966), p. 353.
[2] Leach, p. 753; H. M. Belden, ed., *Ballads and Songs collected by the Missouri Folk-Lore Society* (Columbia, 1940), pp. 402–3. An alternative composer is the unidentifiable Billy Gashade mentioned in some versions of the song.

5

It was on a Saturday night, Jesse was
    at home
  Talking to his family brave,
When the thief and the coward, little
    Robin Ford,
  Laid Jesse James in his grave.

6

How people held their breath when
    they heard of Jesse's death,
  And wondered how he ever came to
    die.

'Twas one of the gang, dirty Robert
    Ford,
  That shot Jesse James on the sly.

7

Jesse went to rest with his hand on his
    breast;
  The devil will be upon his knee.
He was born one day in the county of
    Clay,
  And came from a solitary race.

'Robin Hood and Arthur-a-Bland', or *Robin
Hood and the Tanner*, a broadside printed at
London for C. Sheppard, 1791 (Bodleian
Library, Oxford, Douce F.F. 71, no. 13).

Appendix I

TITLES AND FIRST LINES OF ROBIN HOOD BALLADS

This list of Robin Hood ballads is arranged alphabetically. With the exceptions of the early *Robin Hood and the Monk* and *Robin Hood and the Potter* (both of which are untitled in their original manuscript form), and those versions preserved in the Percy Folio, all the ballads listed below appeared in broadsides or chapbooks of the seventeenth century or later. Other ballads into which Robin Hood's name has been imported but which form no part of the traditional English cycle are omitted. Items preceded by an asterisk have been printed above in this anthology. A separate list of the most common variant titles of Robin Hood ballads has been added and is also arranged alphabetically.

1. BOLD PEDLAR AND ROBIN HOOD, THE (Child 132)
   'There chanced to be a pedlar bold' *15 stanzas*

*2. JOLLY PINDER OF WAKEFIELD, THE (Child 124)
   A. Broadside version: 'In Wakefield there lives a jolly pinder' *11 stanzas*
   B. Percy Folio version: *5 stanzas survive*

3. KING'S DISGUISE AND FRIENDSHIP WITH ROBIN HOOD, THE (Child 151)
   'King Richard hearing of the pranks' *44 stanzas*

4. LITTLE JOHN AND THE FOUR BEGGARS (Child 142)
   A. Percy Folio version: *11 stanzas survive*
   B. Broadside version: 'All you that delight to spend some time' *22 stanzas*

*5. NOBLE FISHERMAN, THE; OR, ROBIN HOOD'S PREFERMENT (Child 148)
   'In summer time, when leaves grow green' *28 stanzas*

*6. ROBIN HOOD AND ALLEN A DALE (Child 138)
   'Come listen to me, you gallants so free' *27 stanzas*

*7. ROBIN HOOD AND GUY OF GISBORNE (Child 118)
   'When shales beene sheene, and shradds full fayre' *58 stanzas*

*8. ROBIN HOOD AND LITTLE JOHN (Child 125)
   'When Robin Hood was about twenty years old' *39 stanzas*

*9. ROBIN HOOD AND MAID MARIAN (Child 150)
'A bonny fine maid of a noble degree' *22 stanzas*

10. ROBIN HOOD AND QUEEN KATHERINE (Child 145)
A. Percy Folio version: 'Now list you, lithe you, gentlemen' *38 stanzas survive*
B. RENOWNED ROBIN HOOD: 'Gold taken from the king's harbengers' *42 stanzas*
C. ROBIN HOOD, SCARLET AND JOHN: 'Stout Robin Hood, a most lusty out-law' *35 stanzas*

11. ROBIN HOOD AND THE BEGGAR I (Child 133)
'Come light and listen, you gentlemen all' *31 stanzas*

12. ROBIN HOOD AND THE BEGGAR II (Child 134)
'Lyth and listen, gentlemen' *93 stanzas*

13. ROBIN HOOD AND THE BISHOP (Child 143)
'Come gentlemen all, and listen a while' *24 stanzas*

14. ROBIN HOOD AND THE BISHOP OF HEREFORD (Child (144)
A. Garland version: 'Some they will talk of bold Robin Hood' *21 stanzas*
B. Scottish version: 'Some talk of lords, and some talk of lairds' *11 stanzas*

*15. ROBIN HOOD AND THE BUTCHER (Child 122)
A. Percy Folio version: 'But Robin he walkes in the greene fforest' *31 stanzas survive*
B. Broadside version: 'Come, all you brave gallants, and listen a while' *30 stanzas*

*16. ROBIN HOOD AND THE CURTAL FRIAR (Child 123)
A. Percy Folio version: 'But how many merry monthes be in the yeere?' *21 stanzas survive*
B. Garland version: 'In summer time, when leaves grow green' *41 stanzas*

17. ROBIN HOOD AND THE GOLDEN ARROW (Child 152)
'When as the sheriff of Nottingham' *33 stanzas*

*18. 'ROBIN HOOD AND THE MONK' (Child 119)
'In somer, when the shawes be sheyne' *90 stanzas*

19. ROBIN HOOD AND THE PEDDLERS (Child 137)
'Will you heare a tale of Robin Hood' *30 stanzas*

*20. 'ROBIN HOOD AND THE POTTER' (Child 121)
'In schomer when the leves spryng' *83 stanzas*

21. ROBIN HOOD AND THE RANGER (Child 131)
'When Phoebus had melted the sickles of ice' *23 stanzas*

22. ROBIN HOOD AND THE SCOTCHMAN (Child 130)
(adapted to form the conclusion of No. 27 and only survives in debased form)
'Then bold Robin Hood to the north he would go' *7 stanzas*

23. ROBIN HOOD AND THE SHEPHERD (Child 135)
'All gentlemen and yeomen good' *28 stanzas*

24. ROBIN HOOD AND THE TANNER (Child 126)
'In Nottingham there lives a jolly tanner' *37 stanzas*

25. ROBIN HOOD AND THE TINKER (Child 127)
'In summer time, when leaves grow green' *42 stanzas*

*26. ROBIN HOOD AND THE VALIANT KNIGHT, TO-
GETHER WITH AN ACCOUNT OF HIS DEATH AND
BURIAL (Child 153)
'When Robin Hood and his merry men all' *23 stanzas*

27. ROBIN HOOD NEWLY REVIVED; OR, HIS MEETING
AND HIS FIGHTING WITH HIS COUSIN SCARLET
(Child 128)
(identified by Ritson, possibly rightly, with *Robin Hood and the
Stranger*: some editions conclude with No. 22, and others with No. 31,
as second part)
'Come listen a while, you gentlemen all' *25 stanzas*

28. ROBIN HOOD RESCUING THE WIDOW'S THREE
SONS FROM THE SHERIFF (Child 140B)
'There are twelve months in all the year' *29 stanzas*

29. ROBIN HOOD RESCUING THREE SQUIRES FROM
NOTTINGHAM GALLOWS (Child 140)
(closely related to No. 28)
A. Percy Folio version: *18 stanzas survive*
B. See No. 28.
C. Garland version: 'Bold Robin Hood ranging the forest all around'
19 stanzas
D. Scottish version: 'Robin Hood's to Nottinghame gane' *25 stanzas*

30. ROBIN HOOD RESCUING WILL STUTLY (Child 141)
'When Robin Hood in the green-wood liv'd' *38 stanzas*

31. ROBIN HOOD, WILL SCADLOCK AND LITTLE JOHN; OR, A NARRATIVE OF THEIR VICTORY OBTAINED AGAINST THE PRINCE OF ARAGON (Child 129)
(usually included in broadsides and garlands as second part of No. 27)
'Now Robin Hood, Will Scadlock and Little John' *58 stanzas*

32. ROBIN HOOD'S BIRTH, BREEDING, VALOUR AND MARRIAGE, A NEW BALLAD OF (Child 149)
'Kind gentlemen, will ye be silent awhile' *55 stanzas*

33. ROBIN HOOD'S CHASE; OR, A MERRY PROGRESS BETWEEN ROBIN HOOD AND KING HENRY (Child 146)
'Come you gallants all, to you I do call' *24 stanzas*

*34. ROBIN HOOD'S DEATH AND BURIAL (Child 120)
A. Percy Folio version: '"I will never eate nor drinke," Robin Hood said' *27 stanzas survive*
B. Garland version: 'When Robin Hood and Little John' *19 or 23 stanzas*

35. ROBIN HOOD'S DELIGHT; OR, A MERRY COMBAT FOUGHT BETWEEN ROBIN HOOD, LITTLE JOHN AND WILL SCARELOCK AND THREE STOUT KEEPERS IN SHERWOOD FOREST (Child 136)
'There is some will talk of lords and knights' *24 stanzas*

36. ROBIN HOOD'S GOLDEN PRIZE, SHOWING HOW HE ROBBED TWO PRIESTS (Child 147)
'I have heard talk of bold Robin Hood' *24 stanzas*

37. ROBIN HOOD'S PROGRESS TO NOTTINGHAM, WHERE HE SLEW 15 FORESTERS (Child 139)
'Robin Hood hee was and a tall young man' *18 stanzas*

*38. TRUE TALE OF ROBIN HOOD, A; by Martin Parker (1632) (Child 154)
'Both gentlemen, or yeomen bould' *120 stanzas*

VARIANT TITLES

1. *Arthur a Bland, a Tanner of Nottingham :* see No. 24.
2. *Bishop of Hereford's Entertainment by Robin Hood and Little John, The :* see No. 14 A.
3. *Famous Battle between Robin Hood and the Curtal Fryer, The :* see No. 16.
4. *Famous Battle between Robin Hood and Maid Marian, A :* see No. 9.
5. *Guye of Gisborne :* see No. 7.
6. *Little John A Begging :* see No. 4.

7. *New Song to Drive away Cold Winter, A* : see No. 25.
8. *Pedigree, Education and Marriage of Robin Hood, The* : see No. 32.
9. *Renowned Robin Hood; Or, His famous archery truly related* : see No. 10 B.
10. *Robin Hood and Friar Tuck* : see No. 16.
11. *Robin Hood and the Jolly Pinder of Wakefield* : see No. 2.
12. *Robin Hood and the Prince of Aragon* : see No. 31.
13. *Robin Hood and the Sheriff* : see No. 29 D.
14. *Robin Hood and the Stranger* : see either No. 27 (according to Ritson) or No. 8 (according to Child).
15. *Robin Hood, Scarlet and John* : see No. 10 C.
16. *Robin Hood turned Beggar* : see No. 11.
17. *Robin Hood's Meeting and Fighting with his Cousin Scarlet* : see No. 27.
18. *Robin Hood's Preferment* : see No. 5.

ROBIN HOOD
AND HIS
Crew of Souldiers.

A
COMEDY 23 Aug.t

Acted at *Nottingham* on the day of His 1661 faCRed Majefties Corronation.
Vivat Rex.

The Actors names.

Robin Hood, Commander.

Little John.
William. } Souldiers.
Scadlocke.

Meffenger from the Shieriffe.

LONDON,
Printed for *James Davis.* 1661.

The Title-Page of *Robin Hood and his Crew of Souldiers*, a comedy acted at Nottingham in 1661 (British Museum, E. 1088, 6).

NOTE ON THE SLOANE MANUSCRIPT LIFE OF ROBIN HOOD

There survives on fos. 46–48v of British Library, Sloane Manuscript 780 (once 715) the earliest known of all prose lives of Robin Hood. Found only in this one manuscript, it was first rescued from obscurity by Joseph Ritson, who used it extensively in the course of his famous and influential introduction to the first edition of his own *Robin Hood* in 1795. Since that date this so-called Sloane 'Life' of the outlaw has often been regarded as an important and independent source of factual information about the origins of the Robin Hood legend; and for that reason it seems worthwhile to add a short note on the 'Life' to this anthology of Robin Hood literature. For reasons that will appear, the text of the 'Life' does not itself merit publication here: it has in any case already been printed, admittedly somewhat inaccurately, by two Victorian editors.[1]

Like so many of the items in the Robin Hood canon, the Sloane 'Life' tends to raise rather more questions than it answers. It appears in a manuscript made up of a variety of items, composed or transcribed at different times, many of which are concerned with the study of alchemy. It is preceded by a didactic poem, written in a late sixteenth-century hand, and is followed by a treatise on the astrolabe in a fifteenth-century script. The 'Life' itself is written in a small and unusually crabbed secretary hand of *c.* 1600 and occupies two and a half folios of the volume. Some lines of doggerel are added on the lower half of the last folio containing the text. The palaeographical evidence therefore suggests that this prose account of Robin Hood was composed towards the end of the sixteenth century, probably before the contributions made to the Robin Hood legend by Munday and other playwrights at the very end of Elizabeth's reign.[2] This particular text appears to be a copy of some original, and was possibly dictated, for proper names such as Plumpton were imperfectly understood. Moreover certain phrases, first omitted, were later written in above the line.

It is immediately apparent that the 'Sloane Life'—despite the claims of Ritson and many of his followers to the contrary—is of little value as an

---

[1] *Early English Prose Romances,* ed. W. J. Thoms (2nd edn., London, 1858), II, 124–37; Gutch, *Robin Hood* (London, 1847), I, 379–89.
[2] Child (III, 129), inadvertently assigned the MS. to 'the end of the seventeenth century' in his discussion of *The Jolly Pinder of Wakefield.*

independent historical authority, either for the supposed details of Robin Hood's 'real' career or for the early history of the outlaw legend. Its only importance lies in its revelation that the materials for 'a life of Robin Hood' available to an ambitious inquirer of *c*. 1600 were already very limited indeed. Like so many English historians through the centuries, the anonymous compiler of this 'Life' was forced to rely heavily on the vague and very suspect generalizations of John Major. Otherwise and except for an occasional folk tradition, all his information appears to have been derived from ballad literature. Most of the 'Life' is indeed no more and no less than a somewhat clumsy but occasionally interesting paraphrase of the *Gest*. The opening sections of the work are of more significance in revealing that the author was familiar with early versions of *Robin Hood's Progress to Nottingham*, *The Jolly Pinder of Wakefield*, *Robin Hood and the Curtal Friar* (confused with Much, the Miller's Son), and *Robin Hood and Allen a Dale* (whose story is applied, however, to 'Scarlock'). It would accordingly seem to follow—despite various opinions to the contrary—that the Sloane Life's identification of Robin Hood's birth-place with the mysterious 'Lockesley' also derived from a now lost sixteenth-century ballad rather than from any genuinely historical tradition; and it was of course to John Major once again that the compiler owed his view that Robin Hood was a contemporary of Richard I. The belief that 'Robin Hood accompanied with one called Little John molested passengers on the high way Temp. Rich. I' was similarly held by the seventeenth-century writer of a few bald notes on Robin Hood now to be found on the last folio (156v) of British Library, Harleian Manuscript 1233. These notes, like the Sloane 'Life' itself, furnish yet one more demonstration that the quest for factual information about the English outlaw has been pursued vigorously but unsuccessfully for well over three centuries.

A SELECTION OF PROVERBS OF ROBIN HOOD

References are to the following collections:

Apperson G. L. Apperson, *English Proverbs and Proverbial Phrases: A Historical Dictionary* (London, 1929).

Oxford *The Oxford Dictionary of English Proverbs*, Third Edition, revised by F. P. Wilson (Oxford, 1970).

Ritson J. Ritson, *Robin Hood: A Collection of all the Ancient Poems, Songs and Ballads* (London, 1846).

Tilley M. P. Tilley, *A Dictionary of the Proverbs in England in the Sixteenth and Seventeenth Centuries* (Ann Arbor, 1950).

Whiting B. J. Whiting, *Proverbs, Sentences and Proverbial Phrases from English Writings mainly before 1500* (Cambridge, Mass., 1968).

1. *AS CROOKED AS ROBIN HOOD'S BOW* (Ritson, p. 26)
I.e. presumably as crooked as Robin Hood's bow when bent by himself. Ritson was able to cite only one authority for this proverb, the description of an old woman in a late eighteenth-century Irish song with 'Her back more crook'd than Robin Hood's Bow'. It also appears among a list of Derbyshire sayings contributed to the *Derbyshire Advertiser* by George Hibbert: *Folk-Lore Journal*, VII (1887), 291.

2. *COME (STAY) AND DRINK WITH ROBIN HOOD* (Ritson, p. 28)
This saying owed its once very general currency to its appearance as an inscription upon inn-signs. Very popular in the north of England, it occurred much farther south, for example on a public-house in Hoxton, Shoreditch, as late as 1839 (Ritson, p. 28).
Of the many variations, the most famous—still prominent above the door of the *Robin Hood and Little John* inn at Castleton, N. Yorks.—reads as follows:

> 'Kind gentlemen and yeomen good
> Come in and drink with Robin Hood.
> If Robin Hood he be agone
> Come in and sup with Little John'

For other examples, see J. Larncop and J. C. Hotton, *The History of Signboards* (London, 1866), pp. 75–6.

3. *COME, TURN ABOUT, ROBIN HOOD* (Ritson, p. 26)

Ritson cited only one source (*Wit and Drollery*, 1661) for this proverb and thought it implied 'that to challenge or defy our hero must have been the *ne plus ultra* of courage'. It seems more probable that to ask Robin Hood to turn about was regarded as an equivalent of attempting the impossible.

4. *GOOD EVEN, GOOD ROBIN HOOD* (Ritson, pp. 25–6; Apperson, p. 535; Tilley, No. E 188; Whiting, No. R 155; *Oxford*, p. 319)

'The allusion is to *civility* extorted by *fear*' (Ritson)

    (a) The clearest (and very early) reference to this proverb occurs in John Skelton's *Why come ye not to Court?* (1522–3, published 1545), line 194:

> 'He saith 'How say ye, my lordes?
> Is nat my reason good?'
> Good evyn, good Robyn Hood!

    (*Complete Poems of John Skelton*, ed. P. Henderson, London, 1959, p. 314).

    (b) An analogous usage ('Yea Robyn Hoode!') occurs in 1559: *The Complete Works of George Gascoigne*, ed. J. W. Cunliffe (1907–10), I, 171.

5. *MANY SPEAK (TALK) OF ROBIN HOOD THAT NEVER BENT HIS BOW (SHOT IN HIS BOW, DID HIM KNOW)* (Ritson, p. 26; Tilley, No. R 148; Whiting, No. R 156; *Oxford*, p. 761)

I.e. many speak of matters whereof they have no personal skill or experience. For the importance of this, the most popular as well as the most historically significant of all Robin Hood proverbs, see Introduction, above p. 2.

Among the many interesting variants of the proverb are the following:

    (a) *c.* 1385?: 'Swich maner folk, I gesse, Defamen love, as no-thing of him knowe; Thei speken, but thei benten nevere his bowe' (Chaucer, *Troilus and Criseyde*, Book II, 11. 861).

    (b) *c.* 1425: MS. of (a) has marginal gloss 'of robyn hode' (*Troilus and Criseyde*, ed. R. K. Root, Princeton, 1926, p. 449).

    (c) *c.* 1450: MS. of (a) reads 'Thei spekyn of robynhod but thei benten never his bowe' (*ibid*).

    (d) *c.* 1400–25: 'for mani, manime seith, spekith of Robyn Hood that schotte never in his bowe' (*Three Middle English Sermons*, ed. D. M. Grisdale, Leeds, 1939, p. 8).

    (e) *c.* 1419–20: 'On old Englis it is said, Unkissid is unknowun, And many men speken of Robyn Hood, And shotte nevere in his bowe' (*Jack Upland, Friar Daw's Reply and Upland's Rejoinder*, ed. P. L. Heyworth, Oxford, 1968, p. 80).

    (f) 1471: 'For many men speketh wyth wondring of Robyn Hood, and of his Bowe, Whych never shot therin I trowe' (George Ripley, *The Compound of Alchemy*, ed. in E. Ashmole, *Theatrum Chemicum Britannicum*, London, 1652, p. 175).

(g) 1670: 'Many men speak of Robin Hood that never shot in his bow;
Many a man talks of Little John that never did him know' (John Ray,
A Collection of English Proverbs, p. 137).

Among other sixteenth and seventeenth-century writers who cited forms of
this proverb were Lyly (*Euphues*, 1580), Munday (*The Downfall of Robert
Earl of Huntington*, 1601), William Camden and Sir Edward Coke (M. P.
Tilley, *Elizabethan Proverb Lore*, London, 1926, p. 259). Thomas Fuller
later vouched for the fact that 'This proverb is now extended all over
England' (*Worthies of England*, 1662, p. 315). For a seventeenth-century
Italian analogy ('*Molti parlan di Orlando, Chi non viddero mai suo brando*'),
see Ritson, p. 26, and *The Macmillan Book of Proverbs, Maxims and Famous
Phrases* (New York, 1948), p. 2001.

6. *ROBIN HOOD COULD BEAR (STAND) ANY WIND (ANYTHING) BUT A THAW WIND (Oxford*, p. 681).

The most probable key to this somewhat mysterious proverb is that it alludes
to the bitterly cold north and east winds around Blackstone Edge in Lancashire (which has a feature known as Robin Hood's Bed). The milder 'thaw'
winds from the south and west were therefore *not* 'Robin Hood's winds' but
rather winds which—by extension—Robin could not 'bear'.

The two references to this proverb collected in *Oxford*, one of *c.* 1855 and
one of 1917, suggest that it emerged quite late and was current only in
Lancashire, Yorkshire and Cheshire.

7. *ROBIN HOOD ROBBED THE RICH AND GAVE (TO GIVE) TO THE POOR*

Although it has never found precise proverbial expression, this concept—
implicit in the story of Robin Hood's befriending of an impoverished knight
as early as the *Gest*—has now become the most ubiquitous, distinctive and
influential of all beliefs relating to the outlaw. See e.g., the late nineteenth-
century comment on Billy the Kid, who 'was good to Mexicans. He was like
Robin Hood; he'd steal from white people and give it to the Mexicans, so
they thought he was all right' (cited by K. L. Steckmesser, 'Robin Hood and
the American Outlaw', *Journal of American Folklore*, Vol. 79, 1966, p. 350).
The first clear statement of the general principle at stake seems to have been
made by John Stow under the influence of John Major: 'poore mens goods
he spared, aboundantlie relieving them with that which by thefte he gotte
from Abbeies and the houses of rich Carles' (*Annales*, ed. E. Howes, London
1614, p. 159). For an unsuccessful attempt to coin a new word formalizing
this sentiment, see *The Church Times* of 9 December 1887: 'Robin-Hoodism:
the robbing of the rich for the sake of the poor'.

8. *ROBIN HOOD'S CHOICE*

The implication is that *no* choice is available or being offered. An apparently
very infrequent variant form (Gutch, I, 59) of the famous *Hobson's Choice*,

a proverbial expression established in the early seventeenth century (*Oxford*, p. 375).

9. *ROBIN HOOD'S MILE* (*Oxford*, p. 681)
I.e. a mile of several times the recognized length.
1559: 'These are Robin Hood's miles, as the prouerbe is'. (The source of this reference appears to be an article in *Notes and Queries*, 12. x. 412, contributed by a correspondent in Lancashire).

10. *ROBIN HOOD'S PENNYWORTHS* (*BARGAINS*) (Ritson, p. 26; Tilley, No. R 149; *Oxford*, p. 681).
The usual meaning (but see (f) below) is a commodity or quantity sold at a robber's price, i.e. far below the real value.
  A very popular proverbial expression in the late sixteenth, seventeenth and early eighteenth centuries. Among many possible examples are:
  (a) 1565: 'Making Robin Hoodes pennyworthes of their copes and vestments' (at St John's College, Cambridge: *Calendar of State Papers Domestic, Elizabeth*, Vol. I, 262).
  (b) 1582: 'The cunning Lawier, that buyeth Robin hoodes penneworthes and yet with some nice forfaitures threatneth the seller with continuall bondage' (G. Whetstone, *Heptameron of Civil Discourses*, T 2).
  (c) 1600: title of a now missing play by W. Haughton (*Henslowe's Diary*, ed. W. Greg, II, 215).
  (d) 1631: 'The moveable goods as they were sold, Robin Hoods peniworths, amounted to more than one hundred thousand pounds' (J. Weever, *Ancient Funeral Monuments*, 1631, p. 104).
  (e) 1662: 'To sell Robin Hood's penny-worths. It is spoken of things sold under half their value; or, if you will, *half sold half given*' (T. Fuller, *Worthies of England*, 1662, p. 315).
  (f) 1670: 'This may be used in a double sence, either he sells things for half their worth . . . or he buys things at what price he pleases' (John Ray, *A Collection of English Proverbs*, p. 191).

11. *TALES OF ROBIN HOOD ARE GOOD* (*ENOUGH*) *FOR* (*AMONG*) *FOOLS* (Ritson, p. 26; Tilley, No. T 53; Whiting, No. R 157; *Oxford*, p. 803).
This particular saying gradually emerged out of a long tradition—dating back to at least the fifteenth century—of regarding tales, jests, fables and songs of Robin Hood as (a) incredible and (b) symptoms of a vulgar and morally suspect taste. Among many expressions of this view that tales of Robin Hood were 'old wives foolyshe tales' are the following:
  (a) *c.* 1405–10: 'gon levir to heryn a tale or a song of robyn hode or of sum rubaudry than to heryn messe or matynes' (*Dives et Pauper*, published 1493, *First Commandment*, Chapter LI).

(b) 1509: 'All of fables and Iestis of Robyn hode' (A. Barclay, *The Ship of Fools*, ed. T. H. Jamieson, Edinburgh, 1874, Vol. II, 155).

(c) 1528: 'to read Robin Hood, and Bevis of Hampton, Hercules, Hector and Troilus, with a thousand histories and fables of love and wantonness, and of ribaldry, as filthy as heart can think, to corrupt the minds of youth withal' (William Tyndale, *The Obedience of a Christian Man*, ed. in *Works of William Tyndale*, ed. G. E. Duffield, Appleford, Berks., 1964, Vol. I, 331).

(d) 1546: 'Tales of Robin hood are goode among fooles' (John Heywood, *Dialogue conteinyng . . the proverbes*, ed. R. Habernicht, 1963, II, ix L1).

(e) 1632: Martin Parker's ballad of *A True Tale of Robin Hood* (above No. 14) was almost certainly so entitled because of the prevalence of the (correct) belief that Robin Hood's tales were largely fictitious (see Child III, 227).

(f) 1670: 'Tales of Robin Hood are good enough for fools' (John Ray, *A Collection of English Proverbs*, p. 137).

12. *TO GO ROUND BY ROBIN HOOD'S BARN*

I.e. to take the longest way round.
The barn was probably the surrounding countryside. The proverb is explained by Cuthbert Bede as 'to go all about the country, first here and then there'. (*Notes and Queries* (1878), 5th Series, IX, 486). See also Gutch, I, 59, and E. M. Wright, *Rustic Speech* (Oxford, 1913), p. 189, who explains the proverb in a similar sense, and gives a list of plants named after Robin Hood.

13. *TO OVERSHOOT ROBIN HOOD* (Ritson, p. 26)

I.e. to make an absurdly extravagant claim.
The expression occurs in Sir Philip Sidney's *Apologie for Poetrie* (probably written in 1580 and published in 1595): 'And lastly, and chiefly, they cry out with an open mouth as if they out shot Robin Hood, that Plato banished them out of his commonwealth': see G. Shepherd, ed., *Sir Philip Sydney, An Apology for Poetry* (London, 1965), p. 123, and W. C. Hazlitt, *English Proverbs and Proverbial Phrases* (London, 1869), p. 425.

Appendix IV

A SELECT LIST OF ROBIN HOOD PLACE-NAMES

The following list of Robin Hood place-names, arranged geographically under pre-1974 counties, provides only a small selection of what seem to us the most important items in an enormous field. The usual criterion for admission to the list is the appearance of the name in question on the Seventh series of 1″ Ordnance Survey maps, to which reference is made by the usual six-figure grid number. Where the name does not figure on the 1″ O.S. map, this reference is given in brackets. References to the 6″ and 25″ Ordnance Survey maps are only provided for those Robin Hood place-names of particularly early date or exceptional historic interest.

The following categories of Robin Hood place-names have been deliberately excluded:

1. STREET NAMES	Several of England's larger towns have one or more streets named after Robin Hood (according to the 1968 edition of *Bartholomew's Reference Atlas of Greater London*, there are at present eleven such names in the capital alone): the majority undoubtedly date from the nineteenth century.
2. INN NAMES	'The Robin Hood' or 'The Little John' continues to be a comparatively popular inn sign although much less so than in the late eighteenth and early nineteenth centuries (see Ritson, p. 28). Most such names are to be found in Yorkshire and Nottinghamshire but there are many examples all over the country, e.g. as far away from Sherwood as the 'Robin Hood Inn' in the High Street of Sheringham in Norfolk. Only a small selection of the older and more interesting of such names are listed below.
3. FIELD-NAMES	A majority of the many Robin Hood field-names still in use are likely to be of early date and hence of considerable interest to the growth of the legend. But as the work of collecting English field-names is still in its infancy, only a few

especially important examples can be included in the lists which follow. For some other examples, see J. Field, *English Field-Names, A Dictionary* (Newton Abbot, 1972).

4. 'ROBIN' NAMES   Innumerable English place-names begin with the prefix 'Robin' (e.g. the many Robinswoods and Robinsgroves in Surrey and Essex); although several are likely to have originated as contractions of Robin Hood names, they have nevertheless been ignored below.

5. PLACE-NAMES OUTSIDE ENGLAND   Robin Hood place-names, like the outlaw legend itself, are naturally not confined to England. Given the popularity of the hero north of the Border, it is somewhat surprising that Robin Hood place-names in Scotland are so infrequent. They were certainly exported by English colonists to many other parts of the world, particularly Australia and the U.S.A. (where there are 11 Sherwoods). Two small towns, one in Maine, one in Australia, are named 'Robin Hood' to this day (for further details, see *The Columbia Lippincott Gazetteer of the World*, ed. L. E. Seltzer (1962 edn.).

To the listing of Robin Hood place-names there is unlikely ever to be a complete end; and it has proved remarkably easy to augment such earlier collections as those of Joseph Ritson (pp. 32–3), James Tait (*D.N.B.* sub 'Hood, Robin') and W. R. Mitchell, *The Haunts of Robin Hood* (Clapham, Yorkshire, 1970). The most recent county volumes of the English Place-Name Society can leave no doubt that there are many discoveries still to be made: the following list is neither comprehensive nor definitive. Is it of any value whatsoever?

In a very general sense, all Robin Hood place-names bear some witness to the influence of his legend; but it needs to be added that very few of the names which appear below can bear the weight of precise historical interpretation. Several of the place-names seem to have originated after 1800; and the great majority of the others are first recorded in maps of the late eighteenth century. All in all, the most likely conclusion—although exceptionally difficult to prove—is that the custom of assigning Robin Hood's name to unusual and bizarre natural features was at its height in the sixteenth and seventeenth centuries; in which case the geographical concentration of these names in Yorkshire, Derbyshire and Nottinghamshire (the most obvious feature of the lists which follow) testifies to the way in which the legend retained its strong local associations for many years. In more recent times the name of the outlaw hero has been applied *ad libitum*, most bizarrely perhaps in such cases as the Robin Hood Golf Course at Hall Green near Birmingham and the Robin Hood Crematorium at Solihull in Warwickshire.

BERKSHIRE

LITTLE JOHN'S FARM   1 mile N.W. of Reading   Sheet 159 SU:698745

A farm between the old Great Western railway line and the river Thames.

ROBIN HOOD'S ARBOUR   in Maidenhead   Sheet 159 SU:852811

A square prehistoric earthwork near Maidenhead Thicket, already called 'Robin Hood's Bower' in the late seventeenth century; for that reason Thomas Hearne put forward the view that the outlaw frequented the Chiltern Hills. See *V.C.H. Berkshire*, I, 204; P.N.S., vol. I (1924), p. 163; Ritson, 1846, p. 30.

BUCKINGHAMSHIRE

THE ROBIN HOOD   An inn 2 miles N.W. of Buckingham   (at Sheet 145 SP:668353)

CHESHIRE

ROBIN HOOD FIELD   5 miles S.W. of Runcorn   (near Sheet 109 SJ:488756)

A field-name within the parish of Helsby, cited by Field, *English Field-Names*, p. 183.

CUMBERLAND

ROBIN HOOD BUTTES   Farlam, 2 miles S.E. of Brampton (near Sheet 76 NY:555587)

A field-name near Eskdale Wood, Farlam. A reference to days' work on a meadow called 'Robin Hood buttes' occurs as early as 1598 (*Cal. of Border Papers*, cited in P.N.S. *Cumberland*, I, 87).

ROBIN HOOD'S CHAIR   Ennerdale Water (at Sheet 82 NY: 101151).

DERBYSHIRE

LITTLE JOHN'S GRAVE   Hathersage churchyard   (at Sheet 111 SK:235819)

The reputed grave of Little John, nearly 14 feet long and under a modern headstone, lies opposite the porch of Hathersage parish church. According to local tradition, Captain John Shuttleworth had the grave opened in 1784 and a thigh-bone of 32 inches in length was discovered there; a now vanished cottage to the east of the church was held to be the place where Little John died (Gutch, I, xiii–xviii, 68, 70). Although these legends attained their wildest elements of fantasy during the course of the eighteenth century, they appear to have originated by the 1650s (P.N.S. *Derbyshire*, I, p. 112; Ritson, 1846, p. 34).

LITTLE JOHN'S WELL   2½ miles S.E. of Hathersage   Sheet 111 SK:267794

A well near Longshaw Lodge and clearly closely associated with a Robin Hood's Well (see below) less than half a mile away. Not included in P.N.S. *Derbyshire*.

ROBIN HOOD   6 miles W. of Chesterfield,   Sheet 111 SK:278721

A small hamlet immediately N.E. of Chatsworth Park and in the parish of Baslow and Bubnell. It apparently derives its name from a Robin Hood Inn (marked on the 1840 Ordnance Survey Map of the area), which probably reflects the cult for such names on the neighbouring Chatsworth Estate (see P.N.S. *Derbyshire*, I, 42).

ROBIN HOOD'S CAVE   1½ miles N. of Hathersage   Sheet 111 SK:244836

A cave, familiar to rock-climbers, among the crags of Stanage Edge north of Hathersage.

ROBIN HOOD'S CHAIR   Hope Dale   (near Sheet 111 SK:213820?)

'a rude natural rock in Hope Dale is his (Robin Hood's) chair': Child, III, 47.

ROBIN HOOD'S CROFT   4 miles N.W. of Hathersage (at Sheet 111 SK:197867)

An old sheep shelter and field under Lead Hill (Mitchell, *Haunts of Robin Hood*, p. 67).

ROBIN HOOD CROSS   3 miles W. of Hathersage   Sheet   111 SK:183802

A medieval wayside cross on the moors one mile E. of Bradwell in Hazlebadge parish. The base of the cross still survives. Possibly originating as a boundary mark, it occurs as 'Robin Crosse' in 1319, and 'The Robin Crosse' in 1640 (P.N.S. *Derbyshire*, I, 118).

ROBIN HOOD INN   6 miles S.E. of Hathersage   (near Sheet 111 SK:320776?)

An inn in Holmesfield parish which appears to derive from the 'Robin Hood' mentioned in an 1820 Enclosure Award (P.N.S. *Derbyshire*, II, 266).

ROBIN HOOD'S LEAP   Chatsworth   (near Sheet 111 SK:260690?)

A chasm on the Chatsworth Estate (Child, III, 47).

ROBIN HOOD'S MOSS   11 miles N.W. of Sheffield   (at Sheet 102 SK:190930)

Moorland overlooking the Derwent Dams in the High Peak (Mitchell, *Haunts of Robin Hood*, p. 68).

ROBIN HOOD'S PICKING RODS 2½ miles S.W. of Glossop Sheet 102 SK:008909

Two stone pillars in a stone socket on Ludworth Moor. Almost certainly originating as a boundary mark, they appear on the 1842 Ordnance Survey Map (P.N.S. *Derbyshire*, I, 154).

ROBIN HOOD'S STOOP 1½ miles S.W. of Hathersage Sheet 111 SK:217805

An old boundary stone, perhaps originally a medieval cross, on Offerton Moor. Later alleged to be the place from which Robin Hood shot an arrow into Hathersage churchyard, over 2,000 yards away (cf. the similar tradition at Whitby, N. Yorkshire, and see P.N.S. *Derbyshire*, I, 156).

ROBIN HOOD'S STRIDE 3 miles S. of Bakewell (at Sheet 111 SK:223623)

A group of broken gritstone rocks on Hartle Moor; the distance between two of the rocks was allegedly the length of Robin Hood's stride or step. Alternatively known as Mock Beggars Hall because of the supposed similarity of the two rocks to chimneys. The name of Robin Hood's Stride appears in an 1819 Enclosure Award (P.N.S. *Derbyshire*, I, 109).

ROBIN HOOD'S TABLE 6 miles N.W. of Chesterfield (at Sheet 111 SK:277755)

Two slabs of gritstone forming a low platform in the upper Bar Brook valley among the moors north of Chatsworth. They lie close to a spring, and according to Mitchell (*Haunts of Robin Hood*, p. 69) were used by a Duke of Rutland who held shooting parties there in the 1860s.

ROBIN HOOD'S WELL 2¼ miles S.E. of Hathersage Sheet 111 SK:267799

A well near Longshaw Lodge, not far from Little John's Well (see above). The name occurs as early as 1809 (P.N.S. *Derbyshire*, I, 112).

ESSEX

ROBINHOOD END 2 miles N.E. of Finchingfield Sheet 148 TL:708366

A small hamlet in the parish of Finchingfield, N. Essex. It occurs in an unpublished deed as 'Robyne Hoods End' as early as 1699 (P.N.S. *Essex*, p. 428).

ROBIN HOOD END FARM 2½ miles N.E. of Finchingfield Sheet 148 TL:710369

Half a mile north of Robinhood End, in the parish of Stambourne. It occurs as 'Robinhood Farm' in Chapman and André's 1777 *Map of Essex* (P.N.S. *Essex*, p. 457).

ROBIN HOOD INN 1 mile W. of Loughton (at Sheet 161 TQ:412972)

An inn at an important crossroads in Epping Forest.

GLOUCESTERSHIRE

ROBIN'S WOOD HILL 1 mile S.E. of Gloucester Sheet 143 SO:841151

A prominent hill (with beacon) in the parish of Matson and overlooking Gloucester: alternatively known as 'Matson Hill' or 'Mattesknoll'. It occurs as 'Robinhoodes Hill' in 1624, 'Robins-wood' in 1777, and 'Robin-Hood's hill' in 1779. For the argument that the name may recall the family of Robins, tenants of the manor in the sixteenth century, but was later changed to the Robin Hood of the ballads by popular etymology, see P.N.S. *Gloucestershire*, II, 168; and cf. Ritson, 1846, p. 33; Child, III, 47; *Statutes of the Realm*, III, 873.

HAMPSHIRE

ROBIN HOOD'S BARROW Bournemouth (at Sheet 179 SZ:070931)

A tumulus in Talbot Woods to the north of Meyrick Park (*V.C.H. Hants.*, V, 134).

HEREFORDSHIRE

ROBIN HOOD'S BUTTS 3 miles E. of Weobley (near Sheet 142 SO:430515)

Two round-topped natural hills (see P.N.S., vols. I, 159; XXV, 65).

HERTFORDSHIRE

ROBIN HOOD HOUSE 3 miles N. of Berkhamsted (near Sheet 160 SP:995134)

Formerly the village inn, the 'Robin Hood', of Little Gaddesden (*V.C.H. Herts.*, II, 208; P.N.S. *Herts.*, p. 37).

KENT

THE ROBIN HOOD or ROBIN HOOD AND LITTLE JOHN 3 miles S. of Rochester Sheet 172 TQ:734627

An inn on the edge of Buckmore Park, not far from the Rochester–Maidstone road.

LANCASHIRE

ROBIN HOOD 5 miles N.W. of Wigan Sheet 100 SD:521115

A hamlet at a crossroads one miles S. of Wrightington (*V.C.H. Lancashire*, VI, 169).

ROBIN HOOD'S BED 5 miles N.E. of Rochdale (at Sheet 101 SD:975165)

A name applied to whole or part of the prominent ridge of Blackstone Edge in the Pennines; neolithic flints have been discovered there (*V.C.H. Lancashire*, I, 215, 253).

ROBIN HOOD'S CROSS   7 miles N.W. of Wigan   (near Sheet 100 SD:519141)
A cross near the village of Mawdesley (*V.C.H. Lancashire*, VI, 196); possibly associated with the hamlet of Robin Hood less than two miles away?

ROBIN HOOD'S HOUSE   5 miles E. of Burnley   Sheet 95 SD:920346
A ruined farm on the edge of Widdop Moor.

LEICESTERSHIRE
LITTLE JOHN   6 miles N.W. of Leicester   Sheet 121 SK:501084
A small hill in the southern part of Charnwood Forest.

LITTLE JOHN'S STONE   Leicester (at Sheet 122 SK:585055)
'Near the Abbey, Leicester, stands an upright ponderous forest stone, which goes by the name of Little John's Stone; but for what reason none can tell' (Thoroton's *History of Nottinghamshire*, ed. J. Throsby, 1797, II, 170).

LONDON
Of the many references provided by *Bartholomew's Reference Atlas of Greater London* (13th edn., 1968) only the two oldest names are recorded here.

ROBIN HOOD LANE   London E.14   Bartholomew 66U
A street name in Poplar (immediately W. of the N. entrance to the modern Blackwall Tunnel) which occurs—as 'Robin Hood's Lane'—in J. Gascoyne's 1703 *Map of the Parish of Stepney* (P.N.S. *Middlesex*, p. 137).

ROBIN HOOD YARD   London E.C.1.   Bartholomew 8B
A small lane off Leather Lane immediately N. of Holborn.

LOST ROBIN HOOD NAMES IN THE CITY OF LONDON, listed in H. A. Harben, *A Dictionary of London* (1918), p. 505, which provides full references:—

ROBIN HOOD COURT   Cordwainer Ward
A court running west out of Bow Lane destroyed during the construction of Queen Victoria Street. Is recorded as early as 1677 and was known as 'Robin Wood's Court' in 1746.

ROBIN HOOD COURT   Cripplegate Ward Without
One of two small courts running west out of Milton Street in 1677, it was converted into Haberdashers' Square shortly before 1720 (Harben, p. 285).

ROBIN HOOD COURT   Cheap Ward and Cripplegate Ward Within
A court running east out of Milk Street, first known by that name in 1810, but earlier recorded as 'Robinson's Court' (1677) and 'Robinhood Alley' (1720–99).

ROBIN HOOD COURT   Farringdon Ward Within
A court running west out of Shoe Lane, first recorded in 1677: it was known as 'Robin-wood's Court' in 1746.

ROBIN HOOD COURT   Queenhithe Ward
A court running south out of Thames Street, recorded from 1677 to 1799, but later destroyed to make Trig Wharf.

NORFOLK

ROBIN FRIEND   1 mile N. of Sheringham   Sheet 125 TG:145435
Flat rocks off the Norfolk coast which appear to have been associated with the Robin Hood legend.

NORTHAMPTONSHIRE

ROBIN HOOD AND LITTLE JOHN   3 miles W. of Peterborough   Sheet 134 TL:140984
The names of two stones in Castor Field near Gunwade Ferry, now covered with thorn-bushes. According to Morton, *The Natural History of Northamptonshire* (1712), p. 551, 'Erroneous tradition has given them out to be Two Draughts of Arrows from *Alwalton* Church-Yard thither, the one of *Robin Hood*, and the other of Little *John*. But the Truth is they were set up for Witnesses, that the carriage of Stone from *Bernack* to *Gunwade-Ferry*, to be conveyed to *St Edmund's—Bury*, might pass that way without paying Toll. And in some old Terriars, they are called *St Edmund's* Stones. . . . They are supposed to be the petrifyd Arrows of those Two Famous Archers'. The two stones in question are indeed nicked at the top, apparently in imitation of arrows and hence perhaps originally as a memorial to the martyrdom of St Edmund: the stones still stand on 'St. Edmund's Balk'. See the references in P.N.S. *Northamptonshire*, p. 233.

NORTHUMBERLAND

ROBIN HOOD'S BOG   1 mile E. of Chillingham   Sheet 71 NU:079261
A bog situated in the woods on the eastern edge of Chillingham Park.

ROBIN HOOD'S ROCK   3½ miles N. of Dunstanburgh   Sheet 71 NU:236273
A small rock formed by a whin point five hundred yards off the Northumberland coast. Usually called Robin Wood's Rock, 'Wood' being a quite common seventeenth or eighteenth-century alternative for 'Hood': see J. A. Steers, *The Coastline of England and Wales* (Cambridge, 1946), p. 454.

NOTTINGHAM

The town most closely associated with Robin Hood from the fifteenth century onwards and one which now abounds with memorials to him, ranging from the modern Maid Marian Way to the frescoes in the cupola of the Council House (1927–9) and the statues on Castle Green sculpted by James

Woodford and unveiled in 1949. Of the several Robin Hood place-names in the modern city, the oldest (all now disused) appear to be the following:

ROBIN HOOD'S ACRE

Mentioned in 1624–5: *Records of the Borough of Nottingham*, ed. W. H. Stevenson (5 vols., Nottingham, 1882–1900), IV, 441.

ROBIN HOOD'S CLOSE

A pasture described as 'Robynhode Closse' occurs in the Nottingham civic Chamberlains' accounts for 1485, 1486 and 1500 (*Records of Nottingham*, III, 64, 230, 254; cf. P.N.S. *Nottinghamshire*, p. 294).

ROBIN HOOD'S WELL, alias ST. ANNE'S WELL

A 'Robynhode Well' near Nottingham is mentioned in a presentment at the civic sessions of 20 July 1500, and is presumably identical with the 'Robyn Wood's Well' recorded in 1548 (*First Report of Royal Commission on Historical Monuments*, 1874, p. 105; *Records of Nottingham*, III, 74; IV, 441). This well was also known as St Anne's Well as early as the sixteenth century, for there are references to a 'Seynt Anne Well' in 1551, and a 'Robyn Hood Well alias Saynt Anne Well' in 1596 (P.N.S. *Nottinghamshire*, p. 20). Situated at the foot of a hill two miles N.E. of the centre of the town, this well was to become one of the most famous of all places associated with the Robin Hood legend; it was visited by a great number of seventeenth- and eighteenth-century travellers who were shown the outlaw's supposed chair, bow, arrows, cap and slipper: see the references in Ritson, 1846, p. 32; Gutch, I, 66; and (especially) Thoroton's *History of Nottinghamshire*, ed. J. Throsby (1797), II, 170 (with illustrations).

NOTTINGHAMSHIRE

'As might be expected in the county of Nottingham references to the Robin Hood story are frequent but none of the names is recorded except in modern maps and documents' (P.N.S. *Nottinghamshire*, p. 294).

(CLIPSTONE, ARCHWAY LODGE) 4 miles N.E. of Mansfield (at Sheet 112 SK:593649)

Built in 1842–4 by the fourth Duke of Portland in imitation of the gateway of Worksop Priory and decorated with statuary of Robin Hood, Little John, Friar Tuck, Maid Marian, Allen a Dale and Richard I (illustrated in Mitchell, *Haunts of Robin Hood*, p. 39; cf. N. Pevsner, *The Buildings of England, Nottinghamshire* (1951), p. 52).

(FOUNTAIN DALE) 3 miles S.E. of Mansfield   Sheet 112 SK:565568

Since the early nineteenth century this wooded area, one of the few vestiges of Sherwood Forest to survive, has come to be identified with the 'Fountains Dale' which the Curtal Friar of the ballad kept 'Seven long years or more': but the ballad of *Robin Hood and the Curtal Friar* clearly confuses the site with that of Fountains Abbey in Yorkshire; and, in any case, Fountain Dale is apparently not recorded as a place-name until C. and J. Greenwood's 1826 *Map of the County of Nottingham* (P.N.S. *Nottinghamshire*, p. 116).

FRIAR TUCK'S WELL   3 miles S.E. of Mansfield   Sheet 112 SK:568568
   A well situated on the east of Fountain Dale.

(PAPPLEWICK)   7 miles N. of Nottingham   Sheet 112 SK:549514
   Allegedly the church at which Allen a Dale was married with the assistance of Robin Hood. This tradition no doubt originates from the appearance of the witch of Papplewick in Ben Jonson's *The Sad Shepherd* (1641).

ROBIN HOOD'S CAVE   2 miles N. of Ollerton   Sheet 112 SK:665707
   A cave near the river Maun in Walesby parish. The name occurs in an Ordnance Survey Map of *c.* 1825 (P.N.S. *Nottinghamshire*, p. 64).

ROBIN HOOD'S CAVE   4 miles S.W. of Mansfield   Sheet 112 SK:510545
   A cave at the foot of Robin Hood's Hills in Sherwood Forest (see below).

ROBIN HOOD FARM   6 miles N. of Nottingham Sheet 112 SK:581494
   A farm towards the southern boundary of old Sherwood Forest. It appears as 'Robin Hood's Farm' in C. and J. Greenwood's 1826 *Map of the County of Nottingham*, and was apparently associated with a 'Robin Hood Bank' of a *c.* 1840 Tithe Award (P.N.S. *Nottinghamshire*, p. 78).

ROBIN HOOD'S GRAVE   7 miles N. of Mansfield   (near Sheet 112 SK:540730?)
   Apparently a cave in Holbeck parish. Appears as 'Robins Grave' in a Tithe Award of *c.* 1840 (P.N.S. *Nottinghamshire*, p. 84).

ROBIN HOOD HILL   4 miles W. of Southwell   Sheet 112 SK:633534
   A tumulus one mile N. of the village of Oxton. Apparently the 'Robin Hood Pit' which appears in an Ordnance Survey Map of *c.* 1825 (P.N.S. *Nottinghamshire*, p. 173).

ROBIN HOOD'S HILLS   4 miles S.W. of Mansfield   Sheet 112 SK:515547
   A group of small hills forming a natural amphitheatre in Sherwood Forest, closely associated with a neighbouring Robin Hood's Chair and Cave (see above). The name is recorded in Chapman and André's 1775 *Map of Nottinghamshire* (P.N.S. *Nottinghamshire*, p. 122).

ROBIN HOOD'S LARDER   3 miles W. of Ollerton   Sheet 112 SK:602675

A large tree, in that part of Sherwood Forest called Birklands, where Robin Hood was alleged to have hung venison on wooden hooks (hence the tree's alternative name of 'The Shambles'). Robin Hood's Larder collapsed in the late 1950s. An even more famous tree, the Major Oak, lies a mile to the east and has also been associated with the outlaw legend (Mitchell, *Haunts of Robin Hood*, p. 35).

ROBIN HOOD'S MEADOW   2 miles N. of Ollerton   (near Sheet 112 SK:645709?)
A field-name in the vicinity of Perlethorpe, mentioned in Field, *English Field-Names*, p. 183.

ROBIN HOOD'S STABLE   7 miles N. of Nottingham   (at Sheet 112 SK:552523)
A cave cut into sandstone one mile N. of Papplewick (P.N.S. *Nottinghamshire*, p. 131).

ROBIN HOOD'S WELL   7 miles N.W. of Nottingham   Sheet 112 SK:497492
A well in High Park Wood to the immediate north of Beauvale Priory and in Greasley parish (P.N.S. *Nottinghamshire*, p. 148).

(SHERWOOD FOREST)   N. of Nottingham   Sheet 112
The most famous of all medieval English forests, extending due north of Nottingham towards Worksop. The name (as *Sciryuda*) occurs as early as 958 (*Early Yorkshire Charters*, ed. W. Farrer, I, 1914, p. 11). For a good impression of its extent at the end of the middle ages (its bounds were regularly perambulated) see *Maps of Yorkshire*, Y.A.S., Record Series, LXXXVI (1933), Plate III. See also Thoroton's *History of Nottinghamshire*, ed. J. Throsby (1797), III, 157–76; *V.C.H. Nottinghamshire*, I, 365–81; *The Sherwood Forest Book*, ed. H. E. Boulton, Thoroton Society, Record Series, XXIII (1965), *passim*.

(THORESBY)   3 miles N.W. of Ollerton   Sheet 112 SK:638712
The rebuilt (1864–75) mansion has a statue of Robin Hood in the forecourt as well as an elaborate wooden fireplace with Victorian carvings of Robin Hood and Little John in the Library.

SHROPSHIRE
ROBIN HOOD'S BUTTS   2 miles N.W. of Church Stretton   Sheet 129 SO:431966
A group of tumuli on the edge of the Long Mynd.

SOMERSET
ROBIN HOOD'S BUTTS   6 miles S. of Taunton   Sheet 177 ST:230144

Three long barrows near Otterford and close to the Chard and Wellington road (*V.C.H. Somerset*, I, 182; III, 532; cf. P.N.S., vols. I, 159; XXV, 65).

ROBIN HOOD'S BUTTS 7 miles S. of Taunton Sheet 177 ST:237128

Another group of five long barrows on Brown Down, a mile S. of those listed above (see the same references).

SURREY

ROBIN HOOD'S BUTTS 3 miles N. of Godalming (near Sheet 170 SU:970478)

Two hills, now known as Budburrow and Rowbury Hills, to the N.E. of the village of Compton. They were called 'Robin Hood's Butts' by Aubrey in 1673 and Coxe *c.* 1726 (*V.C.H. Surrey*, III, 16).

ROBIN HOOD NAMES IN AND NEAR RICHMOND PARK

The association of the Robin Hood legend with Richmond Park probably dates from Henry VIII's patronage of the outlaw's role in early sixteenth-century May Games there. The following selection of names is in order of probable antiquity.

ROBINHOOD WALK Inside Richmond Park (at Sheet 160 TQ:205725)

Occurs as 'Robynhood Walke' in the reign of Henry VIII, and as 'Robyn-hodes walke' in 1548 (P.R.O., Ministers' Accounts and Misc. Books, Land Revenue, as cited in P.N.S. *Surrey*, p. 63).

ROBINHOOD GATE Into Richmond Park (at Sheet 160 TQ:213723)

The S.E. gate into Richmond Park, at the northern end of Kingston Vale. Appears in John Cary, *A New Map of Surrey* (1785), which also shows a ROBINHOOD FARM in the near vicinity.

ROBIN HOOD 2 miles N.E. of Kingston-on-Thames (at Sheet 160 TQ:220720)

An ecclesiastical district outside Richmond Park in the parishes of Coombe and North Ham.

ROBIN HOOD WAY 2 miles N.E. of Kingston-on-Thames (at Sheet 160 TQ:218700)

The name given to the section of the Kingston Bypass (A.3) immediately W. of Wimbledon Common.

WARWICKSHIRE

ROBINHOODS FARM 10 miles S. of Birmingham (near Sheet 131 SP:110705?)

A Farm near Tanworth in the hundred of Kineton. So named in 1830 Ordnance Survey Map (P.N.S. *Warwickshire*, p. 296).

(LOXLEY) 3 miles S.E. of Stratford-on-Avon Sheet 144 SP:259530

A village said to be the birth-place of Robin Hood by J. R. Planché, *A Ramble With Robin Hood* (*Assoc. Archit. Soc. Reports*, VII, 1864, pp. 157–74). Planché elaborated on Stukeley's fictitious attempt to make Robin Hood a descendant of the Fitzooths; and associated Robin Hood with Robert Fitzodo, lord of the manor of Loxley in the late twelfth century (*V.C.H. Warwickshire*, III, 130). Cf. Loxley in W. Yorkshire (see below).

WESTMORLAND

ROBIN HOOD 6 miles S.W. of Shap Sheet 83 NY:528060

A hill on the Shap Fells, which appears on the 1865 Ordnance Survey Map, and as a 'Robin Hood's Wood' on the same site in the 1859 Ordnance Survey Map (P.N.S. *Westmorland*, II, 176).

ROBIN HOOD'S GRAVE 2½ miles S. of Crosby Ravensworth Sheet 83 NY:617106

A cairn on Crosby Ravensworth Fell which occurs on the 1859 Ordnance Survey Map. It may be related to a 'Howe Robin' only half a mile away (P.N.S. *Westmorland*, II, 160–1).

ROBIN HOOD ISLAND 3 miles S.W. of Kendal (near Sheet 89 SD:490885?)

Occurs in a rental of 1836 (P.N.S. *Westmorland*, I, 111).

ROBIN HOOD'S WOOD 3 miles S.W. of Kendal (near Sheet 89 SD:490885?)

Occurs, within Helsington chapelry, on the 1857 Ordnance Survey Map (P.N.S. *Westmorland*, I, 111).

WILTSHIRE

ROBIN HOOD BALL 12 miles S. of Marlborough (near Sheet 167 SU:144474)

A Neolithic tumulus at Netheravon in Elstub Hundred, possibly used as a boundary mark. Occurs as 'Robin Wood Ball' (*sic*) in J. Andrews and A. Dury, *A Topographical Map of Wiltshire* of 1773. See C. Fox, *The Personality of Britain* (4th edn., Cardiff, 1943), p. 15 n. 3; P.N.S. *Wiltshire*, p. 331.

ROBIN HOOD'S BOWER 2 miles S. of Warminster Sheet 166 ST:876424

A circular earthwork in Southleigh Wood just S. of Warminster: see William Worcestre, *Itineraries*, ed. J. Harvey (Oxford, 1969), p. 141.

YORK

ROBIN HOOD TOWER York City Walls (at Sheet 97 SE:602524)

The name by which the northern angle tower of the city wall, between Bootham and Monk Bars, is recorded in 1622 and 1629. The tower was called Bawing Tower in 1370 and Frost Tower in 1485 (A. Raine, *Medieval York*,

1955, p. 6; Royal Commission on Historical Monuments, *City of York*, Vol. II, *The Defences*, 1972, p. 124).

YORKSHIRE, NORTH RIDING

ROBIN HOOD   1 mile N. of Catterick Bridge   Sheet 91 NZ:224004

A small hamlet along the course of the old Great North Road or Roman Dere Street (I. D. Margary, *Roman Roads in Britain*, 1967 edn., p. 429).

ROBIN HOOD'S BAY   12 miles N. of Scarborough   Sheet 93 NZ:952055

A fishing (and now tourist) village on the north side of the bay of the same name. One of the oldest and most intriguing of all Robin Hood place-names, it was in use by at least the early sixteenth century: see 'Robyn Hoodis Baye' in 1544, *Letters and Papers of Henry VIII*, XIX, i, p. 224; Leland's *Itinerary*, ed. Toulmin Smith, I, 51; G. Young, *History of Whitby*, 1817, II, 647. The suggestion that the name was derived from a tumulus called 'Robbed Howe' near the neighbouring village of Sneaton seems doubtful (*V.C.H. Yorkshire, North Riding*, II, 534). A place-name associated, but probably long after its formation, with the Robin Hood ballad of *The Noble Fisherman*.

ROBIN HOOD'S BUTTS   2 miles N. of Danby   Sheet 86 NZ:712114

Three tumuli on Danby Low Moor and others further north on Gerrick Moor towards Skelton (*V.C.H. Yorkshire, North Riding*, II, 336; cf. Ritson, 1846, p. 33 n. 1). Several were excavated by Canon Atkinson in the late nineteenth century (F. Elgee, *Early Man in North-East Yorkshire*, Gloucester, 1930, *passim*).

ROBIN HOOD'S BUTTS   6 miles W. of Barnard Castle   (near Sheet 84 NY:975220?)

Mounds with this name are recorded in the parish of Romaldkirk south of the Tees in S. R. Clarke, *The New Yorkshire Gazetteer* (London, 1828), p. 208.

ROBIN HOOD'S BUTTS   2 miles S. of Robin Hood's Bay   Sheet 93 NZ:963018

Three tumuli, about a mile from the sea and 775 feet above sea-level, south of a beacon at Stoupe Brow. They probably derive their name from Robin Hood's Bay which they overlook. See Teesdale's 1828 *Map of Yorkshire*; Young, *History of Whitby*, II, 647; *V.C.H. Yorkshire, North Riding*, II, 535.

ROBIN HOOD'S HOWL   1 mile W. of Kirkbymoorside   Sheet 92 SE:682869

Apparently a hole or hollow (rather than a hill) on the southern escarpment of the North Yorkshire Moors: see P.N.S. *North Yorkshire*, p. 85; Ekwall, *Concise Oxford Dictionary of English Place-Names*, 1960 edn., p. 254.

ROBIN HOOD AND LITTLE JOHN INN   Castleton   (at Sheet 86 NZ:693081)

Because of its painted sign and inscription (see above, p. 288), now the most famous of all inns named after Robin Hood. The building itself can be dated to 1671 on the evidence of the inscription on the lintel over the door; but no precise date can be given for the origins of the myth (still prevalent in Castleton) that Robin Hood and Little John met here for the last time.

ROBIN HOOD'S TOWER   Richmond Castle   (at Sheet 91 NZ:172007)
The name given—probably only after the fifteenth century—to an eleventh-century tower projecting from the curtain wall of Richmond Castle (*Richmond Castle, H.M.S.O. Guide*, 1953, p. 13).

ROBIN HOOD'S WELL   3 miles S.W. of Wensley   Sheet 90 SE:057866
A well at the source of a hill stream on Melmerby Moor south of Wensleydale.

WHITBY: ROBIN HOOD'S CLOSE AND LITTLE JOHN'S CLOSE   6″ 90 NW NZ:918096
Two adjacent fields immediately W. of Whitby Laithes, recorded as such in a land conveyance of 1713 (Young, *History of Whitby*, II, 647). They owed their names to two monoliths, one 4′ and the other 2½′ high, which stood at the side of the two fields, to the north of the lane that leads from Whitby Laithes to Stainsacre. These stones (a 'Robin Hood's Stone' occurs as early as 1540: *Cartularium Abbathiae de Whiteby*, II, 727) traditionally mark the points at which arrows shot by Robin Hood and Little John from the top of Whitby Abbey reached the ground: see L. Charlton, *History of Whitby and Whitby Abbey* (York, 1779), pp. 146–7; C. Platt, *The Monastic Grange in Medieval England*, 1969, p. 244; *V.C.H. Yorkshire, North Riding*, II, 506.

YORKSHIRE, WEST RIDING
(BARNSDALE)   North of Doncaster   Sheet 103 SE:510130
'the wooddi and famose forest of Barnesdale, wher they say Robyn Hudde lyvid like an owtlaw' (Leland's *Itinerary*, ed. Toulmin Smith, IV, 13). An area of approximately four to five miles from both north to south and east to west between the river Went and the villages of Skelbrooke and Hampole, six miles north of Doncaster. For the significance of the many references to Barnsdale in the *Gest* and early ballads of Robin Hood, see Dobson and Taylor, 'Medieval Origins of the Robin Hood Legend', *Northern History*, VII (1972), pp. 11–20. Places in Barnsdale especially closely associated with the Robin Hood legend are:

(a) BARNSDALE BAR   Sheet 103 SE:511136
The place where the Great North Road forked into two branches, one leading through Pontefract and Wetherby to the extreme north, the other

through Sherburn-in-Elmet to York: a place of ceremonial welcome to distinguished travellers to the north.

(b) BISHOP'S TREE   6″ Sheet   51SW SE:517121
The site of the tree by the side of the Great North Road where Robin Hood was traditionally held to have intercepted the Bishop of Hereford (Child 144).

(c) ROBIN HOOD'S WELL   see below

(d) SAYLES PLANTATION   6″ Sheet 41 NE SE:495171
The site of 'the Saylis', S.E. of the modern Wentbridge Viaduct, to which Little John is commanded to 'walke up' by Robin Hood at the beginning of the *Gest* (Dobson and Taylor, pp. 17–18).

(e) WENTBRIDGE   Sheet 103 SE:488174
The village at the bridge over the river Went mentioned in *Robin Hood and the Potter* (Dobson and Taylor, p. 17).

LITTLE JOHN'S WELL   1 mile N.W. of Hampole   6″ Sheet 41SE SE:499109
A stone well beside the Doncaster–Wakefield Road to the west of Barns-dale. It occurs as 'Little John's Cave and Well' in an 1838 Tithe Award, and as 'Little John's Well' on the 1840 Ordnance Survey Map (P.N.S. *West Yorkshire*, II, 44). It is incised with Little John's name (see photograph in Mitchell, *Haunts of Robin Hood*, p. 4).

(LOXLEY)   3 miles N.W. of Sheffield   Sheet 102 SK:307899
'. . . the fairest pretensions to be the Locksley of our ballads, where was born the redoubtable Robin Hood. The remains of a house in which it was pretended he was born were formerly pointed out in a small wood (Bar Wood) . . . and a well near called Robin Hood's Well' (J. Hunter, *Hallamshire*, London, 1819, p. 3). Also see H. Moll's 1724 *Map of West Riding* (*Maps of Yorkshire*, Y.A.S., Record Series, LXXXVI, 1933, Plate XIV); P.N.S. *West Yorkshire*, I, 225.

ROBINHOOD   4 miles S.E. of Leeds   Sheet 96 SE:326274
A village, now skirted by the northern section of the M.1 Motorway, which has given its name to neighbouring quarries and collieries. It occurs on the 1841 Ordnance Survey Map and an unpublished Tithe Award of about the same date (P.N.S. *West Yorkshire*, II, 138).

ROBIN HOOD'S BOWER AND MOSS   4 miles N. of Sheffield (near Sheet 102 SK:355945?)
The precise site of this place-name appears to be lost. It occurs as 'Robin Hood's Bower, Bower Wood' near Ecclesfield in 1637 (P.N.S. *West Yorkshire*, I, 226).

ROBIN HOOD'S GRAVE, KIRKLEES   4 miles N.E. of Huddersfield   6″ Sheet SE 12 SE:174215

'*Kirkley monasterium Monialium ubi Ro : Hood nobilis ille exlex sepultus*': Leland's *Collectanea*, ed. Hearne, 1774, I, 54. The most controversial of all places associated with Robin Hood, his alleged grave lies in a secluded part of the Kirklees Estate, 650 yards S.W. of the ruins of the Cistercian nunnery where the outlaw is supposed to have met his death (see the ballad of *Robin Hood's Death*). Of the medieval nunnery itself only the reconstructed gatehouse survives relatively intact. Kirklees has been regarded as the place of Robin Hood's burial since at least the early sixteenth century; but the exact date at which the present grave and its successive tombstones came to be precisely located remains mysterious. According to ballad tradition, Robin Hood chose his own burial place by shooting his last arrow from a window in the nunnery ('And where this arrow is taken up, There shall my grave digged be'). Of the voluminous literature, see especially J. H. Turner, *The History of Brighouse, Rastrick and Hipperholme* (Bingley, 1893), pp. 198–205; G. S. Phillips, *Walks round Huddersfield* (Huddersfield, 1848), pp. 29, 46; W. B. Crump, 'The Site of Robin Hood's Grave', *Y.A.J.*, XXXVII (1948–51), pp. 105–6; Ritson, 1846, pp. 13–14; P.N.S. *West Yorkshire*, III, 5. There is a ROBIN HOOD'S COTTAGE in the vicinity (SE:173215).

ROBIN HOOD HILL AND HOUSE   1½ miles S. of Huddersfield   6″ Sheet 11 SW SE:139135

A hill and house at Berry Brow near Almondbury, S. of Huddersfield (P.N.S. *West Yorkshire*, II, 261). The local railway tunnel (SE:141132) is named 'Robin Hood Tunnel'.

ROBIN HOOD HILL   2 miles N. of Wakefield   6″ Sheet 32 SW SE:320237

A hill immediately W. of the village of Outwood. It occurs as 'Robinhoodstreteclose' in an unpublished Wakefield Court Roll of 1650 and as 'Robbin Hood hill' in 1657: there are a Robin Hood House and a Robin Hood Bridge in the vicinity (P.N.S. *West Yorkshire*, II, 158).

ROBIN HOOD'S PARK   4 miles S.W. of Ripon   (near Sheet 91 SE:260690?)

A name apparently applied to part of an estate near Fountains Abbey (P.N.S. *West Yorkshire*, V, 205).

ROBIN HOOD'S PENNY STONE   5 miles N.W. of Halifax   6″ Sheet 02 NW SE:018284

A loggan or rocking-stone on Midgley Moor in the Pennines, immediately N.W. of Midgley. It appears in J. Watson's *History and Antiquities of the parish of Halifax* (London, 1775), p. 27: see P.N.S. *West Yorkshire*, III, 135; Ritson, 1846, p. 28.

ROBIN HOOD'S PENNY STONE   2 miles W. of Halifax   (near Sheet 102 SE:058248?)

A stone mentioned in P.N.S. *West Yorkshire*, III, 129.

ROBIN HOOD'S STONE   4 miles S.E. of Skipton   (near Sheet 96 SE:045465?)

A stone near Silsden, S.E. of Skipton. It occurs in an 1846 Tithe Award (P.N.S. *West Yorkshire*, VI, 22).

ROBIN HOOD'S WELL   6 miles N. of Doncaster   Sheet 103 SE:518120

A well on the eastern side of the Great North Road and in the middle of Barnsdale, this is the most historically significant of all Robin Hood place-names. It appears to be on or near the site of a 'stone of Robin Hood' recorded in a Monkbretton charter as early as 1422 and is first recorded as 'Robbinhood-well' by Roger Dodsworth. Throughout the seventeenth and eighteenth centuries it was one of the most famous halting-places on the Great North Road, celebrated by many travellers. The well-house, in the form of a 'rustic dome' designed by Vanbrugh for the Earl of Carlisle in the early eighteenth century, survives within a few yards of its original location: a spring is still visible to the north. But the hamlet with two good inns of the early nineteenth century has now disappeared. Several references are collected in Dobson and Taylor, pp. 18–19: see also *The New Yorkshire Gazetteer*, ed. S. R. Clarke (London, 1828), p. 208; W. White, *Gazetteer and Directory of the West Riding* (Sheffield, 1838), II, 261, 274; Mitchell, *Haunts of Robin Hood*, pp. 25–6; P.N.S. *West Yorkshire*, II, 36.

ROBIN HOOD'S WELL   1½ miles N. of Threshfield   Sheet 90 SD:979657

A well near the road between Threshfield and Kilnsey in Wharfedale. It has been recorded as 'Robin Hood's Beck and Well' (P.N.S. *West Yorkshire*, VI, 87).

ROBIN HOOD'S WELL   1½ miles N. of Halton Gill   Sheet 90 SD:869786

A well high on the Yorkshire Pennines north of Pen-y-ghent (P.N.S. *West Yorkshire*, VI, 123).

ROBIN HOOD'S WELL (AND WOOD)   Fountains Abbey   (at Sheet 91 SE:276683)

The well now associated with Friar Tuck's combat with, and ducking of, Robin Hood (see the ballad of *Robin Hood and the Curtal Friar* for the references to Fountains). It occurs as 'Robin Hood Wood' in a Vyner land deed of 1734 (P.N.S. *West Yorkshire*, V, 192; *Fountains Abbey*, H.M.S.O. *Guide*, 1970, p. 39).

ROBIN HOOD WELL 5 miles N.W. of Sheffield 6″ Sheet 39 NW
SK:334965

A well in Low Hall Wood, N.W. of Ecclesfield. It occurs as 'Robin Hood's Well' in 1773 (P.N.S. *West Yorkshire*, I, 251–2). Possibly associated with 'Robin Hood's Bower and Moss' (see above).

ROBIN HOOD WELL 2 miles W. of Haworth (near Sheet 95
SE:010370?)

Recorded near the village of Stanbury in the Pennines (P.N.S. *West Yorkshire*, III, 270).

The Victorian Robin Hood: the title-page of the 1850 edition of Pierce Egan's *Robin Hood and Little John* (W. S. Johnson, London).

Select Bibliography

I *Principal Printed Editions of the Robin Hood Ballads*

c. 1510   'A lyttel geste, of Robyn Hode and his meyne, and of the proude sheryfe of Notyngham'. Printed at London by Wynkyn de Worde. A unique copy survives as University Library, Cambridge, Sel. 5. 18. (The best modern editions of this text are those by Ritson, Gutch and Child below).

c. 1510   'A Gest of Robyn Hode'. Without date, place or printer's name; the eleventh and last piece in a volume of printed tracts once in the Advocates' Library, Edinburgh, and now in the National Library of Scotland. Possibly printed by Jan van Doesborch in Antwerp. (The best modern edition is *Nine Tracts from the first Scottish Press, Edinburgh 1508, followed by the two other tracts in the same volume in the National Library of Scotland. A Facsimile with a Bibliographical Note by William Beattie*, Edinburgh Bibliographical Society, 1950, pp. 197–220).

1557–8   'A ballett of Wakefylde and a grene' entered in London Stationers' Registers (Arber, I, p. 76). Probably an early but now lost version of the ballad of *The Jolly Pinder of Wakefield*.

c. 1560   'A mery geste of Robyn Hoode and of hys lyfe, wyth a newe playe for to be played in Maye games very plesaunte and full of pastyme.' Printed at the Three Cranes Wharf, London, by William Copland. (Reprinted by John Farmer, *Robin Hood, c. 1561–9*, The Tudor Facsimile Texts, London, 1914).

1562–3   'A ballett of Robyn Hod' entered in London Stationers' Registers (Arber, I, p. 204). Unidentifiable; but the only Robin Hood 'ballad'—apart from that for 1557–8 above—which can be proved to have been printed before the end of the sixteenth century.

c. 1590   'A merry Iest of *Robin Hood*, and of his life, With a newe play for to be plaied in May-games. Very pleasant and full of pastime.' A reprinting of William Copland's earlier edition by Edward White, London.

1631   Martin Parker, 'A true tale of Robbin Hood, or A briefe touch of the life and death of Robert Earle of Huntington, vulgarly called Robbin Hood.' Printed for T. Cotes, sold by F. Grove, London.

1662   'The noble birth and gallant atchievements of that remarkable outlaw Robin Hood; together with a true account of the many merry and extravagant exploits he play'd, in twelve several stories, newly collected into one volume by an ingenious anti-quary.' Printed at London, for Thomas Vere and William Gilbertson. (Prose versions of twelve of the Robin Hood ballads from the common garland).

1663 'Robin Hood's garland; or, delightful songs shewing the noble exploits of Robin Hood, and his yeomandrie. With new eddition and emendations.' Printed at the Bible in Giltspur Street without Newgate, London, for W. Gilbertson (the earliest datable copy of the innumerable editions of *Robin Hood's Garland*, still being printed in great quantities in the 1820s).

1765 Thomas Percy, *Reliques of Ancient English Poetry* (3 vols., London; and many later editions). Includes the text of *Robin Hood and Guy of Gisborne* and other ballads from the Percy Folio.

1777 Thomas Evans, *Old Ballads, Historical and Narrative* (2 vols., London; later editions of 1784 and 1810). Includes the great majority of the Robin Hood ballads in the common garland.

1795 Joseph Ritson, *Robin Hood: A Collection of all the Ancient Poems, Songs and Ballads, now extant, relative to that celebrated Outlaw* (2 vols., London; of the many later editions, those of 1820, 1832, 1846, 1862, 1884 and 1885 are the most significant). Still the most comprehensive collection of Robin Hood ballads and literary references: includes an edition of the *Gest* and the first printed text of '*Robin Hood and the Potter*'.

1806 Robert Jamieson, *Popular Ballads and Songs, from tradition, manuscripts, and scarce editions* (2 vols., Edinburgh). Contains three Robin Hood ballads, including the first printed text of '*Robin Hood and the Monk.*'

1828 William John Thoms, *Early English Prose Romances* (3 vols., London; and editions of 1858 and 1906). Includes a copy of the 1678 edition of 'The noble birth and gallant atchievements of that remarkable outlaw Robin Hood' (see above).

1829 Charles Henry Hartshorne, *Ancient Metrical Tales; printed chiefly from original sources* (London). Includes a useful printed text of '*Robin Hood and the Monk.*'

1838 William Chappell, *A Collection of National English Airs* (2 vols., London; and editions of 1859 and 1893). Prints the music of nine Robin Hood ballads.

1846 James Henry Dixon, *Ancient Poems, Ballads and Songs of the Peasantry of England* (Percy Society, London). Includes the text of '*The Bold Pedlar and Robin Hood.*'

1847 John Mathew Gutch, *A Lytell Geste of Robin Hode, with other ancient and modern ballads and songs* (2 vols., London; and edition of 1850). A large collection of Robin Hood literature, with 'Musical illustrations of the Robin Hood Ballads' by E. F. Rimbault.

1857–9 Francis James Child, *English and Scottish Ballads* (8 vols., Boston; and editions of 1864 and 1885–6). The forerunner of Child's much more extensive collection (see below).

1864 William Allingham, *The Ballad Book: A selection of the choicest British Ballads* (Cambridge; and edition of 1898). Includes the *Gest* and two Robin Hood ballads.

1867–8 *Bishop Percy's Folio Manuscript: Ballads and Romances*, ed. J. W. Hales and F. J. Furnivall (3 vols., London). The first correct, and still definitive, edition of the Robin Hood ballads in the Percy Folio.

1871–99 *The Roxburghe Ballads, Printed for the Ballad Society* (9 vols., London). Provides (badly edited) printed texts of the Robin Hood ballads to be found in the three-volume collection of Roxburghe Ballads in the British Museum Library: this collection (finally bound in 1774) was originally formed by Robert Harvey, Earl of Oxford, and was augmented by successive owners, including John, third Duke of Roxburghe.

1882–98 Francis James Child, *The English and Scottish Popular Ballads* (5 vols., Boston). Vol. III, pp. 39–233, consists of Child's texts of the *Gest* and the Robin Hood ballads, the standard edition since it first appeared in 1888.

1894 F. B. Gunmere, *Old English Ballads* (Boston). Includes the *Gest* and three Robin Hood ballads.

1897 Andrew Lang, *A Collection of Ballads* (London). Includes three Robin Hood ballads.

1904 *English and Scottish Popular Ballads* (edited from the collection of F. J. Child by H. C. Sargent and G. L. Kittredge, Boston). Includes texts of all the Robin Hood ballads printed by Child, but without critical apparatus.

1910 Arthur Quiller-Couch, *The Oxford Book of Ballads* (Oxford). Includes modernized versions of the *Gest* and eleven Robin Hood ballads.

1912 Frank Sidgwick, *Popular Ballads of the Olden Time*, Fourth Series (London). Contains 'Ballads of Robin Hood and Other Outlaws'.

1948 G. E. Morris, 'A Ryme of Robyn Hod', *Modern Language Review*, XLIII, pp. 507–8. The first printed edition of a fragmentary poem of the early fifteenth century in Lincoln Cathedral Library MS. 132.

1955 MacEdward Leach, *The Ballad Book* (New York). The most useful large modern anthology, including many American versions and variants of Robin Hood and other ballads.

1956   A. B. Friedman, *The Viking Book of Folk Ballads of the English-speaking World* (New York).

1959–72 B. H. Bronson, *The Traditional Tunes of the Child Ballads* (4 vols., Princeton, New Jersey, in progress). Vol. III, pp. 13–71, prints and discusses the tunes of the Robin Hood ballads.

1965   M. Hodgart, *The Faber Book of Ballads* (London). Contains only two of the Robin Hood ballads but is the best of the many small modern ballad anthologies.

II   Robin Hood in Literature

Date	Author	Title	Comments
c. 1377	William Langland	*Piers Plowman*	first reference to 'rymes of Robyn Hood'
c. 1420	Andrew of Wyntoun	*Metrical Chronicle*	assigns Robin Hood and Little John to Barnsdale and Inglewood, *c.* 1283
c. 1446	Walter Bower	Fordun's *Scotichronicon*	assigns Robin Hood to the 1260s
1501	Gavin Douglas	*Palace of Honour*	refers to 'Robene Hude, and Gilbert with the quhite hand'
1521	John Major	*History of Greater Britain*	assigns Robin Hood to the reign of Richard I
c. 1540	John Leland	*Collectanea, Itinerary*	associates Robin Hood with Barnsdale, and his burial-place with Kirklees
1548	Edward Hall	*Union of Lancastre and Yorke*	mentions Robin Hood's role in Henry VIII's Mayings, 1510, 1515
1549	Wedderburn	*Complaint of Scotland*	refers to Robin Hood tales and dances
c. 1560	William Copland	'Playes of Robyn Hode'	two Robin Hood plays appended to Copland's edition of the *Gest*
1569	Richard Grafton	*Chronicle at Large*	assigns Robin Hood, as a disinherited earl, to the reign of Richard I
1586	William Warner	*Albion's England*	later editions present Robin Hood as sympathetic and noble outlaw

Date	Author	Title	Comments
1592	John Stow	*Annales of England*	assigns Robin Hood to the reign of Richard I
1593	George Peele	*Chronicle of Edward I*	Robin Hood and his men appear as dramatic characters in this play
1597–8	Anthony Munday	*The Downfall of Robert, Earl Huntington*	Robin Hood identified as the earl of Huntington
1597–8	Anthony Munday	*The Death of Robert, Earl of Huntington*	sequel to *The Downfall*
1599	Robert Greene	*George A Green*	the tenth and twelfth scenes of this play are based on the ballad of *The Jolly Pinder of Wakefield*
1600	?	*Looke About You*	a 'pleasant comedy' with Robin Hood as earl of Huntington
1609	Robert Jones	*A Musicall Dream*	this song-collection includes 'In Sherwood Lived Stout Robin Hood'
1612–22	Michael Drayton	*The Poly-Olbion*	the 26th song celebrates Robin Hood and his men
1615	Richard Brathwayte	*Strappado for the Divell*	celebrates the contest between Robin Hood and George A Green
1632	?	*The Pinder of Wakefield*	a prose jest-book loosely based on the *Jolly Pinder* ballad
1615	Anthony Munday	*Metropolis Coronata*	a pageant for Lord Mayor's Show, includes a Robin Hood song
1638	Richard Brathwayte	*Barnabee's Journal*	celebrates Robin Hood's well, etc., in Sherwood
1641	Ben Jonson	*The Sad Shepherd*	incomplete Robin Hood pastoral play
1661	Anonymous	*Robin Hood and His Crew of Souldiers*	acted in Nottingham on Charles II's coronation day

Date	Author	Title	Comments
1662	Thomas Fuller	*Worthies of England*	Robin Hood eulogised as a 'worthy' of Nottinghamshire
1714	Alexander Smith	*Lives of Highwaymen, Footpads, etc.*	contains a section on Robin Hood
1727	Anonymous	*Robin Hood and the Duke of Lancaster*	political ballad, with Robert Walpole as Robin Hood
1730	Anonymous	*Robin Hood, An Opera*	as performed in Bartholomew Fair
1734	Charles Johnson	*Lives and Actions of Highwaymen, Murderers, etc.*	contains a section on Robin Hood
1751	Moses Mendez	*Robin Hood : A New Musical Entertainment*	a two-act play with music, as performed at Drury Lane
1784	Leonard MacNally	*Robin Hood ; or Sherwood Forest : A Comic Opera*	as performed frequently at Covent Garden
1800	Frances Brooke	*Marion : A Comic Opera*	as performed at Covent Garden
1813	Sir Walter Scott	*Rokeby*	the 30th canto contains an Allen-a-Dale song
1819	Sir Walter Scott	*Ivanhoe*	with Robin Hood as Locksley
1819	John Keats	*Robin Hood : To A Friend*	poetic lament for the 'greenwood'
1822	Thomas L. Peacock	*Maid Marian*	'romantic' novel
1840	Joseph Cundall	*Robin Hood and his Merry Foresters*	tales for children
1840	Pierce Egan	*Robin Hood and Little John*	frequently re-published version of the legend for children
1843	G. P. R. James	*Forest Days : A Romance of Old Times*	a once popular Robin Hood novel

Date	Author	Title	Comments
1847	Robert Southey	*Robin Hood, A Fragment*	incomplete poem
1855	J. H. Leigh Hunt	*Stories in Verse*	includes four new Robin Hood ballads written by the author
1860	John Oxenford and G. A. Macfarren	*Robin Hood: An Opera*	first played at Her Majesty's Theatre
1872	Alexandre Dumas	*Le Prince des Voleurs*	translated into English, 1903
1873	Alexandre Dumas	*Robin Hood Le Proscrit*	translated into English, 1903
1883	Howard Pyle	*The Merry Adventures of Robin Hood of great renown*	with illustrations by the author
1890	Reginald DeKoven	*Robin Hood: A Comic Opera*	first performed in Chicago; staged in England (1891) as *Maid Marian*
1892	Alfred Tennyson	*The Foresters*	poetic drama, published posthumously
1914	Henry Gilbert	*Robin Hood and His Merry Men*	an English story-book edition of long popularity
1914	E. F. Matheson	*Robin Hood and His Merry Men*	a play for children in two acts
1914	John Drinkwater	*Robin Hood and the Pedlar*	a 'Georgian' verse play
1925	Henry Newbolt	*The Greenwood*	a collection of literary readings relating to Robin Hood
1926	Alfred Noyes	*Robin Hood*	a five-act play in verse
1927	E. C. Vivian	*Robin Hood and His Merry Men*	a 'Charming Colour Book' for children; several later editions
1928	John C. Squire	*Robin Hood*	a 'farcical romantic pastoral'
1929	Kenneth Hare	*The Archer's Chronicle and Greenwood Companion*	an anthology which includes several items relating to Robin Hood

Date	Author	Title	Comments
1930	Enid Blyton	*Tales of Robin Hood*	stories for children
1934	Geoffrey Trease	*Bows Against the Barons*	a novel for children which interprets Robin Hood politically
1938	Anonymous	*The Adventures of Robin Hood*	a novel based on the First National Pictures Technicolor film
1939	Carola Oman	*Robin Hood, The Prince of Outlaws*	children's novel, freely adapted from the *Gest*
1955	Antonia Fraser	*Robin Hood*	for young children, illustrated by Rebecca Fraser
1956	Roger Lancelyn Green	*The Adventures of Robin Hood*	for children, carefully based on earlier ballads. etc.

III   *A Selection of Critical Works*

Arber, E., *A Transcript of the Registers of the Company of Stationers of London* (5 vols., London and Birmingham, 1875–94).

Bellamy, J. G., 'The Coterel Gang: An Anatomy of a Band of Fourteenth-Century Criminals', *E.H.R.*, LXXIX (1964), pp. 698–717.

—, *Crime and Public Order in England in the Later Middle Ages* (London, 1973).

Bessinger, J. B., Jr., 'Robin Hood: Folklore and Historiography, 1377–1500', *Tennessee Studies in Literature*, XI (1966), pp. 61–9.

Birrell, J., 'Peasant Craftsmen in the Medieval Forest', *Agricultural History Review*, XVII (1969), pp. 91–107.

Bronson, B. H., *The Ballad as Song* (Berkeley, California, 1969).

—, *Joseph Ritson, Scholar-at-Arms* (2 vols., Berkeley, California, 1938).

Chambers, E. K., *The Mediaeval Stage* (2 vols., Oxford, 1903).

—, *The Elizabethan Stage* (4 vols., Oxford, 1923).

—, *The English Folk-Play* (Oxford, 1933).

—, *English Literature at the Close of the Middle Ages* (Oxford, 1945).

Child, F. J., ed., *The English and Scottish Popular Ballads* (5 vols., Boston, 1882–98): Child's most detailed discussion of the Robin Hood legend is to be found in the introduction to his edition of *A Gest of Robyn Hode* (Vol. III, pp. 39–56).

Clawson, W. H., *The Gest of Robin Hood* (University of Toronto Studies: Philological Series, Extra Volume, 1909).

Collison, R., *The Story of Street Literature* (London, 1973).

Coote, H. C., 'The Origin of the Robin Hood Epos', *Folk-Lore Journal*, III (1885), pp. 44–52.

Crosland, J., *Outlaws in Fact and Fiction* (London, 1959).

Crump, W. B., 'The Site of Robin Hood's Grave', *Y.A.J.*, XXXVII (1948–51), pp. 105–6.

Dobson, R. B., and Taylor, J., 'The Medieval Origins of the Robin Hood Legend: A Reassessment', *Northern History*, VII (1972), pp. 1–30.

Entwistle, W. J., *European Balladry* (Oxford, 1939).

Firth, C. H., 'Ballads and Broadsides', in *Shakespeare's England*, ed. Sir S. Lee (2 vols., London, 1917), II, pp. 511–38.

Fowler, D. C., *A Literary History of the Popular Ballad* (Durham, North Carolina, 1968).

Frankel, L., 'Zur Geschichte von Robin Hood', *Englische Studien* (Leipzig), XVII (1892), pp. 316–17.

Fricke, R., 'Die Robin-Hood-Balladen', *Archiv*, LXIX (1883), pp. 241–344.

Gable, J. H., *A Bibliography of Robin Hood* (University of Nebraska, Studies in Language, Literature and Criticism, No. 17, 1938).

Gerould, G. H., *The Ballad of Tradition* (Oxford, 1932).

Greene, R. L., *The Early English Carols* (Oxford, 1935).

Gunmere, F. B., *Old English Ballads* (Boston, 1894).

—, 'Ballads', in *Cambridge History of English Literature*, II (1908), pp. 449–74.

Hales, J. W. and Furnivall, F. J., ed., *Bishop Percy's Folio Manuscript: Ballads and Romances* (3 vols., London, 1867–8): the editors discuss the general significance of the Robin Hood ballads in Vol. I, pp. 1–12.

Hargrove, E., *Anecdotes of Archery from the earliest ages to the year 1791, with some particulars in the life of Robert Fitz-Ooth, Earl of Huntington, vulgarly called Robin Hood* (York, 1792).

Harris, P. V., *The Truth about Robin Hood* (London, 1951; new edition, Mansfield, 1973).

—, 'Who was Robin Hood?', *Folk-Lore Quarterly*, LXVI (1955), pp. 288–94.

Hart, W. M., 'Professor Child and the Ballad', *Publications of the Modern Language Association of America*, XXI (1906), pp. 755–807.

—, *Ballad and Epic: A Study in the Development of the narrative art* (Harvard Studies and Notes in Philology and Literature, XI, Boston, 1907).

Henderson, T. F., *The Ballad in Literature* (Cambridge, 1912).

Hill, C., *The World Turned Upside Down; Radical Ideas during the English Revolution* (London, 1972).

Hilton, R. H., 'The Origins of Robin Hood', *Past and Present*, 14 (1958), pp. 30–44.

—, 'Robin Hood', in *Encyclopaedia Britannica* (1971), XIX, pp. 394–5.

—, *The English Peasantry in the Later Middle Ages* (Oxford, 1975).

Hobsbawm, E. J., *Bandits* (London, 1969).

Hodgart, M. J. C., *The Ballads* (London, 1950).

—, ed., *The Faber Book of Ballads* (London, 1965): Introduction.

Holt, J. C., 'The Origins and Audience of the Ballads of Robin Hood', *Past and Present*, 18 (1960), pp. 89–110.

—, 'Robin Hood: some comments', *Past and Present*, 19 (1961), pp. 16–18.

Hunter, J., *South Yorkshire* (2 vols., London, 1828–31).

—, 'The Great Hero of the Ancient Minstrelsy of England: Robin Hood, his period, real character, etc., Investigated and perhaps Ascertained' (*Critical and Historical Tracts*, No. 4, London, 1852).

Jusserand, J., *English Wayfaring Life in the Middle Ages* (London, 1889).

Keen, M., 'Robin Hood, a Peasant Hero', *History Today*, VIII (1958), pp. 684–9.

—, *The Outlaws of Medieval Legend* (London, 1961).

—, 'Robin Hood—Peasant or Gentleman', *Past and Present*, 19 (1961), pp. 7–15.

Kennedy, D. N., 'Who was Robin Hood?' *Folk-Lore Quarterly*, LXVI (1955), pp. 413–15.

Ker, W. P., 'On the Danish Ballads', *Scottish Historical Review*, I (1904), pp. 357–78; V (1908), pp. 385–401.

—, 'On the History of the Ballads, 1100–1500', *Proceedings of the British Academy*, IV (1910), pp. 179–205.

Klapp, O. E., 'The Folk Hero', *Journal of American Folklore*, LXII (1949), pp. 17–25.

Lange, J. de, *The Relation and Development of English and Icelandic Outlaw-Traditions* (Nederlandsche Bijdragen op het Gebied van Germaansche Philologie en Linguistiek, No. 6, Haarlem, 1935).

Lee, Sidney, 'Robin Hood', in *Dictionary of National Biography*, XXVII (1891), pp. 258–61.

Lloyd, A. L., *Folk Song in England* (London, 1967).

Mill, A. J., *Mediaeval Plays in Scotland* (St Andrews University Publications, No. XXIV, Edinburgh, 1927).

Mitchell, W. R., *The Haunts of Robin Hood* (Clapham, Yorkshire, 1970).

Moreland, C. C. 'Ritson's Life of Robin Hood', *Publications of the Modern Language Association of America*, L (1935), pp. 522–36.

Murray, M. A., *The Witch-Cult in Western Europe: A Study in Anthropology* (Oxford, 1921).

Neilson, G., 'Robin Hood', *Notes and Queries*, 7th series, 9 (1890), p. 226.

Nelson, M. A., *The Robin Hood Tradition in the English Renaissance* (Salzburg Studies in English Literature, Elizabethan Studies, No. 14; Salzburg University, 1973).

Oates, J. C. T., 'The Little Gest of Robin Hood: A Note on the Pynson and Lettersnijder Editions', *Studies in Bibliography* (Charlottesville, Virginia), XVI (1963) pp. 3–8.

Owen, L. V. D., 'Robin Hood', in *Chambers's Encyclopaedia* (1950), XI, pp. 733–4.

Pound, L., *Poetic Origins and the Ballad* (New York, 1921).

Ritson, J., *Robin Hood: A Collection of all the ancient poems, songs, and ballads* (London, 1795): the 'Life of Robin Hood' and accompanying 'Notes and Illustrations' in this and most subsequent editions remain indispensable.

Robbins, R. H., ed., *Historical Poems of the XIVth and XVth Centuries* (New York, 1959).

Rollins, H. E., 'The Black-Letter Broadside Ballad', *Publications of the Modern Language Association of America*, XXXIV (1919), pp. 258–339.

—, 'Matthew Parker, Ballad-Monger', *Modern Philology*, XVI (1919), pp. 113–38.

—, 'An Analytical Index to the Ballad Entries (1557–1709) in the Registers of the Company of Stationers': North Carolina University, *Studies in Philology*, XXI (1924), pp. 1–324.

Scattergood, V. J., *Politics and Poetry in the Fifteenth Century* (London, 1971).

Schlauch, M., *English Medieval Literature and its Social Foundations* (2nd edition, Warsaw, 1967).

Shannon, E., Jr., 'Mediaeval Law in *The Tale of Gamelyn*', *Speculum*, XXVI (1951), pp. 458–64.

Shepard, L., *The Broadside Ballad* (London, 1962).

Simeone, W. E., 'The May Games and the Robin Hood Legend', *Journal of American Folklore*, LXIV (1951), pp. 265–74.

—, 'Still More about Robin Hood', *Journal of American Folklore*, LXV (1952), pp. 418–20.

—, 'Robin Hood and Some Other Outlaws', *Journal of American Folklore*, LXXI (1958), pp. 27–33.

Simpson, C. M., *The British Broadside Ballad and its Music* (New Jersey, 1966).

Smith, A. H., 'Robin Hood', *Modern Language Review*, XXVIII (1933), pp. 484–5.

—, ed., *The Place-Names of the West Riding of Yorkshire* (English Place-Name Society, XXX–XXXVII, 1961–3).

Spencer, Lewis, 'Robin Hood in Scotland', *Chambers's Journal*, 9th Series, XVIII (1928), pp. 94–6.

Steckmesser, K. L., 'Robin Hood and the American Outlaw: a Note on History and Folklore', *Journal of American Folklore*, LXXIX (1966), pp. 348–55.

Steenstrup, J. C. H. R., *The Medieval Popular Ballad* (trans. E. G. Cox, Boston, 1914).

Stones, E. L. G., 'The Folvilles of Ashby-Folville, Leicestershire, and their

Associates in Crime, 1326–41', *T.R.H.S.*, 5th Series, VII (1957), pp. 117–36.

Stukeley, W., *Palaeographia Britannica* (2 vols., London and Stamford, 1743–6): 'The Pedigree of Robin Hood earl of Huntington' is printed in Vol. II, p. 115.

Tiddy, R. J. E., *The Mummers' Play* (Oxford, 1923).

Walker, J. W., 'Robin Hood Identified', *Y.A.J.*, XXXVI (1944–7), pp. 4–46.

—, *The True History of Robin Hood* (Wakefield, 1952).

Walker, V. W., *Robin Hood Literature in the Nottingham Public Libraries* (Nottingham, 1933).

Wilson, R. M., *The Lost Literature of Medieval England* (2nd edition, London, 1970).

Wimberly, L. C., *Folklore in the English and Scottish Ballads* (Chicago, 1928).

Wright, T., 'On the popular cycle of the Robin Hood ballads', in *Essays on subjects connected with the literature, popular superstitions, and history of England in the Middle Ages* (2 vols., London, 1846), I, pp. 164–211.

Robin Hood meets Little John: Howard Pyle's illustration from his *The Merry Adventures of Robin Hood* (New York, 1883).

INDEX

Aberdeen, 40

Aeglamour, the Sad Shepherd, 231–6 *passim*

Alice, wife of William of Cloudesly, 261–4, 268–9, 273

Allen a Dale, 159, 172–5, 301, 302, 317

'Aragon, Prince of', 53, 284

archery, 36, 46, 254, 260, 272; contests, 19, 58 n.1, 76–8, 99–100, 107–8, 110 and n.1, 116, 125, 129–30, 143, 259, 271–2; garlands, 108 and n.1, 143; pricks, 130 and n.3, 143 and n.5, 271; wands, 89, 100, 108, 271

arrows, types of, 88 and n.6, 99, 167, 271 and n.9, 272

Arthur, King, 32, 37, 58, 187, 260 n.2

'Arthur a Bland', 166

As You Like It, 43, 223 n.2 and see Shakespeare

Bagford Ballads, 114

Balder, 63

Ball, John, 32

Ballads, 6–7, 10, 46–54, 65–6, 113–14, 124, 183 and *passim*; broadsides, 46–50, 65–6, 150–1, 191–2; Garlands, 46, 51–3, 58–9, 176, 179; American, 134 n.1, 165–6, 170, 278–80; Danish, 10 n.4, 274–7; Scottish, 10 n.4, 195–7, 275; Ballads of Robin Hood: listed 281–5; *A Gest of Robyn Hode*, see *Gest*; *Bold Pedlar and Robin Hood*, 281, 313; *Jolly Pinder of Wakefield*; text, 146–9; 43 n.3, 44, 47, 52, 281, 287, 312, 316; *King's Disguise*, 53, 281; *Little John and Four Beggars*, 52, 281; *Noble Fisherman (Robin Hood's Preferment)*; text, 179–82; 17, 48, 50, 52, 115 n.2, 187, 281, 306; *Robin Hood and Allen a Dale*; text, 172–5; 50, 53, 281, 287; *Robin Hood and Guy of Gisborne*; text, 140–5; 7, 19, 34, 37, 53, 115 n.2, 124, 135 n.1, 203, 204, 206 n.1, 281; *Robin Hood and Little John*; text, 165–71; 53, 281; *Robin Hood and Maid Marian*; text, 176–8; 50, 195, 282; *Robin Hood and Queen Katherine*, 17, 41 n.3, 52, 187, 282; *Robin Hood and the Beggar*, 52, 151, 282; *Robin Hood and the Bishop*, 52, 187, 282; *Robin Hood and the Bishop of Hereford*, 53, 282; *Robin Hood and the Butcher*; text, 150–7; 49, 52, 125, 166, 282; *Robin Hood and the Curtal Friar*; text, 158–64; 52, 115 n.2, 134, 152 n.6, 154 n.2, 180 n.3, 208, 209, 282, 287, 301–2, 310; *Robin Hood and the Golden Arrow*, 53, 282; *Robin Hood and the Monk*; text, 113–22; 8–10, 18–19, 33–7, 66–7, 123–4, 282 and *passim*; *Robin Hood and the Pedlars*, 282; *Robin Hood and the Potter*; text, 123–32; 8–10, 33–6, 66–7, 215–16, 283 and *passim*; *Robin Hood and the Ranger*, 53, 283; *Robin Hood and the Scotchman*, 283; *Robin Hood and the Shepherd*, 52, 134, 283; *Robin Hood and the Stranger*, 151, 166 n.1, 283, 285; *Robin Hood and the Tanner*, 38, 48, 52, 166, 283; *Robin Hood and the Tinker*, 48, 53, 180 n.3, 218, 283; *Robin Hood and the Valiant Knight*; text, 183–6; 50, 53, 138 n.4, 283; *Robin Hood Newly Revived*, 52, 166 n.1, 177, 283; *Robin Hood Rescuing Three Squires*, 49, 53, 283; *Robin Hood Rescuing Widow's Sons*, 283; *Robin Hood Rescuing Will Stutly*, 52, 168 n.1, 283; *Robin Hood, Will Scadlock and Little John (Robin Hood and the Prince of Aragon)*, 53, 284; *Robin Hood's Birth, Breeding, etc.*, 53, 259, 284; *Robin Hood's Chase*, 52, 284; *Robin Hood's Death*, text, 133–9; 7, 19, 184, 284, 309; *Robin Hood's Delight*, 52, 284; *Robin Hood's Golden Prize*, 41 n.3, 48, 52, 284; *Robin Hood's Progress to Nottingham*, 52, 184 n.1, 284, 287; *True Tale of Robin Hood*, text, 187–90; 48, 284, 292, 312 and see Parker, Martin

Bampton (Oxon.), 38

Barclay, Alexander, monk of Ely, 3 and n.2, 41, 292

Barnabee's Journal, see Brathwayte

Barnsdale (Bernesdale, Bernysdaile), 18–24; and see 4, 15, 33, 63, 211, 260 n.2; in *Gest*, 74–80, 85, 88, 94, 98, 111; in other ballads, 124, 142, 144; legal maxim, 3, 18; chapel in, 111; Barnsdale Bar, 24 and n.2, 307–8; place-names in, 307–8

Barrie, Sir James, 200

Bass, Sam, 278 n.2

Beckwith (W. Yorks.), 27

Beckwith, William, 27, 33 n.3

Bell, Adam, 4, 34 n.5, 47, 77, 78, 258–73 *passim*; ballad of *Adam Bell, Clim of the Clough and William of Cloudesly*, 260–73

Bellamy, J. G., 27–8 and ns., 33 n.3, 251 n.2

'Belregard', 252–3

Belvoir Castle (Leics.), 231, 232

Bessinger, J. B., 4 n.4

Bevis of Hampton, 3, 33, 47, 58, 63

Bickhill (Wakefield), 13

Billingham, Thomas, 27

Birth of Robin Hood, Scottish ballad, 195–7

bishops, 31, 80, 94, 172, 174–5, 282; of Hereford, 282, 308

Black Death, 35

Blackstone Edge (Lancs.), 290, 298

Blyth (Notts.), 81, 98 and n.2

Blyton, Enid, 60 n.2, 319

Bolingbroke, Lord, 192–3

Boroughbridge (N. Yorks.), 24, 26; battle of (1322), 13

Bower, Walter, chronicler, 4, 5, 15–16, 18, 40, 315

Brathwayte, Richard, 23 and n.2, 316

Bretoun, Richard, 26

broadsides, *see* Ballads

Bronson, B. H., on music of Robin Hood
ballads, 49 n.1, 134 n.1, 147 n.1, 151 n.1, 166
and ns., 180 n.3, 184 n.1, 315
Brown, Mrs (of Falkland), 55, 195
'Brown Robin', 195
Bury St Edmunds Abbey, 255
butts, 99–100, 129, 271 *and see* archery, Robin
Hood
Byddell, John, printer, 258

Camden, William, 290
Canterbury, pilgrims to, 26, 35
Canterbury Tales, 35 *and see* Chaucer, Geoffrey
Carlisle (Caerlel), 258, 261–8, 270–1; mayor of,
267, 271
Carlisle, Earl of, 23, 310
Castleton (N. Yorks.), 288, 306–7
Cecil, Sir Robert, 4
Chambers, E. K.: on Robin Hood, 12 n.1, 63
n.1, 76 n.1; on ballads, 7, 9 n.5, 34 n.3, 113
n.2; on plays, 38 n.3, 40 n.4, 42–3, 204, 208
n.2, 220 n.2
chapbooks, *see* Ballads
Charles II, 45, 237, 238 n.1, 316
Charnwood Forest (Leics.), 299
Chatsworth (Derbyshire), 296–7
Chaucer, Geoffrey, 2, 26 *and* n.1, 32, 35 *and*
n.3, 43 n.3; *Canterbury Tales*, 35, 88 n.6;
Troilus and Criseyde, 2, 289
Chester, Earl of, *see* Randolf
Chettle, Henry, 221
Child and the Shepherd, The, 123
Child, Francis, J., 54, 147, 166 *and passim*; on
ballads, 6–7, 48, 65, 314; on Robin Hood
ballads, 8, 9, 113, 140–1, 147, 183; on Robin
Hood, 11, 63, 125; on Maid Marian, 41; on
Friar Tuck, 159, 209; on *Robyn and Gande-
leyn*, 255; on Robin Hood plays, 203–4, 209
Clawson, W. H., 8 n.4, 33 n.1, 74 n.1, 152 n.2
Claxton, Thomas, 27
Clerk and the Nightingale, The, 114
Clerk of Copmanhurst (*Ivanhoe*), 41
Clim of the Clough (*Adam Bell*), 258, 260,
263–5, 268–70, 273
Cloudesly, William of (*Adam Bell*), 258–73
passim
Coke, Sir Edward, 26, 290
Coles, Francis, printer, 48, 52 n.2, 146, 158
Coote, H. C., 30 *and* n.4
Copland, William; printer of *Gest*, 37, 71–3,
312; of plays of Robin Hood, 37, 41, 158,
208–9, 215–16, 315; of *Adam Bell*, 258
Coterel family, 15, 27–30
Covent Garden Theatre, 45, 56, 317
Cox, Captain (of Coventry), 47, 259
Crane, R. S., 58 n.2
Croscombe (Somerset), 39
Curtal Friar, *see* Ballads of Robin Hood, Tuck
Curtiz, Michael, 61

Dale, Sir William, 184–5
Davenant, William, 259
Davenport, Robert, 223
Delaney, Thomas, 50
Denmark, 10 n.4, 11, 274–7

Derbyshire, 4, 15, 27; place-names, 295–7
Dicey, Cluer, printer, 51, 53 n.2
Dives and Pauper, 1–2 *and* n, 291
Dodsworth, Roger, 23, 310
Doesbroch, Jan van, printer, 71–2, 312
Doncaster (W. Yorks.), 2 n.1, 18–21, 81, 98,
307–8, 310
Doncaster (Donkesly), Sir Roger of, 13, 20, 78,
112, 133–6, 222–3
Dorne, John, bookseller, 8 n.3
'Douce' (of *The Sad Shepherd*), 231, 235, 236
Douce, Francis, 62 n.3, 71–3
Douglas, Gavin, 45
Drayton, Michael, 45, 146–7, 222, 316
Drinkwater, John, 58, 318
Drury Lane Theatre, 45, 232, 317
Dumas, Alexandre, 60, 318
Dunmow Abbey (Essex), 222
Durham Cathedral Priory, 27

'Earine' (of *The Sad Shepherd*), 231, 235, 236
Earl Bothwell, 275
Ebbesen, Niels, 274 n.2
Edinburgh, 40
Edward I, 14, 24 n.3, 43, 251, 316
Edward II, 13, 15
Edward III, 20, 22, 25, 29
Edward IV, 24 n.2, 44, 62, 177 n.1, 203
Edward VI, 39
Egan, Pierce, the younger, 59–60, 317
Elderton, William, ballad writer, 58 n.1
Eleanor (Elenor), Queen (in Munday's plays),
222, 224, 227–30
Eliot, George, 58 n.1
Eltham, Sir John (in Munday's plays), 221–5
Ely, Bishop of (in Munday's plays), 227
Entwistle, W., 16 n.3, 274 n.2, 275 *and* n.4
Eustace the Monk, 33, 76, 78, 125
Evans, Thomas, 54, 313
Evelyn, John, 23
Evesham, battle of (1265), 16

Fairbanks, Douglas, 61
Father Christmas, 38
Fawkes, Guy, 4
Fawkes, Richard, printer, 47
Fenn, Sir John, 204
Fereby, John, mayor of York, 24 n.2
Ferrybridge (W. Yorks.), 21–2
Firth, C. H., 47 n.2, 180 n.2
Fitz-Aylwin, Henry, mayor of London, 44
Fitzooths, family of, 305
FitzWarin, Fulk, 33, 63
Fitzwater, Lord (in Munday's plays), 44, 221,
222, 226–30
Flamborough (E. Yorks.), 255
Flynn, Erroll, 61 *and* n.3
Folville family, 27–8; Richard de, 30
Ford, Robert, 278–80
Fordun, John, chronicler, 5, 315
Foresters, The, 243–9 *and see* Tennyson
Fountain Dale (Notts.), 162, 164, 301–2
Fountains Abbey (W. Yorks.), 158–64 *passim*,
302, 309–10
Fowler, D. C.: on ballads, 6 *and* n.3, 7, 9, 49,

124 n.3; on *Robin Hood and Monk*, 113 n.3, 114; on Mrs Brown, 55 n.1, 195 n.1
Fraser, Antonia, 60 n.2, 319
Frere, William, 204
friars, 1, 39, 41, 62 n.3, 93, 108, 188, 212 *and* n.1 *and see* Tuck, Friar
Fuller, Thomas, 237 n.1, 290, 291, 317

Gamelyn, Tale of, 33, 76–8, 199
'Gandeleyn', 7–8, 255–7
Garlands, *see* Ballads
Gärtner, Willhelm der, 31
Gent, Thomas, York printer, 52 n.4, 179
gentry, and Robin Hood, 32–3, 36; gentry gangs, 27–8
George (Jorge) St, 18, 38, 40, 59, 187, 204
George I, 191–4
George a Green, 44, 50, 146–8, 222, 232, 316 *and see* Pinder of Wakefield
Gerould, G. H., 30, 48, 180 n.2
Gest (Lytell, Merry) of Robyn Hode, A; text, 71–112; 8–24, 30–37, 223 *and passim*
Gesta Herewardi, 77
Gilbert, Henry, 60, 318
Gilbert of the White Hand (Withondes), 5, 13, 77, 100, 108, 315
Gilbertson, W., printer, 51–2, 146, 158, 313
Gisborne, Guy of, 37, 140–5 *and see* Ballads of Robin Hood
Godberd, Roger, 16
Grafton, Richard, chronicler, 44 n.5, 187, 222, 315
Graves, Robert, 63 n.2, 255
Green, R. L., 61, 319
'Grenelef', 4, 225 *and see* Reynolde
Grey, Reynold de, 16
Grove, F., printer, 150, 155, 187–8, 312
Grundtvig, Svend, 274
Gutch, J. M., 16 n.1, 55 n.2, 123, 286 n.1, 292; Robin Hood anthology, 54 *and* n.2, 313–14
Guy of Warwick, *see* Warwick

Hall, Edward, chronicler, 42, 315
Halle, Adam de la, 42 n.1
Hampole (W. Yorks.), 20, 307–8
Harold, King, 245
Harris, P. Valentine, 13 n.3, 15
Hart, W. M., 9 n.1, 171 n.1
Harvey, John, 12 n.3
Hathersage (Derbyshire), 295–7
Havilland, Olivia de, 61
Hearne, Thomas, 295
Henry III, 14, 16
Henry IV, 25
Henry VIII, 21, 47, 221, 223, 258; May festivities of, 42–3, 304, 315
Henslowe, Philip, 43, 221, 291
Hereward the Wake, 33, 63, 77–8, 125, 245
highway robbers, 24–6, 28
Hilton, R. H., 13 n.2, 31 n.2, 35 n.5, 251 n.1; on criminal bands, 27 n.4, 28
Hjelm, Danish island, 275, 277 *and* n.3
'Hobbehod', 16
Hobsbawm, E. J., 62, 64, 274 n.1
Hodeken, 12, 63

Hodgart, M. J. C., 6 n.1, 275 *and* n.2, 315
Hodr, 11
Holderness (E. Yorks.), 90
Holinshed, chronicler, 222
Holt, J. C.: on Robin Hood ballads, 6 *and* n.2, 10 n.1, 11; on historic Robin Hood, 13 n.2, 14–16; on Robin Hood and gentry, 30–6 *passim*, 275 n.1; on 'Roberdsmen', 26 n.5
Hood, as surname, 11–12; *and see* Robin Hood
'Hood, Gilbert', 60, 222, 223
Huddersfield (W. Yorks.), 19, 78, 309
Hunt, J. H. Leigh, 58, 318
Hunter, Joseph, 13 *and* n.1, 21 n.3, 22, 24, 260 n.2
Huntington, Earl of, as title of Robin Hood, 40 n.2, 44, 59 n.1, 139, 177, 186, 188, 190; plays of, 220–30, 243–8 *and see* Munday
Husbandman, Song of the, 31
husbandmen, 10, 34, 80
Hutchinson, Colonel, 237

Inglewood (Englysshe-wood; Cumberland), 4, 18, 63; in *Adam Bell*, 258, 260 *and* n.2, 261, 267, 268
Ingram, Sir Robert, 15, 29
Ivanhoe, 41, 56–8 *passim*, 60, 62, 198, 244 *and see* Scott, Sir Walter

Jackson, J., York printer, 165, 172
Jacquerie (1358), 30
James IV of Scotland, 123
James, Frank, outlaw, 278–9
James, Jesse, outlaw, 11, 278–80 *passim*; *The Death of Jesse James*, 279–80
Jamieson, Robert, 55, 113, 195, 313
John, King, 16, 44, 192, 201, 222 *and* n.1; in Munday's plays, 222–30 *passim*; in Tennyson's play, 243–8 *passim*
John, Little, *see* Little John
Johnson, Samuel, 54, 138 n.5
Jonson, Ben, 37, 45, 46, 221 n.2, 231–2, 259; *The Sad Shepherd*, 45, 231–6, 302, 316
justices: of the peace, 14; of trailbaston, 250; in *Adam Bell*, 262–3, 265–6, 270–1; in *Gest*, 75, 85–8, 98

Keats, John, 57, 198–9, 200, 317; *Robin Hood* poem, 198–9
Keen, M., 25 n.3, 30 n.2, 141 n.1, 190 n.1, 251 n.1; on historic Robin Hood, 13 n.2, 33 n.3; on Robin Hood legend, 4 n.4, 35 n.2, 63 n.1, 134 n.2; on other outlaws, 32–3, 76 n.1, 125 n.1
'Kendal green', 213
Kendrew, James, York printer, 52 n.4
Kenilworth (Warwickshire), 259
King and the Barker, The, 123
King and the Miller, The, 78
King Edward and the Shepherd, 9, 114
king of England, in ballads, 33, 184–5, 192–4; in *Gest*, 74, 77–8, 102, 104–11; named 'Edward', 104, 107, 111; in *Robin Hood and Monk*, 119–22; in *Adam Bell*, 264–5, 269–73; 'King Henry', 284
Kingston-on-Thames, 39, 304

Kirkby Hill (N. Yorks.), 26
Kirklees (Kyrkesly, Church Lees) nunnery, 19
  and n.3, 21, 59 n.3, 309; in *Gest*, 78, 111–12;
  in *Robin Hood's Death*, 133–9; prioress of, 78,
  111, 133–9, 183, 190
Kirkley Hall, 137–8 *and see* Kirklees
Kirk Smeaton (W. Yorks.), 22
Kirkstall Abbey (W. Yorks.), 27 n.3
Knaresborough Forest (W. Yorks.), 27
knighthood, 10, 14, 82; distraint of, 14, 82;
  Lancashire knight (of *Gest*), 28, 74–7, 80–9,
  98–9, 290; Robin Hood's respect for, 10, 32,
  79–80, 84, 99
Knighton, Henry, chronicler, 20 n.2, 30
Kraljevic, Marko, 274 n.2

Lancashire, 74, 105 *and see* knighthood; place-
  names, 298–9
Lancaster, duchy of, 27; knight of, 74, 82
Lancaster, Robin Hood and the Duke of, 191–4,
  317
Lancaster, Thomas Earl of (d. 1322), 13
Laneham, Robert, 47, 259
Langland, William, 1, 7, 13, 23, 31 *and see Piers
  Plowman*
Latimer, Bishop Hugh, 39
Le Neve, Peter, 204
Lea, Sir Richard (of *The Foresters*), 243–7
Lechmere, Lord, 192–4
Lee, Sir Richard at the (of the *Gest*), 13, 76–8,
  101–5, 108, 110
Legat, Hugh, St Albans monk, 2
Leicester (Lester), Earl of (in Munday's plays),
  227
Leland, John, 21, 306, 307, 315; on Robin
  Hood as *nobilis*, 44 n.5; on Kirklees, 19 n.3,
  309, 315
'Lincoln green', 62, 109, 149, 163, 199, 202
'Lionel, king of raveners', 33 n.3
Lisle, Brian de, 15
Little John (Johnn, Johun), 4, 5, 8 n.1, 18, 45,
  260, 301, 303; ballads of Robin Hood and,
  47–8, 165–71, 281, 284; in *Gest*, 21, 23,
  74–85, 89–97, 99–102, 107–8, 110; in *Robin
  Hood and Monk*, 115–22; in *Robin Hood and
  Potter*, 19, 126–7, 131; in other ballads,
  134–8, 140–2, 145, 147, 148 n.1, 157, 161,
  164, 178, 199, 202; in plays, 38–45 *passim*,
  206–7, 210, 216–25 *passim*, 231–2, 238, 244
  n.1; as yeoman, 34, 165; quarrels with Robin
  Hood, 94, 115–16, 121, 142, 167–8; place-
  names, 288, 293, 295–6, 298, 299, 300, 306–7,
  308
Little John and the Four Beggars, 52, 281
Locksley (Lockesley, Loxley), 183, 185, 287,
  304–5, 308; as name of Robin Hood, 57, 183,
  244, 317
London, 12, 22, 26 *and* n.1, 44, 191; in ballads,
  75, 97, 102, 185, 269; ballad publishing in,
  47–52; May Games in, 39–40; place-names,
  46 n.2, 293, 299–300
'*Looke About You*', play, 44, 316
'Lorel' (of *The Sad Shepherd*), 231, 236

Macaulay, T. B., 25

Machyn, Henry, 39, 214 n.1
MacNally, Leonard, 45, 317
Maid Marian, 3, 39–42, 43 n.3, 159, 188, 199,
  201–2, 301; ballad of Robin Hood and,
  176–8; in May Games, 39–42, 147, 209, 214
  n.1; in plays, 44, 221, 223–30 *passim*, 231–6
  passim, 243–7; in films, 61; street name, 300
Maid Marian, see Peacock, Thomas Love
Maidenhead (Berks.), 295
Maitland, F. W., 29
Major, John, 4, 5, 16, 287, 290, 315
Marchall, Robert, of Wednesbury, 4
Mark, Philip, 15
Marsk Stig, 11, 274–7 *passim*; ballad of, 276–7
Mary, Blessed Virgin (Our Lady), 75, 254;
  invocations to, 97, 162, 257; Robin Hood's
  devotion to, 79, 83–4, 94, 96–8, 115, 116,
  118, 124, 125, 127, 144, 279
Mary Hamilton, 275
masques, 43
Matilda, 44, 221–2 *and see* Maid Marian
'Maudlin' (of *The Sad Shepherd*), 231–6
  passim
May Games, 38–42, 63, 147, 159; and Robin
  Hood plays, 203–4, 208–10, 215–16; at royal
  court, 42, 223, 304; at Wakefield, 147;
  Queen of, 40, 62 n.3
Midge, 161, 173 *and see* Much
Minsterley (Salop.), 41, 62
minstrels, 9, 10, 114, 124, 260
Monkbretton Priory (W. Yorks.), 23, 310
Montfort, Simon de, 16
morris dances, 39, 40–1, 159, 209, 214 n.1, 216,
  225
Morys, Thomas, 26
Much the Miller's Son: in *Gest*, 74–5, 79–80,
  83–5, 94–5, 100, 101, 260; in *Robin Hood and
  Monk*, 115, 118–20; in other ballads, 161, 173,
  287; in plays, 44, 222, 232, 243
mummers' plays, 37–8
Munday, Anthony, 37, 44–5, 220–30 *passim*,
  290, 316; *Downfall of Robert Earl of Huntington*, 223–8; *Death of Robert Earl of Huntington*,
  228–30; *Metropolis Coronata*, 44, 316;
  influence on Robin Hood legend, 16, 44–5,
  176, 223, 286
Murray, Margaret, 63 n.2

Nelson, M. A., 37 n.1
Newbolt, Henry, 56 n.3, 198, 318
Nickson, N., York printer, 133–4
Noble Fisherman, The, see Ballads of Robin
  Hood
Nottingham, 14, 19, 27, 45, 217, 237; in *Gest*,
  76–8, 92, 94, 102–7, 109–10; in *Robin Hood
  and Monk*, 115–17, 120–1; in *Robin Hood and
  Potter*, 124, 127–32; in other ballads, 145,
  150–1, 153–5, 164, 167, 169, 170; archery
  contest at, 76–7, 99–100; castle, 15, 16, 62;
  gallows, 283; mayor of, 15; porter of, 120–1;
  place-names, 300–1
Nottingham, Sheriff of, 14–15, 19, 20, 31, 36, 74
  and see Ingram; in *Gest*, 74, 76–7, 80, 85,
  89–94, 99–104; in *Robin Hood and Monk*, 117,

120–2; in *Robin Hood and Potter*, 127, 129–32; in other ballads, 142, 144–5, 150–7; in plays, 18, 38, 203–7, 222, 225, 243–6; butler of, 90; cook of, 91–2; wife of, 36, 125, 128–32, 153–4, 157; decoyed into greenwood, 76–7, 92–3, 125, 130–2, 150, 154, 156–7; killed, 104, 145, 204

Nottinghamshire, 14–15, 17, 173; place-names, 301–3

Noyes, Alfred, 58, 200–2; *Sherwood*, poem, 201–2; *Robin Hood*, play, 201, 318

Oman, Carola, 60 n.2, 319
Orwell, George, 50
outlawry, 29, 224, 251
Outlaw's Song of Trailbaston, An, 29, 250–4
Owen, L. V. D., 15, 16

Paine, Tom, 55
Papplewick (Notts.), 231, 232, 302
Paris, Matthew, 24 n.1
Parker, Harry, Carmelite friar, 2 n.1
Parker, Martin, 48–9, 187–90, 191, 284; *True Tale of Robin Hood*, 48, 65 n.1, 188–90, 284, 292, 312–13
Paston, Sir John and family, 18, 32, 38, 204; *Letters*, 28 n.3, 204
Peacock, Thomas Love, 56–7, 198, 317
'pavage' (passage), 33 n.3, 126, 216–18
peasants in medieval literature, 31–2
Peasants' Revolt of 1381, 30, 32
Peele, George, 43, 316
Pepys, William, 46, 48, 158 n.1
Percy Folio, 7, 49, 66, 209, 259, 313, 314; ballad texts from, 133–7, 140–5, 146–9, 150–4, 158–61
Percy's *Reliques of Ancient Poetry*, 1, 36, 65, 258–9, 313; influence of, 53
Perth (Scotland), 40
Pierce the Plowman's Crede, 32
Piers Plowman, 1, 10, 32, 114, 315 *and see* Langland
Pinder of Wakefield, 45, 50, 146–9 *passim*, 259; ballad of, 43 n.3, 44, 47, 146–9, 159, 281, 287, 312; play of, 44, 146, 222, 316
Plowman's Tale, The, 32
Plumpton Park (W. Yorks.), 78 n.1, 105, 181, 286
Pontefract (W. Yorks.), 22, 24 *and* n.3, 307
Price, Laurence, ballad writer, 48
Pyle, Howard, 60, 184 n.2, 318
Pynson, Richard, printer, 8, 71–3

quarter-staff, 210 *and* n.2, 243
queen of England, in *Adam Bell*, 270–3

Randolf (Rannulf), Earl of Chester (d. 1232), 1, 10 *and* n.2
Rastell, John, 3 *and* n.3
Reading (Berks.), 39, 295
'Red Roger', *see* Doncaster, Sir Roger of
Reeve's Tale, The, 35 *and see* Chaucer
Reply of Friar Daw Topias to Jack Upland, 2, 289
Reynolde Grenelefe, 4, 90, 92, 100, 225
Reynolds, J. H., 198

Richard I: as contemporary of Robin Hood, 5, 16, 188–90, 287, 301, 315–16; in Munday's plays, 221–2, 225–9; in Tennyson's play, 243–9
'Richard at the Lee', *see* Lee
Richmond Park (Surrey), 304
Ripley, George, 2 *and* n.5, 289
Ritson, Joseph, 45–6, 54–6, 123 *and* n.1, 190 n.1, 191, 286 *and passim*; his *Robin Hood* (1795), 37 [n.1, 53, 59, 62, 176, 188, 195, 313; on ballads, 51, 191; interpretation of Robin Hood, 55–6; on *Robyn and Gandeleyn*, 255; on Robin Hood proverbs, 288–92 *passim*; on place-names, 294
'Roberdsmen', 26 *and* n.5
Roberts, James, printer, 259
Robin des Bois, 60 *and* n.1
Robin et Marion, 42 *and* n.1
Robin Goodfellow, 63
Robin Hood, associations and attributes: arbour, 295; barn, 292; bed, 290, 298; bow, 19 n.3, 288, 301 *and passim*; bower, 42, 295, 305, 308, 311; butts, 295, 298, 303–4, 306; cave, 296, 302; chair, 18 n.1, 295, 296, 301; cross, 296, 297, 299; hill, 298, 302, 305, 309; inn, 23 n.2, 46 n.2, 288, 293, 295, 296, 298, 306–7, 310; larder, 302–3; pennyworths, 291; stone, 23–4, 300, 307, 309–10; street, 293, 299–300; stride, 297; tower, 305, 307; villages and towns, 294, 296, 297, 298, 306, 308; well, 23, 296–7, 301, 303, 307, 308, 310–11; wind, 290
Robin Hood, ballads of; *see* Ballads of Robin Hood
Robin Hood, career of; name of, 11–13, 26, 63, 294; noble ancestry, 44, 59, 61, 223, 305; father, 259; birth-place, 287, 305, 308; historicity of, 11–17, 24, 55; geographical background, 17–24, 307–9; social background, 10, 11, 31–6, 64, 125; Sloane MS. Life of, 172, 286–7; as Earl of Huntington, *see* Huntington; marriage, 44, 284; royal pardon to, 33, 104–9, 122, 241; death, 19, 59 n.3, 62, 78–9, 112, 133–9, 186, 222, 228–30, 279, 309; grave, 19 n.3, 134, 137–9, 229, 302, 305, 309; epitaph, 139, 183, 186, 190
Robin Hood, characteristics; courtesy, 10–11, 32–3, 36, 50, 76, 79, 124, 125, 188–9; generosity to poor, 25, 36, 55, 112, 172, 188, 275–6, 279, 290; hostility to churchmen, 31, 80, 106, 188, 209, 211; loyalty to king, 61, 78, 104, 107, 109; nobility, 5, 33, 44–5, 61, 188, 279; piety, 79, 94, 96, 115, 116, 118, 136 *and see* Mary, Blessed Virgin; religious endowments, 78, 111, 180, 182; respect for women, 79, 132, 136, 138
Robin Hood, legend; 62–4 *and passim*; popularity, 1–5, 36–7, 53–64 *and passim*; juvenile appeal, 58–61; gentry hero, 32–6; peasant hero, 30–2; yeoman hero, 34–6, 98, 127 *and see* yeomen; 'social bandit', 64, 274, 278–9; mythological interpretations, 38, 63–4, 260 n.3; portraits, 62; statues, 19 n.3, 62, 300–1, 303; films, 61–2

Robin Hood, place-names, 63, 293–311 *passim*, *and see* Robin Hood, associations

Robin Hood, plays; 5, 37–43, 316–18 *and see* Munday, Jonson, Tennyson; comic operas, 45, 56, 317; *Robin Hood and the Sheriff*, 37, 140, 203–7, 209; *Robin Hood and the Friar*, 37, 41, 208–14; *Robin Hood and the Potter*, 37, 210 n.1, 215–19

Robin Hood, proverbs; 2, 288–92 *passim*

Robin Hood's Bay (N. Yorks.), 180, 306

Robin Hood's Penn'orths, 43, 291

Robinhood Society, 46 n.2

'Robin Lyth', 255, 276 n.4

'Robin Wood (Whod)', 12, 39 n.1, 298, 299, 300, 305

Robins, Thomas, ballad writer, 151, 155

Robyn and Gandeleyn, 7, 8 n.1, 255–7

'Robynhod', as surname, 12; Gilbert, 12; Katherine, 12; Robert, 12

Rockingham Forest (Northants.), 12–13

Rollins, H. E., 47, 151 n.2, 165 n.2, 179 n.2; on Martin Parker, 48, 187 n.1

'Rosamund, Fair', 177 *and* n.1

Rose the Red and White Lily, 195

Roxburghe, ballads, 48, 314; duke of, 47, 314

Rufford Abbey (Notts.), 27 *and* n.3

Sad Shepherd, The, 45, 231–6, 302 *and see* Jonson, Ben

St Albans Abbey, *see* Legat, Hugh

St Anne's Well, Nottingham, 301

St Mary's Abbey, York, 74–6, 85–8, 96; abbot, 14, 31, 74–5, 82–3, 85–8, 98, 187, 243; cellarer, 75, 85, 94–9; prior, 75, 85, 98, 222, 223

St Winifred's Well (Flint), 138 *and* n.5

Sayles (Saylis), The (W. Yorks.), 21, 22–4, 74, 80, 94, 308

Scarborough (N. Yorks.), 17, 179–81, 306

Scarlett (Scadlock, Scalok, Scarlock, Scatheloke), Will, 44, 202, 284–5, 287; in *Gest*, 74–5, 78–80, 83–5, 94, 100, 108, 110; in other ballads, 116 n.7, 120, 134–5, 142, 147–8, 161–2, 172; in plays, 206–7, 222, 231–5 *passim*, 238–9

Scattergood, V. J., 31 n.3, 32 n.1

Scotland, 252; May Games in, 40; Robin Hood in, 4–5, 40, 195–7, 294

Scott, Sir Walter, 16, 54–7, 65, 198, 317 *and see Ivanhoe*

Segrave, John de, 15

Selden, John, 47

Shelley, P. B., 57

Sheppard, C., ballad publisher, 51

Sherburn-in-Elmet (W. Yorks.), 24, 308

Sheridan, Richard Brinsley, 46

Shakespeare, William, 42, 43 n.3, 46, 147 n.5, 159, 220–1; *As You Like It*, 43 *and* n.3, 223 n.2

sheriff, office of, 14–15, 28–9, 64, 86; in *Adam Bell*, 262–3, 266, 270–1; *and see* Nottingham, sheriff of

Sherwood, poem, *see* Noyes, Alfred

Sherwood Forest, 14, 16, 18–20, 76, 199, 201–2,

294, 303; in *Robin Hood and Monk*, 19, 116, 118 n.1, 121; in other ballads, 150, 156; in plays, 225, 226, 231, 232, 243, 248

Shipton-under-Wychwood (Oxon.), 38

Shooter's Hill (Kent), 42

Shore, Jane, 177 *and* n.1

'Simon Over-the-Lee' (Robin Hood), 181, 182

Skelbrooke (W. Yorks.), 20, 307

Skelton, John, 2 *and* n.5, 47, 289; lost interlude by, 43 n.2, 223; in Munday's plays, 221–6

Slepill (W. Yorks.), 23

'Sloane MS. Life' of Robin Hood, 172, 286–7

Smith, A. H., 23 n.3

Smith, Captain Alexander, 25 n.2, 317

Southey, Robert, 318

Stafford family, 28

Stafford, Robert (*alias* Frere Tuck), 4, 41 n.2

Staffordshire, 4 *and* n.2, 28, 39 n.3

Stationers' Registers, 43, 47–8, 146, 151, 165, 179, 187, 208 n.2, 220, 258, 312

Stellee (*alias* Stutely), William, 171 *and* n.1

Sterndalle, John, 203

Stones, E. L. G., 27 n.4, 251 n.2

Stonor Letters, 28 n.3

Stow, John, 316

Stukeley, William, 46, 59, 203, 204 n.1; pedigree of Robin Hood, 59 *and* n.1, 305

Stutely (Stutley), William, 168 n.1, 169, 171 n.1, 283

Surrey, 4, 304

Sussex, 4, 12

Tell, William, 260 n.3

Tennyson, Alfred Lord, 58, 201, 243–9 *passim*; *The Foresters*, 244–9, 318

Thackeray, William, printer, 52, 188

Tickhill (W. Yorks.), 24 n.3

Tiddy, R. J. E., 38 n.3

Tintinhull (Somerset), 39 n.1

Tollet's window (Minsterley, Salop.), 41, 62 n.3

trailbaston, commissions of, 250 *and* n.1

Trease, Geoffrey, 60, 319

Trent, river, 231, 232

Trent, William a, 142

Trevisa, John, 35

trysting (trusty, trystell) tree, 99, 100, 107, 109, 118, 130 n.8, 141, 152, 154, 267, 268

Troilus and Criseyde, 2, 289

Tuck, Friar (Frere), 40–1, 43 n.3, 159, 188, 202, 301, 310; ballad of, 159–64; in May Games, 40–1, 159, 214 n.1; in plays, 41, 159, 203, 205–7, 208–14, 221–6, 231–2, 243, 248; in *Ivanhoe*, 57; outlaw named, 4, 41; well of, 302

Tudor, Margaret, 123

Tunstall, Bishop, 21

Turnament of Tottenham, The, 9, 114

Tutbury castle (Staffs.), 4

Tyler, Wat, 55–6

Tyndale, William, 3 *and* n.4, 292

Vanbrugh, Sir John, 23, 310

Venables, Piers, 4

Vere, Thomas, printer, 52 n.1 *and* 2, 146, 158, 313

'Verysdale', 88 *and see* Wyresdale
Vivian, E. C., 60, 318

Wakefield (W. Yorks.), 13, 24, 146–9, 229, 308–9; *and see* Pinder of
Walker, J. W., 13 *and* n.2
Wallace, William, 33, 125; *Scyr William Wallace*, 33
Walpole, Sir Robert, 191–4, 317
'Warman' (of Munday's play), 222, 223, 229
Warner, William, 315
Warwick, Sir Guy of, 33, 58, 59 n.5, 63, 187
'Watlinge Strete', 21–3, 80, 94
Wells (Somerset), 39
Went, river, 20, 21, 23, 307–8
Wentbridge (W. Yorks.), 19, 21 *and* n.4, 23, 88 n.10, 124, 126, 308
Westminster, abbot of, 120
Wetherby (W. Yorks.), 24, 307
When the King shall enjoy His Own Again, 191
Whitby (N. Yorks.), 180, 297, 307
White, Edward, printer, 72, 208, 215, 312
White, Thomas, 58
Willenhall (Staffs.), 4, 39 n.3
Willes, Richard, 39
Willie and Earl Richard's Daughter, 195–7
Willoughby, Sir Richard, 27
Wilson, R. M., 10 n.2, 12 n.2, 18 n.3
Wilson, Thomas, York printer, 52 n.4, 183

Winchester, Statute of (1285), 26
Windsor, castle, 222; forest, 57 n.1
Woden, 11, 63
Wood, Antony, broadsides of, 48, 146, 150, 158, 176, 179
Woodford, James, sculptor, 62, 300–1
Worcester, prior of, 39 n.1
Worde, Wynkyn de, 8, 71–4, 312
Wordsworth, William, 59
Worksop (Notts.), 22
Wrangbrook (W. Yorks.), 22
'Wrennok of Donne', 256–7
Wright, Thomas, 123 n.1
Wyntoun, Andrew of, chronicler, 4, 18, 260 n.2, 315
Wyresdale (Lancs.), 75, 88 *and* n.2

yeomen, 34–5; minstrelsy, 7, 9–10, 113, 124, 260; in *Adam Bell*, 258–73 *passim*; Robin Hood a yeoman, 79, 80, 88, 95, 122, 125, 141, 143–4, 218; Robin Hood a friend of, 10, 80
York, 11 n.4, 24 n.2, 26, 35 n.3, 308 *and see* St Mary's Abbey; archery at, 58 n.1; printers of, 52 n.4, 66, 133–4, 165–6, 172, 179, 183; Robin Hood Tower, 305
Yorkshire, 28 n.3; sheriff of, 15, 16; North Riding, 26 n.4, 179–82 *passim*; place-names, 306–7; West Riding, 17, 24, 76; place-names, 307–11